BURNING DOWN THE HOUSE

ALSO BY NELL BERNSTEIN

All Alone in the World: Children of the Incarcerated

BURNING DOWN THE HOUSE

THE END OF JUVENILE PRISON

NELL BERNSTEIN

THE NEW PRESS

NEW YORK
LONDON

Requests for permission to reproduce selections from this book should be mailed to:
Permissions Department, The New Press, 120 Wall Street, 31st floor, New York, NY 10005.

Published in the United States by The New Press, New York, 2014
Distributed by Perseus Distribution

LIBRARY OF CONGRESS CATALOGING-IN-PUBLICATION DATA

Bernstein, Nell.
Burning down the house : the end of juvenile prison / Nell Bernstein.
pages cm
Includes bibliographical references.
ISBN 978-1-59558-956-9 (hardback)
ISBN 978-1-59558-966-8 (e-book)
1. Juvenile justice, Administration of—United States.
2. Juvenile delinquency—United States.   3. Juvenile courts—United States.   I. Title.
HV9104.B4243   2014
365'.420973—dc23   2013043709

The New Press publishes books that promote and enrich public discussion and understanding of
the issues vital to our democracy and to a more equitable world. These books are made possible
by the enthusiasm of our readers; the support of a committed group of donors, large and small;
the collaboration of our many partners in the independent media and the not-for-profit sector;
booksellers, who often hand-sell New Press books; librarians; and above all by our authors.

www.thenewpress.com

Composition by dix!
This book was set in Fournier MT

Printed in the United States of America

2   4   6   8   10   9   7   5   3   1

365.4209
Ber

For Ri'Chard, who knew freedom

For Ruby, Nick, and Tim, who tether my heart to the world

Not everything that is faced can be changed, but nothing can be changed until it is faced.

—James Baldwin

CONTENTS

AUTHOR'S NOTE

Most of the stories in this book, as well as the direct quotations, are drawn from interviews I conducted with young people in and out of locked facilities in various states between 2010 and 2013. A few of the interviews were conducted at earlier points during the many years I have spent working with and writing about young people and the multiple public systems with which they collide. Will Roy conducted crucial interviews in New York, Massachusetts, and California. Carolyn Goosen contributed two interviews from Southern California. All interviews were taped and transcribed, unless they were conducted in a facility that did not allow recording equipment. On those few occasions, quotations are drawn from my handwritten notes. Some of the quotations from adult experts come from presentations they made at public events and conferences, including two organized or co-organized by the Annie E. Casey Foundation, which provided support for this book. The rest of this book comes from long friendships with young people caught up in the juvenile justice system—stories they told me and experiences that I witnessed or shared. For a number of reasons—most pressingly, the deep, and deeply wrongheaded, stigma that is attached to incarceration in this country—I have chosen to use pseudonyms in writing about people who are or have been incarcerated.

When speaking in general terms, I use both the masculine and feminine universal pronoun. In this book, I have used the masculine more frequently simply because there are many more boys behind bars than there are girls. I use the term "juvenile prison" more consistently than the various official euphemisms (training school, reform school, and the like) simply because it is more accurate.

BURNING DOWN THE HOUSE

PRELUDE

The Time Is at Hand

IT WAS TEN P.M. and I was half-asleep when my cell phone began dancing on the bedside table. The texts were coming in rapid fire, too fast for me to read one through, much less to respond, before the next announced its arrival.

> When I was locked up, I could talk to high school kids who came in with the "scared straight" programs. Now that I'm out, I can't get clearance to go into the high schools to speak because I'm a felon.

It took me a moment to recognize the cadence, and, with it, the sender. I've known Jared for nearly twenty years. We met when I was the editor of a San Francisco youth newspaper and he was just emerging from a long sojourn within the correctional circuit, which had taken him from juvenile hall through state juvenile lockup and finally to San Quentin State Prison, where he'd been sent at sixteen on a gun charge.

> We can save lives inside as earthquake relief and firefighters but outside the prison walls we're a bunch of filthy ex-cons.

When I first met him, Jared was a heavily muscled young man who favored dark clothing with oversized hoods, his face set in the emotionless mask of the prison yard. His writing, though, crackled with emotion and

1

furious intellect: page after page of cramped longhand, as if there were not paper enough in the world for all he had to say.

While his first text jolted me out of half sleep into confusion, as the next few came in and I started waking up, I began to catch on. Something had inspired Jared to pick up a thread in a running conversation, neglecting the formality of a transition or hello.

> NELL the time is at hand and we must do our part.
> Just don't play with this shit cuz I am serious about it.

Jared knew I was in the thick of writing this book. He had been generous with his time and insight when I'd asked to interview him.

> Don't get sidetracked sista!
> Don't fail.

No matter how many years had passed since his incarceration, the urgency had not faded for Jared. Nor had the pressure lifted.

> You keep pushing and pushing until you DIE!

Jared had been in trouble with the law since fourth grade. That was when his mother's addiction finally overwhelmed her capacity to care for him. Cast out on his own, the nine-year-old quickly allied himself with a troupe of other children who were "living life solo." By day, they ran errands for drug dealers. At night, they pooled their earnings and piled into a shared room in a single-room occupancy hotel in San Francisco's Tenderloin District.

Jared was done with all that now, working a steady job, engaged to be married, and a devoted father to his two children. He'd been keeping his head up, but he still had two strikes on his record under California's notorious three strikes law. A single misstep could send him back to prison for good.

> I TRUST YOU.
> And "Trust" for me is hard.
> Just write the TRUTH.

Jared had struggled in the years since his release. His ex-offender status had stymied his efforts to find work and housing and get onto his feet, and a lifetime of trauma had set his temperament at a low boil. But now he was doing well. A kid who had lived out his teenage years under the motto *I don't give a fuck* (an existential cry I would hear many times as I spoke with others who had been locked up as kids), he had grown into a man with something to live for: people he loved and could count on, who loved and relied on him in turn.

Do what's right and I gotcha back bud. Know that I am living IT.

Jared was acutely aware of how vulnerable his closest relationships left him. The connections that sustained him held the potential to shatter him, should that third strike fall. The intensity of his drive to see genuine transformation in our nation's merciless justice system—to close down the brutal institutions where he had come of age—came from a sense of personal jeopardy as well as collective injustice.

He had paid his own debt many times over. The time, as he put it, was at hand. He was ready to be free.

Do what's right.
JUST WRITE, Nell. WRITE.

INTRODUCTION

Caging men like animals . . . then expecting them to become better men is fallacious.

—Earl Warren

CURTIS HAD MIXED FEELINGS when he learned he was headed for the California Youth Authority: "terrified and petrified." A sprawling system of violent and poorly managed state institutions, the Youth Authority was home to California's most serious juvenile offenders and, at the time, held wards as old as twenty-five. Curtis was ten years old.

I met Curtis on a brisk fall afternoon soon after his release. Sixteen by then, he was sitting on a bench in a leafy courtyard outside the restored Victorian that housed the Oakland-based Mentoring Center. He had attended the organization's workshops while he was locked up and formed a strong bond with several of the staff. Post-release, the center had become a second home to Curtis.

For the next several hours, Curtis spoke in an urgent, nearly unbroken stream, pausing only to catch the occasional breath. In pressed black slacks and a black-and-white-checked shirt, towing a briefcase stuffed with books and papers, the newly freed teenager seemed at once anxious and exuberant, wringing his hands until his narrative kicked into high gear, then releasing them to gesticulate or pound the bench for emphasis.

When Curtis was arrested for a robbery, he told me, he figured he would do some time in county juvenile hall. No one had ever heard of a child his age being sent to the Youth Authority.

"To me, California Youth Authority is a *prison* for younger people," Curtis said, recalling his reaction when he got the news. "And I was going to prison. I was scared. I was ten years old and I was in the Youth Authority with twenty-five-year-old grown men. I was crazy. I was saying, 'Man, oh my God, they gonna rape me. They gonna kill me. I'm gonna become somebody's woman.' 'Cause I heard so many things about prison, you know."

Researchers have taken to mapping "million-dollar blocks"—pockets of immiseration where we spend that sum or more each year to lock up large proportions of the residents. Less remarked upon is our proclivity for churning out million-dollar kids. On average, we spend $88,000 per year to incarcerate a young person in a state facility—more than eight times the $10,652 we invest in her education. In many states, this gap is even wider. In California, for example, the cost of a year in a youth prison reached a high of $225,000, while education spending dipped to less than $8,000. The young people who rack up the million-dollar tabs behind bars, and the many more we spend hundreds of thousands to incarcerate, generally get the message: that they are at once disposable and dangerous—worth little to cultivate but anything to contain.

Curtis became a million-dollar kid. By the time he left the Youth Authority, the annual cost per youth was approaching its high of $225,000—a figure inflated by the cost of litigation over physical abuse, inhumane conditions, and other violations of children's civil rights. Sentenced initially to two years behind bars, Curtis wound up staying more than six "because of my repetitive negative behavior," he intoned, slipping into the jargon that defined him throughout his adolescence.

"Fighting and things," he clarified. "I cut somebody when I was locked up. Somebody tried to rape me, and I shanked that person in the neck."

Curtis described his experience as a ten-year-old in a high-security facility as akin to being "thrown to the dogs. If you're out there with the savages, then you're gonna have to become a savage in order to survive. 'Cause it's the survival of the fittest in there."

"They treated me like I was an animal," he said forcefully, using an expression I would hear many times from young prisoners, "when I really was just a little child that was misguided, that needed some help and some direction."

California taxpayers spent at least a million dollars constructing this self-described "savage": turning an angry, lonesome, traumatized ten-year-old into a ruthless fighter; driving him crazy with months in solitary confinement to punish him for those fights; and finally medicating him into a stupor to "treat" the new disorders with which he was diagnosed in solitary, where his main form of human interaction was the nurse who pushed the meds cart down the hall.

At last count, 66,332 American youth were confined in juvenile facilities, with the majority—about two-thirds—in long-term placements such as state-run training schools, places like the one to which Curtis was sent at ten. Most of these are boys; about 13 percent are girls.

More broadly, police arrest nearly 2 million juveniles each year, and demographers predict that one in three American schoolchildren will be arrested by the age of twenty-three. All this is so despite the fact that juvenile crime is steadily declining.

The juvenile court was founded at the end of the nineteenth century with the mandate to rehabilitate, not punish, wayward youth. There is little evidence, however, that confining young people does anything to advance this mandate. Instead, for as long as we have locked children away in the name of rehabilitating them, the evidence has mounted that this approach is a failure on all fronts. Sky-high recidivism rates (the percentage of those released who are re-arrested or incarcerated again)—higher than 80 percent in some states—indicate that whatever is taking place inside our juvenile correctional facilities, nobody is actually being "corrected."

In fact, multiple studies have shown that putting youth behind bars not only fails to enhance public safety; it does just the opposite, driving low-level delinquents deeper into criminality and *increasing* the likelihood that they will wind up behind bars again and again. One recent longitudinal study of 35,000 young offenders found that those who were incarcerated as juveniles were twice as likely to go on to be locked up as adults as those who committed similar offenses and came from similar backgrounds but were given an alternative sanction or simply not arrested. A study from the Arkansas Division of Youth Services identified incarceration itself as the single most significant factor in predicting whether a youth will offend again—more so than family difficulties or gang membership. As scholar and author Barry Feld has written, "A century of experience with training

schools and youth prisons demonstrates that they constitute the one extensively evaluated and clearly ineffective method to treat delinquents."

Beyond this central failure, our nation's juvenile facilities do not even
meet their bottom-line responsibility to keep their charges safe. Physical
and sexual abuse are rampant, as are solitary confinement and other practices that erode young people's mental and physical health. Even those
who manage to avoid the most explicit abuses live in isolation, in conditions that are often dangerous and unhealthy and serve further to trauma-
tize young people who often already carry a heavy burden of pain.

We are hurting kids, and hurting ourselves in the process, exposing far
too many young people to inhumane conditions with the sole measurable
result of *increasing* the odds that they will be drawn ever more deeply into
delinquency. A system ostensibly designed to protect and improve children has turned on them instead, scarring one generation after another,
and—after decades of institutional impunity—leaving today's youth vulnerable to practices we would decry were they perpetrated anywhere but
behind prison walls.

Juvenile incarceration is also one of the most glaring examples of racial
injustice our nation has to offer. Studies based on confidential interviews
have found that the vast majority of Americans go through a period of
delinquency at some point during adolescence. Fully 80 to 90 percent of
American teenagers have committed an illegal act that could qualify them
for time behind bars, and one-third of all teens have committed a serious
crime. Most, however, never see the inside of a cell, or even a police car.
Of this group—the kids who get a pass—the overwhelming majority simply grow out of it. By the time they reach adulthood they are crime-free.

Black and brown youth, especially those from impoverished communities, face far different prospects than do their white counterparts on this
front. Those living in poor neighborhoods are subject to what sociologist
Victor Rios calls a "culture of control"—treated with suspicion and harsh
discipline at school, on the street, and even in the community. They also
face discrimination at every stop on the juvenile and criminal justice cir-
cuits. They are more likely than white youth who commit identical acts to
be arrested; to be charged and detained rather than released to their families; to be sentenced to locked institutions; to be kept behind bars longer;
and to be sent back more often (all after controlling for the seriousness of

their acts and other relevant factors). These cascading inequities dramatically curtail the prospects of young people who are already at a disadvantage when it comes to the educational and employment opportunities that serve as the bridge to secure and successful adulthood.

The young people who sit today inside locked facilities are, overwhelmingly, our nation's most vulnerable youth. Disproportionately black and brown and drawn from impoverished neighborhoods, they are more likely to have been victims of violence than they are to have perpetrated it. Incarceration not only exacerbates the vulnerabilities with which they arrive but exposes them to all manner of new challenges: post-traumatic stress syndrome; curtailed education; gang affiliation and a gladiator mentality enforced by prison culture; the unraveling effects of social isolation; and a lifetime of stigma and further isolation.

Counter to the popular notion of the juvenile detainee as vicious "super-predator," young people are far more likely to be locked up for minor offenses than for violent crimes. In 2010, only one of every four confined youths was locked up based on a Violent Crime Index offense (a category that encompasses aggravated assault and robbery along with homicide and sexual assault). At the other end of the spectrum, nearly 40 percent were behind bars due to low-level, low-threat offenses: technical violations of probation, drug possession, minor property offenses, public order offenses, or status offenses (activities that would not be crimes for adults, such as possession of alcohol or truancy). The bottom line is that most confined youth pose little risk to public safety—they're not kids we are afraid of but those we are mad at, to borrow a much-quoted locution.

Whatever the charge, the overwhelming evidence is that whatever mental health, trauma, or behavior problems children may enter with are rarely alleviated and more often exacerbated by the experience of finding themselves caged. Being locked up, many young people I spoke to conveyed in one way or another, undermined not only any faith in their own potential—their sense of connection to and stake in the larger society— but their very sense of self.

The small proportion of young prisoners behind bars for acts that pose a genuine threat to public safety are no exception. While a small number of serious juvenile offenders do need to be confined to protect the public (a much, much smaller number than are currently locked up), juvenile prisons as they are currently managed are not the place even for the so-called dangerous few. By worsening the problems that often contributed to their crimes in the first place, and *increasing* the odds that they will commit more crime in the future, these institutions actually undermine public safety in the longer term.

The wholesale sacrifice of a young person's future that incarceration often reflects is all the more tragic because it is so very unnecessary. Models exist—carefully designed and extensively studied—that improve the prospects of virtually all juvenile offenders, including the most serious. These models—which provide a tight web of support, supervision, and relationship without forcibly removing a young person from home and community—show far better outcomes than do juvenile prisons.

Over the decade I spent as editor of a youth newspaper, I developed friendships with young people that spanned many years and, too often, multiple incarcerations. I attended dozens of court hearings, sometimes speaking before the judge on a young writer's behalf, other times just shaking hands with a weary public defender or brisk district attorney, but either way doing my Ann Taylored best to give my writers the boost in credibility that a white face beside them appeared to confer. It wasn't a fair strategy, nor was it universally effective: despite my weekday vigils in the courtroom, I spent many weekends in visiting rooms.

Watching an ambitious, lively girl or boy—filled with the rebelliousness, vulnerability, spark, and aspiration that mark the adolescent years—unravel behind bars was always wrenching, no matter how many times I had seen it before. But over the years, I also bore witness to something very different. Over and over, I watched young people who appeared to be well along the path to delinquency turn their lives around when they had support in doing so.

The kids I've seen make it have followed various trajectories, but they all have a consistent relationship with at least one trusted adult. Young people struggling with the pull of the street, as well as the trauma that often accompanies it, need someone walking with them as they do the difficult work of changing how they think, act, and react; how they view themselves and others and their own place in the world.

After spending much of the past two decades listening to the young people we dub juvenile offenders—having read the literature, interviewed the experts, and visited juvenile prisons across the country—I have seen a single theme emerge with remarkable consistency: *rehabilitation happens in the context of relationship.*

Every study I've seen on the subject bears this out, as does the life trajectory of every young person whose genuine transformation I've been fortunate enough to witness. Meanwhile, virtually every aspect of our juvenile prison system—designed to disrupt and deny relationships, not foster or forge them—runs counter to this fundamental aspect of human nature.

If you've witnessed true rehabilitation, the fact that our default response when young people veer into trouble is incarceration—the deprivation of relationship—seems more than counterintuitive. Viewed through the eyes of the children consigned to exile when they most need connection, incarceration seems flat-out monstrous. We take young people who have violated a communal norm and we *isolate* them in barren facilities where relationships with staff are minimal and hostile. ("If you wanted attention," a juvenile hall staffer told my friend Eliza—then a sixteen-year-old survivor of more than thirty different foster and group homes, whose vast and helpless loneliness was as unmistakable as an open wound—"you shouldn't have gotten yourself locked up.") Our response when already vulnerable, needy, and impulse-prone youth do *not* adapt well to being isolated from family, friends, and community and commit some sort of infraction on the inside—fighting with one another, breaking a rule, or simply breaking down—is to isolate them further, in solitary confinement, an environment that often succeeds in breaking them entirely.

There is no reform adequate to remedy a conceptual flaw this fundamental. We simply cannot fix a system with recidivism rates that send as many as four out of five juvenile parolees back behind bars within three years of release. The time has come to acknowledge our failures and demonstrate the courage to try something new—the same courage we demand of young people whose terms of probation require them to avoid all that *they* know and begin new lives from scratch.

The challenge is not simply to build a better mousetrap, but to reexamine every aspect of how we address delinquency, from taking on the racial, educational, social, and economic inequities that feed it to ensuring that relationship-focused, community-inspired responses are not just boutique "alternatives" but become the status quo—available to everyone.

The moment is at hand.

Jared was right on point with his literal wake-up call. We are at a crucial juncture when it comes to juvenile justice in this country—a time when the peril we face if we fail to change course is matched only by the surprising possibility that we may succeed.

All across the country, states are shutting down juvenile prisons, often beginning with the most abusive. The rate of juvenile confinement has dropped a remarkable 41 percent since its peak in 1995, with the decline accelerating in recent years. A few states have been hit by a perfect storm—crushing budget pressures; determined campaigns led by young people, their families, and other advocates; damning exposés in the media; defeats in the courtroom; and Department of Justice findings of widespread violations of constitutional rights—and responded by closing not some but *most* of their juvenile prisons.

This shift has not led to a rise in youth crime. In fact, juvenile crime rates *dropped* over the same period. Politicians who back these changes are finding far more support than they expected among a public increasingly soured on wasting tax dollars on failed interventions.

These cuts are rightly heralded as cause for celebration. But any social change that is inspired in large part by a dip in tax revenues is intrinsically fragile. Buildings that now stand empty may well fill up once again, should an improved economy replenish drained state coffers and a fresh onslaught of fearmongering shift the political winds. The wave of closures of juvenile prisons that now appears so promising may be looked back on as just another blip in America's history of pendulum swings on questions of criminal justice—a back-and-forth that has always, to date, returned to incarceration as a first-line intervention. Without a frank acknowledgment of the fundamental failure of our isolation-driven model to improve public safety; an honest reckoning with the devastation incarceration wreaks on young people, their families, and their neighborhoods; and a shared belief that *all* children are *our* children and deserve a chance to flourish, the promise of the current moment could well be betrayed.

As things stand, the United States still incarcerates more of its young people than does any other industrialized nation—seven times the rate of Great Britain and eighteen times that of France—spending a total of $5 *billion* a year to keep kids such as Curtis in juvenile institutions. Even our closest competitor, South Africa, incarcerates its children at one-fifth the rate of the voracious United States.

We continue to countenance racial disparities so extreme as to threaten the legitimacy of our democracy, locking up black teenagers at five times the rate we do whites. We still fill our youth prisons primarily with young people who pose little or no threat to public safety. And we persist in sending them to places where they are likely to be victimized and certain to be isolated, and from which they consistently emerge further disadvantaged—a formula custom-made to send them back to prison again and again.

When something is as wrong as what we are doing to young people behind the walls of our juvenile prisons, it calls for a remedy more immediate and more profound than incremental and partial reform. We don't have the luxury of patting ourselves on the back for simply cutting down on abuse, no more than a parent in family court can get away with telling the judge he is beating his children less often, or breaking fewer bones. When it comes to an institution as intrinsically destructive as the juvenile prison, there is no middle road.

That's not to say we should throw up our hands when it comes to intervening in a young person's delinquent trajectory. Not only do interventions that rely on support and connection rather than isolation and confinement exist; they have been studied closely and found to have great promise for young people and the public. Across the country, scattered jurisdictions have adopted these models with tremendous success, but to date they have been utilized mainly as "alternatives" or small-scale pilot programs, available to only a sliver of those who might benefit. Incarceration, despite these reforms, remains our default response to everything from homicide to shoplifting.

"When will justice come?" Tolstoy is said to have asked and then answered: "When those who are not injured are as indignant as those who are."

My travels through the deep end of our nation's juvenile justice system—the large, state-run, locked facilities—have left me beyond indignant. Along the way I've met many others, including system survivors, their families, and their allies, who are not only outraged but extraordinarily committed to change, many dedicating their lives to answering Tolstoy's question.

Bart Lubow—director of the Annie E. Casey Foundation's Juvenile Justice Strategy Group—argues for a simple exercise he calls the "my child" test. The standard he suggests is simplicity itself: *Would this be acceptable if it were my child whose freedom were at stake?* This intimate yardstick offers the radical shift in perspective that is required to move beyond momentary horror to outrage, shame, and, eventually, action.

Try it for a moment. Picture a child—your own, if you are a parent, or any child you love. Now imagine that child has committed a crime—the worst you can imagine. Murder, mayhem, armed robbery, arson? Perhaps she drives drunk and causes a serious accident. Maybe he gets angry—in defense of a friend or over a girl—and the fistfight that ensues is charged as an assault. Using drugs? Selling them? Bringing them to school? It doesn't much matter, for the sake of this exercise: many roads converge at the prison gate.

Now picture your child, this child whom you love, being called to account for the thing he has done. Do you see him kneeling, cuffed, in a pool of his own urine, denied all but one meal a day and a few hours of sleep? Does the picture include your child being raped or beaten—perhaps both—by the very staff entrusted with her rehabilitation? Can you hold this image as day after day passes? Can you hold it for months? Can you live with it for years?

How would your child respond to these conditions? Might she break down and cry out that death would be better? Picture her, in that case, tossed into solitary; this is where those who speak of suicide are often sent. See her alone in a windowless cell, with a bare cement bunk and a cold metal toilet, huddling naked beneath a single rough blanket.

Might he get into a fight soon after arrival, trying to prove that he is not an easy mark? Imagine him, then, in this same bare cell, not huddling but screaming, unanswered cries of raw and helpless pain (he's been sprayed in the eyes with Mace and then dispatched to solitary without medical care or so much as a shower).

Would this be acceptable if it were my *child?* If the answer is no (and it's a question most of us can answer in an instant), then the edifice must crumble. We must not permit ourselves to settle on *any* child's behalf for piecemeal reform, nor find excuses to turn our faces away until another scandal returns us to attention. Bloodthirsty mass media have encouraged us to think of those in the juvenile justice system as fundamentally other, an alien species that to this day carries the taint of the "super-predator" label even as the research that spawned that politically potent term has been discredited. But we can cast these thousands of young people into dungeons of destruction only when we do not know them.

Getting to know them has left me both hopeful and indignant. It is remarkable how radically the lens shifts when one actually spends time with the young people we all too quickly write off in the political arena and throw away via our criminal dispositions.

"Doesn't it get old after a while?" an acquaintance asked of my work. "I mean these stories—they are heartbreaking, but don't they all start sounding the same?"

Yes and no, I would have answered, had the question not sent me into a defensive silence.

Yes, there is a tragic trajectory from hurt kid to delinquent to detainee to prisoner—and yes, the rough contours of that journey often seem alike. But not the kids! Shear their hair, put them in uniforms, brand them with numbers, and toss out their names; treat them as if they *are*, in fact, "all the same"—try as we might to obscure or extinguish a child's individuality by making him a prisoner, young people will find some way to resist. The will to keep growing is fierce.

Crystal is a ballerina; she dances in her cell. "It makes me feel like I can let all my frustration out," she told me. "Whatever I'm feeling, I put it in my dance."

For an hour every day, Crystal and her unit are let onto the yard for exercise. Why not dance then, where there's space to stretch her arms out without hitting the wall? I thought she'd plead shyness, but Crystal's not like that. She stood in the hallway where we had been talking and spun off in a series of crisp pirouettes, her grace the more stunning because it was stolen.

"They don't let us do that," she said, meaning dance outdoors in the sunlight. "They'll be like, 'What are you doing, Jenkins? What are you doing?' And I'm like, 'Oh, my bad.' " So she does what she can during her one hour of outdoor "large-muscle exercise"—push-ups, jumping jacks, sit-ups, crunches—and then dances alone in her cell.

Before she could say more, our interview was cut short; my guide was approaching to move me along. By the time he arrived, Crystal had slipped back to the bench and composed her graceful limbs into the apathetic slouch that is the young prisoner's fallback pose.

"I dance in my room, though," she repeated in a whisper as I was led away.

Young prisoners like Crystal have been stripped of nearly everything, but even in the most materially and emotionally impoverished environments they manage to aspire. This hidden vein of promise—the hope and ambition young people maintain under the most barren circumstances— glints briefly even in the otherwise bleak federal Survey of Youth in Residential Placement. Despite the fact that their educational opportunities have been sharply curtailed, more than two-thirds of youth in custody aspire to higher education. About half want to go to college and another fifth hope to go further, to graduate school, medical school, or law school. Despite obvious barriers, most youth in custody believe that they will reach the goals they set for themselves. The same is true when it comes to employment. Most youth in custody—88 percent—say they expect to have a steady job in the future.

The question is not whether young prisoners have hopes for the future—in that, like so much else, they are no different from any young person—but whether they will be permitted to pursue them.

Rakim is a mathematician, working out elaborate equations in his head. Darren is a therapist, his empathetic ear taking the place of formal training—the one with whom others share secrets they wouldn't dream of disclosing to a professional on the payroll. Luis is a comic, bringing levity to his unit, and Eliza a paperback scholar, reading history, philosophy, romance, or Westerns—whatever she can get her hands on that day.

The young people who fill our nation's prisons are at once each unique and at the same time—even in the very fact of their individuality—*just like* other young people, captive or free. That a particular teenager is locked up, or has been, changes nothing on that front, no matter how thorough the institutional practices designed to make truth of the lie that they are, to paraphrase my skeptical acquaintance, "all the same."

Once you understand this essential individuality—part and parcel of young people's universal humanity—the notion that delinquent children are somehow expendable, essential as it is to the practice of locking them away, becomes not only ludicrous but genuinely horrifying. We cannot afford to extinguish the light in one more child's spirit.

Just write the truth, Jared urged. I don't take his trust lightly. Any truth I have to tell belongs not to me but to him, to the other veterans of our juvenile justice system whom I've come to count among my friends over the years, and to the many more who offered their time and their trust by agreeing to be interviewed.

Here, then, is the truth as I have come to understand it, after listening to hundreds of young people and their families, speaking with dozens of scholars and practitioners, and reading thousands of pages of documentation of vicious abuse, chronic neglect, and unremitting failure behind the walls of our nation's juvenile prisons:

- Correcting our children does not require containing them.
- Rehabilitation happens in the context of relationship, making our addiction to isolation a surefire route to failure.
- Reform is inadequate to the moral challenge posed by the violence-plagued dungeons in which we keep our children.
- Setting our children free will make us safer, not less so.

We owe young people nothing less than a complete transformation in how we respond when they step outside the law: an end to isolation and a national infrastructure of community-based supports.

This is the truth I hope to honor Jared's trust in telling. It is the truth I have heard and witnessed all across the nation. The time has come to move beyond the long battle to reform our juvenile prisons and declare them beyond redemption. Raze the buildings, free the children, and begin anew.

PART I

Teenage Wasteland

1

INSIDE JUVENILE PRISON

Even if I got away with a few years only, on account of my age, it was forever. It wasn't even possible that Monday should come, when at least I'd get a walk up the stairs. The clock was not made that would pass the time between now and Monday. It was like what we were told about the last day, "Time is, time was, time is no more." And Jesus Christ, even now, I was only locked up ten minutes.

—Brendan Behan, *Borstal Boy*

On the day of our arrival to Oakley, we observed a 13-year-old boy sitting in a restraint chair near the Ironwood control room. Reportedly, he was placed in the restraint chair to prevent self-mutilation. No staff approached him, and he was not allowed to attend school or receive programming, counseling, or medication. This boy had been severely sexually and physically abused by family members . . . prior to being sent to Ironwood. Just before our arrival, he had been locked naked in his empty cell. His cell smelled of urine, and we observed torn pieces of toilet paper on the concrete floor that he had been using as a pillow.

—Findings letter, Department of Justice Investigation
of Oakley and Columbia Training Schools in Raymond
and Columbia, Mississippi, June 19, 2003

THE PLACES WHERE YOUNG people are confined in the United States operate under any number of euphemistic titles, each as soothing as it is implausible: guidance center, boys school, youth ranch, camp. New arrivals test the door and know exactly where they are.

Most get the message long before they arrive. A teenager headed for a state juvenile prison likely rides in a van for hundreds of miles, shackled in leg irons, a belly chain, and handcuffs. He passes the outskirts of his hometown or city and enters an unfamiliar rural landscape. He may ride for hours before he arrives, passing through gates topped with razor wire into a compound inhabited by two hundred or three hundred others, ranging in age from twelve to twenty-four (juvenile facilities hold young people for offenses committed as minors but are often permitted to keep them past their eighteenth birthday). His jaw muscles may tighten as he composes his face in an effort to hide the fear that constricts his gut as his senses fill with what appears to be a prison.

Despite the fact that the very notion of a separate system for juveniles is predicated on the need to keep youth *out* of adult prisons, most state juvenile institutions look and feel very much like the adult correctional institutions they were intended to supplant. Sited in job-hungry rural counties far from most wards' homes, holding as many as two hundred or three hundred uniform-clad bodies, fitted with cell blocks or closely packed dormitories, and surrounded on all sides by angry coils of razor wire, many seem custom-made to inspire the kind of fear the new arrival has been warned by veterans to conceal at any cost.

These institutions are run by the states, and there is certainly great variation among them, from size and site to policies and procedures. But an overriding focus on custody and control and a persistent climate of dehumanization make it possible to offer a broad outline of what a new arrival might generally expect.

After he is escorted into the building (unless these things have already been taken care of at a separate intake facility), he will be photographed, fingerprinted, and, in some states, required to submit a DNA sample. He will be assigned an identification number, which anyone who hopes to reach him by mail will need to use. Before he can enter the general population, he will have to hand over any personal belongings—shoes, belt, watch, jewelry—though most arrive at state facilities from local juvenile halls and so have already been stripped of these effects. Anything that remains will be either stored, mailed home at his expense, or destroyed.

Next, he will be required to strip naked, surrender what is left of his cloth-ing, and submit to a search. He may be ordered to turn this way and that, run his hands through his hair, lift his genitals, or spread his butt cheeks in order to give officers the most thorough view. He may also be asked to squat and cough to expel whatever might be hidden in a bodily orifice.

He will then be required to shower and may have delousing chemicals sprayed on his head, underarms, and pubic area, whether or not he shows symptoms of lice. Next, he will be given a uniform—sweatpants and a T-shirt or baggy khakis, sometimes in bright colors, socks, and under-wear, all of which have been worn by others before him. Here and there, young wards still wear prison stripes.

He may go through an "orientation" in which guards who are not called guards (youth workers, counselors, youth development aides, team lead-ers; here also imaginative euphemisms proliferate) will spell out the offi-cial rules and sometimes the unofficial as well, letting him know he has reason to fear both his neighbors and his keepers. More than one young person paraphrased this part of their orientation as the *Don't be a bitch* talk—a "bitch" being a youngster who shows fear or other weakness, opening himself up to abuse and exploitation. One young man recalled sitting handcuffed with three or four other newly arrived wards while a guard broke it down for them: "You won't die," the guard promised. "You'll get beat up, get unconscious, probably go to the hospital, get your tooth broke, your nose broken, probably get a black eye, but you won't die. So don't sweat it."

Only after these initial rites have concluded will the new arrival be led to a bunk in an open dormitory, or to a narrow cell, which may or may not house a roommate.

If the new arrival is a first-timer, he is likely terrified and struggling not to show it. His stay, he will have been warned on the outside or in county juvenile hall, will be nasty, brutish, and long. Watch out for gangs, he will have been cautioned; everyone's going to want to know what you're claiming. Stick with your own race—especially when it comes to the drug trade inside. Never show fear or walk away from a challenge. *Don't be a bitch*.

Fear is omnipresent inside a youth prison, hanging over the place like a persistent fog. Its companion is boredom, dense and unrelenting, sapping the spirit as one day bleeds into the next and then the next. The days are a carefully synchronized march between cell, showers, cafeteria, school-room, dayroom, yard, and cell, punctuated by the sound of doors swinging open and gates clanging shut. None of this activity seems to counter the omnipresent lethargy that hovers over the place. Lights-out comes finally, a moment to oneself, but many describe this as the worst time of the day, as thoughts of what might have been and fear of what's to come crowd out sleep's relief.

Walk into the dayroom of a state juvenile prison (the common space intended for rest and recreation) and one is hit with a wave of collective ennui so powerful it can be soporific. Lanky teenagers slouch in an open-legged stance in plastic chairs that are, for some reason, always too small to contain their growing frames. Some turn the chairs around and sit back-wards, their heads hunging forward in a posture of surrender, beneath motivational posters peeling from the walls. There may be a game of cards on a bolted-down table, the drone of a television tuned to an approved channel, or laconic conversation, but mostly there is a sense that time has slowed down.

Even when marching or walking in formation—as they are generally required to do—young prisoners often appear to drag their feet, as if in an effort to fill the empty time. The baggy sweats or droopy khaki uni-forms and hospital-style slippers collude to enforce this slow shuffle and heighten the sense of being somehow underwater. The boisterous energy one finds virtually anywhere else that teens congregate is replaced behind bars by a sort of hibernation, as if children kept in cages somehow slowed their metabolism in an instinctive response to the winter of their exile.

In fact, that may be exactly what they are doing, intentionally or not. Young people describe the food inside juvenile facilities in terms of quan-tity, not quality. Growing boys describe themselves as "hungry all the time"—so much so that they do, perhaps, become lethargic.

Will spent six years in juvenile prisons across California. "I don't know if you can call it a meal," he said of the thrice-daily offerings, con-sumed quickly in forced silence. "They feed you enough not to starve, but never enough to satisfy you." The hardest part to get through was the empty-bellied stretch between dinner at five and breakfast at seven.

"Young people are growing, and fourteen hours without a meal is not sufficient," said Will, an athletic six-foot-something who spent his growing years on a prison diet. "You're hungry all the time."

That, he added, was a best-case scenario. During the stretch he spent in a maximum-security lockdown, there was no communal mealtime at all. The delivery of food became, instead, another means of ritual humiliation. Wards were required to lie on their bunks, facing the wall, hands behind their backs, while a guard brought a tray in and set it on the toilet. The boys could lift their heads only once they heard the cell door close. This ritual was repeated when the tray was removed. Those in solitary confinement were granted even less: bag meals consisting of bread, two slices of bologna, Kool-Aid, and a container of room-temperature milk. The more experienced learned to ration the food to make it through the day.

Even out in the general population, the food young people described sounded barely edible, but very few complained about the menu—they spoke of food as fuel, not flavor or comfort. The one specific dish that Will could call to mind was SOS (Shit on a Shingle), a "chunky gravy on biscuits" that my father ate (and called by the same name) as a soldier during the privations of World War II. Will looked forward to it, he said, because it was filling.

Showers, like meals, are a mixed blessing. "I've never seen a group of guys so into their hygiene," Will recalled. "When guys go to jail, they really keep their bodies clean."

Nevertheless, he added, "For me, showering was one of the worst parts of jail." The company of peers and the scrutiny of guards are hard to get used to, as is the three minutes allotted each bather. At one facility where Will spent time, things were made worse by a regimen of "broken" plumbing that mysteriously produced only cold water in the winter months and scalding hot in summer.

School, although legally mandated, does little to break the monotony. Luis was sixteen when he was shipped off to a state facility for violating his probation on an earlier, bungled burglary attempt. On the outside, teachers had urged him to stay in school and fulfill his potential. On the inside it was different. "Very little emphasis on education," said Luis, who spent what would have been his high school years in prison. "Books are

outdated; teachers are pissed off." Groups of one sort or another—Anger
Management is a staple, as are Life Skills and Relapse Prevention—are
sometimes helpful but more often perfunctory. Count to ten, rage-filled
youth are instructed in Anger Management, while those in Life Skills
report being told to watch their step on the outside, or else. (There are
always exceptions—brilliant teachers or dedicated group leaders—but
most youths I spoke with had not encountered them.)

Mental health care may be mandated by law, but that does not translate,
for instance, to therapy. One of the sadder rituals I have witnessed is the
nightly arrival of the "meds cart" on a wing: a nurse rolls in and half the
kids line up without a word, downing handfuls of psychotropics with a
single gulp of water from a flimsy paper cup.

Measuring about nine by eleven feet, a cell (or "room," to use another
common euphemism) in a juvenile prison seems more like a stall than
anything else. Most have minimal bedding—a thin mattress on a bunk
bolted to the wall, a steel toilet and sink. The fortunate may have a desk,
also bolted to the wall, or a locker or shelf to store a few belongings. In
some facilities, large dormitories filled with bunk beds replace individual cells; in others youths have roommates, sometimes bunked four to a
cell. There will also be a yard, sometimes a field, and a gym. Classrooms.
A cafeteria. An infirmary. A chapel. And miles of empty sky—the practice of siting juvenile prisons in remote rural outposts leaves even those
with windows little to see. If the facility is on lockdown—as can happen
because of a fight, gang concerns, or something as mundane as a short-
age of teachers—the dayroom may be empty, while young people spend
twenty-two, twenty-three, or sometimes, despite regulations, twenty-four
hours locked in their cells.

Just as all hospitals or high schools seem to have the same smell, so do
juvenile prisons—the astringent odor of industrial-strength soap mixed
with the sour sweat of fear. Sound echoes hollowly off concrete floors and
cinder-block walls. Every aspect of the institution, cold to the touch and
harsh on the ear, seems designed to convey that those who abide there are
all alone and very far from home.

Rules vary from one institution to the next, but most places require that
wards march three or four across from unit to classroom to meals and back

again. Some also require young people to hold their hands behind their backs when they move together from one place to another, or to do some version of the "chicken walk" (hands folded across the chest and tucked into the armpits). Justified as a means of preempting fights, this odd posture of self-containment also functions to sap any residual dignity.

Most juvenile facilities have some version of "the hole": stripped-down solitary confinement cells, sometimes whole wings of them, used to house the victimized, the victimizer, the vulnerable, the suicidal, or the simply defiant, with little distinction made among them. Youth deemed in need of protection (from themselves or others) or discipline spend up to twenty-three hours a day in these barren cells, with the mattress removed during the day in the name of safety, and meals and education (sometimes worksheets and a crayon) slipped through a slot in the door. When these young people leave their cells for any reason, they must first slip their hands through a slot to be cuffed.

Even in the "general population," the young prisoner generally has little to call his own. There are strict limitations on "personal effects"; even photographs of family are rationed, if not banned. Rooms must be kept military-style neat, although guards may also ransack them in the name of a general search. The young ward will eat, sleep, and shower with strangers, under the eye of yet more strangers and often surveillance cameras, and wake to the sound of a clamoring bell.

"When you walk into the living quarters of a lot of our places, it's very intimidating," a clinician who works with multiple New York youth facilities acknowledged. "When you drove up to the facility, it was a huge campus surrounded by a fence with razor wire," he continued, speaking of a particular institution that had recently been closed. "You had to drive [through] a fence. They closed the gate behind you and then the next gate opened up and you drive through it. Just the physical layout is . . . very intimidating." For those new to institutional life, he explained, the effect was often overwhelming.

He was not talking about the kids who are held in these places, sometimes for years. He was explaining why turnover is so high among newly hired guards.

· · ·

As California's Preston Youth Correctional Facility loomed in the distance, Luis's palms began to sweat and his heart rate accelerated. Instinctively, he balled up his fists, ready to fight before he even stepped off the bus.

"I did not know what to expect," Luis recalled of his arrival at age sixteen. His first stop on the state juvenile circuit was known colloquially as "The Castle" because of its site just beneath the now empty Preston School of Industry, a massive, Romanesque Revival stone edifice in California's Gold Country that housed young offenders until 1960.

Evoking a medieval torture mill more than any kind of industry, the Castle is rumored to be haunted by the ghosts of former wards and an unlucky housekeeper. Ghosts, however, were not Luis's top concern. A slight and handsome teenager with the eyes of a deer, Luis had picked up a gang affiliation in an effort to protect himself inside the local juvenile hall. Until now, though, he had just been testing out the identity. Here, he feared, he might be pushed further. "I thought if it was gonna be hella crazy, then I would have turned crazy and kept fighting and defending the gang that I represent," Luis explained.

Each unit at Preston was named for a different tree, as if the complex were a suburban subdivision. First, Luis went to Cedars, the reception unit. Looking around, he saw no familiar faces—no potential allies but any number of possible foes. As he passed by the Sequoia Unit, empty metal cages loomed before him, used (until subsequent litigation challenged the practice) to hold young men during their legally mandated hour of "large-muscle exercise."

"I was lost," Luis recalled of his arrival at Preston. "Swear to God, I was lost."

Luis was lying on his bunk in boxers and sandals, trying to orient himself by staring at the rows of triple-tier bunks and the locked command center, when he heard a catcall that represented a direct challenge to his local gang. Luis returned the insult, and then it was on. He charged his provocateur at full speed and was ready to fight a second belligerent when guards arrived and hauled him away.

Others shouted taunts as guards escorted him past the showers and down the hallway to Ironwood, Preston's secure unit. It was his first night, and already Luis was on lockdown.

"Where the fuck am I?" Luis wondered. "I am hella skinny, my shirt is off, I am in my boxers still . . . and I am just pondering. Am I going to be this self-proclaimed gangster that goes all out for this stupid set that I am not a part of? That is really just hurting me, not loving me—hurting me in every way possible?"

What was the alternative? The conflicts and alliances that defined life in a juvenile prison held little interest for Luis, who had entered the system an abused kid toying with a criminal identity. But could he survive without the protection of a gang? Challenged within hours of his arrival, he had already landed in solitary confinement.

He tried to fall asleep on the bare concrete slab that served as his bed—he had no blanket and had cast away the shit-stained mattress—but these questions kept him awake deep into the night.

The next day was little better. Released from isolation, he was placed in a cage (an actual metal cage, ostensibly for exercise) with two rival gang members, who told him to plan to "get down" in the showers.

"Shower time, and you are gonna box me when I'm naked?" Luis cast his eyes to the sky: What next? He'd soon find out.

"When kids go to prison in California, it's not pretty," Luis summarized. "I witnessed how COs [correctional officers] would put you in your place, and if you *weren't* in your place, they would beat the shit out of you and put you in your place."

Technically, the young people held in juvenile institutions like Preston are not prisoners. They have stepped outside the lines of the law, but they have not been convicted of any crime. Instead, under the rubric of the juvenile justice system, they have been adjudicated delinquent and mandated to a stay in a state institution in the name of their best interest as well as public safety.

But walk down a cellblock or visit a dorm inside one of these places anywhere in the nation and ask the kids to describe their situation: they will make it clear that they are locked down. The distinction we make between a juvenile facility, by whatever euphemism, and a prison means little to the kid who enters through a sally port and sleeps in a barren cell, watched over by uniformed guards wielding pepper spray, and surrounded on all sides by coils of razor wire.

A national survey by the federal Office of Juvenile Justice and

Delinquency Prevention paints a picture of state juvenile prisons as an environment of nearly unremitting victimization, where young people "experience violence, theft and assault at an alarming rate." The majority of youth in state custody—56 percent—told investigators they had been victimized, most of them repeatedly, at the hands of staff as well as their peers. Sixty-one percent of those who had been victimized reported that they were injured in the process. Nearly half of those surveyed had their property stolen, 10 percent were directly robbed, and 29 percent had been threatened or beaten. Most who were robbed behind bars had been robbed repeatedly, and about a third were injured badly enough to require medical treatment.

All of this conspires to underscore a central message: that the young ward surrenders the right not only to freedom but also to safety and bodily integrity the moment he crosses the threshold. Young people who have been sent to juvenile institutions to learn "accountability" discover that there is a powerful double standard when they are the victims and their keepers are the perpetrators. According to a large-scale federal survey, fully 41 percent of incarcerated youth who told investigators they'd "had property taken by force or threat" reported that a guard was the perpetrator, as did 24 percent of victims of assault. A comprehensive federal investigation into sexual abuse in juvenile facilities found that the vast majority was perpetrated by guards. One in ten youths nationwide had suffered sexual assault at the hands of a staff member, while a far lower number—one in fifty—were sexually victimized by peers. Staff are rarely called to account for these offenses—which are often more serious than those that propelled their victims into custody—and criminal prosecution is particularly rare.

The ward-on-ward violence, at least, may appear self-explanatory: *These are violent kids; what else do you expect?* In fact, the dynamic is more complex. Certainly, some youths are already acting out violently by the time they are locked up, but more are not. Only one-fourth of youth held in state juvenile facilities, ostensibly reserved for more serious offenders, are locked up for Violent Crime Index offenses. But whatever their charge, or demeanor on the outside, new arrivals often feel pressed to make a stark choice: victim or victimizer. Neutrality is rarely an option.

Even as young prisoners are given the message that they must be confined because they pose a threat to society, many live in constant, if well-hidden, fear themselves. More than one-third of youth (38 percent) told federal researchers they feared being attacked while locked up, 25 percent by another resident and 22 percent by staff.

On top of the violence cited above, more than one-fourth of youth in custody reported that staff used "some method of physical restraint on them—whether handcuffs, wristlets, a security belt, chains, or a restraint chair." Another 7 percent had been pepper sprayed, while 30 percent live on units where pepper spray is used. Taken in the name of "safety and security," these and similar measures more often serve to heighten young people's fear and constant vigilance.

Guards often use hands-on physical restraint, not only to break up fights or avert other violence but in response to minor infractions such as horseplay, talking in line, or simply talking back. The most dangerous method is known as "prone restraint." Guards, sometimes two or three, force a youth to the ground and then lie or sit on him until they are convinced he has been thoroughly subdued. A number of young people have died during or shortly after being restrained in this manner, leading a few states to ban the practice.

Also striking is the pervasive use of solitary confinement, given widespread agreement that the practice is damaging and potentially dangerous, especially for youth. Nevertheless, more than a third of youth in custody reported being placed in isolation, more than half for longer than twenty-four hours (a clear violation of international standards).

In a particularly bitter irony, the stricter the means of custody and control at a particular institution, the *higher* the odds that youths will be victimized there, by guards as well as peers. The more often young people are handcuffed, strip-searched, chained, or bound in restraint chairs, in other words, the higher the odds they will also be assaulted, robbed, or raped.

Much of what is done in the name of institutional security only adds to young people's sense of degradation. For Enrique, the frequent room searches were a particular affront. "That's your sanctuary," he said of the few feet of cell space allotted each inmate—"that's our place of peace.

Some guys' floor is so clean, the toilet is spotless, the walls are clean, the bed is made, all your clothes you have are folded neatly, your letters, paper, and pencil, everything is perfect."

During a search, he said, order gives way to chaos. "All your mail is thrown on the ground. Body washes and shampoos are open and [spilled] on the mail. Blankets are on the floor. The blankets you sleep on, and it's on the floor! Your clothes, your boxers, it's on the floor. Why throw it on the floor? Why can't you just put it on the mat?"

For many young people, connection with family—their link to the outside world and the life they knew before—is especially precious. Even in this sacred realm, according to Enrique and others, staff seemed to go out of their way to convey disrespect.

"The mail—some of them hold the mail for years. They throw out the letters," Enrique said. Room searches provided yet another opportunity to insult those on the outside whom young people most love. "The pictures that you have of your family—nieces, girlfriend, grandma—everything is taken out, thrown around. Your letters, your papers? All wrinkled. Your schoolwork, your court letters, it's all mixed up."

In the four years that Enrique was locked up, he went through this more times than he could count, he said. "Sometimes twice a week. Once a week. It happens a lot."

Some young men on his unit registered their objection by tearing out the relevant section of the facility handbook (which calls for guards to leave belongings as they find them) and placing it in full view on top of their lockers. "What are you gonna do? You gonna write a grievance?" guards would mock in response. It was widely understood that grievances went nowhere.

Rochelle was fifteen and pregnant when she was locked up in New York State for fighting. "They treat you like dogs," said Rochelle. "The worst thing about it is the search. When they surprise you out of nowhere, wake you up from your sleep and trash your room. They don't have no kind of respect there. You have to get naked and squat. It is just degrading."

"I never thought I would be someplace like that," said Rochelle, whose pregnancy made intrusions such as squatting naked before strangers particularly humiliating. "It was horrible. I didn't like being away from family. I was trapped. I felt lonely. It was like I was in another world."

Young prisoners learn in multiple ways that their bodies are no more their own than are the cells they maintain so carefully or the uniforms they wear. On top of strip searches and supervised showers (which may come with catcalls or disparaging remarks from guards), some institutions force young people to endure pat searches multiple times each day. At one Florida facility, according to a Department of Justice investigation, youth were subjected to frisk searches more than ten times a day, even when they were under constant supervision, "purportedly for recovery of contraband. During the six month period we reviewed, the most dangerous contraband recovered were pencils."

"Many of the youths informed us that some [staff] were especially intrusive in conducting the searches," federal investigators wrote. "We heard a number of reports of youth being groped by [staff] during the searches. One youth noted, 'Some staff rub on your privates.' Another stated, staff 'touch too much.'"

Reading the results of this investigation, I thought of one of my first visits to a county juvenile hall, where I had gone to conduct a writing workshop for two units, boys and girls. Breaking a rule I had not been informed of, I failed to count all the pencils before we handed them out so they could be counted again before we left.

Because of my mistake, everyone who had joined the class was strip-searched. There was no evidence that a pencil had gone missing, nor that any of the young people subjected to the search had done anything wrong. The error was entirely mine, but no one suggested that I be penalized for it. While the girls and boys who had, moments ago, been my "students" were being stripped naked in front of their keepers, I was on the road, headed for home.

Prison dehumanizes, not as a side effect but as a central function. A child who is forcibly removed from home and society and placed inside a cage receives a powerful message about herself and her place in the world. Assigning a number in lieu of a name; taking away clothing and personal belongings and replacing them with uniforms and cold metal bunks; the bare-bones environment with its spare furnishings, harsh lighting, and round-the-clock surveillance; the lining up and other militaristic affectations; and, above all, the stripping away of human connection—every aspect of institutional life conspires to diminish a young person's sense of herself as someone who matters, to wear down her sense of individuality. Because adolescents are at a stage of life where building a sense of self in relation to others is central to their development, this assault on identity strikes them with particular force.

"When you're in a place where you are segregated, ostracized—a physical environment that is corroding, that is black, that is dark, that is isolated—all these things do something to your brain, to your psyche, to your self-esteem," Luis said. "It is something that your body internalizes, and it is obviously negative. A place that is dark and eerie? This is something that no human being *should* adapt to. We are not made to. You are supposed to be out in the sun, for God's sake!"

The notion of "prison culture" may have the ring of sociological jargon, but inside the gates its pull is undeniable. Each time I drive into a compound surrounded by razor wire, pull up at the guard station to verify my clearance, and leave my identification with the guard at the front desk, I feel as if I've just had my passport stamped at the border.

Young people acculturate, but at a cost. *Treated like an animal, I became an animal.* Over and over, as they described growing up in institutions governed by the law of the jungle—adapting to a culture of captivity and power where the worst thing you could be was somebody's bitch—this is the transformation young people described.

Many referred to the institutions where they spent their teenage years as "gladiator schools" or simply "schools for crime." Their assessment is borne out by the research, which finds that spending time in a state juvenile facility *increases* the odds that a young person will advance in delinquency and that he will go on to be arrested as an adult.

"I saw more violence in those six years [locked up] than I've ever seen," said Will, a rangy, long-limbed young man with wire-rimmed glasses and piercing brown eyes, "even on TV. If you can imagine it, then I've probably seen it."

"The mind games," he elaborated, were "the hardest part. 'Oh, you're new? Here goes a Ramen noodle. Yeah, I'll take care of you.' Then, like a week later: 'Oh, you gotta go stab this dude.'"

Mark was stocky, tattooed, and muscular, a veteran of more locked facilities than he cared to name. "As far as being aggressive and not trusting anybody, that's what the system did for me," he said flatly. "The weak get run over. You gotta be strong and stick to your guns, and you can't trust anybody."

As a teenager inside a California youth prison, Mark was forced to participate in what became known as "Friday Night Fights." Guards would place known gang rivals together in a locked room and stand idly by, watching while captive youth beat each other bloody, intervening only when they'd seen enough, using pepper spray or riot guns to break up the staged battles.

"I know where my anger stems from," said Mark, who struggled with what he called "blackout rages" well into adulthood, "and my inability to trust. If you tell me this is a cup of coffee, I'll turn it over and over and over till I find out what it is."

"Which I'm trying to work out," he added, glancing at his girlfriend—who, he acknowledged, had sometimes been the target of those rages—and seeming to deflate as the anger left his voice and a rueful tone replaced it. "It doesn't happen overnight."

On top of the violence, chaos, fear, and degradation, the defining aspect of life behind bars is isolation. A young person who spends part or all of her adolescent years in a locked facility, away from friends and family, her every action subject to the dictates of strangers, misses many if not most of the central developmental tasks of adolescence: learning to navigate intimate relationships; forming the capacity to make independent decisions; taking on increased responsibility; discovering and expressing one's personal identity. None of these goals can be met in isolation. All require relationship, human connection. That is what prison, by definition, takes away.

Walk a straight line.
Don't be a bitch.
Don't ask questions.
Talk is dead.

Machine down.

These are the lessons young people who are locked up learn instead: to close off their emotions, shut down their intellect, quell their individuality, avoid forming connections, and view all interactions through the prism of power.

Gladys Carríon, the iconoclastic head of New York State's Office of Children and Family Services—which runs that state's juvenile facilities—makes no bones about the impact of severing relationships during the crucial passage that is adolescence (not coincidentally, she is also rapidly shutting down the juvenile prisons under her jurisdiction). "Kids are punished when they're removed from their home," she said bluntly. "We don't have to put them on the chain gang. They're removed. That is punishment. I keep reminding my staff, *that is the punishment*: removing the kid from their family, from their school, and from their community. I don't think you could do anything worse in the formative years of a child, of a young person, than to remove them from their community. We are interrupting their developmental process. We don't need to punish them any further."

Luis offered a related analysis of the impact of incarceration on a young mind and spirit. "Prison makes you hate yourself," he said flatly, as if stating something that was widely understood. "The way prison is developed is to keep you oppressed, and in a state where you cannot believe in yourself. Everyone looks down on you, instead of looking down *at* you and helping you up."

"The way that you are treated, the way that you are stigmatized, the way that you are labeled . . ." Luis trailed off in frustration but quickly recovered his train of thought.

"If society wants to see a decline in victimization, then you need to *help* the person who is hurting," he insisted, "because otherwise, he'll end up turning on himself, and you. That is just our nature."

Jared turned to metaphor to describe the emotional impact of incarceration. Not long after his release, he told me, he went down to the San Francisco Bay and swam out into the open water, just because he could. Intoxicated by the freedom, solitude, and motion, he swam too far and panicked, nearly drowning before he recovered enough to make it back to shore. The sensation of near drowning—the struggle for air, the terror of the depths, and the fear of slipping past the point of no return—was the best analogy Jared could find for the pressure he felt on the worst days behind bars. These were the days when he felt his lungs might implode as confinement sucked the very air out of his spirit.

"That feeling, almost drowning," said Jared, "is the only thing I've ever experienced that even came close to being locked up."

2

BIRTH OF AN ABOMINATION

The Juvenile Prison in the Nineteenth Century

You have to be ever-vigilant every time you deprive someone of their liberty. It should never be done easily or cavalierly—always as a last resort. If history has taught us anything, it's taught us that.
—New York City probation commissioner Vincent Schiraldi

THE STORY OF JUVENILE justice in the United States begins, as does every epic tragedy, as a tale of good intentions.

The story of the juvenile prison begins near the founding of the country, when a group of merchants and civic leaders came together under the banner of the newly formed Society for the Prevention of Pauperism, later renamed the Society for the Prevention of Juvenile Delinquency.

Intending to rescue children from the degradations of the adult prison, Progressive-era reformers wound up with a junior version, which they dubbed, optimistically, the "House of Refuge." In New York, home to the first House of Refuge, the state legislature gave this new institution a mandate as noble as its name. Its managers, according to the law that authorized the New York House of Refuge, were to provide wayward youth—whether delinquent or merely destitute—with education and employment "as in their judgment will be most for the reformation and . . . future benefit and advantage of such children."

By way of these institutions—which soon spread across the nation—the "child savers" diverted countless children from adult institutions. They also gradually gained a power that had heretofore been reserved for the individual patriarch, no matter his means: control over the children.

The Houses of Refuge, author Kenneth Wooden writes, were "a historical milestone in the American family culture. For the first time family centered discipline was replaced by institutional discipline administered by city, county or state governments. Parents, grandparents, older sisters and brothers were replaced by guards and superintendents."

The House of Refuge, in other words—like every manifestation of the juvenile prison to follow—came to function as a mechanism for gaining control over the children of the poor, depriving them of their liberty in the name of their own best interest while skirting the burdensome requirements of due process. The civic leaders who comprised the society had little compunction about placing the cart ahead of the horse, granting themselves control over any child they deemed at risk of delinquency well before the law gave them license to do so.

On January 1, 1825, the New York House of Refuge—the nation's first known juvenile reformatory—opened its doors, with a society board member holding the post of superintendent and a total of nine youngsters under his supervision.

The House of Refuge—like every version of the juvenile prison that would follow—was from its inception a race- and class-driven enterprise, intended explicitly for "other people's children." When the New York House of Refuge opened its doors, the state was at the tail end of a five-fold population increase, due primarily to forty years of Irish and German immigration. Social engineers of the day were quite concerned with the influx of immigrants from Europe, particularly the Irish, whose arrival, they feared, would lead to "a breakdown in the social order and perhaps a lower class revolt against established moral and political authority." In an early example of racial profiling, one training school superintendent offered the following explanation as to why a particular boy had been identified as delinquent: "The lad's parents are Irish and intemperate and that tells the whole story."

Within months of opening its doors, the New York House of Refuge secured from the state legislature an allocation of $2,000 per year, allowing it to harbor greater numbers of young people. According to the *New York Times*, the rapid influx of confined juveniles stemmed "mainly from three sources, viz.: from the children of poor and often vicious emigrants; from the intemperance of parents, and the frequent want, misery and ignorance of their children; and from the existence of theatres, circuses, &c., whose amusements offered such temptations to children as to lead them often to petty acts of dishonesty to obtain the means of gratifying their taste for such performances."

Whatever their offenses, actual or anticipated, children did not have to be tried or even arrested in order to be incarcerated in the early nineteenth century. In New York, agents of the House of Refuge simply roamed the streets of immigrant neighborhoods and rounded up whomever they pleased, consigning children to custody on grounds of anything from impoverishment to delinquency to neglect.

The discovery (or invention) of this large and heretofore untapped population of delinquents proved a fund-raising boon for the fledgling society, which "sought the means of sustaining their institution from the sources which thus supplied them with inmates." That line of reasoning garnered the society $10,000 from the Excise Fund, drawn from liquor licenses and fees imposed on theaters and circuses, and another $8,000 a year from the Hospital and Passenger Fund. The latter was amassed via a per capita tax on new immigrants, collected before they were allowed to disembark; in other words, a pay-in-advance scheme for the cost of housing the delinquents that each boatload of "vicious emigrants" could be counted upon to spawn, according to the advocates of the House of Refuge.

Good intentions notwithstanding, the less-than-charitable motives that drive the worst excesses of the juvenile prison today—racism, politics, and simple venality—were embedded in the institution before the first brick was laid. The popular narrative of a system born out of selfless concern for children endangered on the streets or in adult prisons, corrupted only later by politics and greed, turns out to be, if not a fiction, at best a partial account. The corrupting elements that plague the system to this day were right there in the blueprint from the very start.

Once it had established the need for its services, the society successfully petitioned for a more secure funding stream, augmenting its annual allotments with a supplement of $40 "per head" (or child, as they are otherwise known). Tying funding to population created a built-in incentive for growth, and from then on the charitable endeavor known as the House of Refuge operated under an unspoken maxim that would characterize prison growth well into the next century: *if you build it, they will come*—in ever greater numbers, willingly or not.

By 1860, the New York House of Refuge had gone from nine residents to 560, some as young as eight, and momentum showed no sign of slowing. Having obtained a thirty-plus-acre tract of island land in the East River, the society raised upwards of $400,000 to build a massive institution intended to contain more than twelve hundred children. "The boys' house," per the *Times*, was "an imposing edifice, having a main building, 80 by 100 feet, 3½ stories high, with two wings, each 255 feet in length, making an entire front of 590 feet. The main building, and the terminal buildings at the end of the wings, are each crowned with a dome."

Maintaining an institution of this magnitude was a costly endeavor, but those in charge soon found a way to fund it: they put the kids to work. The "boys of more vicious character, and who would be most likely to contaminate those with whom they might associate" rose at dawn and went to school for thirty to sixty minutes before reporting to work making chair frames, sieves, and rat traps—all "under contract," creating a steady cash flow for the institution. More schooling followed dinner, and then it was off to bed. The "younger and better boys" had a slightly better deal—they were made to work only six hours a day, allowing for an extra hour of education.

The eight- to seventeen-year-olds working these long hours were kept in line by a system of rewards and punishments that bears a striking resemblance to the level systems and behavior modification programs in use to this day. The children were divided into five categories, based on their perceived character ("Class No. 3 are vicious, but a grade better in behavior than No. 4"). On the rewards front, the best of the lot could aspire to a "distinctive badge." The punishment system was more elaborate, ranging from loss of already scant "play hours" to a bread-and-water diet and solitary confinement to "lastly, if absolutely necessary, corporeal punishment."

Only toward the end of its account does the *Times* introduce concerns regarding certain aspects of the newly minted institution.

> While some of the children . . . undoubtedly become attached to the Superintendent and teachers, it is unquestionably true that a large majority are not restrained, by any affection, from acts of violence and insubordination; they regard themselves as prisoners, and as a matter of prudence submit to what they cannot help. . . . The system . . . requires for its highest measure of success what is evidently an impossibility: that one or two men shall become . . . so fully acquainted with the character, disposition and impelling motives of each of 450 boys, as to be able to adapt their instruction and conduct to them in the way most effectually to call out what is good and to subdue what is evil in their natures. . . . If the same number of boys could be broken up into twelve or fifteen families . . . each of those heads of families could attain a far more thorough knowledge of the character, habits and passions of each boy in his charge than can now be done. He would know what temptations assailed each boy with the greatest power, and what influences would be most effective in combating them, and we might hope for a still larger percentage of reformations.

Only one thing, in other words, was needed to improve what the *Times* found otherwise an "excellent institution": an opportunity for the children to form trusting relationships with adults who viewed and knew them as individuals.

When I interviewed wards of the current system more than 150 years later, I asked them what they thought might improve their lives and prospects. The great majority offered the very same answer: trusting relationships with adults who saw them as human beings. However many children longed for this, few had experienced it, despite countless cycles of "reform" over the intervening years.

Beyond noting this central absence of human relationship, the *Times* had only a couple of suggestions: more religious instruction and better monitoring to prevent indulgence in "the solitary vice." The heartbreaker comes when the newspaper begins to editorialize about the young wards' future prospects, warning against the danger of introducing hope into a locked facility.

> Injudicious friends of this, as well as of other similar institutions, often do injury by attempting to encourage the boys that if they do well they will attain to high social position and consideration. . . . It is a fact which it would be better to impress upon the children, that no such high destiny awaits most of them. They may and can become honest, upright, conscientious and hard-working laborers and mechanics; they may be able to provide well for those whom they love, and for the families they may rear, but very few of them will ever attain exalted station, and so far as this ambition unfits them for the sober realities of life, it is prejudicial to them.

There it is in black and white, set forth by the "newspaper of record" right from the start: more religion, less masturbation, and the radical curtailment of hope. This is the best one can wish for those "other people's children" raised by the nation's first juvenile institution, one that would become the model for the sprawling system to come.

So much for the American ideal of equal opportunity—the bootstrap ethos American schoolchildren are told makes their nation unique. The parcel of life allotted to those raised by the state, it was clear from the outset, would be forever limited by the experience of juvenile incarceration and the diminished status that it conveyed. Being "other people's children" got them locked up in the first place, and "other" they would remain for the rest of their days. To tell them anything different—to imply, for instance, that such as they might have a shot at the American dream—would be to do them a cruel injustice.

Later accounts indicate that residents of the earliest House of Refuge were all too familiar with these sober realities. There were regular allegations that the private contractors who paid (some said bribed) house managers for wards' labor abused the children who were sent to work for them. Inside the House of Refuge, violence was "commonplace," and residents regularly registered their protest by rioting, setting fires, or running away.

These problems did not stop the New York House of Refuge from being widely replicated. Between 1750 and 1850, the population of the United States grew from 1.25 million to 23 million. As cities scrambled to keep up with a massive influx of immigrants (and the delinquent children they were expected to produce), similar institutions sprung up across the country. The houses of refuge built in tandem with this wave of immigration, the legal scholar Barry Feld has written, "constituted the first specialized institutions for the formal social control of youth," rising as the "development of a market economy and growth of commerce in cities widened social class differences and aroused fear of the poor."

The juvenile institutions (training schools, houses of refuge, etc.) that opened their doors in the early nineteenth century in cities including Boston, Chicago, and Philadelphia defined their mandate in the language of benevolence but, upon closer inspection, had many hallmarks of the traditional prison, most notably locked cells and a culture of total control.

This culture was often a cruel one. "Children confined in the houses of refuge were subjected to strict discipline and control. . . . Corporal punishments (including hanging children from their thumbs, the use of the 'ducking stool' for girls, and severe beatings), solitary confinement, handcuffs, the 'ball and chain,' uniform dress, the 'silent system,' and other practices were commonly used in houses of refuge."

As Barry Feld has written,

Punitive delinquency institutions have characterized the juvenile justice system from its inception. Historical analyses of the early training schools described institutions that failed to rehabilitate and scarcely differed from their adult penal counterparts. . . . One account of juvenile correctional programs under the aegis of Progressivism concluded: "The descent from the rhetoric to the reality of juvenile institutions is precipitous. . . . No matter how frequently juvenile court judges insisted that their sentences of confinement were for treatment and not punishment, no matter how vehemently superintendents declared that their institutions were rehabilitative and not correctional, conditions at training schools belied these claims."

Never slow to seize an opportunity to control an unruly or unwanted population, the state soon got into the training school business itself, opening public juvenile reformatories to supplement or supplant those run by private charities. Massachusetts jumped in first with the Lyman School for Boys (1847) and the Lancaster School for Girls (1855), and other states soon followed suit. By the end of the nineteenth century, every state in the nation was operating juvenile reformatories. By 1960, there were two hundred training schools across the United States, with a daily population of about forty thousand.

Then as now, the gap between rhetoric and reality when it came to the institution of the juvenile prison was large enough to swallow up the building itself. As historian Joseph Kett has written, "Those who sought to reform juvenile delinquents in mid-19th century America spoke the lofty language of nurture and environmentalism. Reform schools, they claimed, were not prisons but home-like institutions, veritable founts of generous sentiments. In fact, they were prisons, often brutal and disorderly ones."

"As children of immigrants and the poor increasingly populated refuges and reformatories, the conditions deteriorated further," Barry Feld concurred. "In an early version of 'blaming the victims,' institutional managers contended that 'the aliens had only themselves to blame for the decline of the asylum, for they were untreatable or unmanageable.'"

Almost seventy-five years after the New York House of Refuge opened its doors, the Illinois Juvenile Court Act of 1899 codified thinking about juvenile justice for the first time, establishing a family court and giving it authority over delinquent, dependent, and neglected children (with little distinction made among the three).

In passing the act, the Illinois legislature formalized the means by which children might be placed in training schools, providing legal cover for practices that were already widespread.

The legal justification for vesting the state with the power to determine what was best for (certain) children was drawn from a doctrine known as *parens patriae*, or "the state as parent." Derived from English common law, parens patriae was a vestige of the feudal notion of obligations and powers belonging to the king and was originally applied mainly to clear up issues of feudal succession or disperse the property of orphaned minors.

The broad authority judges assumed under parens patriae was based on a presumption of benevolence: the court's actions, however much they might impinge upon a child's freedom or the parental prerogative, were taken in the name of the child's best interest.

The tension between care and control—reflected to this day in the tug-of-war between rehabilitation and punishment—is not, as is sometimes assumed, of recent origin. It was woven into the fabric of the juvenile court from its very inception. On the one hand, many judges did their best to advance the rehabilitative mandate—most famously Denver's Ben Lindsey, who advocated that judges develop a personal rapport with the youth who came before them, and play an active role in surrounding them with support, encouragement, and resources in an effort to boost first their self-esteem and then their prospects in the world.

On the other, the wide latitude granted judges to act in children's best interest, as those judges perceived it, meant that many children were deprived of their liberty without having committed any crime. One reform school investigation found that only one in ten residents had committed an offense serious enough to bring an adult before a judge. The superintendent of a Chicago reform school testified that "courts considered what was best for the welfare of the children and made orders to that effect, often with no formal charge against these children and regardless of the severity of the crimes for which they had been arrested."

Julian Mack, one of the first judges to preside over the Chicago Juvenile Court in the early twentieth century, revealed this tension in his 1909 effort to describe the new court's role: "The child who must be brought into court should, of course, be made to know that he is face to face with the power of the state, but he should at the same time, and more emphatically, be made to feel that he is the object of its care and solicitude."

Mack recommended various means of projecting the latter half of this mixed message: "The judge on a bench, looking down upon the boy standing at the bar, can never evoke a proper sympathetic spirit. Seated at a desk, with the child at his side, where he can on occasion put his arm around his shoulder and draw the lad to him, the judge, while losing none of his judicial dignity, will gain immensely in the effectiveness of his work."

However solicitous the jurist, once a child passed through the gates of the institution to which his erstwhile protector remanded him, the "power of the state" hit him full force. According to a report from the Annie E. Casey Foundation, "From the very beginning . . . the implementation and practice of juvenile justice fell far short of its lofty ideals. The courts relied heavily on 'reformatories,' later known as training schools, where conditions were often more severe and discipline far harsher than their rehabilitative mission implied."

Like the House of Refuge, the juvenile court was an instant sensation, spreading across the nation in the span of a generation. While the new court did spare some children the hardship of time in adult jails, it also provided a legal foundation for placing many more in training schools and other juvenile institutions (an operation previously executed on a more ad hoc basis) while skirting due-process protections.

When the juvenile court judge exercised his discretion, he was protected and empowered by the assumption that he was acting in the child's best interest. On the basis of this presumption, young people could be deprived of their liberty without the protections otherwise guaranteed by the Constitution. Over the following decades, a series of Supreme Court decisions (most notably *In re Gault* in 1967) extended some protections to juveniles—including the right to counsel and to confront their accusers—but others, like the right to a jury trial, remained out of reach.

Well before the Illinois Juvenile Court Law formalized its place in the American legal system, the doctrine of parens patriae had been invoked to justify a child's commitment to a House of Refuge over a parent's explicit objection. In *Ex parte Crouse* (1838), the Pennsylvania Supreme Court rejected a father's challenge to the incarceration of his daughter Mary Ann, whose mother had found her "unruly and unmanageable" and handed her over to the Pennsylvania House of Refuge.

Ex parte Crouse strengthened the legal justification for institutionalizing children who had committed no crime. It also made clear that parens patriae trumped parenthood itself. In rejecting the father's plea for his daughter's freedom and return to his custody, the court held that Mary Ann's constitutional rights were not being violated because she was being held for the purpose not of punishment but of "reformation." If keeping her separate from "the corrupting influence of improper associates" also required separating her from her apparently loving father, that was incidental.

"To this end," the court argued,

> may not the natural parent, when unequal to the task of education, or unworthy of it be superseded by the *parens patriae*, or common guardian of the community? It is to be remembered that the public has a paramount interest in the virtue and knowledge of its members, and that, of strict right, the business of education belongs to it. . . . The infant has been snatched from a course which must have ended in confirmed depravity; and not only is the restraint of her person lawful, but it would be an act of extreme cruelty to release her from it.

As the late legal scholar Sanford Fox has noted, *Ex parte Crouse* "became the precedent for 20th Century cases holding that the juvenile court could similarly commit children without the traditional legal formalities." The decision, legal scholar and advocate Barry Krisberg has observed, "was heavily influenced by the antagonism toward Irish parents who were regarded as corrupt and ineffectual by more established Americans. The courts generally held that the traditional conceptions of criminal law did not apply to the Refuge. The overriding values involved protecting the social order from the potential threat posed by a growing army of impoverished youth."

Understood in the context of the era, as well as the subsequent reality of its exercise, the doctrine of parens patriae had less to do with enforcing the state's obligation to children than with legitimizing its authority over them—an authority greater than that of the natural parent. Once a child was committed to a House of Refuge, house managers generally maintained jurisdiction until he reached adulthood, although few were held that long; most were "bound" as apprentices or shipped out to live with, and labor for, farm families after a year or two of institutional life.

"Juvenile justice is replete with oxymorons," Northwestern University's Bernardine Dohrn has written, "perhaps including juvenile justice itself. None, however, are more ironic than the reform school or the training school—these dismal places where children are incarcerated under the promise of education, learning, schooling. . . . The gap between goals and practice, rhetoric and reality, mandates and options, is enormous."

Dohrn is pointing toward a central flaw in the American system of juvenile justice—a flaw that, despite the traditional narrative of a benevolent system later gone astray, was embedded in the juvenile court from its founding moment. The court had (and has) the power to take away a young person's freedom—the most powerful intervention, short of taking a life, available to the state—in the name of his "best interests" without offering him the basic constitutional protections guaranteed adults.

Advocates are not the only ones who have voiced concern about the gap between rhetoric and reality represented by the training schools. In the majority decision in *Kent v. United States*—a 1966 case that revolved around due process and waiver of juveniles to adult court—the Supreme Court found "grounds for concern that the child receives the worst of both worlds: that he gets neither the protections accorded to adults nor the solicitous care and regenerative treatment postulated for children."

The definition of insanity is doing the same thing over and over and hoping for different results.

I heard this aphorism repeated many times by young people with firsthand experience of the juvenile justice system. Often, they were referring to the errors of their younger selves, not those of their keepers, but it seems an accurate analysis of the history of the training school as well.

For as long as houses of refuge and the like have been in business, inquiries of one sort or another have found them to be both corrupt and corrupting—detrimental, at best, to the children they are meant to serve. But rather than leading us to abandon a failed practice, these investigations have, in the main, inspired little more than further investigation—a cycle that continues to this day.

In 1920, for example, a children's advocacy group launched the first in what would be a parade of investigations into the St. Charles Reformatory, established in Illinois in 1904. The report that followed, according to scholar Bernardine Dohrn, described "the repressed and joyless atmosphere, the rule of silence during meals, and an exhausted staff who worked 24 hours per day." Most significantly, the report noted the failure of the Illinois training schools to provide any actual training to their young inmates.

Just over a decade later, a 1931 legislative report on the St. Charles Reformatory found similar problems and worse. On top of the overcrowding and second-rate education, this next round of investigators found, the staff believed that a fourth of the boys should not be there at all.

The saga continued. By 1939, overcrowding and a "crisis of escapes and runaways" inspired legislative hearings.

In 1941, a boy at St. Charles was beaten to death by two house fathers, an event that inspired another investigation, this one conducted by a "blue ribbon committee." The committee's investigation revealed a brutal environment in which boys were subjected to punishments that seemed the product of a sadistic imagination ("swabbing," for example, in which staff filled a basement halfway up with water and forced the boys to soak it up with burlap and buckets before they were allowed food or rest). The committee ordered a variety of reforms—more recreation, staff training, and the like—but little evidence of actual improvement followed.

In 1949, yet another investigation found an "impossible mixture of feeble-minded, psychotic, dependent, and aggressive delinquents in the same facility."

"In the overall picture," this round of investigators lamented, "we must face the tragic facts of neglect, of suffering, and of the waste of opportunities and money which could be prevented. . . . Conditions exist which reflect grave discredit on a state which had the vision, the progressive motivation, to enact the first Juvenile Court Law in our country."

A half dozen investigations into conditions at the St. Charles Reformatory, in other words, had no perceptible outcome except continued decline. The 1949 report was issued on the fiftieth anniversary of the birth of the juvenile court.

Juvenile justice *reform*, it turns out, has been around almost as long as the juvenile prison. The scandals of today do not, after all, reflect the corruption of a once-grand mission. They are merely the latest in a long line of revelations of state-sanctioned child abuse that stretches back to the dawn of the juvenile prison.

3

OTHER PEOPLE'S CHILDREN

One of the underpinnings of the correction business has been that these kids are very different from the rest of us. That's one thing we have to hit head on. We have to change that attitude and stress that they are the same as the rest of us.

—Jerome Miller, former head of the
Massachusetts Department of Youth Services

What the best and wisest parent wants for his own child, that must the community want for all of its children.

—John Dewey

"DON'T YOU GET SCARED going into those places? Does it worry you ever—hanging out with those kids?"

I've been asked this question more times than I can count, in one form or another, all of which rests on the same central premise: that young prisoners are, without exception, Glock-carrying gangbangers, serial killers, carjackers, or rapists; that this is what it takes for a kid to get locked up in America. My interrogators have much in common with the American public, whose concept of the juvenile offender is curated by the mass media, with their unremitting onslaught of aberrations and atrocities.

In fact, for poor kids of color, getting locked up takes appallingly little. Despite the abiding image of the juvenile offender as "super-predator," young people are far more likely to be arrested for minor infractions than are adults. Even in large, state-run juvenile facilities—ostensibly reserved for the "worst of the worst"—the majority have been sentenced for non-violent acts.

But yes, I get scared going into these places. A prison itself—with its coils of razor wire, clanging metal doors, and uniformed guards—is a frightening place. In most cases, instilling fear appears to be the architectural and institutional intent, and I have by no means developed immunity.

Prisons scare me. Prisoners do not. Call me a hug-a-thug (you wouldn't be the first), but the distinction is based on lengthy experience. Some young prisoners I've met have been reserved to the point of silence, a few have been manipulative, and others prone to anger (as have some I've met among the free) but soulless, frozen-faced predators, as far as I can tell, are merely a figment of the criminological imagination—a potent figment, both politically and culturally, but a figment nonetheless.

Inside the girls' unit where I visited my friend Eliza, I got to know some of the other girls, along with their parents, grandparents, and children. Like Eliza—like the great majority of juvenile offenders—most were not there for committing violent or serious crimes; they were runaways, shoplifters, disturbers of the peace. Most, however, had been the *victims* of violence—beaten by boyfriends, assaulted by strangers, knocked around at home, and *then* brutalized in prison.

The federal Office of Juvenile Justice and Delinquency Prevention's Survey of Youth in Residential Placement offers an overview of what lands youth in juvenile prisons. Contrary to the notion that anyone who makes it to the so-called deep end of the juvenile justice system is by definition a super-predator, the most common route to custody is a property offense (45 percent of those surveyed). Forty-two percent reported status offenses (acts for which only minors can be arrested—running away, truancy, underage drinking), 23 percent "public order" offenses, and 30 percent technical violations of probation. Twenty-eight percent cited drug offenses. (The total is more than 100 percent because young people were asked what led to their current custody situation and many listed more than one offense.)

Twenty-six percent of those surveyed were locked up on assault charges and another 14 percent for a robbery. Only 11 percent of youth in custody were there for the kind of crimes associated with the super-predator image: murder, rape, or kidnapping. Forty-four percent reported being drunk, high, or both at the time of their offense, and 55 percent said they were with a group of other youths.

Studies in New York, Florida, Arkansas, South Carolina, and elsewhere flesh out the national picture, confirming the federal study's conclusion: the great majority of those confined as juveniles pose little to no danger to the public. Another misconception is that youths commit the majority of crime in the nation. In 2008, only 12 percent of violent crime and 18 percent of property crime nationwide were attributed to youths. According to the FBI, youths under age eighteen accounted for just 15 percent of all arrests.

Even this last number is likely inflated by police discretion. According to Lisa Thurau of the Massachusetts-based Strategies for Youth, which works to improve relations between police and teenagers, 21 percent of young people referred to juvenile court in 2005 were sent before a judge on charges of "disorderly conduct" or "obstruction of justice"—vague catchalls that, when it comes to teenagers, are very often euphemisms for what Thurau calls "contempt of cop."

In interviews with police officers over the course of a five-year investigation, Thurau found, "officers have routinely told me they will arrest a youth for being rude, for 'giving attitude' and for not submitting to officers' authority."

"Whether the youth has committed an offense does not determine the outcome," Thurau writes. "This focus on the offender rather than the offense is a characteristic of juvenile justice, and speaks volumes about what and who is viewed as criminal."

This was certainly so when it came to Eliza, who was sixteen when she introduced me to juvenile hall, and the road that brings young people there.

In a literal sense, I drove that road with her—she asked me to take her to turn herself in. The twenty-mile journey took us several hours. We stopped at a bookstore where she picked out a stack of novels—Toni Morrison, Gloria Naylor, Jamaica Kincaid—which I promised to bring in to her one at a time: she was not allowed to carry anything with her when she went inside. At a mall off the freeway, she chose a lunch of ice cream and candy, a child's last meal.

I had known Eliza since she was fourteen, when she wandered into the youth newspaper I edited, sat down at a computer, and released an eloquent, punctuation-free stream of autobiography interspersed with well-informed political rants.

Abandoned by her mother as a baby, Eliza had lived with her great-grandmother until she was eleven, when the state deemed her incorrigible and her great-grandmother incapable and took charge of Eliza's care. By the time I met her, Eliza had cycled through more foster- and group-home placements than she could keep track of before finally deciding she would be better off on her own. She was staying on friends' couches, crashing where she could—part of the uncounted, indoor homeless. Enrolling herself in high school and lying about her age to get waitressing jobs, she had managed to stay under the radar for two years.

Then her mother came back to town with a new boyfriend and asked Eliza to move in and give her one more chance. It was a matter of days before an argument with her mother's boyfriend turned violent. He took his belt off and came after Eliza; she managed, somehow, to throw a television set through the window. Her mother called the police, and when they arrived Eliza was the one who got swept back into the system, sent to juvenile hall and then another group home.

Though she'd promised to try to stick it out until Sunday, when I'd be allowed a visit, I was not surprised to get a phone call from the supervisor, his voice strained. Eliza, he told me, had been threatening to leave, didn't need him or anyone else, could make it on her own. But when he put her on the phone she was quiet, almost squeaky, resigned. Two of the other girls had been after her since the day she arrived, she told me. They "couldn't tell if she's black or white" (in fact she is black, South American, and more), accused her of behaving like she was "all that," didn't approve of the gap between her teeth. They would corner her in the hallways and challenge her to fight, later, in the basement, when no staff were around.

She had no interest in fighting them, no interest in any of the petty power struggles that determine dominion in this tiny, self-referential universe. That disengagement was as central to her unpopularity as her caramel-colored skin or her fancy vocabulary: there's nothing more infuriating than a new kid who refuses to play by the rules. So the other girls kept poking at her, which was hard to take, she reminded me, because she "had a lot of anger"—the loose, swirling kind that barely remembers its source, that simply hovers, until it finds a trigger or a target.

That night's fight started at the dining table. Eliza used a polysyllabic word, showing up her less erudite adversaries, and they either slammed down a dictionary (by their account) or threw it at her (by hers), suggesting she look up those big words of hers. She lunged, they fought, and she wound up ripping out a big chunk of one girl's hair, leaving a gaping bald spot, the quintessential mark of humiliation. (Even a decade earlier, when I spent a miserable year trying to be a "counselor" in a group home myself, "I'll snatch you baldheaded" was the threat of choice when things went sour between the girls.) Eliza took off before police could get there.

When I got to work the next morning, Eliza was already there, asleep on the couch. She woke up and began to bounce around the office, alighting on desks, soaking up all the attention in the room, thirsty for more. "I looove Nell," she announced to nobody in particular when I walked by. The declaration was clearly preemptive: she had screwed up and was afraid that meant I wouldn't love her anymore. That's generally how things happened within the rigid emotional economy of life in "the system"—the umbrella term young people use to describe those agencies and institutions that have come to assume control over their lives.

Eliza regretted her AWOL, though she left not impetuously but because she felt herself backed into a corner—the police were on their way and she wasn't prepared to go back to jail. She did want to go back to the group home, though, and was willing to take whatever medicine was prescribed in order to be allowed to hold on to her last shard of freedom. She felt it was a good placement, relatively speaking, and that had been my impression too—to the degree that any place that takes eight young women, strangers to one another, each carrying her own load of pain and rage, and throws them together in an enclosed space can ever be called a home. Eliza wanted my help in negotiating her return.

Her probation officer, who had not been easy to reach in the past, returned my call immediately when I left a message that Eliza was in our office.

"I've discharged her from the program," the PO informed me, her voice like a door slamming shut. "She needs to turn herself in."

"Needs to" is one of the more frightening euphemisms one hears from representatives of "the system," used to describe actions that they are determined to compel. Eliza may have had no *choice* but to turn herself in, but on her list of needs, which ranged from love and attention to a jacket to a high school education, incarceration was actually pretty low. But until she met this "need," I was told, she could forget about the rest of them. We were talking about an *offender*, I was reminded. There would be no deals here, no bargaining, no "working together" on her behalf. I must deposit Eliza behind bars posthaste and let them do with her what they would.

Eliza took a few hours to consider her limited options, then asked me to take her to juvenile hall. "Slow down," she kept saying as we crawled along the freeway. By the time we reached the exit, we were pressing the forty-mile-per-hour minimum speed limit, and I could sense how much it was costing her to submit voluntarily to a system that had treated her with both indifference and disdain.

The sun was setting by the time we arrived. Eliza was stripped of her clothing and belongings, issued slippers and a thin cotton jumpsuit, and ushered out of sight to shower and be deloused.

After that, I had to grovel and plead for permission to visit, since my role corresponded to none of the categories on the little blue visitors' pass: parent, guardian, custodian. Pointing out that no one else could check those boxes either (except, in theory, the state, which she had fled) got me nowhere with the gatekeepers. They were accustomed to kids like Eliza— not just "other people's children" but nobody's at all. Who was I—who was *she*—to expect special treatment?

For the next six months, Eliza's childhood, actual and legal, ticked away while she sat suspended in a sort of sleep in her darkened room. Every so often—when another group home administrator explained to me why she was not "appropriate for the program," when the guard at the front desk arbitrarily changed the rules, when another court hearing was canceled without warning or explanation—I got just a taste of the rage that is generated when helplessness meets irresponsible power. Your mind looks for avenues, ways out of or around the dead end before you, and then, hitting only brick walls, lashes out. That may be one reason why there is such seemingly random venting in juvenile institutions—the throwing and breaking of things, as well as the viciousness young people sometimes show one another. Legitimate anger is blocked off, dammed, until, as inexorably as water, it finds another outlet.

Each time I came to visit, Eliza's greeting was the same: "Who asked about me?" I brought messages and books and learned to play dominoes. Sometimes, when she was feeling especially hopeless, we would decorate the apartment she hoped one day to have, stocking the refrigerator and filling the closets, building her a home out of images and words.

Most of the time, she sat in her cell and read. "I lived in my books," she told me later, "until I could get away. I read about heroines who were kept in towers. I read about women who survived obstacles, and reading about survivors made me feel like one. If they could leave slavery and defy Rome, so could I."

I believed her, for a time.

NO, WHITE LADY, I DON'T WANT YOUR PURSE.

Jared had emblazoned this slogan on a custom-printed T-shirt. He wore it often on the days he came to work at the youth newspaper office in order to ease his transit through San Francisco's Financial District, where sidewalk crowds parted at his approach.

To my surprise, the shirt did not evoke a hostile, affronted, or even discomfited reaction in its target demographic. Instead, passersby appeared to take it literally. Some did a quick double take as their eyes traveled from his shirt to his face and back again, but few appeared embarrassed to be confronted so baldly with the prospect of their own prejudices. Instead, many visibly relaxed, as if they were taking his T-shirt at its word. The grip on purses loosened and the wake around Jared narrowed.

"How does this make you feel?" I once asked Jared after witnessing this phenomenon.

He gave me that particular half smile that young people reserve for well-meaning adults to whom they are willing to give the benefit of the doubt despite their glaring naïveté.

"It's not about how I *feel*," he answered patiently. "I *feel* like maybe I won't get arrested trying to get to work today."

Remember adolescence? The keen eye for hypocrisy that has not yet acquired the veneer of self-righteousness; the seeking, probing, and

endless philosophizing; the persistent questioning of a status quo that—
because they have yet to make the slow bargain with the world that constitutes social adulthood—teenagers see more clearly than their elders can
afford to? It didn't take the findings of a blue ribbon commission to let
Jared and other black and brown youths know how the world saw them.
For that, they had the "purse clutchers" (their term for the adults who
crossed the street when they approached or shrunk into elevator walls to
avoid getting too close), who are ubiquitous whenever young people of
color have the temerity to step outside their turf.

Race and class, more than anything else, *including* behavior, determine
who gets locked up in this country. As many as 90 percent of *all* teenagers,
according to research based on confidential interviews, acknowledge having committed illegal acts serious enough to warrant incarceration. Most
are never arrested, much less incarcerated. They simply go on with their
lives, growing up and, as they do, growing out of the impulsivity that leads
so many teens to break the law. Young people of color face a different reality. They comprise 38 percent of the youth population, but *72 percent* of
incarcerated juveniles. Multiple studies reveal that this gap is a result not
of differences in behavior but of differences in how we respond to that
behavior—differences grounded in race.

Racism does not merely inform or infuse our juvenile justice system;
it drives that system at every level, from legislation to policing to sentencing to conditions of confinement and enforcement of parole. Harsher
treatment of poor youth of color at every point on the juvenile justice
spectrum ensures that they will be grossly overrepresented in the so-called
deep end: long-term locked facilities. "Your skin is your sin," one young
man I met recalled young wards saying inside one such facility.

In almost every state, youth of color are held in secure facilities at rates
as high as four and a half times their percentage of the population. Black
youths are five times more likely than their white peers to be incarcerated,
and Hispanic youths twice as likely.

Reams of research have left little doubt that so-called racial disparities
result from disparate treatment rather than different rates of criminality.
Across the board, the justice system treats youth of color far more harshly
than it does whites, after controlling for offending history and myriad
other factors. For instance:

- African American youth are 4.5 times more likely (and Latino youth 2.3 times more likely) than white youth to be detained *for identical offenses.*
- African American youth with no prior offenses are far more likely than white youth with similar histories to be incarcerated on the same charges. Specifically, they are nine times as likely to be incarcerated for crimes against persons; four times as likely for property crimes; seven times as likely for public order offenses; and *forty-eight times* as likely for drug offenses.
- About half of white teenagers arrested on a drug charge go home without being formally charged. Only a quarter of black teens catch a similar break.
- Despite the fact that white youth are *more than a third more likely* to sell drugs than are African American youth, black youth are twice as likely to be arrested on charges of drug sales. Nearly half (48 percent) of all juveniles incarcerated on drug charges are black, while blacks make up 17 percent of the juvenile population.
- When charges are filed, white teenagers are more likely to be placed on probation, while black youth are more likely to be placed behind bars. According to research from the National Council on Crime and Delinquency, when white and black youths with similar histories were charged with the same offenses, black youths were six times more likely to be incarcerated in public institutions. Latino youths were three times more likely than white youths to be incarcerated under similar circumstances.
- Unequal treatment determines how deeply a young person will penetrate into the system. African American children comprise 17 percent of the overall youth population, 30 percent of those arrested, and 62 percent of those prosecuted in the adult criminal system. Latino youth are 43 percent more likely than white youth to wind up in the adult system.

These gross inequalities persist despite decades of advocacy and reform efforts aimed at creating a more equitable system. The result has been not a resolution of the racism that drives the current system, nor even a mitigation of the crushing odds young people of color face before the law, but instead the growth of what the W. Haywood Burns Institute calls a "multi-million dollar cottage industry whose primary activity is to restate the problem of disparities, in essence, endlessly adoring the question of what to do about [disproportionate minority confinement], but never reaching an answer."

The federal Juvenile Justice and Delinquency Prevention Act, for instance, was amended in 1988 to require the states to study the problem of racial disparity in juvenile justice and make "good faith" efforts to remedy it. The Department of Justice funded a major effort to reduce racial disparity, and private philanthropy has launched or supported efforts with similar aims. But as Barry Krisberg, director of research and policy at the University of California, Berkeley's Chief Justice Earl Warren Institute on Law and Social Policy, puts it, despite these efforts to "control this entrenched, discriminatory tendency, the problem has only gotten worse."

For far too many young people of color, coming of age is marked by metal detectors and onsite police officers in their schools, security guards following them in stores, the "gang squad" showing up to break up school yard scuffles, purse clutchers, car-door lockers, and many other signals that they are now old enough to be presumed guilty at a glance. In this sense, youth prisons are the end phase of what sociologist Victor Rios calls the "youth control complex," a densely woven net that encompasses everything from fortress-like schools and militarized streets to the child welfare system (a primary feeder of its juvenile justice cousin, and also marked by massive racial disparities) to popular and academic culture, which turned on young people of color viciously in the 1980s and 1990s and has yet to overcome its fear-driven demonization of the hoodie-clad hordes at the gates.

The differential treatment young people of color face from an early age contributes to a particularly insidious cycle. The general public sees only the statistics and the faces on the evening news. The differential treatment that *drives* the statistics, however, is rarely reported. Without this context, the racism that leads black youth to be so grossly overrepresented in the juvenile justice system serves to fuel the racism they face on the street—the assumption that all of them have their eye on the white lady's purse.

The criminalization of adolescence has made way for an unofficial,

largely unacknowledged, but brutally effective apartheid that has so
dehumanized large numbers of poor black and brown children—painted
and treated them as so profoundly "other"—that we no longer need take
notice of their inextinguishable humanity, much less the vulnerability of
their tender years. The more time I spent behind the walls of our juvenile
prisons, the more I came to understand the essential role these institutions
play both in perpetuating this apartheid and ensuring its invisibility; in
concealing behind coils of barbed wire and veils of "confidentiality" both
the most wounded among America's children and the further injuries we
inflict on them in the name of the law.

Curtis was ten years old when he was first sent to youth prison, but he was
no neophyte to the struggle for survival. When he was five, his father kidnapped him and his brother off the lawn of their mother's house. Curtis
remembers being kept in a crack house, where addicts came and went
throughout the day and night. Sometimes his father left the boys alone in
the place for days, without food or money. After eight months, Curtis's
mother obtained a court order and the boys were returned to her.

"All that made me very angry, very bitter inside," Curtis recalled, "but
at the time, I didn't know how to deal with those emotions. All around
me, people would express their emotions through violence, so that was the
only way I knew."

At school, when Curtis felt belittled by a teacher, he would make threats
or throw chairs. At home, a new boyfriend was abusing his mother, just
as his father had. In his neighborhood, he was surrounded by gangs,
drugs, and violence. More than once, he said, his own father threatened
to kill him.

"I had a lot of anger and pain and rage inside, and I did not know how
to channel that energy," he continued. "Gangs, violence, drug addicts,
drug dealers—my whole life was surrounded by chaos."

At seven, Curtis was arrested for the first time, for stabbing a teacher
with a pencil. He spent the afternoon in juvenile hall and then went back
to what he knew. By eight, he was out on the street with his cousins and
their friends. "Their mother was on drugs or their father was in and out of
prison, so they could relate to me. They told me, if you wanna be down
with us you gotta do certain things, like steal radios out of cars, steal stuff

from stores. Do these things if you want to be accepted. So I did those things, and it landed me in juvenile hall. From there I was always in juvenile hall and group homes."

"Eventually, I became totally desensitized. Coldhearted. I really didn't care what nobody was feeling. I just wanted what I wanted. And I progressed in violence."

As Curtis progressed in delinquency, the state progressed in sanctioning him, but no one showed an interest in the reasons for his actions. "Nobody really gave me the attention I needed," said Curtis, echoing many other young people with whom I spoke. "Nobody sat down with me and really tried to understand what I was going through and what I was feeling, and tried to help me get through my struggles and my problems."

"Attention," he reflected, "was my number one goal."

Eventually Curtis arrived at the Heman G. Stark Youth Correctional Facility in Chino—a place the California inspector general later found "conducive to suicide attempts and potentially dangerous to staff," one where wards were Maced as often as four times a day. Over time, Curtis's anger melded with his fear and loneliness to form a toxic rage that became explosive.

"Whether it was shanking someone or beating them over the head with a chair," Curtis said, "I was making a point. The point was 'Don't mess with me.' But at the same time, it was a way of releasing my anger, of channeling that energy."

How does a ten-year-old wind up in a state juvenile institution? Curtis was black, male, poor, and alone, his mother overworked and his father (eventually) incarcerated. Most of all, Curtis was hurting, and violence was the language he had learned to express it. Officially, Curtis was sent to juvenile prison on a robbery charge. The bottom line, however, is that he had, like Eliza, bounced through so many "placements"—foster homes, group homes, and then juvenile halls—that the judge couldn't come up with anything else to do with him. As often happens, the intervention the court selected for Curtis had more to do with what was available than with what was most appropriate.

Childhood trauma such as Curtis experienced is so widespread among the children we incarcerate as to be nearly ubiquitous. The report of the Attorney General's National Task Force on Children Exposed to Violence describes the very trajectory Curtis followed from hurt child to child prisoner, and the damage accrued along the way.

> Children exposed to violence, who desperately need help, often end up alienated. Instead of responding in ways that repair the damage done to them by trauma and violence, the frequent response of communities, caregivers, and peers is to reject and ostracize these children, pushing them further into negative behaviors. Often the children become isolated from and lost to their families, schools, and neighborhoods and end up in multiple unsuccessful out-of-home placements and, ultimately, in correctional institutions.
>
> Many youth in the justice system appear angry, defiant, or indifferent, but actually they are fearful, depressed, and lonely. They hurt emotionally and feel powerless, abandoned, and subject to double standards by adults in their lives and in "the system." These children are often viewed by the system as beyond hope and uncontrollable, labeled as "oppositional," "willfully irresponsible," or "unreachable." What appears to be intentional defiance and aggression, however, is often a defense against the despair and hopelessness that violence has caused in these children's lives. When the justice system responds with punishment, these children may be pushed further into the juvenile and criminal justice systems and permanently lost to their families and society.

Jared's eyes blazed as he described the year when he lost his last connection and learned what it was to survive on his own.

"Nine," he said, letting the word hang in the air for a moment. "That is when I stepped out in the world on my own, with all of my young wisdom."

The tide had begun to recede before that, when Jared was eight and his parents split up. Dad moved out. Mom was using crack. His older brother got locked up. His sister got pregnant and moved in with her boyfriend. Eventually, "it was just me and my little brother. We used to steal clothes off of people's clotheslines from different neighborhoods to have clean clothes to wear to school."

Dinner went from home cooked to canned food to cornflakes to nothing.

Jared learned "what it's like not to have food for three days, and have to go rob somebody."

Jeff Adachi, the public defender of San Francisco and a lifelong advocate for young people in trouble, has heard many stories like this over the years. For him, they point the way to a new question. Instead of focusing only on what "rehabilitates" young people, he proposed, why not look also at what "dehabilitates" and intervene there rather than waiting for a crime? Do most kids remember when and why they began to veer off a safe course and into the realm of delinquency? he wondered. What life events set children on the roads that converge at the prison gate?

"You take a kid who's not good or bad, just tabula rasa," Adachi mused. "And then at some point—what happens? You always hear, 'This kid started having problems when he was ten years old, or twelve years old, or he did really well until he was sixteen, and then something happened.' What if we could go backwards, and find out at what point in time an intervention—intensive family services, say—would have made a difference, and figure out what the problem was for that individual at that point in time?"

No one forgets the withdrawal of home and family, the leaching away of hope. Some kids remember not a sudden breach but a gradual ebb, connections receding like a tide going out, until they wake up one morning to find themselves stranded. Others speak of something more abrupt: a grandmother's death or a parent's arrest, and a childhood swept away with the force of a riptide.

By the time Jared was nine, he had lost everything. "My mom is totally gone on crack. We moved to our grandma's house in the Fillmore. The family sold the house, everybody took their money and started using dope with it, so we didn't have anything. So we ended up in the Tenderloin [District] selling dope."

He soon learned that he was not the only one. "By nine, all those other kids out there were in the same situation. However they got there, we were there on the street, and they became my friends."

Whatever safety these children had lay in sticking together. "If somebody messed with us, we'd jump them." Otherwise, they kept a low profile.

"In kids' minds?" he continued, referring to children like himself and his friends, back then. "It's desperation. A lot of kids' moms and dads aren't there, or they are there and on dope. Or the dad's in jail and the mom's on dope. So these kids have grown up having to fend for themselves—selling some weed or some ecstasy pills or even crack or heroin. That's not *bad*, because they have to take care of themselves, and they're doing what they gotta do. In their minds. But they're still kids."

It wasn't long before Jared was arrested. His tone was flat as he described the treatment he received in what would be a string of institutional placements.

"The absence of love plays a big factor. The group homes. These people don't genuinely care. If I slam a bowl of food down in your face, slam it down on the table, you can feel it," he said. "People forget, these are kids, they need love."

The trajectory Jared described was clear enough. From canned food to cornflakes to starving to stealing; from a bowl slammed on a table to a tray slipped through a cell door.

"And then you got some that are hardened," Jared mused, talking about the kids he grew up with. "For some, it's normal to walk around with a pistol. But for society, that's not normal."

"What are you doing with this .357 Magnum?" he continued, offering an imagined dialogue between "society" and the child.

"I'm going to school."

"Why do you need a gun?"

"Because these dudes from the other side of town go to school and I'm the only person from my neighborhood that goes there and I don't want to get jumped. Or robbed. Or beat up every day."

"And so it's *normal* for some kids," he reiterated, leaning across the table as if to bridge the gap between the world he was describing and what Jared, who is black, dubbed "Caucasian Acres." In this barely hypothetical subdivision, he explained, the actions seen as "normal" on the block where he grew up are met with incomprehension and then incarceration.

Jared had no interest in portraying himself as a victim. He described the "normal" he knew as a child: "pulling runners" (eating quickly, without paying, then literally running) at the all-you-can-eat soup and salad bar at Sizzler to get a reprieve from the bottomless hunger, pooling the day's take with four or five other kids until they had enough to pay an addict to get them the key to a hotel room in a flophouse. But he was not making excuses, much less looking for pity. He was trying, with words, to bridge two realities.

Tough-on-crime hard-liners like to speak in terms of "choices"—good and bad, right and wrong, black and white, lock 'em up. Jared was offering a more nuanced perspective: children make choices from among the options they have—choices that are rational, under the circumstances, yet reprehensible to the denizens of Caucasian Acres.

"But society," he elaborated, "says, 'Throw them away. They're corrupt. They don't have the mind-set of a child.'"

Several years ago, I set out to explore the daily lives of homeless youth in California. Aided by a crew of about forty currently or formerly homeless peer researchers, I heard from kids who'd spent the previous night alone behind a Chevron station, camped along the banks of the Sacramento River, or simply on the street. Despite childhood histories horrific enough to raise the antennae of any sentient social servant, the only adults earning a taxpayer-funded salary who'd ever shown an interest in them had come wearing a badge, shining a flashlight in a kid's face, interrupting scant sleep, gloved hands shaking down precious possessions, handing out tickets the young recipients obviously couldn't pay—tickets that, piled high enough, morphed into bench warrants, landing them finally in juvenile hall. All this for the original sin of being parentless and having the temerity to try to survive anyway.

I'd thought I'd been on the margins before, but hearing from children who slept in public bathrooms when they did not sleep in cells, hearing that there was no system for them but one that criminalized their extreme vulnerability, I was beginning to feel I had stepped out past the limits of my comprehension. "Dirtbag," "fuckup," "lazy," "worthless," "lower than the low," these children had answered when we asked them how others perceived them. Could it be, I wondered, that we had turned on the children? Had we *nothing* to offer the most vulnerable among them but the cold hand of the law?

"What do they want us to do?" one teenager asked bitterly, referring to the officers who wrote him tickets for loitering when he could walk the streets no longer, then placed him in handcuffs when those tickets went unpaid. "Just crawl off somewhere and die?"

How many of the children Jared had grown up with—hungry, lonely, and just about invisible, until the will to survive ran up against the law—had considered that same question in the back of a police car, bound for the one institution that, as I heard over and over, "had a bed waiting for me"? How many understood that the system's meager promise—three hots and a cot—came with a condition: that they slip back into the invisibility that allows the rest of us to enjoy untroubled sleep?

In testimony before the Attorney General's National Task Force on Children Exposed to Violence, Annie E. Casey Foundation president Patrick McCarthy underscored the failures of the system that is often the only one to take notice of children like Jared. "Whether we call them training schools, reform schools, juvenile correctional facilities or youth prisons," McCarthy testified, juvenile institutions

> too often have become places of poor treatment and abuse rather than rehabilitation and hope. Recidivism rates are dismal, suggesting that these institutions fail to protect public safety. Abuse and poor treatment are rampant. . . . The sad irony is that as many as three-fourths of the young people incarcerated in these often brutal facilities have themselves been victims of trauma and violence. . . . And following their incarceration, they are more likely rather than less likely to commit violent acts. You would be hard-pressed if you tried to design a less effective response to a child's exposure to violence than to lock him or her up in overcrowded, loud, brightly lit, depressing, frightening conditions with a large group of other children with similar problems, little or no privacy and no sense of personal safety, and then fail to provide a decent education or an opportunity to build skills; neglect to address the mental health, substance abuse, trauma and family issues that contributed to the delinquent behavior; and then release him or her to the streets with little hope for a future of promise or possibility. This is not a recipe for success.

As they cycle ever deeper into the juvenile and criminal justice systems, many young people lose any faith they may have had that they are expected, or even permitted, to succeed. Success comes to seem the purview of others, reserved for the denizens of Caucasian Acres.

Behind bars, many receive the message that they are destined for failure in explicit terms. "When you're locked up, you're treated like you're nobody. You're constantly reminded that you're nothing, that you're a criminal, that you're never gonna be this, that you're too stupid to do that," recalled sixteen-year-old Birdy, whose father had deposited her at juvenile hall after she ran away for a few days. "They tell you, 'We can go home. You can't, because you broke the law. Only criminals are here. Can't you see? Take a look around.'"

"The probation officers think it's good to be in there—it teaches you a lesson," she said. "It don't teach you a lesson. It makes you worse, because you start believing what they're telling you. I felt like I was a criminal. Once you get put in the system, you consider yourself a criminal. So when you get out, you think, 'Oh well, I've been through it before. Why not again?' I started believing I wasn't gonna be nobody."

"That's a nice way to start building your record," Miranda remembers the booking officer sneering as she took the seventeen-year-old's fingerprints after she was arrested for fighting at school. For young people who are most profoundly alone, violence can become its own sort of language, a desperate effort to communicate their pain by passing it on. But no one asked Miranda what had so enraged her, asked her anything, for that matter, that would have helped them to see her as an individual. If they had, they would have learned that Miranda's combatant had insulted her mother, who had been locked up since Miranda was twelve; that police had picked her mother up for check kiting while Miranda was at school, leaving Miranda to pack a bag and fend for herself, alone and itinerant throughout her adolescence.

"They look at you like you're just gonna keep spiraling down," Miranda said of that arrest, "when maybe you're just an angry teenager. Maybe I just needed to talk to somebody. But nobody cares. Nobody cares."

That children who wind up in juvenile facilities have at some previous point "fallen through the cracks" is a popular metaphor but a spurious analysis. It implies that most children who grow up in impoverished, high-incarceration neighborhoods—who face violence on the streets, in their schools, and sometimes in their homes—have access to functional public systems and community networks, and that those who wind up in trouble simply missed or were missed by these otherwise adequate safety nets.

Spend some time talking with young prisoners and the fallacy quickly becomes clear. The children one meets in juvenile prisons have not fallen through cracks; they have tumbled into chasms. Wandered through deserts. There may not exist a metaphor adequate to the trauma that many have survived.

And then we lock them up, in barren, violent, abuse-filled institutions that are virtually guaranteed to exacerbate the trauma they bring with them and add fresh wounds to old.

4

THE RISE OF THE SUPER-PREDATOR AND THE DECLINE OF THE REHABILITATIVE IDEAL

Here is what we believe: America is now home to thickening ranks of juvenile "super-predators"—radically impulsive, brutally remorseless youngsters, including ever more preteenage boys, who murder, assault, rape, rob, burglarize, deal deadly drugs, join gun-toting gangs and create serious communal disorders. They do not fear the stigma of arrest, the pains of imprisonment, or the pangs of conscience.

—William J. Bennett, John J. DiIulio,
and John P. Walters, *Body Count*

"YOU KNOW WHAT I wish?" my friend Lamont once asked, reflecting on life as a black teenager in the fear-crazed 1990s.

"I wish the older folks would have come out to the stoop and told us to quiet down when we got too loud in the street, instead of always calling the cops on us right off. Or at least come to the window if they were too scared of us to come outside. I wish it was like they used to talk about back in the day, when someone else's mom would take a belt to you if you were causing trouble, because anyone's kid was everyone's kid. Back before everyone was scared of us from the day we stepped outta diapers, and it was just cops, guards, and POs left to raise us up."

Six foot something, dark skinned and almond eyed, Lamont drew attention everywhere he went. He had learned to expect that much of it would be fearful, but that doesn't mean he had come to accept it. Charming, funny, and exceptionally perceptive, Lamont spent a great amount of energy reassuring people that he wasn't going to hurt them. For a young black man coming of age at the apex of the super-predator era, it was no easy task.

As crack cocaine hit the cities and private gun ownership became more widespread, the late 1980s and early 1990s saw an increase in juvenile violent crime. More influential than the trend lines were the individual horror stories, local tragedies that quickly entered the national folklore.

Meanwhile, high-profile researchers crossed crime stats with demographic projections to stir up fears of a coming wave of "super-predators" unlike any seen before—"more savage than salvageable," according to Princeton political science professor John DiIulio, who made his name by playing up the (supposedly) coming menace.

On October 19, 1996, a book called *Body Count*—co-authored by DiIulio, drug czar William J. Bennett, and think-tank director John P. Walters—hit the shelves, and America was formally introduced to our new worst nightmare: our children.

Well, somebody's children, anyway. The "super-predators" portrayed in the book, "kids from 13 to 16 who apparently feel nothing as they kill, rob or rape," were painted as so utterly and incomprehensibly *other* that it is hard to imagine anyone seeing a hint of their own kids in the horrifying image. But that was just the point. The book fabricated a new *breed* of adolescent, not only different by virtue of race or background, but so fundamentally alien as to defy comprehension, much less offer the prospect of redemption. The newly hatched "super-predators" were so "radically self-regarding" and "morally impoverished," according to this line of reasoning, that talk of rehabilitating them was dangerously naive.

"A new generation of street criminals is upon us," DiIulio warned, "the youngest, biggest and baddest generation any society has ever known."

He and his co-authors painted with a broad brush, portraying all "inner-city children" as potential predators, tainted from earliest childhood by the depravity of their clan—"teenagers and adults who are themselves deviant, delinquent or criminal." Given demographic projections, the authors warned, violence would reach unheard-of levels by the year 2000.

The political hysteria of the moment found its perfect spokesmodel in the chubby-cheeked, baby-faced, Ivy League–certified DiIulio, who claimed he had simply been crunching the numbers when evidence of this looming mob emerged on his screen. In fact, the fearmongering of the era was in keeping with a long tradition. As Barry Krisberg of the University of California, Berkeley's Chief Justice Earl Warren Institute on Law and Social Policy has pointed out, "Juvenile justice policies have historically been built on a foundation of myths. From the 'dangerous classes' of the 19th century to the super-predators of the late 20th century, government responses to juvenile crime have been dominated by fear of the young, anxiety about immigrants or racial minorities, and hatred of the poor."

Mass-circulation news magazines upped the ante by illustrating stories on the super-predator "phenomenon" with images of glowering black teenagers. Politicians hopped on the bandwagon, passing legislation that increased penalties in juvenile court or that allowed or demanded that growing numbers of youth be transferred to adult court, where longer sentences and harsher penalties were readily dispensed. The public ate it up, and what would later be revealed as myth quickly became a movement—one that has resulted in an amping up of our response to juvenile crime that spans the spectrum from kindergartners hauled off in handcuffs for school yard scraps to twelve-year-olds sentenced to spend their lives in prison.

The fear on the faces of strangers was not the only thing that let youth of color like Lamont know that they were public enemy number one. All around them, the media were screaming the same message. The super-predators were coming—a generation of young people more ruthless, more vicious, and less amenable to change than any who'd come before. With the adolescent population slated to increase in coming years, these teenage terrorists would arrive in hordes.

Despite the glaring lack of evidence to support the notion that more kids meant more crime, the media latched on to the notion that, as writer Robin Templeton put it, "demography is destiny" with a fervor not seen since the turn-of-the-century heyday of yellow journalism, when William Randolph Hearst's *San Francisco Examiner* tried to outdo Joseph Pulitzer's hyperbolic *New York World* by devoting a full fourth of its column inches to stories about crime.

A century after Hearst found fame and fortune by pioneering "if it bleeds, it leads" journalism, a *Time* magazine headline warned of an imminent "Teenage Time Bomb." The ticking tots were "just four, five and six years old now, but already they are making criminologists nervous," the writers intoned in a widely cited cover story.

"America is being threatened by a growing cadre of cold-blooded teens called 'super-predators,'" the *Christian Science Monitor* echoed. News of their imminent arrival even made its way across the Atlantic, where the London *Times* warned of "The Invasion of the Super-predators"—a generation of American children whose default mode was "remorseless brutality."

By 1996, according to research by the Berkeley Media Studies Group, more than half of all local news stories about youth focused on violence, despite the fact that adults were committing 80 percent of the nation's crime.

The racialized nature of these warnings was impossible to miss. Black teenagers growing up in the midst of this cacophony knew that when Americans heard the word "super-predator," theirs was the face superimposed on the nightmare, and that "inner city" had become a euphemism for wherever "they" might congregate.

Criminologists not only advanced the super-predator rhetoric; they made explicit its racial subtext. In a report to the U.S. attorney general, Northeastern University's James Alan Fox called particular attention to projected growth in the black teenage population—which he estimated would increase 26 percent by 2005—to underscore his warning that "our nation faces a future juvenile violence problem that may make today's epidemic pale in comparison."

"The political demonization of young black males as morally impoverished 'super-predators,'" University of Minnesota Centennial Professor of Law Barry Feld wrote in 1999, "and the depiction of delinquents as responsible offenders have eroded the Progressives' social construction of 'childhood' innocence and vulnerability."

Feld was not talking about something as ephemeral as a stereotype here. As changing attitudes seeped into the cultural bedrock, the rehabilitative premise itself began to crumble. The very idea that minors ought to be treated differently from adults—the founding principle of the juvenile court—was called into question. In an era when action was judged independent of circumstance, what reason was youth not to hold a criminal—much less a predator—"accountable" for his crimes? And holding kids accountable increasingly became synonymous simply with holding them. These were the boom years of the juvenile prison, with new ones springing up in job-hungry rural back posts all across the country.

The super-predator myth not only served to justify already abysmal conditions in America's juvenile prisons; it opened the door both to net widening (criminalizing a larger number of acts and locking up more kids) and to an arms race escalation in the sanctions administered, with each state scrambling to outdo the others in its efforts to "crack down" on kids by increasing penalties in juvenile court and—most significantly—creating mechanisms to transfer many more youths to the adult system.

A number of states went so far as to revise their juvenile codes in order to make explicit their punitive intent. Texas, for instance, promised "to promote the concept of punishment for criminal acts" and Kansas committed to "hold juvenile offenders accountable." Other states made similar changes. The result was that the number of cases heard each year in juvenile court rose 44 percent, from 1.2 million in 1989 to 1.8 million a decade later, despite a steep *drop* in juvenile violent crime.

What had previously been unspoken was now written into law. The fundamental rehabilitative mission of the juvenile justice system and, with it, our collective understanding that young people were different from adults—more vulnerable, more malleable, less able to make reasoned decisions and hence less responsible—buckled under the sustained attack that the super-predator movement represented. The result was unmistakable: not only did rates of incarceration in juvenile facilities increase; more minors were sentenced to adult prisons and jails.

"At the state level, the super-predator myth played an important role in 47 states amending their laws on juvenile crime to get tougher on youthful criminals," Krisberg has written. "Legislators modified their state laws to permit younger children to be tried in adult criminal courts. . . . Legislators also weakened protection of the confidentiality of minors tried in juvenile courts, allowing some juvenile court convictions to be counted later in adult proceedings to enhance penalties."

The bottom line? More young people were arrested—and punished more harshly—for increasingly minor offenses. Even as crime dropped, juvenile incarceration continued to rise.

The super-predator turned out to be little more than the product of an overheated public imagination, but the tough-on-kids legislation this bogey-teen inspired would long outlive him. While the rhetoric may have cooled, the countless young people still sentenced under the harsh adult transfer laws passed in the name of the nonexistent monster suffer the consequence to this day.

While *Body Count* relies on demographic projections and other nods to quantitative research to give its inflammatory rhetoric a veneer of academic credibility, DiIulio tipped his hand in a lesser-known, more personal piece of chest pounding that was published in the *Weekly Standard*.

"Since 1980," DiIulio proclaimed,

I've studied prisons and jails all across the country—San Quentin, Leavenworth, Rikers Island. I've been on the scene at prison murders and riots (and once was almost killed inside a prison). Moreover, I grew up in a pretty tough neighborhood and am built like an aging linebacker. I will still waltz backwards, notebook in hand and alone, into any adult maximum-security cellblock full of killers, rapists, and muggers.

But a few years ago, I forswore research inside juvenile lock-ups. The buzz of impulsive violence, the vacant stares and smiles, and the remorseless eyes were at once too frightening and too depressing (my God, these are children!) for me to pretend to "study" them.

This limitation did not stop DiIulio from expounding on the character and inner life of youth he found too frightening to speak with, even with the massive security infrastructure of a juvenile prison covering his back. Per the professor,

On the horizon . . . are tens of thousands of severely morally impoverished juvenile super-predators. They are perfectly capable of committing the most heinous acts of physical violence for the most trivial reasons (for example, a perception of slight disrespect or the accident of being in their path). They fear neither the stigma of arrest nor the pain of imprisonment. They live by the meanest code of the meanest streets, a code that reinforces rather than restrains their violent, hair-trigger mentality. In prison or out, the things that super-predators get by their criminal behavior—sex, drugs, money—are their own immediate rewards. Nothing else matters to them. So for as long as their youthful energies hold out, they will do what comes "naturally": murder, rape, rob, assault, burglarize, deal deadly drugs, and get high.

What to do? DiIulio had an answer for that one, too. "No one in academia," he wrote, "is a bigger fan of incarceration than I am. Between 1985 and 1991 the number of juveniles in custody increased from 49,000 to nearly 58,000. By my estimate, we will probably need to incarcerate at least 150,000 juvenile criminals in the years just ahead. In deference to public safety, we will have little choice but to pursue genuine get-tough law-enforcement strategies against the super-predators."

It is no coincidence that the man who could coolly propose a near tripling of the number of young people behind bars—who glibly called himself a "fan" of incarceration—was the same man who, when he encountered in person the young people whose fate his words might well determine, found them too unsettling even to approach. This aversion, which exacerbated the public's aversion, is key to understanding how we tolerate the destructive, abusive conditions in our nation's juvenile lockups.

A few years after *Body Count* hit the nation's bookstores, DiIulio started backpedaling.

"If I knew then what I know now, I would have shouted for prevention of crimes," he told the *New York Times* in 2001, not long after George Bush Jr. appointed him director of the White House Office of Faith-Based and Community Initiatives.

DiIulio attributed this ideological shift to an epiphany he experienced while praying on Palm Sunday. In this moment, it was revealed to him that his high-voltage Rolodex had been entrusted to him by God and that he was charged with using it (and any other vestiges of his notoriety) to "bring caring, responsible adults to wrap their arms around these kids."

The predictions that had made DiIulio famous, it is worth noting, had by this time been entirely discredited. Rather than rising precipitously, juvenile arrests for violent crime were steadily decreasing, reaching a low not seen since the 1970s or earlier.

In fact, the super-predator era, and the sweeping changes in law and policy that accompanied it, coincided with a drop in juvenile crime of historic proportion. According to the federal government, juvenile violent crime arrests peaked in 1994 (at more than 500 per 100,000 juveniles) and then began to drop sharply, to fewer than 300 per 100,000 in 1998. Between 1995 and 2004, the juvenile arrest rate for serious property and violent crimes fell fully 45 percent, and the juvenile homicide rate plummeted even further, decreasing by 70 percent over the same period. This drop was not a by-product of tougher laws or longer sentences; researchers who investigated that theory found just the opposite. Juvenile crime was dropping across the board, but the drops were steepest in those states that did *not* jump on the lock-'em-up bandwagon. Those that passed the harshest juvenile crime laws generally saw a smaller decline in the juvenile crime rate.

One would expect that a massive national decline in juvenile crime—combined with clear evidence that locking kids up not only did not *cause* this drop but, if anything, diminished it—would trigger a pendulum swing away from the tough-on-kids pole. In fact, the opposite happened: even as fewer young people committed serious crimes, more and more of them wound up behind bars. The only way to pull off a stunt like this was to lock kids up for increasingly minor offenses. Spurred on by the incendiary language of the super-predator era, that is exactly what we did. In 2004, for example, more than twice as many young people were adjudicated on charges of disorderly conduct as in 1995.

Whether he was motivated by the awkward failure to materialize of his army of doom, or by the discovery that his Rolodex was sacred, DiIulio took pains to dissociate himself from the effects his words had on uncounted young lives. "I'm sorry for any unintended consequences," he told the *New York Times*. "But I am not responsible for teenagers' going to prison."

Yet it was precisely the rhetoric of DiIulio and his colleagues—amped up by the media and abetted by politicians who found in the super-predator trope a golden opportunity to pound their chests and pledge to keep the streets safe by legislating ever-escalating sanctions—that snowballed into a PR campaign against a generation. And that rhetoric had results: teenagers went to prison, by the thousands, for longer and longer terms.

As manufactured fear of youth crime spread across the country, juvenile courts raised the stakes again and again in a struggle to keep up with the harsh penalties that growing numbers of kids faced in adult court, and with what they perceived as public sentiment. "Super-predator thinking threatened the notion that we needed a separate system of justice for kids," the Annie E. Casey Foundation's Bart Lubow observed.

As a consequence, juvenile courts were pressured to show that they weren't "kiddy courts" that "coddled" young thugs. Putting youth in adult courts and prisons upped the ante in terms of society's response to juvenile crime. That meant that those who remained in the juvenile court—albeit for relatively minor offenses, because the heavy hitters were now being transferred to adult courts—were now at the top of the food chain. Hence, juvenile court judges were imposing their highest sentences on cases that, prior to the super-predator, would have been middle-of-the-roaders. In effect, super-predator thinking had a gross inflationary effect on the punishments imposed on juveniles, regardless of court of jurisdiction.

As more children were swept into the juvenile justice system (and pushed out of it, into adult court) the public—steeped in the super-predator rhetoric—began to lose faith in the fundamental tenets of a separate juvenile system. The juvenile court was intended to rehabilitate, but *these* kids, we'd been told, were beyond any such hope. The overheated rhetoric of the era "left no plausible role for the juvenile justice system in stemming the coming tide of super-predators," scholars would later assert.

Just desert advocates promoted the use of punitive laws, policies, and practices in the juvenile justice system, including three strikes laws, determinate sentences, longer sentences, sentencing to boot camps, electronic monitoring, drug testing, shock incarceration, and other punitive measures. Such policies and practices, which deemphasize prevention of juvenile crime and rehabilitation of juvenile offenders, became common in the juvenile justice system through new state legislation.

So it came to pass that less than a century after the juvenile court's inception, the goal of "child saving" was overwhelmed by a powerful movement to recriminalize juvenile wrongdoing—to return the court's focus to a child's decontextualized actions, regardless of his age. Today, all fifty states have provisions for trying juveniles in adult court for a variety of charges—not only acts of violence but in some cases drug possession or even public order offenses. At the same time, large state-run juvenile facilities have been refashioned to resemble their adult counterparts, their rehabilitative mission buried under mountains of hardware and punitive regimes.

Over the course of three decades, as Barry Feld wrote in 1999,

> judicial decisions, legislative amendments, and administrative changes have transformed the juvenile court from a nominally rehabilitative social welfare agency into a scaled-down second-class criminal court for young people. Politicians and the public have repudiated the court's original rehabilitative premises and endorsed punishment of young offenders. Judicial opinions and statutory changes have rejected procedural informality and incorporated imperfectly many of the safeguards of the criminal court. These substantive and procedural reforms have converted the historic ideal of the juvenile court as a welfare agency into a quasi-penal system that provides young offenders with neither therapy nor justice.

As a concept, the super-predator has by now been entirely discredited, but there are some insults you just can't take back. By the time the storm had passed, new laws were in place, new youth prisons built, and a new ethos firmly entrenched. Isolation had supplanted rehabilitation as the primary function of the juvenile facility. The mandate was now explicit: keep *them* away from *us*, whatever it takes.

5

THE FIST AND THE BOOT

Physical Abuse in Juvenile Prisons

There will always be individuals and societies that turn against their children, breaking the natural order Aristotle described two and a half millennia ago. . . . Regardless of their individual motivations, they all rely upon a societal prejudice against children to justify themselves and legitimate their behavior.

—psychoanalyst Elisabeth Young-Bruehl,
Childism: Confronting Prejudice Against Children

DARREN WAS KNEELING, BUT he was not praying.

Baptized Catholic and brought up in the church, Darren had turned to his faith to get him through the early years of a decade-long confinement, including months spent on isolation units.

Now he found himself forced to his knees, hands cuffed behind his back, stripped to his boxers, one in a long row of boys in the same supplicant pose. They would be required to hold this position for two full weeks, their only respite a daily three-hour block allotted for sleep and a quick meal—a cheese sandwich, milk, and an egg.

Darren had just been transferred from one facility to another when a large-scale fight broke out. No effort was made to distinguish bystanders from those who had joined in. Witness, participant, instigator—it made little difference to those doling out punishment, it seemed to Darren, who had been through this kind of collective consequence before during the five years he'd spent locked up. Once individuality has been successfully eradicated via uniforms, strict schedules, regulation of daily activity, restricted contact with the outside world, and prison-supplied numbers supplanting given names, punishing the many for the sins of the few comes to seem logical, if not essential to the all-important end of "maintaining order."

So it was that all the boys in Darren's unit were brought to the gymnasium, stripped to their underwear, and ordered to their knees. They would remain in that posture, bound together in a long row, until the guards chose to release them. Silence was strictly enforced.

Darren was a college student when he spoke with me about his long sojourn through the California Youth Authority (CYA). Earnest and deliberate, he chose his words as carefully as he did his attire—a zip-top blue sweater and matching wool knit cap, a carved silver stud anointing each ear, and the hint of a goatee framing a handsome brown face. There was no apparent anger in his tone, even when he described the worst of the abuses. His voice simply dropped, infused with a quiet, contemplative sorrow.

It was difficult to imagine this poised young man in the supplicant, dehumanized position he had described to me. But formal investigations into conditions at the CYA (now known as the Division of Juvenile Justice) confirmed Darren's account and worse.

During Darren's weeks on his knees, the silence made the banter of the guards difficult to ignore. "They talk and chat and giggle and joke," he recalled, a slight edge creeping into his otherwise even manner, "and you just sit there. I was on my knees for two weeks."

"I lost my religion in there," Darren said, his even tone breaking for an instant. "I just stopped believing."

Prostrate before grown men to whom he might as well have been invisible, listening to the guards laugh and joke among themselves as their charges knelt before them, visibly suffering, Darren silently sought answers. *How can the people here do the things they do to children?* he asked the heavens. No answer was forthcoming.

Abuse of the young inside state-run juvenile prisons is both rampant and extreme. A federal survey published in 2010 found widespread abuse and maltreatment in America's youth corrections facilities. More than a third of youth in secure corrections facilities or camp programs reported that staff used force unnecessarily, and 30 percent said that staff placed youth into solitary confinement or locked them up alone as discipline. About half had experienced some kind of group punishment, as Darren described, and half said staff applied punishment unfairly. Fear of abuse was equally pervasive: 38 percent of youth said they feared being physically attacked by staff or other youth. Twenty-five percent feared attack from another youth, and 22 percent were afraid of attack from a staff member. Many lived in fear of both.

In the context of the juvenile prison, the term "abuse" takes on multiple meanings. The following are just a sample of incidents that have come to light in recent years.

- In Florida, a three-hundred-pound guard crushed a twelve-year-old boy with his body, suffocating the sixty-five-pound child to death.
- In California, groups of correctional officers slammed handcuffed boys face-first into walls or set attack dogs on them, often in full view of security cameras.
- In Louisiana, guards assaulted sleeping children, or entertained themselves by pitting boys in fights against each other, leaving them with broken jaws, fractured eye sockets, and an array of other injuries.
- In New York, children were restrained with such force that they wound up with concussions, missing teeth, spiral fractures, and other injuries. While physical restraint is intended only for situations where a young person poses a danger, these harsh examples were sometimes the result of affronts as minor as taking an extra cookie or laughing against orders. "Workers forced one boy, who had glared at a staff member, into a sitting position and secured his arms behind his back with such force that his collarbone was broken."
- In Georgia, guards assaulted children who were anemic, injured, mentally disabled, and as young as nine. When one boy collapsed during a punishing exercise regime, a supervisor broke his arm.

A boy who talked in line was punched in the ear so hard that his eardrum was punctured.

- In Mississippi, guards ripped the clothing from suicidal girls, then hog-tied them, naked, and tossed them into solitary. They also shackled girls to poles and forced them to run in hot weather carrying logs. Those who threw up from the heat and the strain were forced to eat their own vomit.
- In Arkansas, young people were left naked in solitary with the air-conditioning turned on high, or hog-tied and set outside at night in freezing weather.

According to a 2008 investigation by the Associated Press, thirteen thousand formal abuse claims were reported between 2004 and 2007 by state-run juvenile facilities nationwide. "Of these, 1,343 instances of abuse had been officially confirmed by authorities. Countless more claims had never been investigated properly, or never filed in the first place due to lack of information or functioning grievance systems, and/or the fear of retribution."

In the absence of a consistent reporting mechanism, the best source of information about abuse behind bars often comes from litigation initiated by family members, advocacy groups, or the U.S. Department of Justice. The federal entity charged with enforcing the Eighth Amendment (which forbids cruel and unusual punishment), the Department of Justice is responsible for investigating allegations of abuse behind bars and can sue those jurisdictions in which abuse is egregious enough to test constitutional limits.

A 2011 report from the Annie E. Casey Foundation includes an overview of successful civil rights suits across the country. Abuse is pervasive throughout the nation's juvenile facilities, author Richard Mendel concludes, with documentation of "systemic violence, abuse, and/or excessive use of isolation or restraints" in thirty-nine states plus Washington, D.C., and Puerto Rico, going back to 1970.

In each of these instances, "states have been identified not for one or a handful of isolated events, but for a sustained pattern of maltreatment," according to the Casey report. Fifty-seven lawsuits, many brought by the Department of Justice, have turned up enough evidence of violence, abuse, and other violations to require court-imposed remediation.

The thousands upon thousands of pages of documentation that result from these myriad investigations leave little question that the punishment doled out inside our nation's juvenile prisons is cruel. But as evidence of widespread abuse turns up in state upon state, decade after decade, it becomes increasingly difficult to view it as "unusual."

In New York, a supervisor with that state's Office of Children and Family Services, which oversees both the delinquency and dependency systems, said young people sometimes returned from upstate juvenile facilities with bruises, contusions, or even broken bones. Each time, she would pick up the phone and report these instances of alleged child abuse to a branch of the same agency suspected of inflicting them.

Only a handful of states, it turns out, have *not* been determined to have systematically brutalized the youth in their care. A review of all fifty states found only eight where there was *not* conclusive evidence of system-wide mistreatment.

Reading the results of Department of Justice investigations or class-action lawsuits—catalogues of brutality running on for pages—is a painful experience. But there is also something bracing about the bald exposure of abuses behind bars. Surely, one imagines, once these horrors are exposed both in the press and at the highest levels of our legal system, something will be done about them. Reforms will be instituted, the children made safe.

Those who author reports on abuse in juvenile prisons tend to foster this reformist faith, ending the most chilling investigation with an optimistic list of suggested reforms. The language ranges from academic to outraged to crisply legalistic, depending on the authors, but the recommendations themselves are generally quite similar: conduct further inquiries, form new committees, consult experts, draft protocols, hold trainings, and the like. Beneath these procedural suggestions lies a single mandate: quit beating up the children.

Federal law and a number of court decisions have made it clear that incarcerated youth do not forfeit their human rights along with their liberty. Yet as lawsuit follows lawsuit and consent decrees pile up, abuse remains endemic to our nation's juvenile prisons. It has persisted for decades, despite investigations, exposés, admonitions, and court orders; despite public displays of outrage and official commitments to change.

No matter how vehemently we profess ourselves "scandalized" when another investigation brings new abuses to light, the seemingly gratuitous cruelty of captor toward captive is so widespread, and so long-standing despite multiple reform efforts, that it raises a troubling question: is it even *possible* to eradicate the abuses that occur with such regularity when large numbers of vulnerable young people are held captive far from the public eye? Or is there something inherent to this particular structure that makes such abuses inevitable?

From "chemical restraints" to shield-bearing "extraction teams" to age-old tools like the fist and the boot, today's incarcerated youth face a range of mechanisms of assault that taxes the imagination. The restraint chair, for example, may sound like an artifact from a medieval dungeon, but it is used in juvenile facilities to this day.

Ricardo spent twenty-one months in a Massachusetts Department of Youth Services facility. There, he was strapped into the device—a high-backed, padded contraption fitted out with belts, cuffs, and similar devices—in order, he was told, to address his "anger problems."

"They put you in a fucking room by yourself with the chair in the middle . . . a big-ass room with one chair, and you are strapped down to it. . . . They strap you down and sit you like this"—Ricardo stooped to demonstrate the pinioned position that seemed to be imprinted in his muscle memory—"and you have to sit there for five to six hours by yourself."

"They strap you down," he repeated, his voice rising with a fury the passage of time seemed not to have diminished.

"I am able to speak about almost every event of my life like it isn't me," said twenty-year-old Stephanie, who survived rape, stabbings, and more during the years she spent as a sex worker in order to care for herself and her brother. The siblings had lost their father to AIDS, their mother to addiction, and their grandparents to age, and it had not crossed Stephanie's mind that the responsibility for their care might fall to anyone but her.

Eventually, she landed in an upstate New York juvenile facility. "Really, it was like being an adult," Stephanie said. One girl, she recalled, was restrained on a classroom rug that had been salted so heavily that "maybe an hour later, half her face was all gone. It looked like a third-degree burn. They put a fan across her and told her to 'thug it out.' "

The literature on children and trauma makes clear that one does not have to be the direct victim of violence to experience lasting harm. Witnessing violence can also have long-term effects. "I detach myself out of the situations that happen," explained Stephanie. "So when I speak about the situations, it is like they aren't whole situations for me. I guess it is just years of going through traumatic things."

Like Stephanie, battle-scarred children often find ways to distance themselves from the most profound traumas, describing horrific experiences in tones that are incongruously matter-of-fact. It's different for a parent. No matter how much time has passed, when a mother describes being helpless to protect her child as he is raped, beaten, brutalized, and abandoned by a system that has claimed him in the name of his best interest, her pain is as raw as if she were describing events of a moment ago. One mother recalled the horror and betrayal she felt the first time she was permitted to visit her then twelve-year-old son. Arrested along with two older boys for theft of a car stereo, he'd been sent to what authorities had promised her would be a "therapeutic program."

After almost three hours of driving, her car rounded a bend and the building that housed the putative "program," and her son within it, loomed before her. Razor wire, guards, and weapons filled her vision. "Twelve years old, and my son was in a prison."

After a long wait, she was led into a gymnasium-sized room full of bleachers, packed with boys and men from as young as eleven to their mid-twenties. When she finally located her son in the crowd, she barely recognized the rail-thin boy. His eyebrows had been shaved off, highlighting a round indentation on his temple. He had a huge black eye, a busted lip, and, when she looked more closely, a bruise on his rib cage in the shape of a boot.

"Mom, this is what happens," he told her in a flat tone that scared her as deeply as did his physical condition. "A guard did this. They want you to know who's boss."

When a boy with a swollen face meets his mother in the visiting room and answers her anxious questions with an offhand "That's just the way it is," it is unlikely that he has truly grown immune to suffering. More likely, the alternative to feigning diffidence—to beg her for assistance she is powerless to provide, and see his own helplessness reflected in his mother's face—is simply too painful. A young prisoner is likely to learn early on that those who love him are as powerless as he in the face of the omnipotent "system." No matter how brave a face he may wear in the visiting room, this is a hard lesson. If he can no longer be a child and take shelter in the family, then "taking it like a man" becomes the only option—to protect the mother who cannot protect him and to preserve some shard of dignity himself.

For many parents, the second circle of hell is breached when they try to protest what they may at first assume is an anomalous violation of policy, only to learn, as their concerns are dismissed, that their child's experience is in fact par for the course; that, despite their most passionate advocacy, they truly cannot protect him.

That is, if they are both persistent and fortunate enough to get any response at all from the authorities who now control their children. Many parents describe being treated as criminals themselves: the "type of people" who would raise a delinquent child, and so neither credible nor even worthy of an audience with busy administrators.

The boy with the boot-shaped bruise was being held at the Tallulah Correctional Center for Youth in Louisiana, which teetered at the extreme end of a dismal spectrum. The *New York Times* called it "so rife with brutality, cronyism and neglect that many legal experts say it is the worst in the nation." Broken bones, black eyes, fractured jaws, and gang rapes were daily occurrences. A Department of Justice investigation found that dozens of youths went to the hospital with serious injuries each month.

"It eroded years of parenting that taught my son, as well as my other children, to tell the truth and trust in authority," this mother said of her son's experience behind bars. "It stole any confidence in himself that I had managed to instill. And it taught him at a very vulnerable and too young age that authority can be corrupt, without limits or moral boundaries."

"The worst of all of this is that he seems to believe he has no value to add to the outside world," she continued, "that he deserves the harsh treatment he has received, because he is a bad person."

What, this mother has struggled for years to answer, could counteract a message that had literally been beaten into her child? What will it take to restore his faith in his own humanity, much less that of adults in positions of authority?

Eventually, after intense pressure from parents and other advocates, Tallulah was forced to close its doors. Similar scandals, fueled by lawsuits and family and media pressure, have shuttered some of the worst dungeons in other states as well. But while the phrase "isolated incident" is often invoked when this kind of pressure forces a response from officials, the problem is rarely one of "a few bad apples" among the staff, or among the institutions themselves. Brutality and victimization are in fact often "the way it is" inside juvenile prisons—leaving those sent there scarred by new trauma, which is itself a predictor of future incarceration.

By countenancing this ongoing abuse, juvenile institutions instill a "survival of the fittest" mentality that is in direct opposition to the values that judges tell families their children are being sent away to learn. Trapped within a culture built on fear and impunity, young people are more likely to adapt than to protest—objecting, they learn early, is futile or worse. Adapting to prison culture offers some protection, but the price is steep: a brutal and destructive coming-of-age.

Inside a correctional setting, a child's ability to distance himself from emotion—the "machine down" mind-set—is adaptive. Young prisoners may come to believe that a "me against the world" posture is the only thing that will get them through their time. This defensive stance, while effective in the moment, works against the goal of rehabilitation. To "do time" well can require suppressing the instinct toward empathy, developing an immunity not only to one's own pain but also that of others.

For some, the next step is to go from ignoring another's suffering to inflicting it. Ward-on-ward violence and the psychological manipulation that accompanies it reflect the culture of violence and power to which young people learn to adapt. In an environment designed to strip away all agency, tormenting a weaker neighbor can come to seem the only means of regaining a sense of control.

Louis was eleven years old the first time he was sent to Washington, D.C.'s now-defunct Oak Hill Youth Center, then notorious for its culture of abuse. Oak Hill, said Louis, was "anything goes": a chaotic, *Lord of the Flies*–style environment where it was "your so-called bullies," not the staff, who ran the facility.

"And myself, I can say honestly, I was one of them," he acknowledged.

Louis established his status in the pecking order through the kind of petty domination that can make life miserable for those on the other end. "I would tell somebody, 'Don't go in that shower—that's mine. Give me that tray.' Other stuff, just to take anger out."

As he got older, Louis said, he "started to wise up" and backed off the intimidation tactics. By "taking my anger out on somebody else who's going through the same thing I'm going through," he realized, he was helping to perpetuate the same miserable cycle in which he was trapped.

Roland—whose initiation to a California state facility involved guards offering explicit instructions on how to fight, along with a graphic inventory of the injuries he would sustain—went through a similar evolution.

"At first," he explained, "regardless of anything, I had emotions. I had feelings." But in an environment where, he said, guards entertained themselves by unlocking rivals' cells at night and watching them fight, or dragged youth out of sight of the security cameras before laying into them, emotion soon came to feel like a weakness too costly to maintain.

Before his arrest, Roland said, he had been living a double life: one foot headed for college, the other still cemented to the street. When some homies bent on retaliation offered him a ride home, he was ambivalent even as he got into the car. His instinct was right: he ended up charged along with them in a drive-by shooting.

Once he was behind bars, the fork in the road became all the more distinct: he had to make a choice about how he would do his time. Behind bars, without sunlight or water, the side of him that aspired to something better soon withered, while the streetwise survivor had all that it needed to grow.

"It's hard to explain," Roland began hesitantly, "and people probably will never understand, but it's all mind manipulation in there. If you could use your mind, then you pretty much got it made."

"Every time somebody new comes, you play with them," Roland elaborated, describing mind games that revolved around power and fear. The most common was a basic protection racket. Roland would take a new arrival aside while one of his friends circled, mean mugging the new-comer. Roland would play good cop, showing the new kid the ropes and pointing out danger spots.

"He's not by himself," he'd warn, casting a quick glance at his menacing co-conspirator. "He's got about six homies that will jump up and get you. . . . I could look out for you, but it's going to cost."

"It is what it is in here," Roland would sigh, world-weary, before cutting to the chase: $10 a week. "We shake hands, and it's a done deal."

The problem comes when this kind of skill is learned too well. A young person carries back into the outside world whatever he has learned inside. Empathy, for instance, is too often quashed, replaced by a capacity for disconnection that may be useful in a context of institutional abuse but runs directly counter to the goal of rehabilitation.

Will doesn't play much basketball these days. A dean's list student with a prestigious scholarship that will take him through a PhD, a loving father, and a devoted son who helps care for his much younger brother, he doesn't have much time. But during his six-year incarceration, basketball helped him keep it together. He was a good player, always had been, and the intensity of the competition helped him release the tension he built up in his efforts to be a model inmate.

Will played hard but carefully, watchful to keep his aggression just clear of the foul line. But he did play all out, leaving the court dripping with sweat. That, he assumes, was why the pain was so overpowering when the guards came at him with what they called "chemical restraints": his pores were wide open, allowing the caustic, Mace-like liquid to penetrate more deeply.

It was a particularly fierce game, and Will had gotten into it with a rival player. Words were exchanged, followed by blows. Will swung first.

A watchful young man, Will knew the institution had recently started using a new kind of chemical restraint. It worked as a fogger, emitting a powerful spray intended to clear a room, he recalls, and the label warned against using it at close range. That didn't stop the guards from spraying it directly into both boys' faces, aiming for their eyes, Will said.

According to the complaint in *Farrell v. Harper*, a sweeping lawsuit that successfully challenged practices throughout the California Youth

Authority, this kind of abuse, and more, was commonplace. Per the complaint:

> It is common practice within the CYA for staff and/or guards to slam a ward down, pull his arms behind his back, force a knee into his back, and use excessive amounts of Mace or other chemical agents even after the ward is restrained. Wards also have their heads slammed against walls and rails and are beaten and burned by tear gas canisters and Maced without provocation. For example, a ward was repeatedly sprayed with chemical agents for declining to undergo a strip search after being placed in a holding room. In another example, a ward was knocked unconscious when shot directly in the head with a "foam baton" gun. In a third example, CYA officers placed a handcuffed ward face down on a bed and repeatedly struck his head.

Will had witnessed similar attacks before and heard others scream as the chemical hit the sensitive membranes of their eyes. Still, it was worse than he anticipated. The pain as the caustic substance penetrated his open pores was compounded by the twenty-four hours he was forced to go without medical treatment or even a chance to clean off, the chemical seeping ever deeper as he sat locked in a cell.

"I wanted to see so bad," he recalls of that period. "But whenever I opened my eyes, it just hurt more."

The chemical onslaught was followed by a monthlong stint in solitary: "twenty-three hours a day in a cell by myself. The hour I didn't spend in my cell, I showered and sat in a cage by myself with nothing to do but stare into space. This is what they called recreation. When my mother came to see me, I was put in a fluorescent orange jumpsuit and wore handcuffs accompanied by shackles. The 'peace officers' used to joke and call it jailhouse jewelry."

Outside sources corroborate Will's account, as they do much of what I heard from young people who suffered abuse inside juvenile institutions. California law permits the use of chemical weapons "only to restrain wards, and not for punishment or retaliation." Nevertheless, according to investigators, 272 youths were sprayed with chemical weapons by correctional officers in the course of just one month at a single facility—an average of about ten youths per day at that site alone. The *Farrell* lawsuit also documents young people being put in restraint chairs or, as Will was, isolation or suicide watch cells "for extended periods of time without legitimate justification."

Years later, Will still suffers from the attack. No matter how much lotion he applies, the skin beneath his eyebrows regularly peels: a constant physical reminder of those agonizing hours he spent without treatment or relief.

I asked him how he got through both the protracted pain and the subsequent month in solitary. "That's where hope comes in," he told me—"the idea of the future. You can't deal with the resentment at the time because it's so much, and the situation is still so bad. The only way I was able to deal with it was to think about when I would get out. Hope. Some people use religion. Whatever vehicle, it's about taking your brain out of that moment in time. So I thought about the first time I'd see my mom when I was free. Even something as simple as reading a book is taking my mind off jail. It depends on the person and what you are interested in, but the core value is, you take yourself out of your situation. You can't do it physically, but mentally you can. I'd think about the first meal I would eat when I get out, or wonder what my mom is doing right now."

When a captive speaks of hope, he's talking of a strategy as much as an emotion: a technique to stay human in an environment designed to dehumanize him. If he could conjure the taste of a meal consumed in freedom, or picture his mother going about her day, perhaps he could hold on to a piece of himself.

That prison dehumanizes those held there is a well-known phenomenon; in fact, it's not hard to conclude that this is the institution's purpose. But the more I heard stories such as Darren's and Will's, or watched security-camera videos of guards setting dogs on unresisting boys, the more I wondered about those who went home at the end of each shift. Surely they were not all sadists who had chosen a career in corrections in order to hurt children. Did working inside a prison somehow undermine the human instinct to nurture and protect the young? Was prison life as dehumanizing to the keepers as it was to the kept?

How else to explain the fact that in facilities all across the country, adults who have accepted responsibility for supervising young people turn instead to harming them? Why would the same guards who had always considered Will a "model prisoner" spray a toxic chemical directly into his eyes? And—even more incomprehensibly—how could they allow him to soak in the poison through the night and the following day, then leave him in solitary confinement for a full month after that?

What did they say when they got home and a spouse asked how their day went? What went through their minds as they looked at their own children?

"You tell me we're there to be rehabilitated," Will said when I raised this question, speaking to a hypothetical guard. "You can't teach us that if you're not even connected to us. There's a vast disconnect between the people who are supposed to teach us the right way and us."

In Will's analysis, connection, or relationship, is not only what young people need to rehabilitate themselves; it is also what the juvenile justice system and those who run it—from the front lines up through the administrators and legislators who call the shots—need if they are ever to succeed in meeting their stated goals. But many guards—especially the veterans, including those in positions of leadership—have spent more of their lives inside prisons than have their young charges. As a result, as Darren put it, "They are as institutionalized as we are."

Like any other shift worker, Will observed, prison guards are just trying to get through the day with minimum hassle. "If I were working at this coffee shop, and the coffee filters starting acting crazy, I'd be pissed," he offered when I asked him to help me understand how some of the pleasant, thoughtful officers of the law I had met were capable of the brutality that he and many others described.

"The reason could be, 'You are making my shift harder.' It's not a system set up to care. It's an assembly-line mentality. It's not like we have souls or anything. It's more like we're a product. *This is my occupation and when the machines aren't working right, I have a hard day. It's not like I'm dealing with humans.* I see that everywhere: *Let my shift run smooth, don't act up, I hope all the stirrers are there, I hope the sugar is plentiful in my coffee shop, and if not—there goes my day. My shift is messed up.*

"*My* day," Will repeated, with the emphasis on the "my." "It's very egocentric. Rehabilitation isn't possible. There's not even an avenue for rehabilitation when the people who are supposed to help you are only thinking about themselves."

Vincent Schiraldi, now head of probation for New York City, is the kind of leader who is frequently described as "outspoken" or "controversial"— words that don't quite do justice to his strikingly direct manner. A former watchdog and advocate who jumped the fence to run the institutions he had spent decades challenging, Schiraldi has managed to hold on to a consistent ethos regardless of his role or title: that young people do better in the community than they do behind bars. He has also maintained a distinct indifference to the mores of his new position, continuing to communicate in a straightforward and occasionally profane manner without even a hint of bureaucratese.

Prior to taking the job in New York, Schiraldi ran the District of Columbia's juvenile system. His signal achievement there was closing down the District's Oak Hill Youth Center, "one of the most disastrous and abusive juvenile correctional facilities in the nation," and replacing it with the $46 million New Beginnings Youth Development Center, a light-filled compound that resembles a university campus more closely than it does a traditional institution. He also radically reduced the number of young people in confinement, moving many into community placements or supervision at home.

The D.C. system was in a state of chaos when Schiraldi was sworn in—reportedly the twentieth director in the nineteen years the District had been fighting the *Jerry M. vs. the District of Columbia* lawsuit, which challenged conditions at the crumbling Oak Hill facility. By the time he arrived, Schiraldi said, there were twenty-two court orders in place—as the new boss, he found himself operating under orders A through Q— a testimony both to the optimism of the advocates and the intransigence of the institution.

The first thing Schiraldi did to prepare for his new job was to read through the transcripts of the *Jerry M.* suit. He read of "kids taking their shirts off and stuffing them in the toilet bowl to prevent rats and roaches from crawling up on them and biting them at night." From a report by the inspector general, he learned that "it was easier to score [drugs] in that facility than it was on the streets of the District of Columbia." He spoke of "kids sleeping on cots in dayrooms," or in quarters so hot that those with asthma could not safely remain there.

"Staff malaise and depression" were pervasive, Schiraldi said. "The place reeked of apathy."

The apathy was not limited to Oak Hill. That facility, he observed in a tone that made clear that decades in the field had not quelled his capacity for outrage, "was twenty miles from the nation's capital. Twenty miles from the National Prison Project. Twenty miles from the Justice Department. And this had gone on for decades . . . under the noses of the leaders of the most powerful nation in the world."

"You very clearly had a system where, when there was trouble, you call this 'flying squad' of people who beat the kids up and locked them in their rooms," Schiraldi soon discovered. In addition to what he described as "a thriving sex-for-overtime trade" among staff, he continued, "People were selling drugs to the kids. Pretty much everyone knew who it was—kids and staff—and nobody snitched. People who go to church on Sundays and are nice to their families."

For new staffers, all of this can lead to what Schiraldi referred to as cognitive dissonance—the internal conflict engendered when what one believes, or is told, clashes with perceived reality. Cognitive dissonance can be so uncomfortable that a common reaction is to ignore, or explain away, the dissonant reality, rather than confronting it.

For new staff at a facility such as the one Schiraldi described, this is how the syndrome might play out: "You first go into a unit thinking you're there to help kids, and something like that [e.g., abuse] happens. You've got a moment to make a decision. Do I go along with this? Do I snitch? Or do I quit?" he began.

"The people who don't snitch and don't quit, who stay, who came as good people wanting to help? Now a little bit of evil has crept in. It's like the first time people dropped the pellets in the death canister. I'm sure it feels different the first time than the hundredth time. . . . You're working in a dangerous environment where no one has a plan on how to make it not be dangerous, so you sort of do what you did when you were a kid growing up: when there's physical force involved, you react with physical force."

Noting that abuse has been a fact of life inside juvenile facilities for more than a century, Schiraldi cautioned against demonizing the individuals who work inside them today. "It's important to put ourselves in that spot and not just cluck or shake our heads at what staff end up becoming like, because the power of that indoctrination—and the power of the cognitive dissonance and rationalization that goes on for staff, when this is all they've ever seen in their lives—cannot be overstated," said Schiraldi, who recalled being "indoctrinated" himself as a recent college graduate working in a group home. "It's the banality of a particular form of evil that really does set in, and it sets into the good people and the bad people alike."

During my travels, I had a conversation with a clinician who worked for a large state juvenile system in the throes of a major reform effort. He spoke of another kind of dissonance: the kind that can ensue when staff who have been indoctrinated (as Schiraldi put it) into one way of doing things are abruptly told that way is wrong and asked to make radical and rapid changes.

"It's hard to consider and practice something new when there's no room to slow down or to practice," he began, attempting to explain staff resistance to reform. "If you make a mistake, you're going to get called to [the] child abuse [registry], you're going to be fined, you're going to be put on administrative leave—and you're working sixteen hours a day."

When I pressed him to be more specific about what kind of "mistakes" might trigger a call to the child abuse registry, he seemed to acknowledge that the term "mistake" as he was using it could encompass child abuse ("I'm not saying that they're not valid calls, because they are"). But given the difficult working conditions, he also cautioned against blaming the individual.

Many staffers, he pointed out, were working in "an environment where there's chronic stress and violence," where "kids come in with violent behaviors and attack people."

"From a trauma-informed perspective," he told me, skating between the first and second person, "to attack back, to protect myself" is "a natural reaction. . . . You move from the frontal lobes, where you process and understand what's going on, to the hind brain, which is the primitive brain."

"I think the lack of staffing, and the burnout, all contribute. . . . I don't think you can blame it on individual staff. We're all accountable for our own behavior, and that's what we tell kids, too, but at the same time, we need to look at the bigger picture and say, 'What has happened here?' Because nobody says, 'I want to grow up to be a child abuser,' right?"

Just as no child, I thought, says, "I want to grow up to be a prisoner." The young people who *lived* inside the same environment of "chronic stress and violence" that the clinician had cited, it seemed, to excuse staff violence—children who could not go home at the end of a shift—were rarely viewed through this "trauma-informed" lens. They were not granted the latitude to make "mistakes" under pressure—not when they were sentenced, often after childhoods filled with violence and trauma, and not when they were on the receiving end of "discipline" behind bars so harsh that it would qualify as child abuse were those subjected to it seen as fully human.

In fact, when it comes to the kids, the legal and cultural shifts of recent decades have increasingly *foreclosed* consideration of "the bigger picture" the clinician referenced, requiring the courts to demand "accountability" absent the sort of context he advocated when it came to abusive guards.

We're all accountable for our own behavior, and that's what we tell kids, too. . . .

Like all adolescents—all people, for that matter—incarcerated youth respond more powerfully to actions than they do to admonitions. They do as we do, not as we say. How, then, I wondered, could we expect youth to keep their cool behind bars when even the adults in charge could not? Is it reasonable to demand they do better than the adults around them at acting from their "frontal lobes" when we now know that this region of the brain (responsible for capacities such as connecting an action to a consequence, or considering its impact on others) is not fully developed until the mid-twenties? Can we expect young people to demonstrate this kind of control despite, in many cases, lifelong histories of trauma, "chronic stress," and the strain of incarceration in a chaotic, unpredictable environment—one that, per this clinician, was taxing enough for the guards to drive them to violence?

Guards were to be excused because they sometimes worked double shifts. The kids lived in the same environment 24/7. But when—"from a trauma-informed perspective"—the adolescents slip into the "hind brain," they face consequences far harsher than the guard, who may have his pay docked.

Even as the abuses inside juvenile facilities started to become more comprehensible to me, this glaring double standard continued to rankle. It was hard not to wonder how many lives might be different if the kids we consign to abusive institutions were offered even a small percentage of the "second chances" their keepers are granted.

When he described his own dealings with young people, this clinician sounded both wise and compassionate. He spoke of instances when he had relied on patience and communication to help young people calm themselves, rather than reflexively turning to physical restraint. He had listened and talked his way through outbursts to which others might well have reacted with force. Nevertheless, his implicit plea for a "trauma-informed" pass on reporting guards for child abuse remained disconcerting.

What, I wondered, did this double standard do to young prisoners' moral development, their sense of the broader social contract, and their own stake in it? If a "trauma-informed perspective" was used to justify crimes *against* youth in custody, committed by adults who possessed near-complete authority, was it reasonable to expect those same youths to internalize the lesson that growing up means being "accountable for your own behavior"?

"Indifference, to me, is the epitome of evil," the author and concentration camp survivor Elie Wiesel has said. For Darren, the indifference of the guards who went about their shifts as if it were just another day at the mill, seemingly oblivious to the suffering of the boys who knelt at their feet, remains the most difficult aspect of his incarceration with which to come to terms.

It should not be surprising that Darren's struggle would include questioning his own faith. In the same interview, Wiesel elaborated on the corrosive power of the kind of disregard Darren had faced. "The opposite of faith is not heresy, it's indifference," he said. "The opposite of life is not death, but indifference between life and death."

According to the U.S. Office of Juvenile Justice and Delinquency Prevention, eleven thousand young people engage in suicidal behavior in juvenile facilities each year. In California, a recent study calculated the rate of suicide attempts in juvenile halls as close to twenty-four per thousand youth in custody.

That so many young people seek to end their lives in the loveless, hopeless void of juvenile prisons—that they lose faith not only, as Darren did, in God and man, but even in the value of their own lives—would likely surprise neither Wiesel nor Darren.

Darren had been baptized and raised in the Catholic Church. His most traumatizing experiences, which took place inside the institution charged with his rehabilitation, caused him to question, and for a time nearly abandon, his religion. Just like the child who hides his suffering from a parent who is powerless to help, letting go of his faith seemed preferable to crying out to a God who would permit such inhumanity.

This kind of crisis of faith, Darren said, was a "common theme" behind bars. "People lose their religion in there."

Darren's faith may have been shaken, but his seeker's nature remained. While he was locked up, Darren began attending Native American religious ceremonies, "exploring, trying to find answers to the questions I was asking spiritually, mentally."

I asked Darren what those questions were, what he was seeking as he looked to new gods and theologies.

"How can people in here do the things that they do to kids?" he responded. "To us?" During the two weeks he spent on his knees, boys who could not make it to the twice-daily bathroom calls were forced to urinate where they knelt and to clean it up themselves as best they could or else face a beating.

"God let the people in here do the things that they do to the kids," Darren said, leaving the rest unspoken.

Despite a decade behind bars in a barren and abusive environment, Darren emerged with both ambition and compassion, as well as a powerful sense of mission drawn from his own suffering. Today, he works as a liaison between local businesses and homeless people, mediating solutions intended to prevent his clients from ending up behind bars. Darren, in other words, is one of the "beat the odds" kids whose stories the public is so hungry to hear.

Darren is far from alone in his post-prison achievements, and stories like his are as important as those of kids whose lives are derailed by their experience behind bars. But the beloved trope of the "kid who beat the odds" is double-edged. It inspires us but also soothes our collective conscience, allowing us to avoid asking why the odds are so stacked to begin with.

"What I would like," said Darren, who is acutely aware of both the value and the risks inherent in holding himself up as an example, "is to dissect the explanation *behind* the odds."

"Think about it long term," he continued. "The population we are dealing with now are adolescents. I was an adolescent, still [needing to be] nourished, still developing. And these were the things that were orienting my disposition."

"Some people going through this situation," Darren warned, slipping into a first-person plural to indicate his ongoing solidarity with those still behind bars, "we're going to be the backlash. We don't have the fundamental necessities for communication. We got nothing to lose."

During the months he spent on an isolation unit, Darren had listened helplessly to the cries of a boy in another cell as guards beat him for kicking at his door. It was clear to Darren that the boy was not deliberately trying to be provocative; like everyone else on the unit, he was simply desperate for some kind of human contact. How could the guards not see this? How could they answer his plea only with violence? And God— the God Darren had worshipped without question for as long as he could remember—where was He amid this desolation?

The fashionable café was quiet on this spring afternoon, its clientele a mix of underemployed twentysomethings inking their thoughts into moleskin notebooks and thirtysomethings tapping away at laptops. If Darren turned heads, it wasn't because he stood out but because he so perfectly fit in, his sunglasses perched just so atop his knit cap, framing a handsome and animated brown face.

At thirty, Darren was bright with promise and ambition, determined to turn even his deepest traumas into something of use to others. It was difficult to imagine him locked for months on end in an isolation cell, struggling to hold on to his humanity as well as his sanity.

"The question," he asked, "is where is the public when this is going on? When I heard that a kid got beat up by the staff, I would wonder. . . . It was a kid being 'defiant,' since he was kicking the door. But we are all social creatures. If you were locked up . . ."

Darren let the rest of this sentence go unspoken, but his intent was clear. He was joining the many who ask those who have not been there to imagine; to try, at least, to place ourselves in the shoes that kicked the door.

"The kids would do things to act out, to get attention or social interaction," Darren said, trying to explain why a boy would kick his door when logic and experience told him it could bring only a beating, "since we are social creatures. To get some type of contact—unfortunately, in that type of fashion."

"What does it take to be normal again, after having your humanity stripped away by the Nazis?" an interviewer once asked Elie Wiesel. "What is abnormal," Wiesel responded, "is that I am normal. That I survived the Holocaust and went on to love beautiful girls, to talk, to write, to have toast and tea and live my life—that is what is abnormal."

Darren and I were sitting at one of the café's outside tables, and he grew quiet for a moment as two mounted police officers passed by on quarter horses, their chestnut coats gleaming in the near-dusk light.

"That's pretty," Darren reflected, growing silent for a moment as he followed the horses' brisk transit through the intersection, then up a hill, and finally out of sight. I remarked on his ability to enjoy the horses' beauty rather than reacting reflexively to their uniformed riders.

"You take it for what it's worth," he answered with a rare smile. Then the moment passed, and he picked up where he'd left off.

6

AN OPEN SECRET

Sexual Abuse Behind Bars

By acquiescing in an act that causes such suffering to a living creature, who among us is not diminished?

—Rachel Carson

"ANSWER THE QUESTION," THE officer ordered.

Lamont was eight years old at the time of this impromptu interrogation. He'd been riding his bike near his home in San Francisco's heavily policed Hunters Point neighborhood when a squad car pulled up and stopped him in his tracks.

Local police suspected Lamont's older brother of being a gang leader and wanted details about his activities and whereabouts. It was not the first time this officer or one of his colleagues had pulled Lamont off his bike or stopped him on his way home from school, demanding information he did not possess. But this time the officer upped the ante.

"Answer the question, or I'll take you to jail," he growled. "You'll get raped there, and have babies out your butt." It was a threat the third grader was inclined to believe, coming, as it did, from the voice of authority.

There is no way to overstate the corrosiveness of the lesson Lamont learned so early: that the law is a force of violation, not protection. And the officer's threat, while obviously exaggerated, was anything but empty. More than 12 percent of juvenile prisoners will experience sexual assault behind bars, and many more will live in fear of it each day they spend locked up.

In 2010, the Department of Justice's Review Panel on Prison Rape released its report on sexual victimization in juvenile correctional facilities. The report highlights findings of the National Survey of Youth in Custody, based on confidential interviews with more than nine thousand young people in 195 facilities across the country.

The survey found that 12 percent of juvenile prisoners—more than three thousand young people—had been sexually abused at least once over the previous year. In some facilities, as many as 30 percent of the wards had been abused within that time frame.

About one in fifty youth in the study reported being sexually abused by other youths. A much higher number—one in ten of *all* incarcerated minors—had been abused by a member of the staff. Dayrooms, kitchens, bathrooms, laundry rooms—no place, it appeared, was off limits to uniformed predators. Sexual abuse rates are higher in juvenile than in adult prisons, per the report, specifically because of the frequency with which guards assault their young charges—the proclivity of adults, in other words, to prey upon the young.

The study—the first of its kind to rely on confidential interviews rather than official reports—found a rate of sexual assault that was more than seven times higher than reported in a 2008 Justice Department investigation based on sexual abuse claims filed with facility administrators. This gap underscores the degree to which sexual abuse in juvenile prisons generally goes unreported, and so underestimated.

The 2010 Department of Justice study belies the common perception that new arrivals must watch out for other inmates, making clear that their guardians pose a far greater threat. "In essence," the *New York Review of Books* summed up, "the survey shows that thousands of children are raped and molested every year while in the government's care—most often, by the very corrections officials charged with their rehabilitation and protection."

Sexual assault, needless to say, is traumatic for anyone, regardless of age, but children are particularly vulnerable to post-traumatic stress syndrome and other lasting effects. According to the authors of "Defending Childhood: Children Exposed to Violence," victims of childhood sexual abuse may go on to "detach physically and psychologically, leading to symptoms of psychological dissociation, such as 'blanking or spacing out,' or acting on 'automatic pilot' without conscious thought, as a way of escaping overwhelmingly intense feelings of fear, horror, rage, and shame."

Lamont's initiation may have been particularly early and gratuitously graphic, but it was otherwise unremarkable. Many young people in high-incarceration neighborhoods learn to associate the law with sexual violation as early as they learn to look both ways before crossing the street.

The widespread understanding that incarceration is likely to include the threat of sexual violation is among the darkest aspects of our juvenile prison system. Everyone who has any connection at all with these institutions—and many who do not, as evidenced by the cliché status of "don't drop the soap" jokes—knows it takes place, yet we profess ourselves scandalized each time a new spate of violations is revealed. The truth is closer to what Lamont learned at the knee of the neighborhood beat cop: rape behind bars is part and parcel of the punishment.

"Certain staff 'like' you," Cherie ventured tentatively. "Certain staff might rub up on you."

Otherwise direct and open about her time behind bars, Cherie shifted to more stilted language as the conversation turned to sexual abuse. She chose each word with care, avoided naming names, and grew vague with her pronouns—was she talking about her own experience, what she had witnessed, or both?

"I heard some stuff . . . ," Cherie continued with uncharacteristic hesitance. "A couple of different instances, know what I'm saying, where a couple people got taken to get abortions."

These girls, she clarified, had not entered the institution pregnant. Pregnant girls were forced to identify themselves by wearing pink shirts, while the rest wore blue. Cherie recalled one girl who turned up in pink after she had been locked up for quite some time.

"It wasn't no boy . . . ," Cherie clarified, her point unmistakable.

Sexual abuse, Cherie learned, was part of the underground prison economy. A girl whose keepers "liked" her could, if she acceded to their sexual demands, win small privileges that are highly valued in the culture of deprivation that exists behind bars. She might get out of her cell when others were confined, receive extra phone calls, and even gain access to a more private shower (private except for the presence of her abuser). Her diet might be supplemented with treats from the free world, the rough prison soap replaced with scented scrubs and lotions.

"It's all on the tip of my tongue," one girl responded when a newly arrived Cherie inquired about the source of the largesse bestowed upon her. When Cherie did not immediately understand, the young woman cut to the chase: she received these small privileges, she explained, in return for performing oral sex on a correctional officer.

According to Cherie, uniformed predators selected their prey from among the most vulnerable and isolated girls. "The ones they knew wouldn't say nothing" were seen as "fair game," she explained.

"A girl doing five or six years, knowing she ain't got no family?" Cherie elaborated. "They're gonna watch and see. If she ain't got nobody? She's perfect."

"If I was in there longer, I wouldn't have been above it," she added. "'Cause I didn't have nobody. That's how I know."

"That's exactly the thing," she continued in a tone of discovery. "Just think about it—what I came from, my mom strung out on drugs, no help, you feel me? All the shit [that goes on behind bars], you're that far away, you gonna do what you gotta do to survive. It's always been like that. That's why so many girls get into trouble in the first place."

It's always been like that. According to the Department of Justice report, young people who have been sexually abused prior to their arrest are especially likely to be targeted again behind bars. Nearly 25 percent of young people who had been sexually assaulted before their incarceration were abused again while in custody. Fully 65 percent of those who had been sexually abused at a previous correctional facility were targeted again at their next destination.

The cycle does not stop there. Among those young people who reported having been abused by staff, 88 percent had been abused repeatedly. Twenty-seven percent had been assaulted more than ten times and 33 percent by more than one employee. Among those victimized by other youth, a similar pattern emerged: 81 percent had been sexually assaulted more than once and 43 percent by more than one person.

Roland, who spent time in various California state facilities, explained how this latter cycle is perpetuated. Ward-on-ward assaults, according to Roland and others, are—like those by staff—generally met with impunity. Even investigation, in Roland's experience, was more or less unheard-of. Staff, he said, simply "let it happen. . . . They turn their back. Too much paperwork. Too much questioning."

There are also power differentials among wards (albeit of a different order than those between wards and guards). "I knew some people that got sexually abused by other wards," Roland said. "If you are about fourteen, you got guys who are about two hundred pounds, no fat, nothing but muscle, and they grab you and are like, 'Ey, you about to do this and that,' and you're like, 'No,' and they are like, 'You gotta do it' . . ." He left the rest unspoken.

In this sort of scenario, the most a young target might hope for is to be moved out of range of the initial perpetrator. Even when this happens, according to Roland, "the word always gets around. . . . 'He's a gay, he did oral this, he did that.' So it kinda just follows 'em everywhere, even if they move institutions, 'cause word goes through the grapevines. It is better communication [behind bars] than out. Somebody moves, he tells everybody everything. Somebody else moves, and he confirms it." At that point, a victim's fate is sealed.

Sexual abuse is so deeply entrenched in prison culture that it has spawned not only its own subgenre of humor but also its own law—necessary, apparently, despite the fact that both sexual assault *and* the sexual abuse of minors are already illegal.

Passed unanimously by Congress in 2003, the Prison Rape Elimination Act (or PREA) established the National Prison Rape Elimination Commission, tasked with recommending a set of standards to the attorney general. Those recommendations were duly submitted, then sat in a file while six years—and countless more assaults—passed by. In 2009, the attorney general finally officially acknowledged the recommendations, at which point a working group was formed to review them. Toss in time for public comment, and it was May 2012—fully ten years after PREA was signed into law—by the time the Justice Department finally released its "Final Rule to Prevent, Detect and Respond to Prison Rape."

While advocates welcomed the PREA rules, few young people I met had so much as heard of them, and none believed any system existed to which they might have recourse in the face of a sexual assault.

Their lack of faith is well founded. "There are outs all through it," said a parent and advocate who had long looked forward to the release of the PREA rules. "Outs for the state. Outs for the federal government. . . . There are loopholes throughout that entire thing. It looks pretty on paper, but there is nothing about it that is binding that I saw."

She is right: the new rules are not actually binding. Only federally run facilities are required to adopt them, while states may opt out, though those that do will be docked 5 percent in federal prison funding (an amount that speaks volumes about the value placed on the safety of this particular group of children).

"There is language that says 'try' not to put kids in solitary confinement," she added with a mirthless laugh. "That's a good way to hold people accountable!"

The very fact that the new rules call for "a zero-tolerance policy" when it comes to the sexual abuse of children speaks volumes about the blind eye that has been turned to date. So does the suggestion to "terminate" those staff members who assault the youth in their care. While one would think that firing rapists would not require special legislation and regulation, a full quarter of all *known* staff predators (a small percentage of the total, based on evidence that most abuse goes unreported and that prisons rarely substantiate charges against staff even when a report is made) not only have avoided prosecution but have kept their jobs, giving them continued access to their victims as well as to new ones.

A report from the Office of the Inspector General underscored the lightness with which sexual abuse of incarcerated youth is treated. "Even when prosecuted," investigators write, "the punishments for sexual abuse of inmates are not significant. Of the 65 subjects who were convicted of sexually abusing inmates, 48, or 73 percent, received a sentence of probation. Ten of them, or 15 percent, were sentenced to less than 1 year incarceration. Only 5 of them, or 8 percent, were sentenced to more than 1 year incarceration. One of them, or 2 percent, was required only to pay a fine, and another one's sentencing is pending."

The double standard reflected in these figures is mind-boggling. When young people on the outside commit acts similar to those for which guards receive, at most, probation—and more often no sanction of any kind— they are considered serious offenders and are punished far more harshly than are predatory guards. Under civil commitment laws, they may be confined indefinitely—even forever—if a court determines that they are "sexual deviants" who are unlikely to be rehabilitated (despite the fact that juvenile sexual offenders have far lower recidivism rates than almost any other group). Under the federal Adam Walsh Child Protection and Safety Act of 2006, children who have been adjudicated delinquent for a wide range of "sex offenses" designated as serious (including, bizarrely, public urination, as well as consensual sex between two minors that is prosecuted as statutory rape and posting naked pictures of one's underage self online) find themselves, in addition to whatever immediate sanction is imposed, on long-term public sex offender registries. These youth, according to a Human Rights Watch study,

> are stigmatized, isolated, often depressed. Many consider suicide, and some succeed. They and their families have experienced harassment and physical violence. They are sometimes shot at, beaten, even mur- dered; many are repeatedly threatened with violence. Some young people have to post signs stating "sex offender lives here" in the win- dows of their homes; others have to carry drivers' licenses with "sex offender" printed on them in bright orange capital letters. Youth sex offenders on the registry are sometimes denied access to education because residency restriction laws prevent them from being in or near a school. Youth sex offender registrants despair of ever finding employment, even while they are burdened with mandatory fees that can reach into the hundreds of dollars on an annual basis.

Residency restrictions can make finding housing so difficult that fami- lies are driven into homelessness. And the stigma never lifts. A boy adju- dicated for a sex offense at age ten may find, at age forty, that he is barred from dropping his own children off at school or hosting a birthday party at his family's home. As a result of the registry requirements, children of onetime juvenile sex offenders find themselves "harassed and ridiculed by their peers for their parents' long-past transgressions."

Imagine what this double standard must look like to a teenager convicted of a sex offense and sent to a facility where the odds that he will be
abused by a guard are about one in ten—and the odds that the guard will
experience any consequence at all are negligible.

The Office of the Attorney General reported that prison staff who sexually abuse inmates "often do not believe they will be caught, and even
if they are caught do not believe they will be punished. Moreover, staff
can generally conceal their actions because . . . they control the prison
environment. . . . In some cases, prison staff will cover for abusive colleagues by serving as alibis or lookouts. Moreover, staff know that wards
are reluctant to report sexual abuse, and that even if they do, they are
unlikely to be believed."

In 2006, Human Rights Watch and the American Civil Liberties Union
released a report on girls in New York State custody. The interviews in
the report reveal the widespread culture of impunity that has allowed the
sexual abuse of incarcerated youth to continue unabated for so long.

Ebony V. was repeatedly abused by staff at two New York State facilities. Her story illuminates in painful detail both why girls who have
already been victimized are especially vulnerable and why so much abuse
by staff goes unreported.

"Ebony V. stated that girls at Lansing [Residential Center] known to
have previously been commercially sexually exploited, as she was, are
at risk of being targeted by male staff members," the researchers wrote.
"When asked to describe this targeting, Ebony V., who was 16 at the time
of her incarceration, described the conduct of male staff, including her
abuser, who was her facility-assigned counselor."

Ebony's first-person account cracks the veneer of the report's otherwise formal language with its detail and directness.

> The male staff would flirt with me, like [the abuser]. [He] continu-
> ally made me repeat my story in detail, he made me do things I did to
> them to him. He said what I was I would always be that. When I said:
> "I'm going home, I'm not doing this anymore." He said, "You like
> doing this, you like having sex." . . . It was very exploitative in there.
> I was living better than I was on the street but I was still living street
> life in there. I was still being sexually exploited by the staff there. A

staff member had sex with me. . . . Even when I was in there, he was under investigation for inappropriate behavior with girls on the unit.

"At that time my body had been through so much trauma that it didn't matter," Ebony told investigators when they asked why she had not reported the assaults to facility administrators. In addition, the fact that Ebony's abuser was already under investigation for assaulting the girls in his care, yet had continued access to Ebony and others, sent a clear message about the indifference with which she would be met if she did file a complaint.

The message that staff could do with her what they would was conveyed in myriad ways. Once, Ebony recalled, another staff member walked into her abuser's office and caught him in the act. Instead of intervening, or reporting what he saw, he simply bolted: "He said: 'Oh, oh, oh, oh I'm sorry' and closed the door."

The double standard that caused her to be arrested for prostitution (despite the fact that she was below the age of consent), then placed in the custody of a guard who made her reenact the very acts for which she had been arrested, was not lost on Ebony. According to the HRW/ACLU report, Ebony

> ran away from an abusive home and was prostituted by a man in his thirties. She was arrested on a prostitution charge and held in the Lansing facility, where she was again sexually exploited. Contrasting what she viewed as the justice system's lenient treatment of adult men who buy sex from children with its harsh treatment of commercially sexually exploited girls, Ebony V. said: "The system is made for us to fail. Put it like this: A young person like me can get arrested and get put away for a year and a half, then another year for what adults did to her. A lot of times it's not our fault, it's an adult's fault and they treat us like adults in there."

At a hearing held by the National Task Force on Children Exposed to Violence, Sheila Bedi testified about her efforts working for the Southern Poverty Law Center on behalf of incarcerated children in Mississippi and Louisiana. Noting that "the vast majority of [incarcerated children] have committed very low level offenses," Bedi underscored the pervasive double standard that turns a blind eye to the far more serious crimes committed *against* these young people, who are in captivity (and thus easy prey) ostensibly as a result of their own far lesser transgressions.

Bedi described the experience of a sixteen-year-old girl who "was left alone with a staff member who was under investigation for sexually abusing another resident in that facility. She was brutally sexually abused, and that same staff member went on to abuse three other girls before he was finally removed from his position."

"In that same facility," she offered by way of comparison, "seven girls were shackled for over a month because they were an alleged runaway threat." Meanwhile, the serial rapist on staff faced no legal penalty at all and was offered multiple "second chances" to victimize more girls before finally—only after ongoing pressure from advocates—being taken off the job.

Young people in juvenile prisons are especially vulnerable not only to abuse itself but to deep and lasting trauma as a result. Many have been sexually victimized already when they enter, and few have seen those who abused them face any kind of legal consequence. When they are themselves locked up and the jailer takes a turn with their now-captive bodies, the message is clear. *Who would believe a girl like you? You put yourself in this situation. You've got only yourself to blame.*

In testimony before a 2010 House Committee on Education and Labor hearing on "Meeting the Challenges Faced by Girls in the Juvenile Justice System," Rachel offered a vivid account of the lasting effects of being victimized behind bars.

Rachel started out by smoking marijuana to "ease the pain" after her mother's death. At fifteen, she was arrested after a fight with another girl and placed on probation, where she was required to report to a day center but offered neither treatment for her drug use nor support for the loss and grief that triggered it. Unsurprisingly, she failed the drug screenings and was sent to an upstate facility where, she was told, she would be able to get treatment.

Instead of the promised treatment for her drug problem, all Rachel found upstate was a predatory staff member eager to exploit it—to abet and encourage the very behavior for which she was in custody in order to gain sexual leverage over the teenager.

> After a few months on campus, a male staff member on campus who was in his 30s initiated a sexual relationship with me in exchange for bringing me drugs. In order to meet up, the staff member would arrange for me to leave the campus and pick me up in his car down the road from the facility. He would then transport me off campus to a local hotel. These activities were never documented and or questioned and although the staff member who I had the relationship with was eventually fired, it was only because he screened positive for drugs—not because he was sexually exploiting me.

When Rachel was first arrested, she was a grief-stricken teenager who smoked marijuana to drown out her sorrow. By the time she was released, her addiction untreated and her trauma exacerbated, her "behavior began to spiral out of control," she testified. "I started using heavier drugs and then began soliciting my body to support my growing drug habit. It got so bad that I left home and lived on the street, being sexually exploited by adult men in exchange for money or drugs. Eventually I became pregnant with my daughter and I was arrested for prostitution."

In testimony before the National Prison Rape Elimination Commission, Chino, a youth organizer and campaign coordinator for New York's Prison Moratorium Project, described the sexual abuse she witnessed and experienced during eight separate incarcerations.

At thirteen, after getting into a fight with a boy, she spent a little over a month at the Spofford Juvenile Center in the Bronx, on a floor that held boys as well as girls. "I immediately noticed that the male corrections officers seemed too nice to the girls, and were overly familiar with them—putting their arms around them, or touching them on their face, shoulders or waist, and letting the girls touch them," she testified. "I saw these same corrections officers give these girls candy or extra food, and let them out of their cells when they were supposed to be on lockdown."

That was not the worst of it. What Chino described next sounds more like the aftermath of war than the administration of justice.

The corrections officers allowed certain boys to enter the cells of girls that the corrections officers did not like or said were not behaving well. I was aware of this because I often heard girls screaming in fear at 2 or 3 o'clock in the morning, followed by figures in red jumpsuits running past my cell. Only boys wore red jumpsuits. In my one month at Spofford, three different girls told me they were raped by boys who corrections officers allowed to go into their cells. I was terrified and did my best to keep a low profile so that I would not be targeted.

At fifteen, Chino was arrested for assault and sent to Bedford Hills Correctional Facility, an adult prison. When an older woman took the younger girl under her wing, getting Chino moved closer to her own cell, offering her cigarettes and food, and coming to her rescue when she got into a fight, the teenager gradually came to trust her. Then her erstwhile protector began touching her, following her into the shower, and trying to kiss her. When Chino went to guards for help, they told her they could not move her unless her life was in danger.

"Early one morning you go to take a shower," Chino continued, using a distancing second person to tell a painful story,

> and when you're washing your hair, the older woman runs up on you and punches you in the face. You're stunned and your nose begins to bleed; she pins you up against the wall and shakes a sawed-off broomstick at you and tells you that she is going to "take" what is hers, meaning that she wants to have sex with you one way or another. You're terrified and on top of everything, you're naked. . . . Even though you want to die right now, you pull her closer to you despite your bloody nose, close your eyes and kiss her. You're devastated, but at least you kept from being raped.

Chino's next stop, the adolescent unit at Rikers Island, was also rife with abuse. Male guards watched the girls shower, and "girls who had no money in their commissary would suddenly have things that are highly coveted in prison—like cigarettes and candy. When I asked the girls where they got those things . . . a girl would say that [a] corrections officer was now 'her man,' meaning that he was giving her those items in return for sex and sexual favors."

Again, this was not the worst of it. "In addition to sexual misconduct and coercion, there were also instances where girls were viciously attacked and forced to have sexual intercourse. One of the lowest points in my life was when a male corrections officer at Rikers raped one of my friends there." Terrified, the girl did not report the rape.

These events, Chino told the commission, left a lasting mark.

Even though a number of years have passed since I was in custody, I still struggle with the memories of the attempted sexual assault against me, the rape of my friend, and male corrections officers taking advantage of girls they were supposed to be protecting. To this day, I have trouble sleeping through the night, I can't undress in front of other people, and I am very uncomfortable with sexual intimacy. . . .

Please understand that even for someone like me who was able to fend off a vicious attack, the struggle to move on with life—without being consumed by rage—is a difficult one that I must manage on a daily basis. Something was stolen from me that I cannot get back, and I speak out today to prevent other young people from going through this.

Not once in Chino's saga of abuse and degradation was there even a hint that a guard might face consequences. The impunity granted to sexually abusive guards sends their victims a strong message about how little they are valued. Unprotected, young people learn they are unworthy of protection. Stigmatized, they learn that "what they get" is their own fault.

In a particularly telling example of this attitude, a Louisiana parish defended itself against charges that a guard repeatedly raped a fourteen-year-old girl in custody by arguing that she wanted it. According to court papers, lawyers argued that the guard "could not have engaged in sexual relations within the walls of the detention center with [the victim] without cooperation from her."

"These girls in the detention center are not Little Miss Muffin [*sic*]," one official told the local paper. The age of consent in Louisiana is seventeen.

Sexual assault is merely the extreme end of a spectrum of violation that is part and parcel of life behind bars. The full-body contact that can occur during a restraint, for example, regularly re-traumatizes already victimized youth. Commonplace incursions such as being ogled in the shower, humiliated during strip searches, fondled during pat downs, subjected to "cavity searches," and forced to use toilets without doors all underscore the message that young prisoners have lost not only freedom of movement but the most basic right to privacy and bodily integrity.

The HRW/ACLU report offers multiple examples of staff touching girls, watching them dress and shower, and taunting them about sex. "They ask things like, have you ever had sex? How did it feel?" Wendy M. testified. "The girls can't do nothing about it, because if you complain, you'll be overruled."

The report includes a detailed description of agency protocol for conducting a strip search:

> The girl is required to take off all of her clothes. The staff member then performs the following: visual examination of mouth; visual examination of the nose and ears; resident runs fingers through her hair and staff visually examines; resident lifts arms to expose armpits to visual examination; visual examination of hands, between fingers, bottom of feet and between toes; resident lifts breasts to expose areas to visual examination; resident separates body folds or creases to expose areas to visual examination; resident removes any sanitary articles from body or clothing, i.e. tampon, sanitary napkin; resident squats and coughs deeply to dislodge any articles concealed in the anus or vagina; resident bends over and spreads the buttocks to expose the anus and vagina to visual examination; staff search of each article of clothing.

These strip searches required no probable cause, or even suspicion. They were routine procedure whenever girls returned from the doctor, dentist, or other appointment. "Strip searches are performed regardless of how little time was spent away from the facility, and even though children are always monitored by facilities staff and almost always handcuffed and shackled when they are taken outside facility grounds."

"You get strip searched any time you have shackles and handcuffs on," Devon A. told investigators. "It feels like a violation."

A teacher who works with juveniles held in an adult jail writes of "the everyday rape of random body searches—on the block, coming back from court, before seeing family on a visit. As Marcus, a seventeen-year-old who never shied away from speaking his mind, put it, 'Being searched by police makes you feel dirty. They make you strip down, bend over, and . . . you know. They call it cavity search. I call it rape.' "

One of the lesser-known facts about sexual abuse in juvenile prisons is how frequently the perpetrator is a woman and the victim a boy. According to the Department of Justice, 10.8 percent of males reported "sexual activity" with facility staff, compared to 4.75 percent of girls.

Roland, who spent nearly seven years journeying among various California State facilities, said sexual contact between staff and wards was commonplace. Roland characterized these incidents as primarily transactional: youth traded sexual acts or access for various forms of contraband, from a T-shirt to a burrito.

Even if staff are caught in the act, he said, consequences are rarely serious. "Other staff be seeing it and they write a report and she don't come to work no more. Then you happen to see her while you're at visiting and she's in another job duty, and you ask what happened."

The answer, he said, is often that she has been transferred because she is under investigation. "A lot of the female staff go under investigation for sexual contact with a ward." Roland had not encountered a scenario in which these incidents might lead to anything more serious than a transfer, however—much less to criminal charges.

Roland did not seem to be aware that the kind of exchange he described is illegal. One can hardly blame him. In its comprehensive report on sexual abuse in juvenile facilities, the Department of Justice itself evinces a similar lack of clarity about what constitutes "consent" on the part of captive youth.

The authors tip their hands early on with this reassuring spin: "Violent sexual assault in juvenile facilities was relatively rare and facility staff, for the most part, did not victimize juvenile offenders." (This is the same investigation that revealed that 12 percent of youth experience one or more instances of sexual abuse in a given year, primarily at the hands of guards.)

Only half of those youth reporting sexual abuse, they observe, described physical threats, force, coercion, or "unwanted genital contact."

"The remaining incidents involved *sexual relations* between staff . . . and confined youth" (emphasis mine), concludes the federal agency charged with protecting incarcerated youth, splitting hairs more finely than does the law itself, which defines sexual contact between adults and those below the age of consent as illegal (just as it does sex *between* minors, as teenagers who find themselves behind bars for having sex with their also underage girlfriends learn the hard way). When the adult involved is in a position of authority, these boundaries are often—on paper, at least— even more explicit.

But in the through-the-looking-glass world of the juvenile prison, anything short of physical force or coercion is described by the Justice Department as "sexual relations"—a term that implies a kind of consent that minors are legally unable to grant.

That the very agency charged with protecting the rights of incarcerated youth would misconstrue, or misrepresent, the law—which makes clear that there is no such thing as "sexual relations" between adults and minors over whom they have authority—speaks volumes about the culture of impunity and victim blaming that persists to this day, no matter how many new laws and regulations are put in place.

As Lovisa Stannow, executive director of the watchdog group Just Detention International, has pointed out, "Testimony from the [Department of Justice] report makes clear that many youth corrections administrators consider staff sexual abuse of detained youth to be largely consensual, or the result of youth manipulation. The Department of Justice perpetuates that view by insisting that most staff sexual abuse of juveniles is not 'violent.'"

"These are teenagers and children we're talking about," Stannow writes, "and corrections staff have immense power over their lives. They can influence when juvenile detainees are released; they can put them in solitary confinement; they can house vulnerable youth with inmates who are known to be violent or sexual predators; they can even deny these kids basic hygiene items. The very notion of any sort of consensual sexual relationship between juveniles and adults in such circumstances is grotesque."

"People think rape is rape only when someone has a gun to your head," one young survivor wrote in a letter to Just Detention International. "Prison officials don't need a gun; they already have full control over you."

"Every act of sexual contact between a staff member and a detainee, under any circumstances, is a crime in all 50 states," Stannow continued. "If the detainee is a minor, it is also child abuse. The Panel failed to acknowledge these basic legal facts in its report."

When it comes to denial, this is the tip of the iceberg. In its report, the Department of Justice's Review Panel on Prison Rape described what it called "competing narratives" presented by corrections administrators to explain (or discount) the widespread abuse of male wards by female corrections officers.

"One narrative is that sophisticated older youth manipulate young, vulnerable female staff into emotional relationships that evolve into sexual ones. The other narrative is that female staff members who are unable for a variety of reasons to build satisfying personal relationships with men gravitate, by design or by default, to juvenile facilities, where they find young men who are only too ready under the circumstances to enter into relationships with them that have a sexual component."

It is hard to know where to begin to unpack these "narratives," both of which involve insulting assumptions about all involved, and both of which describe sexual contact between guards and wards as "relationships"— again, despite the fact that this contact is clearly criminal. While the sexist assumptions are different from those evoked when male guards abuse incarcerated girls, the bottom line is the same: either way, the kids are to blame. In the view of the Review Panel on Prison Rape, young males who are (by law, anyway) victims of sexual abuse at the hands of female guards are characterized either as smooth operators who take advantage of "vulnerable" young women (who just happen to control their every movement) or as hard-up, perpetually horny boys-will-be-boys who are "only too ready" to service their captors. Female guards in this portrait are either helpless, easily manipulated creatures unable to resist their "sophisticated" young charges or desperate spinsters who cunningly pursue a career in juvenile corrections because they are sexually unfulfilled.

If the very panel tasked with remedying the epidemic of sexual abuse behind bars fails to acknowledge that sexual contact between a juvenile prisoner and an adult guard, whether obtained via violent assault or the promise of a burrito, is *intrinsically* abusive in a setting where consent is doubly impossible (because the victim is a minor, and because he or she is entirely under the power of prison staff)—fails, for that matter, to acknowledge existing law—it should not be surprising that young people also might be confused by the experience. In the context of the extreme powerlessness juvenile prisoners experience, it may be preferable to accept the official narrative—to see oneself as "getting over" by trading sex for cigarettes—than to see oneself as a victim with no rights or recourse.

That youth sometimes come to believe the party line, with its haunting echoes of historic attitudes toward rape victims everywhere—*you know you wanted it; a girl like you; you were asking for it*; and the like—sends a troubling message about what these young people have learned behind bars about justice, power, and the sanctity of their own bodies. When representatives of the law engage in illegal conduct, victimizing their young wards with obvious impunity—when even the federal body charged with stemming this contact implicitly endorses it by imputing to captive youth a capacity to "consent" that does not exist under the law—it erodes any prospect that young people will carry from their incarceration an enhanced respect for the law.

In early 2007, the *Texas Observer*'s Nate Blakeslee opened Pandora's box with an article on sexual abuse at the West Texas State School in rural Pyote, Texas.

Blakeslee has a reputation for exposing horrors hidden in plain sight (his early coverage of racism and police corruption in Tulia, Texas, ignited a national scandal), but this story was troubling not only for what Blakeslee reported—the ongoing sexual violation of youth in state custody—but also because of how many people in positions of authority had known about what was going on for years and allowed it to continue.

The saga began when a source gave Blakeslee a copy of a hundred-page report by the Texas Rangers (the investigative arm of the Texas

Department of Public Safety) on sexual abuse at the West Texas State School. Egregious as it was, that report, it would turn out, was only the beginning.

As Blakeslee reported, two high-ranking West Texas State School officials—assistant superintendent Ray Brookins and principal John Paul Hernandez—had both been accused of having "sexual relations" with a number of students over a period of years. Investigators had "collected dozens of statements from students and staff, conducted polygraph tests on students, and collected DNA samples from semen-stained carpet and furniture at the school." Neither man, however, had been arrested, and—until Blakeslee came along—the public had little knowledge of what was going on.

"The abuse was real," Blakeslee wrote. "Internal agency documents describe in considerable detail numerous incidents of sexual misconduct that TYC [Texas Youth Commission] administrators were able to confirm at the facility. The story of how the scandal in Pyote unfolded—or failed to unfold—raises a number of troubling questions, among them how these two men avoided prosecution and how the story has stayed under the radar for so long."

The answer to these questions is tragically familiar. After receiving multiple complaints and warnings from other staff and administrators about the two men, facility superintendent Chip Harrison responded by "admonishing" and "counseling" them—suggesting, for example, that they do their best to avoid spending time alone with their young charges in unsupervised areas.

This low-key approach did not prove effective. Eventually, two students approached a volunteer math tutor and told him that Brookings had victimized them and other students.

Alarmed, the tutor made a call to the Texas Rangers. "Within three weeks," according to Blakeslee,

TYC administrators in Austin had documented the following allegations, according to internal agency records: that Brookins had performed oral sex on an 18-year-old student; that he had watched another student masturbate; that he had inappropriately touched at least two other students; and that he talked to students about sex toys, penis pumps, and masturbation. They also learned that Hernandez was alleged to have had numerous sexual encounters with at least four students, aged 17 to 20, and that he had allegedly performed oral sex on each of them. . . . It seemed that the abuse had been going on for quite some time. The boys apparently did not come forward sooner, agency investigators concluded, because of the control the two men had over their release date and access to privileges within the facility. By early April, the inspector general of the agency had determined to his satisfaction that each of the allegations against the men was true. Hernandez was informed that he was about to be terminated, and he resigned. (Brookins had resigned almost immediately after his suspension.)

With that kind of evidence in hand, Blakeslee wrote, it looked like the two men were headed for prison, and the state toward a major scandal. "Instead, the case disappeared. The two suspects were never arrested, and details of the investigation were never reported in the papers. Hernandez and Brookins quietly left town."

The state may have been done with the unpleasant business at Pyote, but the media were not. After Blakeslee's story broke in February 2007, the *Dallas Morning News* jumped on board with a series of its own, starting at the West Texas State School and moving on from there "as the scope of the scandal expanded to the entire agency and its prisons throughout Texas."

What had happened at West Texas, it turned out with a little digging, was far from anomalous. The Texas Youth Commission had received 750 complaints of sexual misconduct since 2000, most of which had garnered no response.

Texas offers a particularly sweeping example not only of the ubiquity of sexual abuse inside juvenile prisons, but also of the indifference and impunity that foster it. According to the *New York Review of Books*, the 750 incidents that were reported were

generally thought to under-represent the true extent of such abuse, because most children were too afraid to report it: staff commonly instructed their favorite inmates to beat up kids who complained.

Even when the kids did file complaints, they knew it wouldn't do them much good. Staff covered for each other, grievance processes were sabotaged, and evidence was frequently destroyed. Officials in Austin ignored what they heard, and, in the very rare instances when staff were fired and their cases referred to local prosecutors, those prosecutors usually refused to act. Not one employee of the Texas Youth Commission during that six-year period was sent to prison for raping the children in his or her care.

Texas also offers a particularly vivid example of the difficulty—perhaps impossibility—of reforming one aspect of a system without addressing the culture as a whole. The state did eventually respond to the wave of sexual assault allegations. Texas Rangers, investigators from the Attorney General's Office, and officials from the Texas Department of Criminal Justice were dispatched to every Texas Youth Commission facility. The commission established a twenty-four-hour abuse-reporting hotline. Thousands of calls came in.

The reforms that followed the sex abuse scandal in Texas appeared as sweeping as the scandal itself. Prior to the revelations, Texas had been neck and neck with Florida for the dubious distinction of the nation's most prolific jailer of its children. Today, the juvenile justice systems in both Florida (which went through a series of sex scandals of its own) and Texas are in a state of flux.

Within days of Blakeslee's story, Texas governor Rick Perry dismissed Texas Youth Commission chairman Pete C. Alfaro and called for the resignation of the acting director. In March 2007, Perry signed Senate Bill 103, which spawned various new offices and entities, each charged with keeping state employees from raping the youth in their care. So it was that Texas found itself with a new Office of the Inspector General, an Office of the Independent Ombudsman, a Release Review Panel, a treatment program, a Parents' Bill of Rights, and a new special master to oversee the besieged commission. Employees were required to go through training on how to create an assault-free environment, and thousands of cameras were installed in state facilities.

Finally, the state—which had already granted counties incentives to keep low-level juvenile offenders in their communities—passed a slate of reform bills that abolished both the Texas Youth Commission and the Texas Juvenile Probation Commission and transferred their powers to a newly created Texas Juvenile Justice Department and an independent ombudsman.

The population in state facilities plummeted, from three thousand in 2007 to about twelve hundred in 2011, and nine state facilities closed their doors entirely. Texas—so recently a glaring example of a system run amok—now seemed the very model of a modern justice system.

Then all hell broke loose again.

It is hard to argue with the drop in population that was triggered, at least in part, by the revelations of sexual abuse. But by 2012, the system appeared once again in shambles, with reports of chronic violence and chaotic conditions at the state's remaining facilities.

In the five years since lawmakers approved sweeping reforms, youth-on-youth assaults have more than tripled at state-run juvenile prisons, to fifty-four assaults per one hundred youths in 2011. Youth assaults on staff have more than tripled as well, to thirty-seven confirmed assaults per one hundred youths.

At the Giddings State School—lauded in John Hubner's 2008 book *Last Chance in Texas* for what he described as a groundbreaking therapeutic program—youth-on-youth violence increased by 145 percent between 1997 and 2011, to eighty-one assaults per one hundred youths. The number of youth-on-staff assaults resulting in injury skyrocketed at Giddings as well, from eighteen in 2007 to seventy-two in 2011.

The staff at Giddings responded by breaking out the pepper spray: 216 documented uses in 2011, compared to 74 in 2007, at a facility that had recently been touted as the crown jewel in the Texas system.

"It's nuts that it's taken us five years just to go from one broken system to another," Senate Committee on Criminal Justice chairman John Whitmire—an architect of the original reforms—told the *Austin American-Statesman*.

The collapse of the Texas reforms may be "nuts," but it is also instructive. While all the ingredients for change appeared to be in place—scandal, advocacy, litigation, media pressure, new leadership, and of course the budget crunch affecting legislatures nationwide—one key element was missing: a genuine shift in values.

The lengthy and concerted effort to hide the sexual abuse plaguing the system rather than address it offers a powerful clue that the eventual reforms were rooted first and foremost in political embarrassment. That these reforms so quickly unraveled reveals a central challenge to reforming a system built on secrecy, impunity, and an abiding disregard for the children in its care. Reforms that are not built on a foundation of values— of *valuing* the children in whose name they are enacted—may help some of the children some of the time, simply by reducing the number subjected to the trauma of incarceration. But without a deeper shift in the way these children—and our obligation to them—are perceived, not only do those who are behind bars remain in danger, so do the reforms themselves. An uptick in the economy combined with a newsworthy crime by a young person under community supervision and the pendulum could all too easily swing back once again.

In 2008, Cherie Townsend took over as the Texas Youth Commission's executive director. Townsend was well regarded within the reform community, and her appointment raised hopes for the state's beleaguered system. She lasted four years before retiring in 2012. By that time, she was under fire for everything from rising levels of youth violence in Texas State facilities to continued allegations of unsafe conditions.

Two years after Townsend came on board, the federal Department of Justice released its report on sexual abuse in juvenile facilities. Along with its survey of abuse nationwide, the report homed in on a handful of facilities identified as best and worst. Two of those on the "worst" list were located in Texas. At the Corsicana Residential Treatment Center, the sexual victimization rate was a stunning 32.4 percent: one in three kids at the facility. The Victory Field Correctional Academy in Vernon was the third worst, with one in four youth reporting sexual assault at the hands of a staff member.

Townsend told the *Texas Observer* she was "disappointed" in the federal report, which did not reflect the changes that had taken place since she came on board with what she called a "zero tolerance" approach to sexual abuse.

Fair enough—the report was based on data from 2008. Far more troubling is Townsend's assertion that because the federal survey was anonymous, many of the kids were lying—and that many of those who called her own newly installed hotline (part of the "zero tolerance policy") were also making things up.

"We know that when you install phones, kids give hotline tips all the time, and they'll often [make an allegation and then] say, 'No, I'm just kidding,' " she told the *Texas Observer*.

"It's a way of getting attention," deputy TYC director of youth services James Smith alleged, calling the claims of abuse "overwhelmingly" false.

Smith's testimony before the federal panel placed the blame squarely on the kids. For example, the training his staff received around "professional boundaries" focused, by his description, on protecting naive staff from the predatory youth in their care. "While initially to the staff it's flattering or it sends a sense that they are developing a good relationship with the kid, unfortunately for the kid, it's a door opening for them to maybe perhaps take advantage of the staff or create a situation."

Because of young offenders' tendency to "create situations," Smith explained, the training was needed to help staff understand that "there [are] traps that you need to be aware of and while it may be well-intentioned on your part, it could certainly be perceived on the youth's part as an opportunity. And so we are looking to enhance our training, especially for our female staff, because we do have some young men who are very sophisticated."

The "traps" set by wily youth, according to Smith, included nefarious maneuvers such as using a "pet name" or referring to a favorite staff member as "mama."

Both Townsend and Smith continued to advance this bizarre line of reasoning in interviews with the *Texas Observer*. According to the *Observer*, Smith advanced the argument that "some young men from urban areas are so 'sophisticated' that they may have skills in 'grooming' female guards to be sexual partners. Staff members have to learn, he says, how 'kids can sometimes try to manipulate them.' "

Townsend was equally sympathetic to her easily manipulated staff, explaining to the *Observer* that it is "not about staff who are predators and intending to harm. It's often about crossing boundaries. . . . [Staff members] get into what they think is a positive relationship, and it crosses a line."

Corsicana superintendent Laura Braly stuck to the party line—the kids were to blame. "Almost every kid you talk to here has some sort of sexual victimization in their past," she told the *Observer*. The result, she explained, is that "they are highly, highly sexual. . . . You don't know how to express yourself any way other than through sexuality, and you interpret everything as being sexual."

"If somebody walks by and touches them on the shoulder," she continued, "they go, 'I've been sexually assaulted.'"

The problem with this argument (beyond its eerie echoes of the victim-blaming, *she asked for it* attitude that shamed and silenced rape victims on the outside for decades) is that it makes no sense. Experts say that false testimony or "misunderstandings" at the level documented at Corsicana would be extremely unusual. On top of that, across the nation, juvenile facilities hold large numbers of young people who enter with a history of sexual victimization. While further abuse is far too common at a large number of facilities, few have a rate of reported assaults that tops 30 percent. Even accounting for an excess of "low self-esteem" among TYC employees (one of the qualities Smith said makes his staff so easily "groomed" by the sophisticated youth they are tricked into violating), the argument that cadres of teenage seducers are luring trained staff into sexual encounters for their own unnamed purposes borders on the laughable—if the consequences of this attitude were not so tragic for the youths who are abused and assaulted inside Texas facilities, then blamed by top administrators for their own victimization.

As the federal report's authors delicately point out, "some widely accepted recommended practices did not necessarily correspond with an institution's incidence of sexual victimization." All the policy and procedure in the world, in other words, won't get guards to keep their hands off the kids as long as the overall culture of an institution is one of disrespect and coercion.

The report bolsters this analysis by way of a very different example as well—the Missouri Division of Youth Services Fort Bellefontaine facility. This institution lacked all the trappings of protection—no PREA coordinator, no PREA-specific policy, no orientation for residents on sexual victimization, and no specific policies on dealing with its aftermath—but nevertheless boasted the lowest victimization rate of any facility surveyed.

In a remarkable bit of testimony, Missouri Department of Youth Services director Tim Decker did his patient, methodical best to explain to the panel how it was that—despite a lack of policies, protocols, or procedures prohibiting them from doing so—he nevertheless managed to keep his staff from raping the kids in their care.

It was not, he explained, simply a matter of telling them not to (although staff in Missouri do in fact receive extensive training on "boundaries"). Rather, it was part and parcel of the larger Missouri Division of Youth Services culture, which focuses on rehabilitation, not punishment, and relies on small, homelike settings rather than large institutions.

In Missouri's youth facilities, Decker told the panel, "Young people are in the constant presence of caring staff, learning firsthand what it means to have healthy relationships with peers and adults."

According to Decker's testimony, "Many aspects of traditional institutional and correctional practices in juvenile justice include punitive and coercive approaches that devalue and objectify young people, creating fertile ground for safety issues and sexual victimization. It should be no surprise that if the way we control the kids is through coercion that we will . . . have a growth of other coercive behavior such as sexual victimization."

"Sexual victimization in institutions cannot be effectively dealt with in isolation or as a singular issue," he elaborated. "At the core, all forms of institutional abuse create a lack of safety for young people, staff, and eventually for the public, because young people get released without having the root causes addressed."

"Culture trumps everything," Decker summarized, using one of his favorite maxims. Neither education, nor detection, nor investigation, nor discipline, he said, is as effective as creating an environment of trust and mutual regard.

"A humane culture of care," he concluded, "is ultimately what keeps young people safe, not hard work, fences or cameras."

7

THE HOLE

Solitary Confinement of Juveniles

It's an awful thing, solitary. It crushes your spirit and weakens your resistance more effectively than any other form of mistreatment.
                              —John McCain, senator and former POW

"I SEE HOW THEY do them bitches."

Direct, outspoken, and quick to laughter, Cherie in this instance was skirting a sensitive question: Was she ever placed on suicide watch during her time in a state facility for girls? Her response seemed at once answer and evasion. But the details that eventually spilled out made it clear why, no matter how low she might have felt, she would never have allowed herself even to hint at the kind of desperation that gets a girl put on suicide watch.

"Little broad talking about 'I wanna kill myself'? They open her door up, rushed her, five of them, grabbed her, dragged her to the other place, stripped her butt naked, put a wool blanket in there, and she was in that room for four days, no clothes, none, *no* clothes—only a wool blanket, and the room she was in."

The "other place" was a barren isolation cell—the treatment of choice for those whose despair was deemed a danger. Harsh as it is, the widespread use of solitary confinement is the natural end point of a juvenile justice system that is predicated from the very start on isolation.

There are many ostensible rationales for solitary confinement inside juvenile prisons.

> You can place a child in solitary confinement for his own safety: to protect him from others whose real or threatened violence staff cannot contain.
>
> You can place a child in solitary upon his arrival, in order to evaluate him, no matter how thick the file that arrives with him.
>
> You can place him there as punishment, for violations of procedure as well as acts of violence. You can lock a child down for possessing a pencil.
>
> You can place a child in solitary as punishment for the acts of others—entire units or even facilities may be on "lockdown" because of anything from gang concerns to understaffing.
>
> Should he land in an adult prison, you can lock a child down to ensure that there's "no trouble" while you execute another prisoner. ("Pre-gas, then gas, then twenty-four more hours," one young man recited.)
>
> You can place a kid in solitary for talking about killing herself, despite evidence that this may be the best means there is to push her over the edge.

The rationale may vary, but the mise-en-scène does not: a room, perhaps a bunk, a metal toilet, and a door—a door that doesn't open, except for an hour or two a day of "large-muscle" exercise. Sometimes the door has a slot at the bottom, so that even the guard who brings food, or the teacher toting worksheets, can slip in the legally mandated sustenance without mitigating the child's solitude by so much as a glance.

Young people's description of the conditions inside solitary confinement are remarkably consistent: small cells, often windowless, with little besides a metal toilet and a concrete slab for sleeping. Some youths are allowed a thin mattress, while others are given one only at night.

Individual facilities often devise means of making conditions even worse. In Rhode Island, for example, a federal district court described a juvenile corrections institution that "maintained a dark, cold solitary confinement room where boys were held for as long as a week, wearing only their underwear, and without toilet paper, sheets, blankets, or changes of clothes." Other facilities restrict the diet of those in disciplinary confinement to a "baked nutritional loaf," meant to sustain life while remaining as unappetizing as possible.

Solitary confinement exists in the American imagination as a punishment reserved for the profoundly dangerous—our Hannibal Lecters: those so irredeemably violent that even our highest-security prisons can barely contain them. Or we think of it as something that takes place somewhere distant: Abu Ghraib, Guantánamo, offshore "black sites" where unspeakable torments are administered to enemy combatants. We rarely imagine it as a home for children, despite the fact that this use is commonplace.

Our ignorance is fortified by official obfuscation. There are as many euphemisms for solitary confinement as there are justifications for using it on the young: "ad seg," "time-out," "special housing," "room time," "room restriction," "special management programming," "protective custody," even "reflection cottages." Of the many names for solitary confinement, "dead time" may be the closest to reality. But as the Youth Law Center points out, no matter the nomenclature, "it all comes down to the same thing: a young person locked, alone, in a tiny room."

The American Friends Service Committee calls the practice "no-touch torture. . . . No one who has ever experienced more than the briefest time in solitary would call it anything else, because it was designed to destroy the mind and break the spirit."

The American Academy of Child and Adolescent Psychiatry opposes the practice as well, asserting in a 2012 policy statement that "the potential psychiatric consequences of prolonged solitary confinement are well recognized and include depression, anxiety and psychosis. Due to their developmental vulnerability, juvenile offenders are at particular risk of such adverse reactions. Furthermore, the majority of suicides in juvenile correctional facilities occur when the individual is isolated or in solitary confinement."

These examples are part of a long line of similar protests over the course of at least a century. Oscar Wilde served two years' hard labor in a British jail in the late nineteenth century on charges of gross indecency. The writer was so appalled to witness children locked alone in empty cells that as soon as he was released he wrote to the *Daily Chronicle*.

This terror that seizes and dominates the child, as it seizes the grown man also, is of course intensified beyond power of expression by the solitary cellular system of our prisons. Every child is confined to its cell for twenty-three hours out of the twenty-four. This is the appalling thing. To shut up a child in a dimly lit cell, for twenty-three hours out of the twenty-four, is an example of the cruelty of stupidity. If an individual, parent or guardian, did this to a child, he would be severely punished. The Society for the Prevention of Cruelty to Children would take the matter up at once. There would be on all hands the utmost detestation of whomsoever had been guilty of such cruelty. A heavy sentence would, undoubtedly, follow conviction. But our own actual society does worse itself, and to the child to be so treated by a strange abstract force, of whose claims it has no cognizance, is much worse than to receive the same treatment from its father or mother, or someone it knew. The inhuman treatment of a child is always inhuman, by whomsoever it is inflicted. But inhuman treatment by society is to the child the more terrible because there can be no appeal.

More recently, the United Nations special rapporteur on torture Juan Mendez called for an "absolute prohibition" on the practice of keeping juveniles in solitary confinement and has deemed anything over fifteen hours in solitary torture for adults. "Considering the severe mental pain or suffering solitary confinement may cause" to juveniles especially, he warned, "it can amount to torture or cruel, inhuman or degrading treatment." The United Nations Rules for the Protection of Juveniles Deprived of their Liberty forbids the practice as well, in a 1990 resolution supported (but not followed) by the United States.

The United States has chosen to flout international standards on this as it has on other matters of criminal justice. Young prisoners in America are routinely isolated for weeks, months, even years. A comprehensive national survey by the U.S. Department of Justice found that 35 percent of youth in juvenile corrections facilities had been subjected to solitary confinement. Despite differing euphemisms for the practice, the Office of Juvenile Justice and Delinquency Prevention found that "room confinement remains a standard procedure in most juvenile facilities."

State data are hard to come by, often turning up only when litigation demands it. But what does exist indicates that the practice of placing juveniles in solitary confinement is frequent and routine.

- Youth in Ohio facilities spent an average of fifty hours in solitary over the course of a single month, a year *after* investigators insisted that "the extended . . . use of isolation (i.e., segregation) must be immediately revisited and dramatically changed."
- In California, where a major reform effort is under way and many facilities have closed, there is evidence that solitary confinement may actually be a growing problem in those that remain open. "Incredibly, the practices from 10 years ago persist today, as youth languish in windowless 8.5 x 11 feet cells."
- In New York City, nearly 15 percent of adolescents between the ages of sixteen and eighteen spend at least part of their pretrial detention in solitary confinement.
- Investigations of Illinois's juvenile facilities found that youths were frequently placed in isolation "for transgressions as minor as eating a guard's food." A 2011 visit to Illinois Youth Center St. Charles found injured or sick youth housed in solitary rather than the institution's inadequate infirmary. A separate look at the Harrisburg facility found 122 instances of solitary confinement within a single month.
- In Georgia, mentally ill youth locked in isolation units "were restrained, hit, shackled to beds and even toilets, put in restraint chairs for hours, and sprayed with oleoresin capsicum (OC) spray or pepper spray by staff."
- A survey undertaken at the Texas State facility at Giddings in March 2012—well into a major statewide reform effort—found that 87 percent of youth surveyed had been "confined to [their] room as punishment," 45 percent on ten or more occasions.
- In New Jersey, reports emerged in the mid-1990s that girls at a state facility were being drugged with psychotropics and then tossed into "seclusion," while those at the state's main boys' facility were subject to "extreme" isolation. In 2010, the Juvenile Law Center filed suit on behalf of two young people held in solitary,

one of them for fifty days and another for 178. "T.D." entered
with a history of suicide attempts, according to the suit. "Juvenile Justice Commission's response to T.D.'s deteriorating mental
health status was to confine him in a seven by seven foot cell with
no view to the outside world for nearly seven months. T.D. was
often forced to sleep on a concrete slab and was denied access to
books, personal belongings, peer interaction, recreation, and exercise." The second plaintiff alleged that he was placed in isolation
under similar conditions for a total of fifty-five days for being the
"victim of repeated assaults by other youth, or for minor behavioral infractions such as cursing. . . . Notably, when either T.D.
or O.S. asked for services, they were warned that such gestures
or requests would only extend the period of time they would be
secluded."

• In Mississippi, girls who misbehaved or were placed on suicide
watch were "stripped naked and left in a windowless, stifling
cinder-block cell, with nothing but the concrete floor to sleep on
and a hole in the floor for a toilet."

Although solitary confinement is legal, its humanity is dubious, especially when it comes to children. All manner of international guidelines
and declarations on the human rights of children have deemed placing
them in punitive solitary confinement cruel, inhuman, and degrading.
A 2012 report from Human Rights Watch and the American Civil Liberties Union determined that "the conditions that accompany solitary
confinement . . . constitute violations of fundamental rights."

Unable to justify the practice, administrators often resort instead to
obfuscation. "We don't like to call it isolation," the head of a system under
fire told a television reporter. The regulations in her system explicitly
allowed for youth to be kept in their cells for twenty-one hours a day, but
an internal audit found even those limits were regularly exceeded: some
were locked in their cells for all but forty minutes a day.

"They say that he's not going there for punishment," said a mother
whose son had showed her the scars from his suicide attempts when she
visited, calling them "his ticket to freedom" (by which he meant death).

"We want to protect him, so we're going to put him in solitary," this mother was told when she called the facility to protest—despite the fact that solitary confinement had *triggered* the suicide attempts administrators later used to justify it. "It is all backwards, you know."

"Backwards" is exactly the right word. Solitary confinement is a standard response to concerns that a youth is suicidal, despite the fact that half of all young people who kill themselves in juvenile facilities do so inside solitary cells.

Martín was fifteen the first time he was arrested and sent to a Massachusetts Department of Youth Services facility. Fights, he said, were a regular occurrence. Engaging in them carried consequences, but so did ducking out of them: life could be intolerable for a boy who had shown fear.

The punishment for fighting, however, was even worse. "They put you in a dark room. It is a cell, but no lights are on, or they keep you in your cell and they take everything in there out. They would leave you there for a whole day. You would sleep on the metal, the plain metal."

If "a whole day" seems lenient, consider the fact that Martín was in solitary long enough, or frequently enough, to witness multiple suicide attempts by those in neighboring cells. One boy, he remembers, tried to kill himself by jumping off the top bunk headfirst and smashing his head on a bolted metal table.

Darren spent about a year banished to "ad seg," or administrative segregation—one of the various euphemisms for solitary confinement. His brief stretches of daily "recreation" consisted of pacing inside a metal cage. That, said Darren—who was otherwise more inclined to analyze than to condemn the treatment he had experienced behind bars—"is inhumane."

"Inhumane" may be an understatement. The American Correctional Association, which establishes professional standards for adult and juvenile facilities, limits the isolation of juveniles to a maximum of five days. Forcing Darren to endure a year in ad seg seems all the more excessive given the precipitating offense: he refused to take medication prescribed by prison doctors for psychiatric conditions that were diagnosed only after he was locked up.

Darren had demurred for two reasons. The first, he explained, was the advice his mother had given him before he went away. "I'm my mom's son, and my mother told me not to take any medicine. I refused medication, so the board decided I was 'not taking responsibility for my actions' and 'not participating in the program.' So I was in isolated programs for a year at a time."

The other reason Darren refused to swallow the handful of pills prescribed him was that he had no reason to believe they were medically necessary. Prior to his incarceration, no one had so much as hinted that he might be mentally ill. "I didn't want to take medications when I knew there was nothing wrong with me," he explained, without any apparent rancor. "I knew there was nothing wrong with me; I was making conscious decisions to be rebellious."

The new diagnoses he was given seemed at best situational. "ADD, post-traumatic stress disorder, and some type of anger issues," he recited dryly. "I'm pretty sure if you were fourteen years old, you would be angry too, if you were locked up" for a ten-year stretch. "I had a lot of issues, but they had a problem distinguishing between *child* behavior and *criminal* behavior. In addition, I was an adolescent going through my hormones. I understand that a kid can be traumatized going through that situation. . . . But I feel that the way they were dealing with it was ineffective."

"Ineffective" seems generous. Putting young people in isolation for any period of time, experts concur, is one of the surest means there is to *induce* psychiatric symptoms. Darren spent multiple months-long stretches in ad seg for his refusal to swallow psychotropic medications and to accept the labels that came with them. Even if he had suffered from, say, attention deficit disorder—much less the collection of diagnoses he was disciplined for rejecting—it is hard to imagine a surer way to exacerbate it than long-term isolation. That Darren would be placed in this vulnerable position because, ostensibly, he was showing signs of mental illness is beyond counterintuitive.

As with Darren, it was the quest for some sense of control that landed Cherie in "the other place." It brought her, in fact, to the very cell she'd mentioned when speaking of the girls who had been forcibly placed in solitary after talking about suicide. Cherie was banished for seeking a different escape route: a return to an out-of-state treatment center where her life had been more bearable.

It was a reasonable goal, but Cherie was offered no positive way to pursue it. Instead, she walked a knife's edge of rebellion behind bars, refusing to go to school and breaking as many rules as she could in the hope she would to be returned to court to be reevaluated, and perhaps moved to a "placement" more appropriate than prison. For a while, she had so many write-ups she was dropped down several phases, to use the behavioral-modification terminology Cherie had internalized, losing most of her phone privileges and gaining only more hours exiled to her cell. When she was allowed out of her room, no matter how briefly, she was required to wear a bright yellow jumpsuit, a humiliating reminder of her reduced status.

Rebellion, Cherie learned quickly, came at a price. When she refused to wear the yellow jumpsuit, she wound up "just like that girl I told you they had on suicide watch. They put my food in there and locked me in. It was summer, hot as fuck in there, and I'm in my room burning up. Can't come out. Only could have one book."

Cherie learned a crucial lesson from the experience: no matter how miserable she might become, she would keep it to herself. She would never, no matter what, so much as hint at ending her life.

"You feel me? 'Cause they would have put me in this unit for the crazy bitches. Them bitches *was* crazy—I mean, like, really lonely. I did what I had to do to make myself get up out of there."

The experience taught Cherie not to speak of suicide, but it also gave her reason to consider it. She swears she will kill herself if they try to send her back.

The question of what exactly constitutes torture has been a matter of some debate of late, leaving the leaders of the free world at odds. Waterboarding, sleep deprivation, religious and sexual humiliation: all have been condemned and all have been defended in the context of the debate over how far to go to address the threat of terrorism. Amid this controversy, the international consensus that the use of solitary confinement is a form of torture is all the more striking.

The United Nations is not the only body to have taken up the issue. U.S. courts have also spoken, albeit less definitively. As far back as 1890, the Supreme Court teetered on the brink of declaring extended solitary confinement unconstitutional. Writing for the majority in a case brought by a man who had been kept in solitary confinement for a month, Justice Samuel Miller observed that "a considerable number of the prisoners fell, after even a short confinement, into a semi-fatuous condition, from which it was next to impossible to arouse them, and others became violently insane; others, still, committed suicide; while those who stood the ordeal better were not generally reformed, and in most cases did not recover sufficient mental activity to be of any subsequent service to the community." All this, the Court found, raised "serious objections" to the practice.

About a century later, the federal judge charged with oversight of the California Youth Authority (now renamed the Division of Juvenile Justice) in the wake of a sweeping class action insisted that the Division of Juvenile Justice limit the use of isolation to those situations when it was "absolutely necessary." Despite this court order, juveniles inside California correctional facilities continued to be held in isolation, often with little respite.

A U.S. federal court has also ruled on the issue. That ruling, coming out of a Texas civil suit, limits solitary confinement to three hours for juveniles—three hours more than the UN would call humane, but the closest we have to a national standard.

This standard meant little to Curtis, who spent a year in solitary before his twelfth birthday. Or Jared. Or Cherie. Or Will. Or Darren.

Many of the young people I interviewed had personal experience with solitary confinement. Of all the aspects of incarceration they described to me, "the hole" emerged as the most difficult to withstand. Their accounts of the experience were strikingly similar: solitary is so dehumanizing, they told me in one way or another, that personality itself can begin to erode.

When I first met Eliza she was fourteen, a veteran of dozens of foster and group homes who had recently decided she'd do better on her own. A young man who worked for the youth newspaper I edited brought her to my desk one afternoon, promised I would be dazzled by her genius, and then left me to listen to a long, diffuse stream of ideas and anecdotes that bore out his claim.

At the time, Eliza was living on and around Berkeley's Telegraph Avenue, bunking with college students in dorms or apartments when they'd have her, and in doorways or parks in between. She was in pain—to think otherwise would be unforgivably sentimental—but she was also, somehow, all right. Surviving was something she'd grown used to, and she was buoyed not only by friends but by dreams.

More than anything, Eliza wanted to go to college. She knew she was smart enough and held on to a deep faith in the power of education, instilled by her adored great-grandmother. Education, she believed, was the bridge back to mainstream society, where, for all her bohemian trappings, she most hoped to find refuge. To say she faced obstacles during her teen years is an understatement: she had no money, no family support, and nowhere stable to live. But the years passed, and though she never stopped careening from one place to another, she managed not only to survive but to keep growing.

On top of her myriad strengths, she had one formally documented achievement: a GED. It was the sole benefit she'd drawn from a stint in juvenile hall, where she'd been kept for six months "awaiting placement" in yet another group home.

Throughout her years of wandering and waiting inside cells, higher education had remained her holy grail, and once she turned eighteen she honed in on college with a hungry intensity. She called me the day she enrolled in community college, exuberantly listing the courses she'd chosen: communications, music, history, and art. She was performing regularly as a rapper and spoken word artist at local clubs and had just been promoted from cashier to waitress at an upscale hamburger place. On a good night, she could bring home $100. She was renting a room in a friend's apartment while she saved up to buy a used sailboat from a friend. She could live in the cabin and sail on the bay—a home of her own and a vessel of freedom all at once. Once she caught up on her general education credits, she hoped to transfer to Juilliard, because she had heard that Samuel L. Jackson and Robert De Niro were among the alumni.

"I'm looking for a harbor," she said, and it took me a moment to realize she meant it literally.

Eliza's high spirits lifted my own. Her confidence gave me hope not only for her but for all the other kids I knew who'd been labeled "at risk"—of delinquency, recidivism, addiction, unemployment—all those written off as least likely to thrive.

Perhaps that is why her next call came as such a blow. I hadn't heard from Eliza for a few weeks by then, but I wasn't worried. I figured she was busy with school, caught up in the whirl of the new semester.

She wasn't.

Along with registering for classes, Eliza had submitted paperwork for financial aid. As an "independent student," a ward of the state with no parental support, she knew she was entitled to the full package. What she didn't know was that her run-ins with the group homes had left her a memento: an open warrant. Until she cleared the warrant, there would be no financial aid, no college.

Eliza was offered two options for closing out the warrant: weeks of community service or three days in county jail. The community service would have set her enrollment back by a full semester. If she did the jail time she could still make it to the first day of school. After what she had been through, she figured, what more could they do to her?

There was, as it turned out, more they could do to her.

The jail dorm she entered was at triple capacity, and Eliza had a face that launched a thousand battles: eccentrically pretty, ethnically ambiguous, and radiating a directness often read as a challenge in institutional settings. Then there was her "attitude," a survival skill that had calcified from a habit to a trait. She had just three days to get through and saw no need to bow down to a dormitory despot in order to ingratiate herself, much less be initiated into a hierarchy in which she had no interest.

The fight that followed was more or less inevitable. Eliza had learned to stand her ground at an early age, but she hadn't yet developed the capacity to walk away. A little girl alone is tremendously vulnerable, and she had been through things at which she'd only hinted. She had made it clear, though, that she was done with being victimized, that no one would ever lay hands on her again.

Perhaps that was what landed Eliza in the cold cell: the fury she brought to what might otherwise have been an ordinary scuffle, and the fierceness with which she struggled when guards came to break it up. So much of her daily energy went into bottling up her anger that, once she lost control, there was no turning back.

Cold cells are intended, ostensibly, for the dangerously psychotic, to keep them from hurting themselves or those around them. They also are intended to break the human will. The CIA has used them to extract information from terrorism suspects, a practice that has been condemned as torture. But even the CIA shows more caution than Eliza was offered. According to an ABC report on the harshest interrogation practices used in the so-called war on terror, a prisoner cannot be placed in a cold cell unless the decision has been "signed off at the highest level—by the deputy director for operations for the CIA." Eliza, as far as she could tell, was just tossed in the cell.

A cold cell may be the size of an ordinary cell, but it generally lacks even the meager amenities of that already barren space. The chamber Eliza described had no bed, no toilet, nothing—just tiled walls and a drain in the floor. As is common practice, Eliza was forcibly stripped of her clothing before she was thrust into the cold cell. Then she was left there— naked, freezing, alone, and unheard.

The door had barely locked behind her before she started screaming. At first, she screamed in anger, as others had before her, but this girl's cries had a startling volume and intensity, a piercing tenor that the guards found intolerable. If she wanted out, she recalls being instructed, she'd have to stop that screaming.

Had she been able to hold on to her composure, as she'd been determined to do when she walked in the front gate to dispatch her three-day debt to society, Eliza very likely would have stopped screaming. But by then it was too late. It wasn't a question of defiance or willful disobedience. Inside the cold cell, Eliza was simply beyond the reach of reason.

Eliza's chest constricted and she felt like she was dying. She pounded her fists against the wall for hour after hour, long after her strength would normally have given out. And the screaming—she just could not stop screaming. Eventually, someone from jail psych showed up to sedate her. How much time had passed, Eliza could not say; in the cold cell, time quickly lost all meaning. But once she had been medicated into submission, Eliza finally managed to stop screaming. And then they let her out— just as they had promised.

The girl they carried out was not the one who'd entered. Her eyes had a distant look, her tone a blank emptiness, which were unfamiliar. When I visited her soon after, I had never seen a spirit so utterly flattened.

Later, when she could, Eliza told me more about what happened in the cold cell. "I regressed," she explained.

Shortly after her eighteenth birthday, Eliza had requisitioned a copy of her dependency court file, a thick stack of documents dating back to her infancy. She'd known that her mother, adrift in her addiction, had abandoned her repeatedly when she was little. She had not known how early this abandonment had started, nor just how extreme it had been. According to the records, child protection workers had discovered Eliza alone in her crib—naked, filthy, famished, and trapped. Her mother had routinely left her behind when she went out to score. If a foray proved successful, she might be gone for days.

Many youth who are placed in solitary confinement are survivors of abuse and other trauma. "Placing them in solitary confinement exacerbates already fragile conditions, sometimes with devastating results," the Youth Law Center's Sue Burrell has written. "This is especially so for the many youth who have already experienced abuse, neglect, or previous institutionalization. Locking them away subjects them to re-traumatization."

A staff psychiatrist at a California prison put it even more bluntly. "It's a standard psychiatric concept," she told a researcher. "If you put people in isolation, they will go insane."

Inside the cold cell, Eliza unraveled. Trapped, helpless, naked, and alone, stripped of control and deprived of all comfort, she'd felt time spin backward. Some deep part of her returned to early childhood, reliving the primal terror of a baby left to starve and the bottomless solitude of her earliest cage: her crib. In this regressed state, Eliza instinctively did what she had as a baby: she screamed. She screamed and screamed and screamed until, finally, somebody came for her. That is one part of the experience that she recalled clearly: the sound of her own cries as they echoed off the walls.

In the years since Eliza's sojourn in the cold cell, she has struggled with addiction and stints in psychiatric hospitals. She became involved with an older man and gave birth to twin girls. The last time I saw her, we met at a half-empty shopping mall outside the welfare office. After enduring more than she was willing to say, she had recently taken the girls and moved into a domestic violence shelter. She no longer dreamed about college. All of her energy was focused on survival.

Not long before the cold cell, Eliza had called to celebrate enrolling in college. I remarked on how far she had come and asked what she thought accounted for her tenacity, her seemingly unshakable sense of herself. "My distrust for authority saved me," she had replied. "Whether I was in jail or not, I was always free because I never thought I belonged there. I never let anyone convince me I did."

The last time I saw her, listlessly pushing her double stroller through the empty mall, Eliza was pondering a different sort of question: *Why did he hit me? Did I deserve it? I must have done something, for people to be able to do these things to me . . .*

Curtis, who was sent to the California Youth Authority at the age of ten, was repeatedly consigned to an isolation cell for fighting—an activity he found hard to avoid as the smallest kid in the building. In all, he estimates, he spent a year in solitary—twenty-three hours a day in his cell, his main human contact the nurse who brought him medication twice a day. If Curtis banged on the walls or threatened suicide, a psychiatrist might eventually materialize. Otherwise, there was no one. "Education" came in the form of worksheets and crayons slipped through the door.

According to Human Rights Watch and the American Civil Liberties Union, this is common practice. "Young people in solitary confinement . . . commonly reported being denied access to adequate education. Youth in some facilities were regularly provided with a packet of educational materials for in-cell self-study, but often their completed work went ungraded and their questions unanswered."

"While solitary confinement is harmful to all human beings, it is especially so for children," the Youth Law Center's Sue Burrell wrote in testimony submitted to a congressional subcommittee investigating the practice. "For youth locked in a tiny room, a moment is an eternity, and it seems that the confinement will never end. And because youth in such confinement lack the maturity to put their current circumstances into a long term perspective, many feel hopeless and depressed. . . . The message conveyed to them is that they are worthless and beyond all help."

Sentenced as an adult and sent to San Quentin State Prison at the age of seventeen, Jared was, like Curtis, the youngest prisoner in the building. Also like Curtis, he quickly found himself in solitary confinement.

"Imagine being locked in a bathroom for twenty-three hours," he ventured in an effort to convey the feeling to someone who had not experienced anything like it. "You come out for breakfast and you come out for dinner and then once a week you get to go outside for two hours on the yard."

Jared was not placed in isolation because of any infraction. It was simply "procedure," he explained, which required that all new arrivals be segregated in order to be "screened" before entering the general population: "Screening—like who are you, do you have AIDS, are you detoxing off some kind of drug, where's your mind at? Do you have some kind of mental health issue where they have to isolate you from the general population because you ain't right upstairs? They have to figure all that stuff out, and it's a long process."

Jared had been screened several times already, at juvenile hall, at the Youth Authority, and presumably during the process that led to his being adjudicated as an adult. Nevertheless, screening him once again upon arrival at San Quentin took forty-five days, all of which he was required to spend in a locked cell, allowed out only for brief periods each day.

How, I asked Jared, did he hold it together?

"You figure it out," he answered. "It's like somebody throws you in the water and either you drown or you swim." It was left to him to devise some means to structure the empty days. "Do push-ups and sit-ups, read, meditate. You gotta structure this in your mind. If not . . . for me, I would've went crazy."

"It split me," Jared said of the experience. "I had to split who I am and create a part of me that was able to cope with being isolated."

Curtis used a similar term—"fragmented"—to describe his mental state. "I felt like I was cut into pieces," he said.

In this, Jared and Curtis had much in common with other youth trying to survive in solitary. Researchers have found that the experience of isolation is so devastating that many find ways to dissociate from their own emotions. Like so much else learned behind bars, it's a habit of mind that may be useful—even necessary—in the moment but can have damaging long-term consequences as young people try to build lives on the outside.

"One of the paradoxes of solitary confinement," physician Atul Gawande observed in a much-discussed piece in the *New Yorker* magazine, "is that, as starved as people become for companionship, the experience typically leaves them unfit for social interaction."

Some "begin to see themselves primarily as combatants in the world, people whose identity is rooted in thwarting prison control," psychologist Craig Haney told Gawande.

Gawande described a study of monkeys kept in isolation from birth. Once they were released into the company of other primates, they tended to "go into a state of emotional shock." Those isolated longest never recovered. A monkey released after just three weeks refused to eat and starved itself within days. According to psychologist Harry Harlow, who conducted the study, twelve months "almost obliterated the animals socially. . . . They became permanently withdrawn, and they lived as outcasts—regularly set upon, as if inviting abuse."

"We are social not just in the trivial sense that we like company, and not just in the obvious sense that we each depend on others," Gawande elaborated. "We are social in a more elemental way: simply to exist as a normal human being requires interaction with other people."

"Children," he added, "provide the clearest demonstration of this fact."

Research conducted by Human Rights Watch and the American Civil Liberties Union confirmed this assertion. "Many of the young people interviewed spoke in harrowing detail about struggling with . . . serious mental health problems during their time in solitary. They talked about thoughts of suicide and self-harm; visual and auditory hallucinations; feelings of depression; acute anxiety; shifting sleep patterns; nightmares and traumatic memories; and uncontrollable anger or rage."

Alyssa spent four months in protective confinement at sixteen: "It may sound weird but I had a friend in there that I would talk to," she told the researchers. "She wasn't there, but it was my mind. And I would talk to her and she would respond. . . . She [would tell] positive things to me. It was me, my mind, I knew, but it was telling me positive things. . . . It was a strange experience."

Sometimes youths turn to maiming themselves in solitary. "I'd see the blood and I'd be happy. . . . I did it with staples, not razors. When I see the blood and it makes me want to keep going. I showed the officers and they didn't do anything. . . . I wanted [the staff] to talk to me. I wanted them to understand what was going on with me," one young person told the researchers.

Those who hoped to communicate with their keepers via self-harm were sorely disappointed. One young man who took to cutting himself with a razor reported being further sanctioned for "making the room unsanitary."

"That's when I started going crazy," he reported. "I guess I was fighting two wars—myself and then the officers."

Facilities that rely on solitary confinement justify it as necessary for individual and institutional safety. In testimony before a U.S. Senate hearing on solitary confinement, Federal Bureau of Prisons director Charles E. Samuels spelled out the official perspective: "The use of restricted housing, however limited, remains a critical management tool that helps us maintain safety, security, and effective reentry programming for the vast majority of federal inmates housed in general population."

The argument that the use of solitary confinement improves institutional security is contradicted by the evidence. In fact, jurisdictions that have made a coordinated effort to *reduce* the use of solitary confinement have seen a marked improvement in institutional safety.

In 2007, for example, the Bexar County, Texas, Juvenile Probation Department joined a privately funded initiative aimed at building an environment where control is maintained via positive relationships rather than brute force and isolation. Over the next four years, as the institution reduced its use of solitary confinement by approximately 40 percent and mechanical restraints (e.g., handcuffs, leg irons) by half, it experienced a 30 percent reduction in injuries and more than a 60 percent reduction in suicide attempts. Other benefits included less staff turnover and improved relationships with youth. These findings not only demolish "institutional safety" as a justification for solitary confinement; they make the notion of using it as an attempt to *prevent* suicide appear patently absurd.

Corrections administrators who do not use solitary confinement consistently make the same case against the "institutional safety" argument. Isolation is not only counterproductive, they say; when there are strong and trusting relationships between staff and youth, it is unnecessary.

Missouri—which runs some of the safest and most effective juvenile facilities in the nation while largely eschewing solitary confinement—may offer the clearest counterpoint to the argument that solitary has any value as a safety measure. Widely acclaimed for its network of small, noninstitutional placements, Missouri's juvenile justice system ranks far better on recidivism and other measures of effectiveness than those in other states. According to a recent study, only 8 percent of the youth who passed through Missouri's system wound up in the adult system within five years of their release—a rate that is dwarfed by that of most other states.

Mark Steward, who retired as director of Missouri's juvenile justice system after seventeen years and now works with other states to replicate the Missouri Model, has said that Missouri facilities virtually never use isolation, retaining only seven isolation rooms in a system with more than seven hundred beds. Over a ten-year period, Steward has maintained, none of the state's five regions has used an isolation room more than five times, and some have not used theirs at all.

Tim Decker, Missouri's current director, told me the same thing: isolation is almost never used in his facilities. The trusting relationships youths form with staff and one another within the intimate, carefully designed therapeutic programs make that kind of extreme measure unnecessary.

Eddie Figueroa, the director of New York State's Red Hook Residential Center, shares Decker's perspective. Figueroa, who has been at Red Hook for twenty-nine years, knows each young person there by name and views the kids in his care not as bad seeds but as "fallen angels."

"Room confinement" (the preferred euphemism in the New York system) does not exist at Red Hook, Figueroa said. "If a kid is having a problem, I'll say, 'Come with me,' " a simple yet powerful invitation conveying a message that runs directly counter to banishing kids to isolation cells. Then he talks with him. Very often, he said, that is all it takes.

"We'll come out here," he said, gesturing to the courtyard where we stood among carefully tended flower beds. "My thing is, if I can't talk to them, I'm in the wrong business."

"Don't do nothing stupid," Figueroa might tell a kid who is about to blow up (or already has). "Just call time-out. Go walk. Ten or fifteen minutes later, you're going to feel a whole lot better than you do now." It is a simple message that, conveyed with the affection Figueroa radiates in all his interactions, is remarkably effective at keeping all involved safe.

Solitary confinement, in Figueroa's view, does just the opposite, by undermining any potential for trust between a young person and facility staff. "If they want to blow off some steam," he continued, referring to the sort of outburst that can land a kid in solitary elsewhere, "you don't have to lock them up for that. I equate [doing] that to—imagine a lion in a cage. You poke it, you make fun of it, go 'Ha, ha, ha.' One of these days, you stick your arm out and it's going to rip your arm off and have you for lunch."

In 2012, the Senate Judiciary Subcommittee on the Constitution, Civil Rights and Human Rights held a hearing with the stated goal of "Reassessing Solitary Confinement." Senator Richard Durbin, the committee chair, contextualized the discussion with the dramatic assertion that "America has led the fight for human rights throughout the world." America also, the senator noted, leads the world in the incarceration of its citizens, with "by far the highest per capita rate for prisoners in the world."

"What do America's prisons say about our nation and its values?" Durbin asked. "What does it say when we consider how we treat the people who are in prison?"

The senator pointed to a replica of a solitary cell, which he had stepped inside for a few minutes—not long enough, he acknowledged, to allow him even to imagine "what it must be like to spend extended periods of time, hours, days, weeks, months, years in that confining space." He quoted a man who had inhabited a similar space at a so-called supermax prison. That inmate, said the senator, "fairly described it as being like a space capsule, where one is shot into space and left in its isolation."

"If I had one request to my colleagues on this judiciary committee," Durbin implored, "it is to visit a prison. Do it frequently. See what it's like."

In Durbin's plea I heard echoes of the many young people who expressed the wish that the prosecutors, judges, and legislators who share the power to send them to juvenile prisons would pay even a brief visit to those places; that they would make some effort to understand the impact of their decisions.

Durbin observed that since the "tough on crime" 1980s, the use of solitary had become much more widespread, leading to "an alarming increase in isolation for those who don't really need to be there," especially vulnerable groups such as children.

As the senator wrapped up, however, his rhetoric deflated. Early in the hearing, he had spoken directly to the sister of a boy who killed himself in solitary. But he made no further reference to the notion of a ban on the practice—something he had, quite movingly, told the young woman might have saved her brother's life.

"That's why I've advocated for change in the Justice Department's new prison rape standards," he intoned instead, "to help ensure that sexual assault victims are only placed in solitary when absolutely necessary."

This profoundly limited closing recommendation leaves out the vast majority of youth subjected to solitary, whether for punishment, protection, administrative convenience, or the simple whim of a guard. It even leaves the door open to subjecting sexual assault victims to the torture of solitary confinement as long as it has been determined to be "absolutely necessary."

Once again, the prospect of "reform" appears to elude even the reformers, vanquished before the battle has even begun. The solitary confinement of juveniles can be "reassessed" again and again—in reports, hearings, investigations, statements, and so on—but unless it is actually *curtailed*, no amount of talk or paper will make any difference to the children who endure it to this day, every day.

In the face of overwhelming evidence that placing youth in solitary confinement is not only counterproductive but tantamount to torture, the best even those political leaders most concerned about the practice can offer is a call to mitigate just slightly a practice they concede is both abusive and criminogenic. This speaks volumes about the depth of the struggle against entrenched institutional cultures and practices.

Meanwhile, the use of solitary confinement persists in juvenile prisons across the country—despite lawsuits, federal inquiries, advocacy campaigns, media exposés, hearings, and more. The persistence with which these institutions cling to the practice raises a troubling set of questions: Why *are* those who run juvenile institutions so reluctant to give up their isolation cells? If those who run our juvenile prisons perceive a practice that is considered torture under international law as essential to the function of those institutions, what does this say about their attitude toward the children in their care?

If—as the continued reliance on isolation in juvenile facilities indicates—solitary confinement is a tool our nation's juvenile prisons cannot or will not do without, then scrambling to find an alternative means of sanctioning young prisoners (or protecting them, sorting them, assessing them, etc.) may be a fool's errand. If we want to get the kids out of solitary, we need to get them out of these places altogether.

8

"HURT PEOPLE HURT PEOPLE"

Trauma and Incarceration

The greatest terror a child can have is that he is not loved, and rejection is the hell he fears. . . . And with rejection comes anger, and with anger some kind of crime in revenge for the rejection, and with the crime guilt— and there is the story of mankind.

—John Steinbeck

The saddest part of a juvenile judge's job is watching the progress of a tiny victim as he or she is molded by the system into a delinquent and eventually a criminal.

—Estella May Moriarty, Circuit Court judge,
Fort Lauderdale, Florida

"Gabrielle, what is it?"

Her mother's voice was strained as she struggled to reach this daughter so diffident and distant, to penetrate the enforced separation of the visiting room table, and then the greater chasm of all those years of silence.

"It's like you don't care," said the mother to the child who had been so early exiled, so traumatized that caring was a luxury dispensed with long ago.

"Like you have a death wish, or a wish just to say . . . ," her mother struggled on. "Just talk to me," she exhaled, hinting at defeat.

Just talk to me. The words hung in the air. How many times—as a lonesome child, a teen on her own, a rape survivor, hostage, gangster, gunshot victim, perpetrator, ward—had Gabrielle longed to do exactly that? How many times had she *tried* to talk, to ask for help or just to be heard, to tell her distant, drugged-out mother what had been done to her and what she had done in order to survive it, only, each time, to be silenced or ignored?

Mom, I'm here. I'm alive . . . I am your kid . . . I am right here, whether you notice me or not. For years, this script had played inside Gabrielle's head. But now she was grown, and one strike away from going away for life. She carried four bullets inside her body, lodged too deep in her legs and hip ever to be removed. Just as unremitting were the psychic wounds—years of physical and sexual abuse in her father's home, drugs and neglect in her mother's, and the unremitting violence of life on the street.

Was she now supposed to forget all of that—the years lived in loneliness, silence, and radical self-reliance?

Drugs had come first for her mother for so many years that Gabrielle had long since stopped looking to her for help or protection. Where there might have been connection there was scar tissue instead, formed in the wake of one assault after another, woven by now into a protective emotional carapace she could no more easily shed than she could her own skin.

And now, when she'd just about shut down completely—when the damage was done and her life was on the line—her mother was speaking to her as one might a young child, asking her tenderly where did it hurt.

Mom, I'm here. I'm alive . . . I am your kid . . .

Through all the years of enforced invisibility, all the times she'd been rebuffed or ignored or coerced into silence, Gabrielle had never lost the longing to be known. Now she weighed the options—the safety of silence or the risk of revelation—and discovered she was brave.

"Do you remember trying to kill yourself in front of me?" Gabrielle began.

"Not really."

"Do you remember why I came back from Texas?"

"Not really."

"Do you remember me being a kid?"

"No, Gabrielle. Not really."

"You were so high that you remember none of this," Gabrielle persisted, holding her mother's gaze across the table. "But I was sober, Mom. These are the things that I do remember. . . ."

Walking onto a juvenile unit is like entering a trauma ward, an emotional MASH unit where the gore is no less visceral for being interior. While only a minority of the young people we incarcerate have committed violent crimes, most have themselves been the victims of violence: assaulted as children; raped as adolescents; shot, shot at, or stabbed on the street. The teenagers we put through the trauma of incarceration are, with a few exceptions, traumatized already, hurt children now formally consigned to what they call "a world of hurt."

In 2010, the federal Office of Juvenile Justice and Delinquency Prevention released its Survey of Youth in Residential Placement, a sweeping look at the histories of young people inside the nation's juvenile facilities. The nationally representative survey of 7,073 souls revealed that childhood trauma was so pervasive as to be nearly universal. Seventy-two percent had been directly victimized ("had something very bad or terrible happen to you"), and nearly as many had witnessed extreme violence ("seen someone severely injured or killed"). Thirty percent had been sexually or physically abused. For a quarter, that abuse had been "frequent or injurious." None of these categories was mutually exclusive.

Among girls, trauma is especially pervasive and is frequently described as a "pathway" into the juvenile justice system. According to the U.S. Congress, "Most of these girls [who enter the juvenile justice system], up to 73 percent, have histories of physical and sexual violence, and their entry into the criminal and juvenile justice system is linked to their sexual and physical victimization." One heartbreaking example comes from a study by the Oregon Social Learning Center, which found the average reported age of "first sexual encounter" for girls in the juvenile justice system to be 6.75.

In 2012, the federal Office of the Attorney General released its *Report of the Attorney General's National Task Force on Children Exposed to Violence.* The head of the task force, Robert L. Listenbee Jr., was later appointed to head the federal Office of Juvenile Justice and Delinquency Prevention. This makes the task force's conclusions on trauma and juvenile justice all the more striking.

The vast majority of children involved in the juvenile justice system have survived exposure to violence and are living with the trauma of that experience. If we are to fulfill the goals of the juvenile justice system—to make communities and victims whole, to rehabilitate young offenders while holding them accountable, and to help children develop skills to be productive and succeed—we must rethink the way the juvenile justice system treats, assesses, and evaluates the children within it. . . .

The relationship between exposure to violence and involvement in the justice system is not a coincidence. . . . When young people experience prolonged or repeated violence, their bodies and brains adapt by becoming focused on survival. This dramatically reduces their ability to delay impulses and gratification, to a degree even beyond that of normal adolescents. Youth who are trying to protect themselves from more violence, or who do not know how to deal with violence they have already experienced, may engage in delinquent or criminal behavior as a way to gain a sense of control in their chaotic lives and to cope with the emotional turmoil and barriers to security and success that violence creates.

Research on brain development over the past two decades has shown that the areas of the prefrontal cortex responsible for cognitive processing and the ability to inhibit impulses and weigh consequences before taking action are not fully developed until people reach their mid-20s. . . . Science reveals that the developing brain, in early childhood and throughout adolescence, is very sensitive to harsh physical and environmental conditions. Traumatic violence, in particular, can delay or derail brain development, leaving even the most resilient and intelligent child or adolescent with a severely diminished capacity to inhibit strong impulses, to delay gratification, to anticipate and evaluate the consequences of risky or socially unacceptable behavior, and to tolerate disagreement or conflict with other persons.

A caveat: kids behind bars are individuals, each with his or her own unique history and character—no more or less so than anyone else. Many young people doing time were neither abused nor neglected as children, and most—including those who have grown up amid violence—have family who love them and are heartbroken when they are locked up. Generalizations do a tremendous disservice to the thousands of families that are fighting for their children's lives and freedom every day.

Respecting the diversity of young people's experience does not, however, require ignoring the devastation many have experienced. Too many of the young people we try to hold "accountable" via isolation enter our youth prisons already overfamiliar with rejection, isolation, and profound and chronic trauma. Being tossed into a cage serves only to underscore the despair and sense of worthlessness the trauma they have lived through has often instilled.

As I listened to young people who were or had been incarcerated describe childhood worlds in which not only emotional needs but even the most basic survival needs often went unmet, unless they found a way to take care of things themselves, where the street corner supplanted the backyard and adults in authority saw them as a number or a nuisance, a tragic cycle revealed itself. The brutal bottom line, these young people showed me, is that by relying on incarceration to address an ever-widening range of youthful misdeeds and larger social ills, we are isolating children who are already alone.

Gabrielle came as close as anyone I met to being bereft from the very beginning. Violence and abuse had suffused her whole family—fifteen siblings and parents in two states—for as long as she remembered.

Her mother, a doctor, got hooked on Oxycontin too early for her daughter to know a "before." By the time she developed a tolerance and was looking for something harder, she'd connected with a new man who was able to supply it. Cocaine, crystal meth, heroin, crack—"anything she could get her hands on, my Mom did it." By the time it became clear that the boyfriend was abusive, Mom was in too deep to find her way out. The decades of domestic violence that followed became one more secret for the kids to carry.

If there was little respite in Gabrielle's childhood, there were fleeting moments when rescue felt possible, when hope seemed to hover for a moment like a taunt. Once, her mother nodded out at work and someone made a call to Child Protective Services. Social workers whisked the younger children into foster homes. Then they sent them back.

"Oh, we were wrong, she was just sleepy," Gabrielle mocked, imitating the social workers who couldn't, or wouldn't, see past the middle-class trappings of her home. The house to which they returned her was "perfect on the outside"—her stepfather's vintage Cadillac gleamed at the curb, and a genuine picket fence framed the front yard—but inside was mayhem.

"If you walked in, you'd be like, 'What the hell just happened?' They [her mother and stepfather] are in there fighting, the closet doors are broken again because they have thrown each other into them—it was terrible."

Even through the narcotic haze, Gabrielle's mother understood the need to get her daughter out. Soon after the close call with Child Protective Services, Gabrielle found herself on a plane to Texas, bound toward the home of a stranger—her father.

Gabrielle's mother had walked out on him when she was pregnant with Gabrielle. Nine years later, Gabrielle stood in his doorway, a small stranger wearing a face he had struggled to forget. In the little girl who looked to him for rescue and protection, all he could see was everything he'd lost. For years, he had been powerless to vent his pent-up venom. Gabrielle's arrival loosed the genie from the bottle. Each time he beat his daughter, he used her mother's name.

A vessel for his violence until she grew old enough to run from it, Gabrielle would carry the force of her father's fury with her when she hit the streets, pumped as full of its explosiveness as a live grenade.

But first, when she was around eleven, the beatings tipped into sexual aggression. Gabrielle did all she could to fight off her father's incursions. If she could get her arms free, she went for his face—a mark might raise questions, and that would get him off of her. If his live-in girlfriend was at home, she'd shout so loudly that her father took to covering her face with a pillow.

The battle over Gabrielle's developing body stretched on for two years. Meanwhile, at school, her older brother, who'd come with her from Los Angeles—"the white sheep of the family," favored by their father, who'd had a chance to bond with him before their mother left—had become a target. His skinny frame, glasses, and schoolboy demeanor acted as a clarion call to the local bullies. Gabrielle fought often in order to defend him—or, if she got there too late, to avenge him—protecting her brother with all the fierceness and devotion no one showed on her behalf.

When a football player jammed her brother into a locker, Gabrielle "went nuts." Years of repressed anger found a target in her brother's oppressor. But she was younger, smaller, and—despite her rage—no match for him. She stumbled home from school that day with several broken ribs.

By the next morning, she was in too much pain to rise and dress for school. That was the first time her father succeeded in raping her, pressing on her broken ribs until the pain overrode her capacity to resist. It was also the last. As soon as her father left the house, Gabrielle packed up everything worth selling and, pushing past the pain, staggered out the door.

Research on treatment for childhood trauma indicates that the most important element is the environment in which treatment is offered. "Traumatized kids need to feel like they're in a safe and stable environment," one researcher summarized.

It is hard to imagine anyone arguing that a juvenile prison is anything close to a "safe and stable environment." Yet a history of abuse not only routinely leads a kid to lockup; it is sometimes even used to *justify* incarcerating the most wounded and vulnerable young defendants. A judge who can be convinced that a child has significant support from her family and community—a safe home and neighborhood to which she can return—may take that into consideration in deciding to place that child on probation rather than consigning her to a locked facility. In the more common inverse, children whose homes and communities are deemed unsafe or inadequate—vulnerable children from under-resourced neighborhoods—may be locked up explicitly because of their profound disadvantage. With nowhere else to send them—prison beds are far more available than therapeutic alternatives, not to mention programs that support struggling families—judges wind up relying on locked facilities, where abuse and further trauma regularly follow.

"Childhood victimization can have long lasting effects. One of which is higher risk of juvenile delinquency," Robert Listenbee—now the director of the federal Office of Juvenile Justice and Delinquency—has said.

Will, who spent six years in California youth facilities, agrees. "Hurt people hurt people" is the way he puts it.

"I believe people are born good," he elaborated. "You don't wake up one day [wanting to hurt people]. Usually people who end up in jail have been victims of other things. You gotta *be* hurt to hurt somebody else."

The correlation between childhood exposure to violence and subsequent incarceration has been firmly established. Taken together, the research tells a story that tracks closely those I heard from young people across the nation. The kids we consign to our violent, abusive, degrading youth prisons—from whom we strip away human connection, enforcing their aloneness and endorsing their estrangement—are drawn from the ranks of the youngest walking wounded. Traumatized, brutalized, beat down, and abandoned, they have grown up too often with little to counter the message conveyed with such force behind bars: that they are worthless, hopeless, something less than human.

Leslie Acoca has interviewed more than 3,200 incarcerated girls and women in eighteen states. Among incarcerated girls, she and others have found, childhood abuse is "nearly universal." In 1998, Acoca was part of a National Council on Crime and Delinquency research team that interviewed girls in the California juvenile system. Ninety-two percent had experienced one or more forms of abuse. Nearly a third had been forced to leave home, most often between the ages of twelve and fifteen (a direct path to being *perceived* as delinquent, since homelessness itself is often treated as illegal). Forty percent had been raped or sodomized or both (starting, on average, at age thirteen), and a third had been molested or fondled (average age: five). Forty-five percent had been beaten or burned and one in four had been shot or stabbed.

This kind of trauma is highly correlated with drug use, school failure, and gang affiliation—themselves highly correlated with incarceration.

The most troubling element of Acoca's account may be what the girls reported *without* being asked. "The maltreatment of girls within the juvenile justice system was not an intended focus of the . . . study, nor was it an articulated question with the interview protocol. Nevertheless, many girls reported experiencing emotional, physical, and sexual intimidation and/ or abuses within the juvenile justice system that mirrored and exacerbated those they had previously suffered at home and on the streets. Some of these abuses were directly observed by researchers."

The presence of researchers did not, for example, inhibit "procedures in which a group of girls was strip-searched and their private parts visually examined in an open space where they could be, and were, casually observed by male staff members."

"These experiences seemed to reinforce the girls' perception, born for many with their experience of sexual violation at home and on the streets, that they did not have the right or the power to protect their physical boundaries," Acoca writes.

Girls reported treatment that bore a striking resemblance to the degradations they had already experienced. Staff called them "hood rat," "slut," and "little hooker" and threatened physical violence at the first sign of noncompliance. "Once girls have crossed the threshold into the juvenile justice system, they become vulnerable to multiple additional violations, beginning at the moment of their arrest and continuing through detention," Acoca writes. "The abuses that a majority of girl offenders have experienced in their homes, in their schools, or on the streets are often mirrored and compounded by injuries they later receive within the juvenile justice system."

The trauma girls experience inside locked facilities, in other words, exacerbates the very wounds that propelled their entry—as destructive a cycle as one can imagine.

After Gabrielle fled her father's house, a friend's mother helped her purchase a plane ticket back to California—the only destination she could think to name. She tried several times to tell her mom what had happened in Texas, but her mother would not hear her. "It just made her get higher. She got higher, and she got higher, and she got a little bit higher."

Less than a week after she returned from Texas, Gabrielle left her mother's house for good, this time with no destination in mind. Because she was raised under the ethos *What happens in the house stays in the house*, it did not cross her mind to call Child Protective Services. She was too young to work a legal job, though, or to apply for public support. That left selling dope.

Gabrielle was good at it right from the start. She paid a drug client to sign the lease on an apartment, invited a friend to move in to keep her company, and soon found herself the doyenne of "one great big party house."

"I was out on my own, in my own little world," she recalled, "and I did everything I felt was good for me."

Violence, for example, felt good for her—so far, it was the only thing that had kept her close to safe. "I was probably the most violent girl out there," she said, sounding neither proud nor ashamed of the years she spent gangbanging.

Chronic violence of the sort that Gabrielle grew up with can stymie children's development in myriad ways. Uncertain when violence will take the life of someone close to them (by young adulthood, Gabrielle had lost nine of eleven brothers), they may protect themselves by avoiding close connections. Many become hypervigilant, alert to threats both real and perceived. With their guard always up in anticipation of the next attack, their relationships fray or disintegrate entirely, leaving young survivors, as Gabrielle described it, "in [their] own little world"—more alone and, paradoxically, more vulnerable than ever.

Gang affiliations may come to seem the only safe allegiance. The strength in numbers they provide buffers traumatized youth from feelings of powerlessness and helps them feel less vulnerable to further victimization. But gangs offer this sense of safety and connection at a price, pushing members into a cycle of escalating violence and eventual incarceration.

"It's what I knew," Gabrielle said of her own trajectory. "From in my mom's house to out of my mom's house . . . wherever I was, it was violent. Going back and forth to Texas and L.A., here and there, everything was violent. So I thought it was normal to be that way."

A December 2012 Department of Justice report suggested that children exposed to violence may turn to violence themselves as "a source of power, prestige, security or even belongingness." For those like Gabrielle who grow up knowing nothing else, violence can become its own sort of language, a means of being heard when words and tears don't matter. If Gabrielle became, as she put it, "extremely extreme," perhaps she was shouting particularly loudly.

Children raised amid physical violence and psychological trauma frequently spin into a self-destructive cycle that catches adult attention only when it tips into delinquency. Even then, that attention is limited to labels and sanctions: "bad," "delinquent," "troublemaker," or the more clinical "lacking character and positive motivation."

As a result, few adults get past asking, "What is wrong with you?" and ask the question that trauma researchers have identified as essential to healing: "What happened to you?"

Young people rarely miss the fact that their own offenses draw a sort of attention that offenses against them do not. As a training document aimed at juvenile court judges instructs,

> victimization, particularly victimization that goes unaddressed, is a violation of our social contract with youth and can create a deep disregard both for adults in general and the rules that adults have set. Distrust and disregard for adults, rules, and laws place youth at a much greater risk for delinquency and other inappropriate behaviors. . . . System professionals would benefit from recognizing that imposing only negative or punitive consequences will likely do little to change the youth's patterns of aggression, rule breaking, and risky behaviors because such a response does not address the impact of traumatic stress on the child.

Had there been any room for "What happened to you?" in Gabrielle's trajectory, in other words—much less had the adults who committed crimes *against* her ever been held accountable—her life might have followed a very different course. Both Gabrielle and those she would go on to harm or to frighten might have been saved unnecessary grief.

Those who work in law enforcement are not blind to the trauma their young charges have experienced. Those most sensitive to the connection between trauma and delinquency may find themselves faced with a variant of what New York City probation commissioner Vincent Schiraldi called cognitive dissonance. Their job is to hold young people "accountable" and foster better "choices," with little room to take into account the larger context: that young people who wind up arrested and incarcerated have often grown up in environments so barren, so devoid of opportunity, that those "better choices" are out of their reach.

Jason Druxman is supervising probation officer of San Diego County's Youthful Offender and Community Transition Units. As California empties out its state juvenile prisons, he is working hard to implement a treatment-based model at the local level while struggling to keep up with the influx of young people who were, just a few years earlier, the responsibility of the state.

Square jawed and clean-cut, with a military bearing, Druxman looks like a younger, taller Tom Cruise. He wants very much to believe that every kid is "reachable," but experience, he has found, sometimes tests that faith.

"I go to the homes," he began, "and I can tell you, what I see is so depressing." Druxman described a house where three siblings, all on probation, were recently injured in a gang shooting. Their mother had just died and their father was newly paroled.

"Realistically, how do you expect a youth to progress in that type of situation?" he asked heatedly. "Most of these homes we go into . . . they don't have a bulb in their lights! How is the youth supposed to even study? Or sleep, when there are cockroaches? I don't know how any of these youth are going to succeed."

"Prostitution is a huge problem for our girls," he told me later as we toured the facility, quietly pointing to Crystal, the delicate young woman in sweats and jail slippers who dreamed of becoming a ballerina. Crystal had told me that she no longer cried: her twenty-six-year-old pimp had warned her that crying was evidence of weakness, so she had learned to hold back tears when she was beaten or raped. "Oh well, okay, it happened, forget about it," she told herself each time. "Keep going. Keep moving forward."

I asked Druxman how a traumatized girl like Crystal could be arrested for an act to which, under the law, she was too young to consent. Prostitution, he clarified, was not usually the "immediate trigger" for a girl's arrest. More often she might be arrested on a vagrancy or drug charge. "But we know that they are being abused," he reiterated. "A lot of times they get out and they get sucked right back into that environment, and they are being abused by an individual. So that is a big educational point that we are trying to focus on with our girls."

I asked him to clarify this one for me also: how does one "educate" girls out of being abused when their abusers are so rarely called to account? Were the girls being held responsible even for their own victimization?

"Kids are victims, essentially," he ventured. "But the fact is that they are making choices, and unfortunately, the safety of the community has to come first."

How, I wondered, did this heartsick ballerina pose a threat to community safety? But I didn't have the heart to keep badgering Druxman, whose compassion for the kids was so unmistakable, even if it sometimes collided with the mandates of his job.

Gabrielle did not have the good fortune to run into a Jason Druxman. Despite regular arrests, no one ever inquired into her home life, much less took the time to "educate" her on the perils of being abused. The only ones asking any questions were the cops, and "What happened to you?" was not on their agenda. Instead, Gabrielle grew accustomed to the handcuffs and to biding her time in juvenile hall until a woman she paid to pose as her mother arrived to bail her out.

"Nobody cared at that moment. 'Just another violent individual.' That's how it was. . . ."

Roland's earliest memories of his Southern California childhood include going to the park, shopping with his parents, and trying to shield his mother from his father's fists.

"For the average immigrant family, we were living [the high] life," he said—a life built on his father's earnings as a drug dealer. "We had every game console you could think of, everything was nice, but it's not all about that, because deep inside, we were hurting. Even till this day, I hurt, because of my path."

Roland was six or seven when he began to notice how anxious his mother would grow as the sun began to set. Nightfall meant his father could come home at any moment. "Once I was old enough to realize he was hitting her, it was like, 'Man, what do I do?' It was every time he came home drunk—almost daily. Maybe two days out of the week he was sober."

By the time he was eight or nine, his two older brothers had moved out of the house, and Roland had become his mother's main protector. "I am a child," Roland remembers. "I want to play, I want to have fun. I want to go out and play soccer, play baseball, football." But whenever he made a move for the door, his mother begged him to stay.

I am a child. Roland repeated that phrase often, always in the present tense, as he described the travails of his early childhood. Sometimes he seemed to be reminding himself as well as his listener of something those around him did not seem to recognize, mourning the childhood he was not allowed to have.

"She would cry, I would sit there—bored, mad, but I knew it was my duty to sit there."

Sooner or later, Roland's father would come home. "He'd be hitting on my mom, grabbing her by the hair, tossing her, throwing stuff at her, and I would always try to jump in—knowing I wasn't going to do anything. I couldn't affect him. I was a child. He was a 220-pound guy. I would run in, he would hit on me, and I would fall to the ground and start crying. Bleeding. I knew it was always going to happen, but I kept trying and trying and trying. He would always just dust me off. . . . I would fall to the ground. My mom was crying. Sometimes I'd be crying and she'd end up falling next to me 'cause my dad's beating her up in front of me."

Like Gabrielle, Roland recalls a few pivotal moments when it seemed as if an adult might recognize his suffering and offer him some respite. More than once, when Roland came to school with bruises and scratches, a teacher pulled him aside and made a phone call home. But his terrified mother was adept enough at lying—"He's an aggressive kid," she'd tell the teacher, and he liked to roughhouse or fight with his sisters—that no one looked deeper than that initial call.

As Roland got older, he realized that the time for tossing a football in the street had passed him by. His cousins were dealing openly right down the block, and drugs, guns, and violence suffused his community.

When Roland was eight, a drug-trade colleague of his father's—"a big guy, tattoos everywhere"—tried to assault him sexually. Roland's screams were loud enough to scare the man off, but his already acute sense of looming danger was heightened even further. Like everything else, Roland kept the incident to himself: *Don't ask, don't tell* was the family ethos.

At school, he would hang back and watch the other children playing. "I would look at them and wonder if they went through the same thing. That kid right there with a smile on his face—I wondered if his dad comes home drunk all the time. I wondered if his dad beats him up, you know?"

"Violence at home, drugs, alcohol, verbal abuse, that incident [of sexual assault]—it all just bottled up inside as a child," said Roland. "How do you let that out? What's your outlet? You don't have an outlet."

"I was fresh, I had good clothes, good shoes, but inside I was bumming it. I had nothing," Roland recalled. "So that made me feel like an outcast. It made me feel different, like I didn't belong. And that feeling was traumatizing. I was traumatized, and emotions were all bottled up inside. Emotions of anger and anguish. Feeling—I don't know, you can't explain it—it was eating me up inside, but eventually the monster I have inside, the demon, is going to explode."

When Roland was thirteen, a cousin introduced him to marijuana. The warm, pungent smoke seemed to appease the demon. It left Roland "numb, feeling nothing," relief enough that soon he was smoking regularly. "I was feeling empty, I was feeling hurt, and I wanted to substitute that with something else."

As with any palliative, the drug's powers weakened the more Roland used it. "After a while, smoking so much weed, it becomes nothing to you," he explained. "Your thoughts keep coming back like it's normal." And "normal" as Roland knew it had become intolerable.

A talented student, he started skipping school and hanging out in the park, talking to girls, smoking, or wandering aimlessly. Sometimes he would walk the streets all day. Before long, he connected with a gang.

A handsome Latino with buzz-cut dark hair and a diamond in each ear, Roland walked, a decade later, with the residual hint of a swagger, offset by a quick and disarming smile. "I wanted to belong and feel like I am powerful," he said of his teenage self. "Having a gang behind me, knowing I was protected—that made me feel like I belonged."

For the first time, said Roland, "I started feeling good. Belonging to a crowd, I didn't feel different anymore. I felt like, 'Man, they are just like me.' They showed me the love my father doesn't show me."

Being in a clique also gave Roland the opportunity to fight—an activity that provided more relief than getting high had. "I wanted to feel different. I wanted to release everything I felt inside, and what was the best outlet? Adrenaline. The adrenaline released everything."

He and his cohorts would walk the streets, sometimes twenty strong, in search of trouble. When they found a group that they thought they could take, they would taunt, shove, and otherwise provoke them until words turned to blows and a full-scale fight ensued. "The norm, I guess, with most teens," Roland added.

"Everybody has their own reason why they do it," he said of the street brawls that soon became a habit. "Some of them do it because they are bored of their simple lives, or they wanna be cool. Some want respect. . . . I did it because I was hurting inside and I wanted the outlet. Fighting, being aggressive, not caring—that became my outlet. All my anger was being released right here."

The more deeply Roland got involved in gang life and the violence that accompanied it, the more he believed he was "where I belonged." As he made the transition from victim to perpetrator, he picked up the *I don't give a fuck* mentality. Comfortable, concealing, a shield from unwanted emotions, the attitude fit him like a well-worn sweater.

Roland was out with his eighteen-year-old brother when someone ran up on the older boy with a baseball bat. The first blow missed, and Roland was on him, throwing the kid to the ground and beating him with his own bat. "It was self-defense in a way," he says now, "but I know I used too much aggression. We could have run. I didn't have to grab the bat and hit him."

"When you recognize from the bench a lifetime of trauma in the delinquent acts of a teenager, you have become part of the solution," Attorney General Eric Holder, a former judge, has said. Few young people I met recalled a judge or anyone else in power even hinting at this kind of recognition. As the juvenile court has increasingly come to resemble its adult counterpart, "What happened to you?" has become increasingly unlikely to enter the equation. Fifteen-year-old Hispanic male. Assault and battery. Off Roland went to juvenile hall, and then to a county-run camp in California's Lancaster County.

"It stopped me for about a month or two," Roland said of that first incarceration, which lasted six months, "but then I got comfortable. I got used to it again. I was like, fuck it."

"Fuck it" meant robbery, more fighting, knives. It meant harder drugs—crystal meth, crack cocaine. It meant going to school only on test days, just scraping by, despite the fact that, secretly, Roland liked to learn.

"Deep inside I kept telling myself, what am I doing? What am I doing? Why can't I just go to school and do what I gotta do?" He would promise his counselor, as well as himself, that this time he meant it; he was turning things around. "Then I would meet up with my friends, and I'd do the same thing."

Roland was "frozen"—a common condition among poly-victimized children, for whom trauma is not a single event but a chronic condition. "What is wrong with you?" Roland's probation-assigned counselor kept asking. She saw the bright underachiever sitting in front of her—the diffident teenager wasting his potential—but didn't ask the questions that might have revealed the hurt child hovering beneath the tough-guy facade, the eight-year-old who lay beside his battered mother, her warm blood and hot tears mingling with his own.

Anger, antisocial feelings, lack of self-control. Lack of affection or weak supervision from parents. Lack of role models. Poor academic skills. These are the risk factors for juvenile delinquency. They are also signs and symptoms of childhood trauma.

"In order to recover from the blows which social life inflicts upon them, human beings need a haven of peace, which is normally provided in the family," the Austrian psychoanalyst August Aichhorn explained in a 1922 lecture on juvenile delinquency. "When the individual has such a haven, his instinctual life is able to manifest itself within socially acceptable limits. But if he lacks this refuge, his mental equilibrium . . . becomes more easily disturbed, and, given the appropriate disposition, delinquency results."

When the family not only fails to provide a safe haven but is itself the place of greatest danger, the trouble that follows should come as no surprise. But like Gabrielle and so many others, Roland made the transit from victim to perpetrator without anyone making the connection, anyone asking, "What happened to you?"

"You're a great kid," his probation counselor told him often. "You're smart. What are you doing?"

"I don't know what to tell you," Roland answered. "This is who I am. This is what I do."

Like Gabrielle and Roland, Luis was victimized for years, coming to the attention of the authorities only when he caught a court charge himself.

Luis grew up in a rural county with immigrant parents. At home, he said, "there was plenty of abusive behavior inflicted towards me, in every possible way a human can receive such negativity. It was also done to my mother, and also my brothers, but for some reason I, being the oldest, witnessed and experienced the most."

"With these traumas I experienced," he went on, "I felt different. I felt I couldn't cope and that there was just something wrong with me."

"So I carry that with me," he said.

A slim, delicate-featured twenty-year-old Latino in a crisp button-down shirt and jeans, Luis detailed with precision the abuse he experienced at the hands of his father.

"Physically, he bombed on me since I was three or four. Open hands, sometimes he'd throw a fist in there, and he used his legs a lot. When he hit me, he used what felt like the steel part of the belt, and he would sit there whacking for hours."

You just spilled that barbecue sauce. You are a fucking idiot. Each time Luis's father laid into his son, he made sure to communicate that the child himself was to blame.

"That shit fucked me up," Luis said—a crisp summary of the link between childhood victimization and subsequent delinquency. "Obviously, I hate my dad's guts. He fucking abused me my whole life. It's a good thing he didn't rape me, or I'd be a serial killer."

Luis and his brothers were, in his words, "welfare babies," growing up in a household where not even groceries could be taken for granted. But because they lived in "the poor section of the rich part of town, I grew up around, predominately, a lot of white people. And I say 'white' in the White Wonder Bread culture sense. People who go and have careers, success, financial wealth, and material things, and doing some type of appropriate activities. I grew up with those types of folks around me."

Living on the outskirts of what looked to him like paradise, reminded every day of his own exclusion, Luis reached a conclusion.

"My life was bullshit," he determined before his thirteenth birthday. "I needed to make myself feel like [my better-off neighbors], because that would be happiness."

Luis was too young to cross the tracks on his own. But if he couldn't change his reality, he could change how he experienced it. He "found a different way to get there—to get to happiness—which was smoking bud and drinking."

At twelve years old, he got high for the first time, mixing Bacardi and Jack Daniel's with marijuana a friend skimmed from his dad's stash. "And that began my journey," Luis said—a trajectory he likens to "a big motherfucking snowball going downhill."

Luis started skipping school and acquired a new group of friends who were doing the same. When these friends started talking about breaking into the home of a neighborhood bully, the snowball just kept rolling.

The break-in attempt was a wholesale fiasco. One kid tried to pry open a window. Luis took a couple of steps into the backyard, then, uncertain, retreated. Somebody managed to get into the garage. Then they heard sirens.

Luis got away but wandered back to the neighborhood a few hours later, hoping to pick up a video game from a friend. He arrived at his friend's house to find the police there. When they turned their attention to Luis, he answered their questions without hesitation. "I had at that time what I call a square mind-set," he explained. "I was not entrenched in negative gang culture or whatever you want to call it. I was just a pothead skater kid. And so I told the cops, I did this, X, Y, and Z."

"I really didn't give a fuck," he offered by way of explanation.

Listen for that phrase—what others describe as the *I don't give a fuck* attitude—for you'll hear it referenced over and over by young people whose lives have given them little reason to feel otherwise. Its simplicity is deceptive, its meaning multilayered.

I don't give a fuck about me—no one else does, so why should I?

I don't give a fuck about you—how can I, when I can't even care about myself?

I don't give a fuck what happens to me—could it get any worse than it already is?

Go ahead, lock me up. Bring it on.

Over and over, young people described to me the onset and lingering effect of the *I don't give a fuck* mentality. In a no-win paradox, some said it propelled their criminal acts and led to incarceration, while others said it was inspired *by* imprisonment.

The more I heard it described, the more it seemed this nihilism functioned as an anesthetic, self-administered by young people whose circumstances hurt too much to face with an open heart. Young people who live in the tightly restricted world of prison—stripped of control over their environment and actions—often learn to control the only thing they can: their emotional response. If they can get to that place of *I don't give a fuck*, can convince themselves that nothing really matters (an exercise made easier when life has shown them repeatedly how little *they* matter), they've tapped the source of an existential opiate, a palliative the price of which they may learn too late. The more skilled they become at constructing defenses, the harder it is to drop them, to regain even a glimmer of the openness of spirit that makes adolescence such a vivid, transformative time among the free.

Understanding the nihilism that can afflict traumatized children opens the door to imagining alternatives—responses that address "What happened to you?" along with "What did you do?" How might it change a young person's actions if, from his earliest contact with adult authority, he got the message that, yes, he *did* matter? If we helped her imagine a future that was bright enough to make freedom worth the fight? If kids are wreaking havoc because they don't give a fuck, what possibilities might open if they *did*—if we addressed their trauma rather than exacerbating it, and set our minds to helping them find reasons to care?

Barry Krisberg of the University of California, Berkeley's Chief Justice Earl Warren Institute on Law and Social Policy has been considering questions like these over decades spent talking with and advocating for incarcerated youth. "When I asked kids [inside state facilities] questions like, 'Did staff physically or verbally abuse you?'" Krisberg observed, "They'd ask, 'Worse than my parents, the foster homes, county juvenile hall?' By the time they are here, they figure this is what happens to them."

"What if we really did intervene at young ages, find the kids who are being abused?" Krisberg continued. "Our general response to kids is to throw them away, not engage and work with them."

"If you don't address what gets them to that place where they're twenty years old in shackles," he said bluntly, "then you're having a conversation about trash removal—what's the cheapest waste-removal strategy?"

"More important from a moral and political point of view is to describe who kids are, what they have confronted, their hopes and dreams for the future, and what we can do to help."

The night the murder happened (that is how Roland talks about it, using a passive construction), Roland was standing at a fork in the road—or maybe, in retrospect, at the edge of a cliff. A childhood filled with abuse and domestic violence—the protracted, futile effort to protect his mother from his drunken father's blows—had set him on what he had come to accept as his "path," toward drugs, delinquency, and a bone-deep hopelessness. But now, with the help of a supportive counselor, he was starting to feel that internal compass shifting, pointing, however tentatively, toward a different path.

He was two weeks off parole and two months away from graduating from high school. His grades were good, and his counselor was pushing for him to go to college—something he was starting to think might be possible. "Even though I was living a double life," he said, "I was trying. I thought I found a map for my success, for my happiness. I thought I was going to do a one-eighty and just live life."

"In my mind, I had good intentions. I was like, '[College] might be the key. . . . Man, this is gonna be it, I'ma do it,'" he recalled. "But even though I had those good intentions, I was still doing what I was doing, which was gangbanging."

That's where Roland was, standing at the crossroads, when the call came in. He was hanging at a friend's house when his friend's cell phone buzzed: *Something happened. We are going to retaliate. We're coming to pick you up.*

Roland demurred. *Nah, I'm good . . . I'll walk home.*

No problem, his friend told him—the crew was on its way and they could drop him off at home . . . if that was what he really wanted.

It was late, and the neighborhood was rough—Roland wasn't too thrilled at the thought of the walk home. But he had a bad feeling about riding with the crew. He was shaking his friend's hand, saying his good-byes, when his homeboys pulled up in a truck, ten strong.

Wussup, fool, you going with us?

Nah, I'm about to leave.

Come here, man, we gon' give you a ride, we gonna drop you off.

"And I was, like, you know what, let's do it . . ."

Roland's description of the rest of the evening has a passive, dreamlike quality. They rolled by a park and someone spotted a group of rival gang members. The driver hit the brakes and everyone ran out.

Even in the heat of the moment, Roland remained split: "I remember telling myself, man, something's not right. But I felt good. . . . *Well, this is who I am, we are retaliating for whatever reason, but justice is being done . . .*"

"I'm thinking, 'Man I just got myself into some bullshit. But fuck it.' I ran . . ."

From beneath a barrage of punches and kicks, the kid they were attacking seemed to be looking straight at Roland. "I remember looking at his eyes," Roland said. "There was blood everywhere . . ."

Roland swung his leg back to get in one good kick. "I just wanted to make sure I did something." He missed, and his shoe flew off. He remembers thinking it was some kind of sign. Then there were sirens, and everyone was running back to the truck. As the truck screeched away, Roland heard one of his friends crowing, "I got that fool. I stabbed him."

That was when Roland realized his white T-shirt was soaked through with blood. What the fuck was going on? What had they done?

At six thirty the next morning, the phone woke him up.

"You fools are stupid," a girl he knew was hissing, raw fury in her voice. "You fools killed somebody yesterday. He was thirteen years old. He fucking died."

Roland felt paralyzed. Over years of violence, he had never faced head-on the taking of a life. Drive-bys were one thing—shots might ring in the dark, but you'd be long gone before you had to face the consequences, and you could never be sure who had done what. Looking a boy in the eye as he bled out—that was something different, horrible and new.

For nearly an hour Roland just sat there, trying to muster the energy to flee. "I was, like, man, this shit is over. I'm going to jail for something I didn't do. . . . At the moment, I'm trying to justify 'I didn't do it.' But I am just as guilty as everybody else. I was there. I could have prevented it from happening. I could have opened my mouth."

It took a week for the police to catch up with Roland—a week in which he could barely eat or sleep. *Murder.* The word rang incessantly in his mind. *Murder* and *Why now?* and *Thirteen years old* and *Dead.* He had been so close to a different kind of life, and now two lives were over—that of the boy they had killed and his own life along with it.

When the knock came on the door a week after the crime, Roland lay down on the floor and waited. He had a pack of spearmint gum, he remembers. Mechanically, he unwrapped one piece after another.

I'm going to jail for life, he remembers thinking. *This might be the last gum I ever try.*

"I am going to detain you."

Luis froze as the words left the judge's mouth. His unsuccessful robbery attempt had taken him no farther than a few steps into an unfamiliar backyard. Now he was headed for juvenile hall. It was February 14, 2005. Luis was fifteen years old.

"My heart shook," he recalls of the moment he heard the judge's order. "I didn't know what to do."

Luis was trembling so violently as he was led from the courtroom that the bailiff asked him if he was okay. The truth, Luis understood already, would win him at best a moment's pity—the last thing he needed as he struggled to steel himself for dangers yet unknown.

"Yeah," he answered brusquely, trying to keep his voice from betraying him. It was the first lie he'd told since the misbegotten robbery attempt, but it would not be the last. Surviving behind bars, he learned very quickly, would require reinventing himself inside and out. The trauma he would experience while he was locked up—compounded by all he had weathered already—would launch him on a journey from "pothead skater kid" to card-carrying delinquent.

Slight to this day, Luis felt tiny as he entered the building where he would spend the following year. "Everyone was hella big. It was all shut off by brick. There was no sunlight in there, just bright-ass white lights."

As soon as he entered the general population, the questions began to fly: Norteño? Sureño? What gang was he claiming?

Terrified of being victimized, Luis made a decision: "I have got to start gangbanging for real, because I'm in the hall now. If I'm not down with it, then my life is threatened. If I am not with the culture in there that is aggressive and paranoid and more, then I am going to be eaten."

"It feels like a shark tank," Luis said.

Luis had known violence since he was very young, but mainly as a victim. Behind bars, the balance would shift. "I tried to prove myself immediately," he recalled. He claimed a small gang that was identified with his neighborhood, nodding at street names and pretending to recognize nicknames. He started to fight to establish credibility, taking on all comers with a manic persistence in order to make up for his size and lack of backup. He learned never to back down, flailing away until staff broke things up—interventions that constituted anything but rescue. "They would literally slam me on the ground, Mace me, and then *they* would fuck me up."

As Luis came to understand that those in charge were, like his father, more likely to hurt than protect him, his new persona hardened into something like identity. A familiar transition was under way: *I don't give a fuck about me* combined with *You don't give a fuck about me* to create that most destructive and pervasive of worldviews: *I don't give a fuck. Period. About you, about me, or about anyone else. I just don't give a fuck.*

"Originally," Luis said, "I was a pot-smoking abused kid with some trauma issues. But when I went to jail, I had to defend myself. I felt that if the system was so fucked-up that they couldn't help me, then for damn sure the other fucked-up youth weren't going to help me. But you know what? They are not going to pick on me anymore. I am not going to get taken advantage of anymore. . . . I am going to fuck you all—whoever comes against me."

This attitude offered some protection but also exposed Luis to new dangers. He caught charges for fighting on the inside and landed next at a state-run boot camp. "The only course of action that they had for me was negative reinforcement: *We are going to give you more punishment.* What the fuck—it was not hitting the core. They gave me a stricter boot-camp program. I still didn't give a fuck."

Young people sometimes describe being abused in juvenile facilities with a kind of victimized bravado. The drill sergeants at boot camp were "like ex-Marines," Luis recalled. "They slammed me and tripped me and Maced me while I was down. I would try to fight someone, or someone would fight me, and I wouldn't stop fighting. The staff would literally have to slam me on the ground, and then they would fucking fuck me up."

"I am fully gangster now," Luis recalled of the shaven-headed, reconstructed self who emerged on probation the next time around. "I am on it, I am with it, I am willing to do anything. Don't care about the consequences."

Incarceration, in other words, had done its work on Luis. The kid who had trembled his way into juvenile hall, who had been naive enough to return to a crime scene out of eagerness to play a favorite video game, was buried now beneath a veneer of bravado.

Far from being rehabilitated, Luis emerged a newly minted nihilist, the *I don't give a fuck* attitude imprinted on his soul like the freshly inked tattoos on each of his arms (one honoring his mother, the other claiming his 'hood). It was a passage one young person after another described to me, often using the same wording—*I stopped giving a fuck*—to describe the moment when they let go of hope and surrendered to prison.

"I kind of felt helpless," David remembered of his first days in juvenile hall, coming down off drugs and alcohol and waking up to the seriousness of the charges he faced. But soon, like Luis, he experienced an "excuse the language, but for lack of a better phrase, *I don't give a fuck* moment. I don't give a fuck. I don't care. . . . It was a dark time, because when that disconnect happens in my head, I really don't care about consequences. I don't care about anything."

For Luis, David, and many others, that *I don't give a fuck* moment is a crucial rite of passage, dividing the dreams of childhood from the reality of prison. "I became a man at fifteen, when I went into the system," Luis believes. "My cutoff [from childhood] was 2005, when I got locked up."

By "man," Luis appeared to mean a manufactured gangster, constructed as efficiently as if that had been the juvenile justice system's explicit intent, rather than the phenomenon it is meant to prevent. Building a gangster from the bits and pieces of an angry, wounded kid is, it turns out, no challenge at all. Take a hurt kid, look away from his wounds and allow them to fester, then drop him into a building where further trauma is just about inevitable. The next thing you know, he's covered in ink and claiming his block.

Danielle Sered, founding director of the Brooklyn-based restorative justice program Common Justice, sees this cycle frequently. In fact, it is one of the things that motivated her to launch her organization.

Sered grew up in Chicago in the 1980s, surrounded by the ravages of the crack epidemic: "It was so clear to me what incarceration did to people and to communities. People would go away and come back, and most often, something in them had been damaged. But it wasn't the will to commit crimes. It was the thing that connects us to each other. There are some people with a strength of heart and spirit that could come through even [incarceration] fully intact, but most people couldn't. For most people, that thing in us that connects us to each other, that makes us care about each other, is the thing that is under the greatest attack in a prison. So unless someone is really self-aware, or really naturally inclined to protect that part of themselves, it's hard to make it through without that being damaged."

"People came home, and they were hurt. . . . They expressed that hurt in all sorts of ways, and hurt more people, and went back [to prison]. We saw what it did to their families to have them gone. We saw what they suffered in that experience. And we saw what they did when they came back."

At first, Sered assumed that incarceration "must be bringing the victims some peace. We must at least be doing this because [those who were imprisoned] really hurt somebody, and that's what that person [who was hurt] wanted."

"But as I started listening to victims of crime, and paying attention to my own experiences, the experiences of my loved ones, of the people around me, it became very clear that our needs for safety and justice and peace were *not* being met by someone being incarcerated. So then the whole thing just seemed very silly. . . . It's expensive, it's bad for all parties, and it doesn't work."

Luis was living out the cycle Sered described. Learning to fight protected him from being targeted by his peers but jettisoned him ever deeper into the justice system. Aside from infractions committed inside facilities ostensibly devoted to his rehabilitation, his sole charge was that initial attempted burglary. Those few steps into a neighbor's backyard would draw him, like a river to the ocean, into the heart of the California Youth Authority, a state system ostensibly designed to contain the most serious offenders.

During the latter years of his incarceration, Luis became a student of the system in which he was enmeshed. "If you look at the history," he said, "juvenile justice was created to be rehabilitation. Parens patriae—it meant that the state was going to rehabilitate you, out of the hands of your parents because they couldn't control you. That's where our juvenile justice system comes from."

"Definitely, the [court] was not doing that shit," Luis concluded. "Hell no. They treated me like a monster, and I became the monster. You can't teach someone values unless you *show* them values. The only course of action they had for me was negative reinforcement. *We are going to give you more punishment, more time.* . . . A few fuck-ups later, you go to YA [State Youth Authority]."

On the day he was first released from juvenile hall, Luis said, a year after the break-in, his probation officer taunted, "I *love* your case. You have done so much shit inside juvenile hall that if you fuck up, you are going straight to YA. And you know what's going to happen then."

The PO's prediction was fulfilled within the month. It was, Luis remembers, his twenty-ninth day of freedom, and he was out with his brother when two police cars pulled up, flashing their lights.

"You got anything on you?" one officer asked.

Luis did: a four-inch kitchen knife, wrapped in a bandanna.

"Good-bye, dog," Luis called out to his little brother from the back of the cruiser, unable to wave because of the handcuffs. "I'm going to YA."

"You like fighting?" a guard asked Roland, looking him over. "Well, you're gonna love it here."

"I'm not a bitch," Roland responded carefully. "I gotta do what I gotta do."

Roland had been sentenced to juvenile life—he would be locked up for seven years, until his twenty-fifth birthday. Now he was trying to make it through intake without identifying himself as either troublemaker or target. The guards whose job it was to orient him and five other new arrivals seemed glad to break it down.

They would face violence at the hands of fellow inmates, the handcuffed boys were told, and when they did there would be no recourse. All the institution had to offer was this brief induction, a CliffsNotes distillation of the law of the jungle: "If you fight one individual, he has three friends that are going to jump in, so there ain't no one-on-ones anymore. So you better make friends soon, because this one person you going to fight has two friends, these two friends each have two friends, these two friends of two friends have two friends. So your whole time here you're going to fight. So make sure you pick a good fight, and make sure you make friends before that."

What the fuck? Roland thought. *These were the* guards *talking?*

"This ain't like prison," the intake officer reassured the newcomers. "There's no stabbing. Only slicing [with razor blades]."

Man I'm scared. . . . I'ma have to fight, I'ma have to fight. Roland began to gear himself up internally, silently giving himself a critical once-over. His first thought was that he needed to bulk up. "You need to have some sort of meat in order to fight while you in jail. In order to take somebody's punches."

On the unit, Roland wasted no time learning the ropes. The guards, he said, could unlock each cell via remote control and would entertain themselves on a slow night by clicking several locks along a hallway filled with youths who had been primed to fear one another.

"Every time the door opens, you'll jump up to make sure nobody's coming to your room," Roland recalled. "You'll be sleeping and the door opens, somebody's running to get you. [Or] you'll be laying down and sometimes you'll hear two doors open, and you just hear fighting. *Pow pow pow.* . . . Come on, really? Are the doors going to open on accident? No. [The guards] do it because they so bored in there, they want some type of entertainment. That's what we are."

Some of the staff, Roland added matter-of-factly, would beat the kids up themselves. "The staff, all they do is work out in the gym 'cause they in the jail setting, so they walking all big and muscular." Sometimes, Roland alleged, two staff members would gang up on a single ward, manipulating events so that the security cameras did not tell the full story.

"Say the staff just went inside to punch me in the face. The other one, all you see in the camera is him running in." The paperwork might say that the young target in this scenario had tried to choke the first guard, and the second had heroically come to his colleague's rescue. "Little do they know, the staff punched me and the other one jumped in."

Other times, Roland said, assaults were more straightforward: a ward mouths off and the staff "just punch him in the face and close the door."

Roland entered the Youth Authority in a different frame of mind than did Luis. The violence that had suffused his childhood had risen to the surface, and what Roland could not contain he passed on to others. He had become a danger and required intervention in the name of public safety as well as his own future—a perfect candidate, theoretically, for the juvenile justice system.

The intervention Roland received within that system, however, could not have been more counterproductive. Rather than helping Roland to quell or control his anger, every aspect of his experience behind bars seemed custom-made to exacerbate it, to turn a hurt and rageful kid into a full-grown menace.

Today, Roland understands he made a choice while locked up: "Instead of . . . telling myself I'ma do good, I said, 'I can't be a bitch.'" But just as on the outside, young people in prison make choices from among the ones they have. The bitter lesson Roland learned behind bars—hurt or be hurt—did nothing to counter what he had learned on the street and in his violent home. Instead, it reinforced that terrible dichotomy.

"If you back down in YA, you're pretty much a target," he explained. "If you let somebody step on you, everybody going to step on you and you going to be that welcome mat. That was crossing my mind—that was not going to happen; it's not. . . . I was like, I'm going to go in there and if somebody look at me wrong; if somebody said, 'You're a bitch'; if somebody laughs at me, I'm gonna fight. I'ma prove to them I'm not a bitch. Sure enough I walked in, people are looking, I'm like, 'What the fuck'—started fighting."

The same drugs and gangs with which Roland had grown up now suffused the culture in his new environment. The same ethos—predator or prey—held sway. And the "counselors" whose job was to support his rehabilitation had much in common with his abusive father: "If you're doing something not right, they're going to pepper spray you and tackle you to the ground."

When Roland's probation officer had told him he was a smart kid who could go to college, he started to see himself as someone with a future. Inside the Youth Authority, he got a different message. Again, he adapted to these expectations.

Young people in general rise or fall to meet adult expectations. A system that expects violence, dishonesty, and minimal potential from and for the young people under its care is likely to get just that. A system or intervention that manages to communicate higher expectations—one that holds *aspirations* for those in its care, that wants more for them than, at best, not to recidivate—will not only get better responses from those in its custody; it is much more likely to win their respect. And mutual respect is key to working with young people toward not just compliance but genuine transformation, to helping them meet the various demands imposed upon them but also, ultimately, to find and pursue goals of their own. To grow up, in other words.

9

THE THINGS THEY CARRY

Juvenile Reentry

Society takes upon itself the right to inflict appalling punishment on the individual, but it also has the supreme vice of shallowness, and fails to realize what it has done. When the man's punishment is over, it leaves him to himself; that is to say, it abandons him at the very moment when its highest duty towards him begins. It is really ashamed of its own actions, and shuns those whom it has punished, as people shun a creditor whose debt they cannot pay, or one on whom they have inflicted an irreparable, an irremediable wrong.

—Oscar Wilde, *De Profundis*

Breathe in, breathe out, count to ten . . .

"It's useless!" David exclaimed, shaking his head in frustration at the recollection. "I've been to three anger managements and I still got an anger problem."

Behind bars, David had busied himself amassing vocational certificates: food handling; culinary arts; heating, ventilation, and air-conditioning. He took classes on interview skills, wrote practice résumés, filled out sample job applications, and read self-help books in his spare time—did everything he could to prepare himself for life on the outside.

No one had promised David his post-prison path would be easy. But neither had anyone warned him of the truth about the stack of certificates he had worked so hard to gain—that they would have the value of Monopoly money once employers learned he had earned them behind bars. Now, as one application after another garnered no more than a glance, David's faith in the future was rapidly deflating.

"Reentry"—returning home from a time behind bars—is where the rubber hits the road when it comes to juvenile justice policy and practice: the moment when the efficacy of incarceration itself is tested. For far too many young people—in fact, the great majority—it is also where the tires blow.

A review of multiple studies found that 70 to 80 percent of youth released from juvenile facilities are rearrested within two or three years. The long-term picture is even bleaker. In New York, for example, 89 percent of boys released from state facilities in the early 1990s went on to be arrested as adults. A South Carolina study reached similar conclusions: 82 percent of youth who were incarcerated as juveniles ended up in the adult system down the line. Most ominously, a Montreal study found that involvement in the juvenile system was the single strongest predictor of adult incarceration. "Holding other factors constant, youth incarcerated as juveniles were 38 times as likely as youth with equivalent backgrounds and offending histories to be sanctioned for crimes they committed as adults."

That most of those who are locked up as teenagers return to prison as juveniles, adults, or both amounts to something greater than a failure of reentry planning. It reflects the failure of the entire enterprise. If juvenile incarceration sends the great majority of those affected—many of whom first enter the system on minor charges—into a gauntlet of escalating sanctions, it is failing at its central mission: to enhance the safety of the free and improve the prospects of those whose freedom has been taken.

Each year, roughly one hundred thousand young people under age eighteen are released from secure juvenile facilities. According to the National Juvenile Justice and Delinquency Prevention Coalition, many "are placed back into neighborhoods with few youth supportive programs, high crime rates, poverty, and poor performing schools. Public safety is compromised when youth leaving out-of-home placement are not afforded necessary planning and supportive services upon reentering their communities, increasing the likelihood of recidivism."

More services are certainly needed, but reentry plans and programs, even if available, rarely get to the root of the problem. Young people returning from juvenile facilities face a daunting array of challenges, both external and internal, from limited employment prospects and curtailed education to post-traumatic stress and an institutional mind-set that may have helped them get through prison but works against them on the outside. In this context, the fact that the majority do *not* manage to stay free—that being locked up as a juvenile, no matter how minor the initiating offense, so often leads to a cycle of escalating recidivism and re-incarceration—is hardly surprising. Given the obstacles juvenile incarceration places in young people's paths, the greater surprise is that *any* manage to stay free.

"It's like being naked in a snowstorm," Cherie said of her return to the "free world." Seven years out of a juvenile facility, she had only just managed to get her record sealed and obtain her first job, working at McDonald's for minimum wage. In Washington, D.C., David was facing that same blizzard.

David was seventeen when he was convicted of armed robbery. Now he was twenty-two. He had done his time, learned his lesson, and was ready to begin anew. That was all he wanted now—an honest life, a decent living—he said with an earnestness that bordered on desperation. Wasn't that the point of those years behind bars—to teach him exactly this lesson, instill these very goals? But now, in a cruel twist, he was learning that *because* of his time locked up and the stigma that came with it, the goals he had so successfully internalized were out of his reach.

"That's where most of my anger comes from," David said. "Everywhere I apply, it's like, 'Your background, your background.' That's the only thing I hear back from the jobs. 'You meet the qualifications, but your background check . . .'"

David has good reason to worry about his job prospects. A number of studies document the negative impact that juvenile incarceration has on future employment—not only immediately post-release, but well into adulthood. The National Bureau of Economic Research has found that being locked up as a juvenile reduced total time spent working over the following decade by 25 to 30 percent. Even fifteen years down the line, those who had been incarcerated as teens worked significantly less than those who had not. Further research has found that a criminal record cuts in half the chance that an applicant will get a return call, much less a job offer. If the applicant is black, the negative effect of a criminal conviction is even more extreme. In D.C., where David, who is black, was trying to find work, the *Washington Post* has reported that nearly half of the District's former prisoners are unemployed.

The negative relationship between juvenile incarceration and subsequent employment affects not only individuals but entire communities. The National Bureau of Economic Research found that incarcerating large numbers of young people from a particular neighborhood has "a negative effect on the economic well-being of their communities. Places that rely most heavily on incarceration reduce the employment opportunities in their communities compared to places that deal with crime by means other than incarceration."

The national tendency to rely most heavily on incarceration in poor neighborhoods of color creates a vicious cycle for the youth who grow up in, and return to, these communities. "Areas with the most rapidly rising rates of incarceration," according to the same research, "are areas in which youths, particularly African-American youths, have had the worst earnings and employment experience."

The crooked bottom line? Unemployment leads to incarceration, which leads to unemployment, which leads to incarceration—a cycle that buffets those most likely to face job discrimination to begin with.

Perhaps this despair-inducing cycle had something to do with why David found the anger management class such a bitter pill to swallow. It wasn't just that he had the curriculum memorized, having been through similar courses repeatedly, starting at age twelve. The problem, he explained, was that he was angry for a *reason*. And that reason—economic desperation and the helplessness he felt to escape it by legal means—was the same at twenty-two as it had been at twelve. Swallowing his anger would not put food on the table.

Locked up for the first time at the age of twelve, David had spent nearly half his life to date behind bars, only to find himself, post-release, facing the very dilemma that had propelled him into delinquency to begin with. He was broke—survival broke—and he could not get a job.

David is the oldest of four children raised by a single mother. His anger was born early on, from doing without and feeling helpless to do a thing about it. "You ain't making it. You're barely getting school clothes, and once you get older . . . you hear from your peers, 'You're dirty,' or 'You keep wearing the same thing.' So that starts putting in your head, 'I want to hustle.'"

Seeing his mother struggle was particularly hard to handle. "She cared, but as a single mother, she can only do so much. I was getting tired of her having to ask people for stuff."

David was still in grade school when he took it on himself to help provide for his own needs and those of his family. "In my environment, you can do that," he explained. "Where I'm from, you can do it at twelve. . . . You can't really get a job at that age—you're too young. [So] you gonna hustle. You gonna rob."

Later on, locked up in a series of juvenile institutions, David was offered a different lens on the world, and his own place within it. Crime, he was taught—even what felt like a crime of survival—was not inevitable; it was a *choice*. He was accountable for his actions, no matter the circumstance. The good news, he was promised, was that making better choices would lead to better outcomes.

Over time, David accepted—even internalized—this ethos. He has not yet given up on it, but his post-prison experience has made it hard to keep the faith. With every "good choice" he makes, each job application he seeks out and submits, comes not only rejection but the same disheartening message: not "Sorry kid—keep trying," but "Sorry, kid—don't bother." Once they learned about his criminal record, it seemed to David, potential employers made it clear not just that he was out of luck this time around, but that he was out of the running before the race even began. He was trying to stay hopeful, or at least patient, but with each rejection he felt more like the desperate, unemployable twelve-year-old who got locked up the first time than the new man his stack of certificates attested he had become.

The "post-prison punishment" young people describe comes in many forms, but our widespread unwillingness to offer a second chance in the form of a job is among the most insidious. It reveals the gaping hole in the story we tell ourselves: at bottom, we do *not* believe that reformatories reform. Those young people who walk out the gates and into a wall learn that "paying their debt to society" is a fool's errand. That debt, many learn, will be with them forever, accruing compound interest and blocking their prospects everywhere they turn.

The young man rejected from more jobs than he can count comes face-to-face with a cruel reality: our nation—founded on a belief in new beginnings—does not believe in the possibility of redemption, at least not for all. The scarlet *C*, mark of the convict, can never be erased.

Because David was charged as a juvenile, there was light at the end of the tunnel: once he was off probation, he could petition to have his record sealed and then renew his job search without the barrier of the "ex-con" label. The problem was the distance of that light. He had three full years of probation ahead of him, longer than he could get by without a source of income. A different kind of kid might see that as a setup.

The temptation of quick money had not dissipated, David admitted. It assailed him "every day." But he had not succumbed, he said adamantly, and did not intend to.

What kept him afloat was his closest relationships. "When I start feeling that way, I call my girlfriend or a friend. Or I call my mother, and say, 'Ma, I'm tired. I'm tired of not being able to get a job.' She's still getting help from welfare. I'm the oldest son, so to see my mother still struggling after so many years—I mean, what's next? I'm tempted every day to get back out there and get some fast money, but I'm not about to go back out there. I look at the risks: *I'm about to leave my family again. They're gonna be struggling worse. I'm about to do some more time. This time I can never see the streets again.*"

So David counts to ten, and he calls, and he breathes, and he waits. Three years is a long time, but eventually he will be off probation. After that, under D.C. law, he must wait two more before he can petition to have his juvenile record sealed. *Then*, he believes—he has to believe—he will find work and begin his new life.

Until then, one wonders how exactly he is expected to manage. No matter how deeply he breathes, he cannot live on air.

The myriad practical challenges young returnees face—from the quest for work and housing to the rules and requirements of probation—are only the beginning. There is also the internal battle: the struggle to reclaim their humanity after the psychological conditioning that prison life entails.

Will has struggled with shaking the old rules and rebuilding himself. "The skills you learn in jail to survive are the opposite," he explained, of those likely to lead to success on the outside, whether in college, at work, or in personal relationships.

A true Californian with a multiethnic background that spans several continents, a dean's list college student with a prestigious scholarship, and a loyal ally to old friends who have not left the 'hood, Will fits in seamlessly wherever he goes while maintaining an unmistakable sense of himself. Since his release, Will has been successful by just about any measure. On the inside, however, he remains conflicted: saddled, he said, with habits of mind that got him through the years in the California Youth Authority but now just get in his way.

Fifteen the day he entered the Youth Authority, Will was twenty-one by the time he was released—officially a man. On the outside, six years had passed, but for Will it felt as if time had frozen. "I thought everything would be the same," he recalled.

His first weeks of freedom were a time of disillusionment. When he tried to reconnect with old friends, he discovered that many had moved on without him. Many of those released from juvenile prisons, he pointed out, enter as adolescents and emerge as adults from systems that can keep them until their twenty-first or even twenty-fifth birthday, depending on state law. These are the very years when most young lawbreakers who are *not* incarcerated grow out of delinquency.

Those who are locked up during this period lose years that are crucial both developmentally and pragmatically. Late adolescence and early adulthood are periods of rapid brain growth, when the adult brain—with its more sophisticated capacity for decision making, independent thinking, and looking toward the future—develops, a process that is profoundly affected by a young person's environment. Rather than spending these years laying the foundation for life as an adult, young prisoners live them in a state of suspended animation, where the focus on survival dwarfs all thought of the future, and the otherwise gradual transition from dependence to self-sufficiency is undermined by the enforced dependency of prison life.

"Juveniles and young adults may be incarcerated during a key developmental phase of adolescence," according to the *Journal of Juvenile Justice*.

"Lacking the necessary skills to cope with adult responsibilities when they are released, many youth face unemployment, school re-enrollment challenges, and homelessness upon release."

"The transition getting out is actually harder than being in jail, in my opinion," said Will. "They bring you in as a youngster and let you go as an adult, so you've never had the opportunity to be independent. You go in at fifteen, sixteen, you're still dependent on your family. You go into a system and you're dependent on *them* for food and shelter. Then all of a sudden they let you out. I was twenty-one when they let me out. So at twenty-one, now all of a sudden you're a grown man and you got to learn all these things for yourself."

Dating, for example—the romantic relationships young people may pine for in prison—can seem infinitely complex. It's not just the stigma of a criminal record. There are also all those missed years to make up for. "You're in an environment that is all males," Will explained. "Then when you get out and try to connect with a woman on an intimate level, it's tough." He doesn't just mean emotionally. Even the practical aspects have to be relearned—or learned for the first time.

Will was twenty-one and had not been on a date since he was fifteen. "I was a kid," he said, laughing a bit at his adolescent innocence. Back then, "all you had to do was ask a girl, 'Will you go with me?' and it'll be all right. But now if I ask a girl, 'Would you go with me?' she'll be like, 'Where, and in what car?'"

"It's not about just your relationship with the girl anymore," he has since learned. "It's about what you can offer her. When you're grown, it's like, 'Does he live by himself? Does he have a car? Does he have money?'" Few recently released young men can answer these questions in the affirmative.

Even worse than the difficulty connecting with others was the unsettling sense that Will had somehow lost touch with *himself*, that prison had transformed him in fundamental ways. *Walk a straight line, be quiet, if you want to earn your privileges.* A quick study, Will found he had internalized all too well the ethos of submission and conformity that prison life demanded.

"Here," on the other hand—by which he means both the whole of the world, where he has had to learn anew to make his way, and, particularly, the unfamiliar environment of a college campus—"you have to speak out to get what you need."

Will understood this intellectually, but overcoming years of indoctrination and habit was another matter. "It's not just the isolation," he explained. "It's the personality traits. I developed traits in there that are not useful to me out here."

He spoke, for example, of the erosion of individuality in an environment where there is "just one set of rules to follow from someone I don't even know. . . . *Talk is dead*. With no *why*. I am very inquisitive. 'Why do I have to be quiet?' You can't even ask. If you tell me, 'Will, it's okay to use the bathroom,' that's what I go off of. Why wasn't it okay half an hour ago?"

Even when the guards were not watching and gauging his behavior, other young wards were. As a result, Will said, "Now, sometimes I don't feel motivated unless I am feeling watched, to where, if I am by myself, I will be real lazy. In order for me to be motivated to act, I need to feel like I am being watched."

"To this day," he acknowledged, being alone was hard for him, as was acting independently—much as he had ached for that very independence during the years behind bars. "I don't feel right unless I have someone telling me, 'This is the right thing to do.' Someone who's watching me. Am I walking in a straight line? Even when I am by myself, I am wondering how do I look, am I doing the right thing?" Will said, describing the sense of "constant surveillance" that his experience behind bars had etched into his consciousness.

"Even to this day, I really care what people think of me," he revealed—a concern that his direct and confident manner masks entirely—"and I don't even know why."

The mind games and power plays that are part of getting by in prison, Will believes, eroded his ability to take others at face value. "When people are being nice to me now, or trying to be courteous, I always get kind of—like if people offer me something, there has to be an ulterior motive. That's another internalized idea I got from jail. I can't just receive something from somebody as a gift without feeling like there's something attached to it. 'What do you want from me?' I don't trust genuine giving."

Allowing the experience of incarceration to calcify into an identity—difficult to resist within a system and a society that encourage, if not enforce, this very identification—is, Will implies, the greatest impediment to recovering one's freedom. Shaking off that identity is central to the struggle to reenter the world as something other than an "ex-con."

At bottom, said Will, "a lot of it has to do with language. We own stuff, as if it's our identity. Like when I say, 'I am angry,' as if that is who I *am*, when really, I *feel* angry. It is temporary. Or when you are in jail: 'I *am* a convict.' No, you're not. You made a mistake and you had to do some jail time. But you should not identify with those kinds of labels."

"Once you identify, you internalize those things," Will continued. "So people come out, like, 'I am a convict.' That is so internalized, you can't break away from that. How can you expect to be a normal member of society when you have got that stigma? . . . A lot of people I talk to aren't even aware of it—that this subconscious idea is actually a motivating factor for why they are still having problems out here."

"If I am, five years from now, still talking about something a CO [correctional officer] did years ago? He's not even thinking about me and here I am still mad because, I don't know, he yelled at me or looked at me the wrong way. I don't want to give them that power. I want to be out here talking about 'Yeah, I was in prison but I went to college, I did this and that.'"

For now, his continuing struggle to find his footing has led him to a conclusion that is at once heartbreaking and hopeful in its clarity and logic: "It doesn't make sense to take a kid *out* of the community to show him how to live *in* the community."

Throughout history and across cultures, the transition from child to adult has been marked by rites of passage: bar mitzvah, confirmation, walkabout, vision quest, graduation, prom, fraternity pledge, and more. Anthropologists describe these rites of passage in terms of phases: separation, transition, and, finally, reincorporation. "Reincorporation is characterized by elaborate rituals and ceremonies, like debutante balls and college graduation, and by outward symbols of new ties: thus in rites of incorporation there is widespread use of the 'sacred bond,' the 'sacred cord,' the knot, and of analogous forms such as the belt, the ring, the bracelet and the crown."

Those who are locked up during this pivotal transition experience separation, but there are for them no "rites of incorporation." Instead of the bond and the knot, the ring or the crown—symbols of inclusion, connection, and status—they wear only the brand of the ex-offender. Over and over, as this identity leads to repeated exclusion and rejection, they learn that for them there may be no "reincorporation."

Two in ten, bro. Two in ten.

Will and Luis—two young men who had managed to stay free in a state with a juvenile recidivism rate that topped 80 percent—gave each another an ironic fist bump along with this sardonic congratulation. *Two in ten, bro. Gotta represent.*

Only two of every ten youths who get locked up, they are saying, are expected or even *allowed* to stay free. Those who do become the poster children, role models, heroes—the boy who comes back from the war with, to borrow from Salinger, "all his f-a-c-u-l-t-i-e-s intact." Carrying the weight of living for those they left behind in prison while proving to the world that they are more than "ex-offenders," some show signs of a premature weariness that resembles survivor's guilt.

Will and Luis were doing well enough that they could afford a joke, however bitter, about the bleak odds those in their position face. For others, there is only fear. Fear, in fact, seemed nearly universal among those I met who had recently been released. Those who are still on parole or probation feel it intensely—the fear that they could be sent back to prison for a "technical violation" of the terms of their parole, losing their precarious freedom for an act, such as associating with the wrong people, that would not be considered a crime were they not marked as ex-offenders. Even for those who have finished their probation, this anxiety can be as hard to shake as the stigma of having been locked up. It is worst of all for those who have accrued "strikes" in a state such as California, which allows juvenile strikes to justify decades-long sentences even for minor crimes down the line.

Tony, for example, left prison with two strikes. He had been out for several months when I met him, but the fear had not faded. He woke each morning "terrified I could be sentenced to life in prison for anything. Just being at the wrong place at the wrong time, not even committing a crime, because there are cases of people being sentenced to twenty-five to life for doing not much of anything."

The fear alone is burden enough. But on a deeper level, Tony understands his status as a "second-striker" as a stain he can never erase. That he and those in the same boat can be locked up, perhaps for life, for actions that would draw only minor sanctions for others sends a strong message that they are fundamentally and irredeemably other, part of a criminal caste to whom different rules apply.

No matter how well Tony is doing, his freedom feels contingent. He deals with this by being constantly watchful, restricting his activities in order to avoid any hint of danger.

"There are places I have never gone," he explained. "Like a club. There is no point for me to go clubbing. Say there is a bunch of rowdy people. Maybe some of them . . . just want to pick up hot girls. And if I just so happen to be casually talking to one [girl] and this idiot is trying to—you know, he's drunk and all—I'm going to [get into it with] this dude because I want to look good for this girl. *No.* I'm not going to put myself in that situation. And I never will."

Tony appeared certain of his own willpower: he would not let his guard down, nor make himself vulnerable. But he also understood how much lay beyond his control. "My concern is the stigma that is attached to an ex-felon, an ex-con," he explained. If people—especially authorities—learn he has two strikes, he fears, that is all they will care to know. "They are not going to think, 'You were only a kid.' . . . So if I was at the wrong place at the wrong time, something happens, who is our first suspect? Me, right? 'Let me see your ID. . . . Okay. You're coming in.' "

Researchers have studied the thorny issue of juvenile reentry from virtually every angle, trying to figure out why our nation's youth prisons have such a dismal track record when it comes to turning out returnees who are able to regain their footing and find their way to a stable life.

Darren, whose analytic bent allowed him to squeeze an education out of his incarceration, offered a new and challenging theory as to why so many young ex-prisoners—his co-defendants, for example—wind up back in prison. Several years out, Darren did his best to keep up with the five others who had been sentenced along with him, but it was no easy task. All but one were incarcerated, scattered in adult institutions across the state, part of the 70 to 80 percent of underage prisoners who emerge "uncorrected" from their stays in juvenile correctional facilities.

Given the experiences that shaped their thinking during the crucial adolescent years, Darren proposed, some may be making a conscious decision not to participate in a society they feel has given them no reason to trust its fundamental tenets: that if they play by the rules, they will be treated fairly; that hard work now will pay off later; that the basic components of the American dream—work that pays, relationships that last, and those famous American freedoms—might be within their reach. If nothing in their experience has taught them this lesson, and no one in authority ever held out such a hope, *is* playing ball a rational choice?

In his own life, Darren has offered a vociferous *yes*. Working as a liasion between homeless people and businesses while attending college, he is determined not to let the decade he spent behind bars deter or define him. But the fact that so few of the friends of his youth have taken the same route is, to him, entirely comprehensible.

"I have friends who don't want to work, they don't want to pay taxes, because of the traumatizing experiences they had within the infrastructure of the system," he explained. "They are conscious as to why they choose the position in society that they do, after coming through an experience like that."

"Not only that," he continued, "but some have the perspective that people who were paying taxes that paid for [their incarceration] were responsible, so if they do harm to those people, they don't really care, because they feel like [the taxpayers] failed *them* in the first place. That's a position that some of these young so-called prisoners, re-enterers, violators, hold."

There is a dreadful simplicity to the phenomenon of juvenile recidivism as Darren presents it. Consider, he challenges, what is asked of children raised by prison guards, who come into adulthood chained, cuffed, beaten, and treated as less than human. Darren remembers vividly the way the guards who spent two weeks watching over kneeling, handcuffed youths joked and laughed in the face of their suffering, as if these young people mattered so little that they were not just invisible but entirely dispensable. Just as the child raised in the glow of a parent's loving gaze learns empathy, a child raised under the hostile stare of the prison guard—or, worse, his clear indifference—draws from that experience a sense of what one human being owes another. What strength must it take for this latter child *not* to learn to emulate his keepers; not to lose the capacity for empathy; not, once freed, simply to take what he needs but has never been given, or even permitted to earn.

Behind bars, Jared learned to inhabit a radical present. "From when they take the lock off the gate and say it's time to come out to when it's time to go back in the cell, you're not worried about tomorrow," he recalled. "Just worry about today. That becomes big: just one day at a time."

At the same time, prison demanded constant vigilance, a split self always watching the angles. "Anything could happen at any time. You're watching everybody and everybody's watching you. You're *watching* everybody watch you watch them."

It has been years since Jared walked out the gates. Still, he said, "I gotta watch everything." Like Tony, he left with two strikes under California's three strikes law, and the slightest altercation could send him back for life. Jared described the hypervigilance this knowledge required of him, sharing the anxious cadence of his internal monologue: *Who's the guy on the corner over there? Why is his left arm stiff? Why is he wearing that jacket when it's eighty degrees outside? Say he's posted at the stop sign. Or the light turns green, and he's still standing there. Maybe I don't want to walk over there. Who are these three dudes coming down the street? Where are they from? Look at how they dress.*

It struck me again how readily the habits of thinking essential to adapting to life behind bars could become maladaptive post-release. Incarceration not only fails to rehabilitate young minds; it more often warps them, damaging young people's spirits in ways that are difficult to repair. "One day at a time" may get you through a sentence, but it's not going to get you into college, much less through it. The capacity to live and think only in the moment is not a quality valued by employers, and habitual mistrust makes it hard to forge new bonds both professionally and personally. On top of the multiple external barriers Jared and others faced—the stigma of a record, the barriers to employment—those who fared best in prison often had it hardest on the outside, having adapted all too well to an artificial reality whose values and mores were in direct conflict with those of the larger world.

No one was more aware of this than Jared himself. He described sitting in a restaurant with his girlfriend, waiting to pick up a takeout order. Suddenly Jared realized he was sitting with his back toward the door. Absorbed in conversation and very much in love, he'd let fall his cloak of watchfulness and granted himself a fleeting taste of freedom. But the moment he realized that he had let his guard down, however briefly, he froze back up again. On the surface, he remained relaxed and engaged, continuing to talk with his girlfriend, but his mind was no longer with her. Instead he was distracted by a tense inner dialogue between his past and present selves.

You're sitting with your back to the door.

Don't trip. Nobody's going to come through that door trying to do anything to you. Don't worry about it. There's nobody here to harm you.

"I'm looking at all this stuff. I try not to let that leak out, to be obvious. But that's in my head."

Jared's girlfriend may not notice these small lapses in attention, but she knows him well enough to be attuned to behaviors he picked up behind bars. "One of the biggest things she says is that I always look at somebody with a prison mentality—like they're trying to punk me, as in bully me, or get over on me, or belittle me in some way. Because I've got to have my respect. . . . If there's no respect or if the respect ain't reciprocal, I don't want to deal with you. I will survive another day without you in my life."

Jared laughed drily before returning his attention to the lasting effects of his incarceration. "I don't have many friends. I got one, one friend. I have no other friends, and I can't say that's by choice. It just is. But I'm not walking around, 'Hey, you want to be my friend?' I'm not doing that."

There was a pause while Jared seemed to think this through. "Maybe that's part of the prison still stuck inside."

"There's stuff that gets instilled in you from going to places like [prison], and it never leaves," he continued pensively. "There's no way to unlearn it. It's like eating with a fork. You ain't going to unlearn that. It just ain't going to happen."

The tension is strongest when he's out with his girlfriend. His love for her, he understands, is his Achilles' heel. "The wolf recognizes the wolf," he began, contemplating the protectiveness he feels when he is with her—an emotion strong enough to threaten his sense of control. "I'm not trying to be the wolf. I don't want to be a wolf. But I can definitely recognize the wolf. I don't want to be that. God forbid one of these knuckleheads says something to her . . ."

"I'm a human being," he added abruptly, as if that had somehow been called into question. "I want the same things that you want. Basic human needs. I want love, you know? I want to be able to go to the park and hold hands with my girlfriend, or watch my kids play. I want to go to the movie theater. I want to feed my family."

"Yeah, that's another one," he said with increasing heat. "Poverty and crime—they're directly connected, which is basically connected to education. You don't have education, you're not getting a good paying job, unless somehow you get lucky."

In a few short sentences, Jared had summarized the vicious cycle that overtakes the youngest prisoners—those whose lives are quite literally arrested before they have truly begun. Inside juvenile lockups, many young people come to see—are *encouraged* to see—education as a holy grail, the only way there is to beat the revolving door. For those few who can find the means to pursue it—especially those who make it into and through college—education can in fact fulfill this promise. A door to employment and a buffer against recidivism, a diploma also functions as an antidote to stigma, debunking the notion that its holder will never be more than an "ex-con." It is also extraordinarily difficult to obtain, given the myriad barriers that young returnees face.

"Ten years ago today, I got out of the California Youth Authority battered and bruised by such an ignorant system," Will recently posted online, alongside cap-and-gown photos from his community college graduation in which he is clearly exultant. "Today, I just got accepted to UC Berkeley. A cold cell didn't help me change. Education did! BOOKS NOT BARS! I AM RIDING HIGH RIGHT NOW AND LOVING EVERY MINUTE OF IT!!!"

Few of his cohorts will experience this crucial rite of passage. Even as research confirms that education is key to staving off recidivism, so does it document the myriad ways in which juvenile incarceration *curtails* education—not just putting it on hold but often ending it entirely. Fewer than 15 percent of kids who get locked up in the ninth grade will make it through high school, and many will never return to the classroom at all. Completing the vicious cycle, an individual without a high school degree is three and a half times more likely to be arrested than is a high school graduate.

Researchers who have investigated why it is so difficult to resume an education that has been interrupted by incarceration point to delays in records transfers, lack of specialized services, inadequate planning, and poor coordination among agencies. Then there is the fact that some juvenile offenses are grounds for expulsion. Justice for Families—an organization comprised of parents and other relatives of young people who have been involved with the justice system—interviewed one thousand family members about their experiences. Sixty-nine percent reported that they faced obstacles when they tried to get their children back into school after release, despite the fact that truancy is often a probation violation as well as a new offense—one of the many catch-22s young returnees face.

I am a human being, Jared had said. *I want the same things that you want.*

Work, love, play, family: these are the bricks from which a life is built. For Jared and so many other young people, being locked up as teenagers had pushed these goals out of reach, again in a vicious cycle that lasted long after they walked out the gates: an interrupted education curtails employment prospects, making it hard to support—and so to form—a family.

That juvenile incarceration was, in the moment, profoundly dehumanizing was something my conversations with young people had made painfully clear. What I had not quite understood was how a youthful incarceration might shape a life indefinitely; that despite the rhetoric of rehabilitation, clean slates, and new beginnings, what is stripped away behind prison walls is so very hard to retrieve.

PART II

Burning Down the House

10

A NEW WAVE OF REFORM

A crisis is a terrible thing to waste.

—Paul Romer, professor of economics, Stern
School of Business, New York University

THE STORY OF JUVENILE justice is often told in terms of pendulum swings between the opposing goals of rehabilitation and punishment. These swings, however regular, have been limited in range. Whether we tell ourselves that what goes on behind the gates of the juvenile prison is intended to punish or to heal, the legitimacy of placing children in locked facilities is not fundamentally challenged.

Still, after decades during which the growth of the nation's youth prisons seemed inexorable, we find ourselves today in the midst of a shift of a magnitude that would have seemed inconceivable even a decade ago. Across the country, the number of juveniles who are incarcerated is plummeting. But whether the current era will be remembered simply as a particularly vigorous swing of a familiar pendulum or heralded as a moment of genuine transformation remains to be seen.

Over the course of a single decade, the number of juveniles confined in local and state facilities in the United States dropped 39 percent, from a high of 108,802 in 2000 to 66,332 in 2010—a low not seen since 1985. So far, this trend shows no sign of slowing. In fact, it has picked up speed in recent years. Fewer juvenile prisoners means fewer juvenile prisons: between 2007 and 2011, eighteen states closed more than fifty facilities in all.

States that were notorious for the fervor with which they locked up their

young—California, Louisiana, New York, Illinois, Texas, and others—
have shifted course, some radically. In some of the nation's largest and
most prison-happy states, the reductions in juvenile incarceration rates
have been particularly dramatic. California, for instance, cut the daily
population in state-run juvenile facilities from about 10,000 in 1996 to
922 in June 2012—a drop of more than 90 percent. Likewise, in the years
since the Texas Youth Commission was rocked by a sexual abuse scandal
in the mid-1990s, Texas has closed nine state-run youth corrections facilities. The number of young people in Texas state juvenile institutions went
from 4,700 in fiscal year 2006 to 1,500 in 2012.

This good news is tempered by the fact that conditions in many state
facilities remain inhumane and intolerable. Beyond this central wrong lies
an array of other concerns. In California, which has achieved its population cuts largely by transferring responsibility for young lawbreakers from
the state to the counties, an emerging issue is "justice by geography." Some
counties are responding to the new mandate to keep kids near home with
imagination and courage, asking multiple local agencies to collaborate to
devise effective community-based responses. Other counties, however,
are spending state funds now earmarked for local juvenile justice efforts
to build new lockups or expand those that exist. While it is too soon to say
with any certainty how the big picture will shake out, recent research indicates that despite the massive cuts at the state level, when local placements
are accounted for, California still incarcerates more youth than any other
state in the nation. The state's juvenile incarceration rate (the percentage
of the youth population that is locked up) remains among the highest in
the nation.

A related concern is whether conditions in local facilities—existing or
new—will be significantly better than those in the state lockups they are
replacing. A recent class action lawsuit against California's Contra Costa
County does not auger well on this front. The suit alleges that juveniles
with mental health problems are held in "unconscionable conditions" in
that county's juvenile hall—most egregiously, that mentally ill youth are
kept in solitary confinement without regard to their condition, sometimes
for months.

According to Laura Faer of Public Counsel, one of several groups that
collaborated on the suit, overall conditions at the juvenile hall resemble

those in maximum-security prisons—exactly the situation the shift to the counties was intended to remedy. Wards "are routinely locked for days and weeks at a time in cells that have barely enough room for a bed and only a narrow window the size of a hand," Faer told a reporter.

The suit cites California law, which declares that juvenile halls exist for the purpose of rehabilitation and "shall not be deemed to be, nor treated as, a penal institution [but as] a safe and supportive homelike environment."

One problem that has *not* come up as states close large congregate facilities is a rise in juvenile crime. Juvenile crime rates have been declining across the board, and violent crime fell 27 percent among juveniles nationwide between 1997 and 2007. Try as they might to claim credit for this trend, the tough-on-tots crowd can't make their case. Juvenile crime rates have dropped across the country, but the drop has been steepest in those states that have *reduced* their reliance on juvenile incarceration. The throw-the-book-at-'em regions have seen more modest declines.

As they shut down large institutions, states including Texas and California have passed new laws that limit state-level confinement to those who have committed serious offenses (felonies in Texas and serious and violent felonies in California). New York is moving in a similar direction with the 2012 Close to Home Act, which calls for New York City to send only the most serious juvenile offenders into state custody. The city will keep the rest under local jurisdiction, relying on contracts with community agencies. Even before Close to Home went into effect, New York had closed eighteen of its thirty-two state facilities.

This shift has opened the door to questions we have, until recently, barely dared consider. Do we actually *need* the juvenile prison—at least in the large-scale, state-run form we have tolerated for so long? Or have its costs, both financial and human, finally become so exorbitant, and the harm it wreaks so evident, that we might just find we can get by without it?

For the moment, these questions remain unanswered. But the changes that have taken place over the last decade are significant enough to warrant asking them not just theoretically but in the political forum.

The shift of the last decade also cries out for some kind of explanation. The flaws in the institution of the juvenile prison are certainly not breaking news. In fact, there is evidence that these places have been hurting kids since they first opened their doors under the House of Refuge banner in the 1800s. This long-standing evidence of harm to children, however, has not previously inhibited us from dispatching children to state institutions. Even when the ideological pendulum swung toward rehabilitation, it did not lead to the kind of large-scale closure of facilities we are seeing today.

The rationale for closing these costly, inhumane failures has been laid out in the preceding pages and made by countless scholars and survivors again and again. The question before us is not so much "Why?" as it is "Why *now?*"

If one were to autopsy the fifty-plus juvenile prisons that have closed in recent years, one would find not a single cause of death but, most often, a combination of contributing factors. When one draws the lens back to encompass those states that have undergone the most dramatic changes, a formula, or recipe, begins to emerge.

First there is scandal: misuse and maltreatment of children that goes beyond the ordinary, and some means of ensuring that these events reach the public eye.

In Florida, there were bodies: a secret graveyard behind one of the state's oldest facilities, and stories of boys beaten until bits of their flesh became stuck to the walls. In Pennsylvania, there was bribery: judges caught lining their pockets with kickbacks in return for sending children to for-profit prisons for negligible offenses. In Texas, revelations of widespread sexual abuse blew up into a scandal that engulfed much of the system. In Arkansas, an exposé in the *Democrat-Gazette* revealed that young prisoners were "routinely degraded; verbally, physically and sexually abused; hogtied; forced to sleep outside in freezing weather," and more.

The prison's own panopticon began to turn against it, as security cameras captured footage of guards brutalizing the children in their care—breaking ribs with their boots as they stomped the bodies of their unresisting charges, or setting dogs upon terrified boys who had thrown themselves to the floor in an effort to protect their faces from the animals' teeth. As images such as these turned up on the evening news, the message was increasingly difficult to miss: parens patriae was not, after all, a very good parent. In fact, all too often, it was very bad indeed.

The lawsuits that followed were as inevitable as they were unwinnable for the state defendants. There were dozens of them, all across the country, alleging violations of civil rights in multiple facilities or entire state systems. Armed with evidence of sickening abuses and inhumane conditions, the plaintiffs regularly prevailed. These legal victories brought not only more bad press but sweeping consent decrees that threatened the status of juvenile prisons as self-governing fiefdoms, above the laws and conventions by which others were bound.

The federal Department of Justice sent its own investigators, filed its own lawsuits, and succeeded in obtaining oversight over systems found to be violating the Constitution. This litigation and the mandates it generated drove the cost of confinement higher and higher.

Researchers of all stripes joined in the fray, offering study after study challenging both the practice and the premise of juvenile incarceration by demonstrating that locking up teenagers not only failed to rehabilitate them but actually led to *more* crime. Young people were leaving juvenile facilities with post-traumatic stress symptoms and a hatred of authority that was hard to overcome. Few had received more than the most perfunctory education, further reducing their prospects upon release. The burden of a record, combined with the opportunity cost of all those lost years, made them virtually unemployable. That recidivism rates had reached 80 or nearly 90 percent in some states was hardly surprising in the context of the growing body of research detailing the ways in which juvenile incarceration damaged both the prospects and the psyches of those subjected to it.

Keeping the growing pile of research and scandal from slipping back under the radar required concerted advocacy on many fronts. Foundations and think tanks issued reports and recommendations; public-interest and community groups held rallies and public fora; and the families of the children whose lives were at stake began to join together, their collective voices helping topple some of the worst facilities (in Louisiana, for example, family advocates not only closed a particularly horrific institution but won changes system-wide).

Each of these elements is important, but none is new. Scandal and exposé have dogged the juvenile prison since its inception, and advocates and lawyers have struggled for decades to gain a foothold against the seemingly impenetrable monolith. Sometimes they have succeeded, and a particularly notorious institution has been forced to clean up its act. Occasionally, a full-blown pendulum swing has been triggered.

Change of the current scale, however—a 40 percent drop over the course
of a decade—*is* something new. Making it happen has required a conver-
gence of the various forces listed above, but also something more. All signs
point to the most powerful motivator in American history: money.

As the number of juveniles in state institutions crept ever upward in the
late 1980s and early 1990s, so did the cost of keeping them there: an average of $241 per young person per day, or $88,000 per year, and as high
as $225,000 in some states. This alone—the fact that we could support
about ten kids a year at a public university for the cost of keeping one in a
juvenile prison—might not in itself have been enough to tip the balance.
Prison budgets have long been considered untouchable, and a public fed a
steady diet of terrifying anecdotes, spurious research, and inflammatory
rhetoric could generally be convinced that no price was too high to keep
the barbarians behind prison gates. Even as the cost of locking up (mainly
low-level) offenders drained public coffers so deeply that it threatened
the education of millions of children, politicians dared not risk appearing
"soft on crime."

But finally—with the system weakened, wounded, and visibly
wobbly—came the knockdown blow. The national economy imploded,
tax revenues plummeted, and states that had long considered their corrections budgets sacrosanct started going broke.

As the American economy took a nosedive of a scale not seen since
the Great Depression, legislators finally succumbed to the inevitable. Not only were our juvenile prisons brutal, inhumane, and entirely
counterproductive—all things that had been evident for quite some
time—they were now, finally, out of our price range.

By 2010, the Great Recession had sparked the greatest dip in state revenues ever recorded, with a total state budget shortfall of $191 billion.
By 2011, 46.2 million Americans were living below the poverty line, the
highest number since the government began keeping track. With unemployment rising, housing values falling, and poverty spreading, increasing tax revenues was not a viable option for addressing budget shortfalls
that threatened basic services relied on by the free. In desperate late-night
sessions, legislators cut ever more deeply, leaving crucial social services,
public salaries, and education budgets decimated.

Still the shortfall gaped.

Each time legislators and their staff brought out the blue pencil, hoping they might find something left to cut, the same previously sacrosanct line item loomed ever larger. Mass incarceration, long treated as the last standing entitlement, finally came to be seen as a cost too high to bear.

Whether state leaders were making a virtue of necessity or were genuinely convinced by the mountain of evidence against youth incarceration, political rhetoric started to shift. Maybe those guys from the think tanks were on to something after all with their talk about getting "smart on crime"—moving beyond the tough-guy rhetoric and taking a look at what actually worked when it came to juvenile justice, as well as the high cost of persisting with what did not. Whatever the motivation, a number of politicians adopted the "smart on crime" slogan—an intentional play on the "tough on crime" ethos—as their own.

Also influential was a wave of studies that delved into the structure and development of the adolescent brain. Advances in imaging technology allowed researchers to demonstrate conclusively that the brain was not fully developed until early adulthood. The more recent of these studies established that the frontal lobe, which governs rational decision making, does not fully mature until the mid-twenties. Advances in magnetic resonance imaging allowed neuroscientists to track the continued development of the prefrontal cortex through adolescence and into the mid-twenties. This part of the brain, which grows rapidly during these years, "is involved in complicated decision-making, thinking ahead, planning, comparing risks and rewards"—all functions with tremendous bearing on crime and its cessation. These discoveries underscored empirical evidence that most young people grow out of delinquency on their own as their brains mature—if they are spared the trauma and lasting stigma of juvenile incarceration.

"Much adolescent involvement in criminal activity is part of the normal developmental process of identity formation and most adolescents will mature out of these tendencies," researchers at the National Research Council wrote in 2013, summarizing the implications of more than a decade's worth of studies. "This knowledge of adolescent development has . . . direct bearing on the design and operation of the justice system, raising doubts about the core assumptions driving the criminalization of juvenile justice policy in the late decades of the 20th century."

By underscoring the biological roots of teenage impulsivity, this new wave of adolescent brain research not only called into question the legitimacy of assigning adult culpability to teenagers, it also cast new light on the effect of incarceration in any form—including in institutions ostensibly designed for juveniles—on the developing mind. Confining young people at this crucial developmental juncture, researchers argued, deprived them of the opportunity to develop critical thinking and decision-making skills—exactly the skills they would need to steer clear of crime in the future—at the very moment when their brains were primed to acquire them. The law had long recognized that growing adolescents had a right to physical exercise even when confined; without it, their developing muscles would atrophy. Now scientists were raising similar concerns about the developing brain. What lasting harm might ensue when young people, kept in an environment where every decision was made for them, were deprived of the right to exercise *that* organ?

The technology that allowed brain research to advance may have been new, but what it revealed was not. The understanding that teenagers are *biologically* different from adults, that their developing minds made them both more malleable and less culpable, was central to the invention of the juvenile court, with its presumption that juveniles possessed a particular amenability to rehabilitation. After falling out of favor in the 1980s and 1990s, this notion was not only back on the radar in the early twenty-first century, it now had hard science to support it.

Jay Blitzman, a Massachusetts juvenile court judge who is known (like the avuncular judges of Ben Lindsey's era) for stepping down from the bench to work out dispositions face-to-face with young people and their families, is thrilled to have this hard evidence of what he has long understood.

"What's exciting," Blitzman said, "is that now—over one hundred years after the creation of the first juvenile courts—we have the psychological research, the brain imaging, the scientific research to support the intuitive notion that the founders of the system had around the turn of the century: that kids are not little adults. So this mantra, 'kids are different'— there is now meat on the bone."

The Supreme Court, Blitzman pointed out, cited adolescent brain research in key decisions that undergird safeguards for juveniles. *Roper v. Simmons* (2005), which abolished the death penalty for juveniles; *Graham v. Florida* (2010), which barred mandatory sentences of life without parole in noncapital cases; and *Miller v. Alabama* (2012), which extended the protection against mandatory life sentences to all juveniles, regardless of offense, all relied on the understanding that there were fundamental differences between the adolescent brain and that of adults.

Writing for the majority in *Miller*, Justice Elena Kagan established that "mandatory penalties, by their nature, preclude a sentencer from taking account of an offender's age and the wealth of characteristics and circumstances attendant to it. Under these schemes, every juvenile will receive the same sentence as every other—the 17-year-old and the 14-year-old, the shooter and the accomplice, the child from a stable household and the child from a chaotic and abusive one."

By elaborating on the various ways in which youth matters under the law, these Supreme Court rulings offer broad implications for jurisprudence as a whole. "All of these cases cite the [brain] research that I've alluded to," Blitzman emphasized. "So it's now accepted that, yes, kids are different."

"That doesn't mean we give them a pass," Blitzman clarified. "It doesn't mean that they shouldn't be held accountable. But they have got to be held accountable in a way that is proportionate to where they are developmentally. And you've got to look at each kid individually, which is again part of . . . the way the system was intended."

Several years ago, a state legislator explained to me the difficulty of taking a strong position when it came to juvenile justice. He could vote against a new "tough on crime" law, he told me, without too much risk to his political future, but voting to rescind or even amend an existing one would be going too far. All it would take to end a political career was one teenage Willie Horton. The legislator could do more good in the long run, he told me, if he colored inside those lines.

He might have done better had he actually tested the public mood before deferring so quickly to voters' imagined bloodlust. But when it came to understanding the shift in public opinion, he was far from the only politician to be behind the curve. "Advocates for juvenile justice reform . . . are used to hearing from legislators that they have to appear 'tough on crime' in order to address their constituents' public safety concerns," according to the National Juvenile Justice Network. "However, many recent studies and polls about public attitudes toward youthful offenders . . . suggest that the public is often ahead of their representatives in understanding that the toughest posture on youth crime is not necessarily the smartest one."

Multiple polls bolster this conclusion: Americans believe (correctly) that rehabilitation and treatment are a more effective means than incarceration to reduce youth crime. They are even willing to pay more taxes if that is what it takes to offer young people—including those charged with acts of violence—the support they need to move forward with their lives. (In fact, extra taxes are unnecessary: incarceration is the costliest intervention of all.)

The more deeply pollsters probe, the clearer it becomes that the public consensus has shifted since the fear-infused 1980s and 1990s. The Center for Children's Law and Policy, for example, conducted a national telephone survey in which 89 percent of those surveyed agreed that "almost all youth who commit crimes have the potential to change" and more than 70 percent believed that "incarcerating youthful offenders without rehabilitation is the same as giving up on them." Eighty percent "favored reallocating state government money from incarceration to programs that provide help and skills to enable youth to become productive citizens." Fewer than 15 percent saw incarceration as an effective means of addressing delinquency.

Strikingly, 62 percent favored "assigning nonviolent youth to live in their own homes, receiving counseling and other services under the close supervision of a caseworker, rather than in large juvenile facilities"—an accurate description of several evidence-based interventions that have shown great success with juvenile offenders.

It has taken politicians a while to catch up with the public, but legislators on both sides of the aisle have adopted the new catchphrase: in place of chest pounding about being "tough on crime," many now speak in measured tones of the need to be "smart on crime." And consigning children to large institutions that closely resemble the adult prisons where far too many will eventually end up is increasingly difficult to pass off as "smart."

The first time I encountered Gladys Carrión, then the commissioner of New York's Office of Children and Family Services, she was standing behind a podium at a symposium on the legacy of another iconoclastic administrator, Jerome Miller. A legend among the juvenile justice cognoscenti, Miller is best known for closing down every last training school in the state of Massachusetts during his tenure as director there forty years ago.

Barry Krisberg described Carrión as "the contemporary Jerry Miller. A child advocate who used to be a legal aid lawyer, she's *for* the kids. She cares about them. It's pretty rare in this juvenile justice world that you'd have someone who cares that deeply for the youth and their families."

Like Miller, who was a psychiatric social worker on the Ohio State University faculty when he was appointed to run the Massachusetts system, Carrión did not arrive as an up-through-the-ranks system veteran. Born and raised in the Bronx, she started her career as an attorney at Bronx Legal Services and had become a senior vice president at United Way of New York City when she was tapped for her current job.

Carrión may not be a typical administrator, but she can talk like one when she needs to, breaking down the state's complex, multilayered system and its equally arcane taxonomy like a born bureaucrat. But that is just housekeeping. Once she gets going on her true subject—the kids—her commitment is unmistakable, as are the reasons she is both loved and loathed with such personal intensity.

As commissioner, Carrión oversees the child welfare and juvenile justice systems for the state of New York, along with a hodgepodge of other human services. Hewing to the legacy of Jerome Miller, she is working as fast as she can to do herself out of a job (at least when it comes to running juvenile prisons).

For a lifelong crusader such as Barry Krisberg, there may be no higher praise for a public official than likening her to Jerry Miller. While no other state has managed to dismantle its juvenile incarceration apparatus as thoroughly as did Miller in the 1970s, his efforts were broadly influential. After Miller turned Massachusetts on its head, other states followed suit, albeit more cautiously, closing institutions and moving toward community alternatives until the advent of the super-predator turned the tide again.

As the newly appointed head of the Massachusetts Department of Youth Services, Miller was tasked with running a network of juvenile institutions that one historian described as "nightmarish outposts of abuse and neglect, where callous state workers meted out punishment destined only to reinforce . . . antisocial behavior." Miller entered a reformer and departed a revolutionary, having lost faith in the prospect of turning the state's militaristic reform schools into healing environments.

Miller may have given up on the institutions but not on the kids. Doing them justice, he came to understand, would require far more than tinkering—or even restructuring. "Training staff in new methods of supervision or therapy techniques, reorganizing the department, and reclassifying the youngsters wasn't likely to have much lasting effect," Miller wrote in *Last One Over the Wall*, his account of his experience in Massachusetts, "without a reordering of the goals and values behind the actions."

In that book, Miller recalls the day he realized that this kind of shift in values was not going to happen without drastic measures. He'd just gotten word that a frustrated supervisor at the Lyman School—the state's oldest reform school—had locked two boys in cages in the basement and driven away with the keys.

"It hit me with the full force of conviction: our months of training, meetings, and working with staff and administrators were not going to make the difference I wanted," Miller writes. "As I looked around the department and the superintendents, directors of education, chaplains, planners, and others in leadership roles, I saw that most would be there long after I left. They could outwait and outlast me. I'd made a mistake in concentrating on making the institutions more humane. The idea of *closing* them seemed less risky."

As far back as 1662, Massachusetts distinguished itself as the first colony to execute a juvenile. In 1646, it enacted the first Stubborn Child Law, which legitimized the practice of executing the merely incorrigible. Faced with this long-standing culture of punishment and control, and intractable resistance from many who currently staffed and ran the state's juvenile facilities, Miller decided that bold action was required.

Perhaps it was the extremity of what he had seen—youth who tried to run away from the Industrial School for Boys, for example, had their ring fingers broken and were relegated, naked, to "The Tombs," isolation caverns with neither toilets nor windows—but when Miller made his move, he did not stint on drama. He took the brass locks off the isolation rooms at one newly closed institution, had them mounted, and gave one to Governor Frank Sargent, one of the few in power who did not oppose his efforts.

Over the course of eighteen months, Miller managed to close all the state's reform schools, replacing them as quickly as he could with a network of group homes and family supports. In the process, he became an icon to those committed to transforming the juvenile justice system, many of whom were in attendance at the symposium forty years later.

Despite the forty years that separate the two, Miller and Carrión share a similar mix of devotion to the kids and a seeming indifference to their own political futures. "As a new commissioner five years ago, I inherited a juvenile justice system that, by any measure, had been broken for many, many years," Carrión told the audience at the symposium on Miller's legacy, "an agency unwilling to take the necessary steps to implement meaningful change. Despite the death of a young person under restraint, numerous investigations and reports all documenting the grievous conditions and failures of both management and staff to protect and adequately meet the needs of youth in custody, few in government were paying attention, and the voices of the advocates fell on deaf ears."

"Much to my surprise, no one was suing us," she noted drily.

"That has been remedied," she added, after an impeccably timed pause.

There is, recall, a recipe for closing juvenile prisons, a constellation of elements that together trigger change. Lawsuits, scandals, exposés, and advocates; falling juvenile crime rates and empty state coffers: the right mix can close an institution. Line them all up and the places fall like dominoes. The fly in the ointment is the question of values. Are we shutting down youth prisons because it is, for the time being, practical? Or are we freeing children because doing so is *right*? The answer may determine whether the changes that have taken place over the past decade turn out to be just another pendulum swing or the beginning of the end of the juvenile prison.

In many ways, New York resembles other states that have cut the population of their juvenile prisons. Scandals, investigations, exposés, and advocates, as well as the ubiquitous budget concerns—all the ingredients that have combined elsewhere to shut juvenile prisons—are part of the mix in New York as well. But there is also something different happening in New York: the changes there are driven not just by practical concerns but by deeply held values that, while not universal, cut across multiple agencies and are shared by their leaders. And values—a willingness to acknowledge the depth of the wrong being done to children in the name of the law and the visceral connection to those children that the Annie E. Casey Foundation's Bart Lubow hints at when he speaks of the "My Child Test"—may be the secret ingredient that turns a recipe for reform into a formula for revolution.

In the years before Carrión's appointment, John Mattingly, who retired as commissioner of the New York City Administration for Children's Services in 2011, worked closely with the city's probation and education departments to develop a continuum of community-based and alternative programs intended to keep youth out of the state's notorious upstate facilities. This effort laid the groundwork for the state facility closures that followed. In 2010, Vincent Schiraldi—previously the director of D.C.'s Department of Youth Rehabilitation Services and a lifelong advocate for youth in trouble—was appointed commissioner of the New York City Department of Probation. Schiraldi brought with him a strong personal commitment to keeping young people "close to home," a phrase that became the name of a legislature-supported initiative to keep New York City youth in or near their homes, in the care of voluntary agencies rather than state facilities.

Carrión herself is also clearly driven by values, not by politics— especially when it comes to the fate of New York's most vulnerable young people. Fearless, self-assured, and blazingly direct, she is the kind of administrator frequently described as a "charismatic leader." A Bronx native of Puerto Rican descent, she wears her hair in a layered bob that accentuates the roundness of her face. Only when she stands does one realize she is perhaps five feet tall—a good deal shorter, in any case, than most of those with whom she has gone toe-to-toe in her crusade to remake New York's scandal-ridden juvenile justice system.

Carrión began her tenure in 2007. By the time I sat down with her in the cool of her Manhattan office in the summer of 2012, New York State had closed down eighteen facilities and halved the number of juveniles held in state institutions. Perhaps most remarkably, Carrión had managed to help divert some of the $74 million she estimates has been saved by the closures into a dedicated funding stream to support community-based alternatives to incarceration.

From the beginning, Carrión and her allies were stepping into a firestorm. In 2006, Human Rights Watch and the American Civil Liberties Union released a report calling New York's "among the most hostile juvenile justice agencies we have ever encountered." The report included damning testimony from girls in New York State facilities. "When they restrain kids . . . [t]hey'd have rug burns all over their bodies," said Stephanie, who was sent upstate at age sixteen. "They hold your arms back and they purposefully push your face in the rug. They have their knee in your back and your arms all the way back." (A young woman interviewed for this book described witnessing a similar scenario while she was locked up in a New York State facility.)

In November 2006, a particularly forceful restraint left fifteen-year-old Darryl Thompson dead at New York's Tryon Residential Center. According to *New York* magazine,

> The boys had been on lockdown for two days—prohibited from playing basketball or doing much else—and it looked like lockdown would continue through the weekend. "Am I going to get my rec?" Thompson asked. "You guys won't give us our rec!"
>
> An aide charged into the bathroom. Whether he pushed Thompson first or vice versa is a matter of dispute, but there's no question what happened next: Two aides pinned the teenager facedown on the tile floor, while a third man cuffed his wrists behind his back. Thompson stopped breathing, left the prison in an ambulance, and never came back.

Despite the fact that the medical examiner ruled Thompson's death a homicide, the staff members involved were never indicted. Instead, the state settled with the boy's family for $3.5 million.

In 2007, the newly appointed commissioner visited Tryon for the first time. After she left, she sat in her car and wept.

In 2008, a video of a Tryon aide punching a boy in the face started making the rounds.

In 2009, the U.S. Department of Justice threatened to take over New York's juvenile prison system after investigating Tryon and two other state facilities and uncovering "a litany of abuses: employees restraining kids so often and with so much force that kids had endured concussions, broken teeth, and broken bones."

New York governor David Paterson had by then piled on with his own investigative body, the Task Force on Transforming the Juvenile Justice System, chaired by John Jay College of Criminal Justice president Jeremy Travis. That body reached the sweeping conclusion that "New York State's current approach fails the young people who are drawn into the system, the public whose safety it is intended to protect, and the principles of good governance." Young people in New York State facilities, the task force concluded, lived in dismal conditions, received little counseling and barely cursory education, and risked physical abuse on a regular basis.

At this point, one might think that Commissioner Carrión had herself a mandate. But the politics of incarceration are not so straightforward. Carrión faced resistance right from the start, especially from those with the most to gain from the status quo—politicians representing the upstate counties that had come to rely on juvenile prisons for jobs and many of those who held those prison jobs. Complaints from facility staff included the assertion that Carrión's effort to reduce restraints like the one that left Darryl Thompson dead at Tryon was leading to more violence inside the institutions.

"It's easy to say, 'Well, you're the commissioner. You tell people what to do,' " Carrión reflected. "It doesn't work that way."

Trying to change the culture at a place like Tryon, she found, was virtually impossible. "What I discovered was that despite all the training in the world—literally thousands of hours of training—the behavior of staff didn't change. Young people continued to be abused there, and mistreated, and injured, along with staff."

Barry Krisberg visited Tryon as a consultant to the state and was so appalled, he recalled, that he told his hosts, "It's a good thing I'm working for you guys, because if I was working for the Department of Justice, I'd be reading you your rights."

Their reaction was telling. "They asked me to put it in writing," Krisberg recalls. "They were completely open and helpful."

Even as they struggled to improve conditions at places like Tryon, Carrión and her team were continuing the efforts that Mattingly and others had started to reduce the demand for space in locked facilities by creating alternatives in the community. Deputy Commissioner Felipe Franco, who heads up the Office of Children and Family Services Division of Juvenile Justice and Opportunities for Youth, believes this effort has put New York in a particularly strong position when it comes to shutting down facilities. "Because there was enough investment in the front end in preventative services, [the commissioner] was actually closing empty beds, not just transferring kids from the custody of the state to the community," Franco pointed out. "The kids were *already* in the community . . . [so] she had the luxury to close the facilities."

This planning, along with Tryon's persistent "failure to change," created the criteria for closing it, Carrión said. That is exactly what she did: closed down Tryon and, over time, seventeen other state facilities. When unions resisted, citing state law that called for a year's notice, she cleared the kids out anyway and staffed an empty building until she could close the doors for good.

"I think it's difficult for people to grasp how heroic the closure of those facilities really is," said New York probation chief Vincent Schiraldi. "The status quo has its own power in a way that is very difficult to understand until you really prick it and make it bleed."

When Carrión arrived, the state was running a system that, in her words, was "grounded in punishment and compliance, and relied on restraint and the use of force to impose order." More than 60 percent of youth from New York who were in custody were being held for misdemeanor-level offenses (85 percent when it came to the girls). The overwhelming majority of those in institutions were young people of color, an injustice to which Carrión reacts viscerally. "It literally broke my heart to go in and look at these kids that are all black and brown," she told a reporter of visiting her own facilities. "And I'm thinking, these could be my kids. They look like my son. They look like my nephew. There are all these black and brown faces, and I can't stand it."

At the symposium, she told those assembled that "it became evident that too many young people were being placed in state juvenile institutions because of mental health needs or other social service needs, not because these young people pose a significant threat to public safety." Despite this, she continued somewhat heatedly, no one "thinks twice about depriving the young person of their liberty. Not a second thought."

"These young people clearly could be served in their community. The harm that we were inflicting on already troubled youth was evident in the poor outcomes and the high recidivism rates that characterize the system."

New York had been spending "$272,000 a year [per youth] to operate a failed system," Carrión emphasized. "We know that incarcerating young persons is not in their best interest."

These are fighting words in the upstate regions where that $272,000 per kid was keeping local economies afloat. But Carrión is very clear about whom she considers her constituency. "I am not running the Economic Development Agency for upstate New York," she has been quoted as saying. "I will no longer export black and brown kids to finance the upstate economy."

As an administrator, Carrión is not only exceptionally responsive to critics of her locked institutions, she is foremost among them. Rather than moving cautiously, she has proven herself a master of the crisis opportunity. As one critique after another poured in, Carrión found ways to leverage even the most scathing to glean resources for the youth in her care.

Carrión had been commissioner for less than two years when the Department of Justice issued its report on four state institutions plagued by allegations of excessive use of force. That investigation found that staff "routinely used uncontrolled, unsafe applications of force" that resulted in "an alarming number of serious injuries to youth, including concussions, broken or knocked-out teeth, and spiral fractures." The victims of these assaults were children and young teenagers (in New York, only those aged seven to fifteen can be found delinquent; those sixteen and older are treated as adults), the majority of whom were not hardened criminals but simple misdemeanants. In some cases it had taken nothing more than a child's mocking laughter or defiant silence to provoke a beating, investigators found.

The Department of Justice praised Carrión's efforts to rein in these abuses, but overall, she summarized, "they found that our system practices, grounded in a punitive correctional model, violated the constitutional rights of children in our care."

The thirty-two-page report (three years after its publication, Carrión remembered the exact length of the document) was "devastating. At least it was for me."

Nevertheless, she said, recovering her normally brisk tone, "this commissioner did not oppose the investigation by the Department of Justice. . . . We settled right away."

Instead of seeing the report as an obstacle, Carrión saw an opportunity to "focus public attention on the failures of the system" and "leverage needed resources to reinvest in the system. There was no other way I was going to get resources to do half of the things that needed to be done."

Rather than trying to brush the report under the rug or minimize its findings, Carrión waved it like a battle flag. She was carrying that flag when she met, at her request, with senior members of the judiciary—men and women with the power to send youth to the very facilities the report had savaged. Her facilities.

"Everything in that report is true," she told the judges. "I don't know how often you visit these facilities, but when you go, what you see is really not what's happening there. There are no services."

Next, she went after any misconceptions the judges might have held about the kids. Her "secure facilities," she told them—those reserved for the most serious offenders—did house young people who posed a real danger. But the remaining facilities—nonsecure or limited secure, in New York State terminology—did not. Instead, kids were being held there "because they had serious mental health needs. They had educational deficits. Every other system had failed them and we were the system of last resort. [But] they weren't causing a significant risk to public safety."

If they did not pose a threat, she asked the judges, why are you sending them to me?

For their own good, the judges responded. They were remanding youth into state custody because it was the only way those youth could receive mental health services.

"There are none in my facilities," Carrión informed the judges.

"At that point," she recalled, "I didn't even have a psychiatrist. There was *no* [staff] psychiatrist for the system. I had contract psychiatrists, and very few of those, and [the judges] didn't know. They absolutely didn't know. This was all new information."

Despite her successes in reforming New York's system, Carrión's outrage has not dimmed with experience. "These places are never going to be good," she said, echoing Jerome Miller's assessment of large state lockups decades earlier. "It doesn't matter what we do."

For the very small number of kids who genuinely posed a threat, Carrión elaborated, everything possible should be done to make the places where they were confined both humane and therapeutic. Beyond that, she insisted, "Young people should never be tied to these places for services. That's inappropriate. You don't deprive your people, your children, of their liberty in order to get services. In order to go to school, right? I make that argument and it's incredible to hear even some judges who really feel like it's appropriate to send kids to training schools in order to get them into sports. It's just unbelievable."

Carrión's meeting with the judges did have an impact. After the meeting, the deputy chief judge issued a memo quoting her almost verbatim. The memo, according to Carrión, underscored that state facilities must be used only as a last resort, reserved for those who posed a genuine risk to public safety.

"After that meeting, the judges almost had to stop sending kids to me," Carrión recalled. "They just stopped. . . . It was very important to cultivate that [relationship], because they control the front door."

When Carrión met further resistance to the culture change she envisioned, she reached out to the *New York Times* and other media to ensure that they were well informed about "the failures of the system, the punitive culture, the abuse, the lack of effective services and supports, the high recidivism rates, the exorbitant cost to the taxpayers."

State and national media were quick to take the bait, running stories and editorials highlighting the failures of the New York system, especially its overreliance on institutional placement.

"People said, 'What?'" Carrión recalls, with just the faintest hint of mischief, of the public outcry that followed. "'You can't continue to do that!'"

Public outrage may have helped advance her goals, but it did not, Carrión acknowledged, "make me popular with my staff. I was not welcomed in any facility. But I still went."

Somewhere along the line, Carrión found time to read Jerome Miller's book. "It's incredible what the similarities were," she said, pointing to "the craziness that goes on when we try and do the right thing."

Felipe Franco was more specific. "The commissioner has gone through everything Miller said in the book," Franco told me. "When people were trying to sabotage our efforts, they allowed [youth] to escape. Restraints went up. Everything that she went through, she had already read about."

"She might not have taken the job if she had read the book" sooner, he added drolly.

Actually, she probably would have—Carrión does not appear one to duck a challenge—but Franco's quip points to something else that Miller and Carrión have in common: a willingness to lose their jobs rather than compromise their values.

"It requires a tremendous sense of urgency," Carrión conceded. "You really, really have to care about young people and be committed that this can't continue one day longer. You have to *feel* it. In every young person in my facility, I see my son or daughter; I really do. There can only be one standard. The standard we have for our own children is the standard that we need to have for young people that we institutionalize."

Vincent Schiraldi appears to have heeded Miller's advice as well. When he started out in D.C., he gave each member of his executive team a copy of *Last One Over the Wall*. Then he went about closing the District's scandal-ridden youth prison, replacing it with a sparkling, smaller, model facility complete with its own charter school and a large sculpture in the lobby made from melted guns. He also moved kids to the community at a rapid clip, despite virulent opposition from the *Washington Post*, among others.

"I came in with an opinion," Schiraldi conceded, in a bit of an understatement. "I thought it was important to let folks know it was a new day."

The day before I met with Carrión, I toured the Brooklyn for Brooklyn Initiative, one of her proudest achievements. By building a network of neighborhood programs, some residential and others that served kids in their homes, the initiative aimed to keep city kids in their homes and communities rather than shipping them upstate.

I told the commissioner what one young man had said to me when I'd asked him about the pros and cons of life in the airy Brooklyn brownstone where, for the moment, he was mandated to stay.

The best thing about being there, he'd said, was he had learned to control his anger.

The worst was so obvious it barely bore mentioning, or so his tone implied: "I'm not with my family."

Carrión surprised me once again with her willingness not only to accept criticism, but to raise the stakes.

"I think what no one understands in my system," she said, "is the deprivation of liberty at any level is, for a kid, correctional. Right?"

When it comes to adults, she observed, "We make a big thing, as we should, about depriving people of their liberty. We don't think about that when it comes to kids. We really don't see it as a deprivation of their liberty."

The problem with this perspective is that it allows placement in a locked facility to become a default response rather than a last resort. "One way or another," Carrión came to understand, the intertwined systems she supervised (child welfare and juvenile justice) could "keep [kids] forever, without the protections of due process."

"We want them to finish school. We want them to have a home. We want to 'fix' them. We never think about the fact that we are depriving them of their liberty. And that is huge. There is a high bar one has to meet in order to be able to do something like that. I am constantly surprised by how lightly we deal with that."

"When I take kids away from their families, I need to do a whole lot better," she said, "because I've taken this very drastic step. So the state has a tremendous responsibility to do better."

How much better, realistically?

"We have to want for each child what we want for our own sons and daughters," Carrión replied. "There has to be a single standard. These children *matter*."

Carrión's idealism is balanced by a strong sense of realism. She is doing her best to sell off the facilities she has shut down, or hand them over to the counties, so that the state will not be able to reopen them down the line should the political or fiscal tide shift once more.

"Change must be transformative, systemic, and sustainable," she insisted, "so that you have a hard time undoing this after I leave."

The battle to close the institutions is anything but over. In many ways, it has only begun. Despite the steep decline in recent years, America still leads the industrialized world in the rate at which we lock up our young. As things stand, the recent drop in juvenile incarceration looks more like a stock market correction than a revolution: the current number of youth in confinement is almost identical to that in the mid-1980s, right before that era's pendulum swing swept thousands more youth behind bars. Even accounting for the recent drop in population, state institutions today hold far more young people for nonviolent offenses such as truancy, low-level property offenses, and technical probation violations than they do those who pose a threat to public safety. Finally, changes inspired in great part by financial concerns are extremely vulnerable to shifts in the economic tide.

At the same time, a remarkable opportunity lies before us. If we succeed in building on the changes of the past decade, we will have made great progress. But if we find the courage to go even further—to acknowledge the moral and political bankruptcy of large-scale juvenile prisons and then act on that knowledge—we might finally transcend the long effort to reform a failed system and galvanize a movement to shut it down instead.

11

A BETTER MOUSETRAP

The Therapeutic Prison

At first I was very bitter, but I learned how to "program," a term used by correctional staff that means you have the ability to adjust to the loss of freedom well. . . . Now that I think about it, I don't believe learning how to cooperate with the policies and procedures that are imposed in a locked facility is a positive quality that children should acquire. Nevertheless, that was what I was expected to do.
—Marilyn Denise Jones, MEd, *From Crack to College and Vice Versa*

"WOULD YOU CALL THIS a prison?"

Riley, seventeen, had been inside Minnesota's Red Wing Correctional Facility for ten months when he asked me this question. He had reached Level Four on the facility's behavior scale—the second-highest level—and would soon be heading out. After a series of short-term furloughs to test his newfound stability, he would be free for good in a matter of months.

Riley and Kent, nineteen, had been given the task of showing me around the place. When Riley surprised me with this question we were standing in a hallway, idled for a moment by the piercing blare of a siren indicating that someone was being taken to the security unit, where troublemakers were kept in twenty-three-hour isolation. The sound, Riley explained, signaled "stop movement"—no one could leave where they were until the all clear had sounded.

The temporary lull sent my tour guides into a reflective state. For the past few hours, they had been showing me around Red Wing, a place Riley called the safest he had known. Their pride in their temporary home was unmistakable. Now Riley wanted to know what I made of what they had shown me.

In recent years, many of the states engaged in reform efforts—the same ones, by and large, that are cutting back on their use of juvenile prisons— have also been working to change the culture of those that remain: to use therapeutic concepts and modalities to refashion their youth prisons, including retraining staff to consider themselves adjuncts to their young wards' healing rather than agents of power and control.

Red Wing warden Otis Zanders proudly showed me a map of the country with clusters of brightly colored pins, representing the many jurisdictions that had sent delegations to visit Red Wing in the hope of replicating its model.

Missouri—which has run small, therapeutic facilities for thirty years— is likely the most-visited system in the nation, with a separate institute dedicated to supporting replication efforts. But few states are prepared to turn wholesale to the Missouri Model, which entails eliminating large, prison-like facilities and replacing them with smaller, group home–like settings. For those seeking some sort of a compromise—a therapeutic model at an existing site, for instance—Red Wing offers a promising example.

Whatever the model or scale of the facility, the effort to create a therapeutic prison reflects a new twist in the decades-long back-and-forth between punishment and rehabilitation. This long-standing dialectic is now giving way to a third rationale for incarcerating young people. That rationale is "treatment."

Ideologically, this looks like progress. Punishment (or its milder cousin, "accountability") assumes that a young person is bad and must be made to suffer in order to pay for his crimes. Rehabilitation assumes, more generously, that he is merely broken, and prison is the workshop where he will be repaired.

A treatment-based model, sometimes referred to as a "therapeutic milieu," starts from a variant on this latter premise: the young people who enter these facilities are traumatized—hurt and in need of healing, with or without their consent. This appeared to be the guiding philosophy at Red Wing. It had a good reputation—I had heard praise from local advocates as well as those from the law enforcement side—and I hoped at Red Wing to see what a successful therapeutic prison looked like.

Riley's question hovered in my mind throughout my visit, first to Red Wing and later to other institutions that were trying to import a therapeutic milieu into a correctional setting.

The success of this approach appeared to vary widely, depending in great part on the level of commitment of administrators and staff. But beyond these variations lay a deeper conundrum: can a locked facility truly be a therapeutic environment or are the intrinsic contradictions too profound? If your freedom is taken in the name of treatment rather than punishment, are you, as Riley had wondered, not *really* in prison? Or is there no method or modality powerful enough to counter the loss of liberty that is the defining characteristic of that institution?

Edwin M. Shur raises some of these questions in his book *Radical Non-intervention: Rethinking the Delinquency Problem*. It is important, Shur writes,

> to recognize that when, in an authoritative setting, we attempt to do something for a child "because of what he is and needs," we are also doing something to him. . . . Whatever one's motivations, however elevated one's objectives, if the measures taken result in the compulsory loss of the child's liberty, the involuntary separation of a child from his family, or even the supervision of a child's activities by a probation worker, the impact on the affected individuals is essentially a punitive one. Good intentions and a flexible vocabulary do not alter this reality. . . . We shall escape much confusion here if we are willing to give candid recognition to the fact that the business of the juvenile court inevitably consists, to a considerable degree, in dispensing punishment.

Would I call Red Wing a prison? It certainly didn't look like one. The Romanesque brick-and-stone structure with its arched entryways and pristine lawns bore little resemblance to the stripped-down compounds I had seen elsewhere. As Kent, who had been there for twenty-two months, pointed out, it could easily be mistaken for the campus of one of the elite universities after which its living units are named (Stanford, Brown, Harvard, Yale). The tour buses that pass through the picturesque region along the Mississippi River often stop by the facility, which visitors admire as a historic site.

Even the drive to Red Wing is idyllic. Fifty miles of classic green-gold farmland, dotted with barns and grain silos, separate the facility from the state's urban center of Minneapolis–St. Paul. As one draws closer, passenger cars give way to pickups and tractor-trailers. Red Wing itself rises up from the fields like the Emerald City of Oz: towers and turrets emerging out of nowhere, hinting at a place that is a world unto itself.

When they fenced the institution in the late nineties, superintendent Otis Zanders told me, it created consternation in the community. A square-shouldered, round-faced black man in a crisp suit and tie and wire-rimmed glasses, Zanders had run the place since 1996. Now he was preparing to retire. Before the fence went up, Zanders said, "walkaways" would show up in town from time to time and break into houses, but that didn't stop the locals from opposing the fence on aesthetic grounds. "Red Wing is a tourist town," he explained. The building was "part of their identity."

The beauty at Red Wing is more than skin-deep. Youth have access to healing amenities including a sweat lodge and a ropes course. Community volunteers arrive in such numbers that they sometimes appeared to outnumber the kids (eighty came through in the month that I visited, almost exactly the number of youth in custody at the time). The boys repay the kindness by escorting the older volunteers to swing dances and stopping by nearby senior facilities to play bingo with the residents.

With a capacity of 131 serious and chronic male juvenile offenders, Red Wing offers everything on the contemporary treatment menu: cognitive/behavior restructuring and skill development training, restorative justice and a therapeutic community. The walls are postered with motivational images and inspirational mottos, many of which the young men spontaneously repeated as they tried to describe the ethos of the place. I had never seen a facility quite so steeped in slogans, nor met a group of young people who seemed so thoroughly to have internalized the writing on the wall.

Each resident goes through a risk/needs assessment upon entry, out of which an individual treatment plan is devised. Monthly and quarterly reports track progress toward completion, and those on the way out depart with a personalized relapse-prevention plan. There is mental health treatment available, a specialized unit for sex offenders ("Yale"), and another for those with substance-abuse issues. The residents volunteer in and out of the facility, participate in religious services, have access to high school and work-readiness programs, and participate in community service. All in all, Zanders told me, they are "programming" sixteen hours a day. "There is a schedule like in college," Kent elaborated. "You are active all day, and learning."

Red Wing has a blue-blood pedigree to match its highbrow facade. Built at the end of the nineteenth century, it can trace its roots directly to the House of Refuge movement. Originally named the Minnesota State Training School for Boys and Girls (the girls were transferred out in 1976), Red Wing operated under that title until 1979, when the state changed its name to reflect the shifting mentality of the times.

To this day, however, according to Zanders, "the name 'State Training School' still lingers in the vocabulary of senior staff and local citizens," as does the institution's longtime mandate: "to change the attitudes, values, and behavior of youth committed to the institution so they might be returned to the community to live with dignity, and feelings of self worth."

At the same time, as Riley pointed out, "There are cameras and security everywhere. . . . Patrol everywhere, so you don't go over the fence."

For the moment, Riley himself appeared in no hurry to reach the other side of the fence. "When the cops put me in handcuffs I was relieved," he confessed. "It is hard out there. I was involved in gang activity and on the run from the police. It was stressful, with enemies and the police."

Kent's experience of arrest was more traumatic. "They beat you up," Kent explained matter-of-factly. "I was bit by a dog even though I was on my knees with my hands up. They let the dog come up and bite me."

This experience highlights one of the challenges faced by Red Wing and the similar cities on a hill that I visited in other states. No matter how much effort had gone into creating a kinder, gentler prison, these boutique institutions remained embedded in a larger system that rarely shared their values.

Young people who wind up in a state facility such as Red Wing generally pass through local juvenile detention centers first—institutions that are often dominated by a traditional, punitive culture. Before that, there are encounters with the police, whose main focus may not be on instilling "dignity" or "self-worth." After being set upon by police dogs en route to Red Wing, Kent, for example, acknowledged, "I have a hard time respecting authority and the law."

"Especially if they say they are 'just doing their job,'" chimed in Riley. "Sometimes they are the antagonist."

This led to discussion of Red Wing's secure unit, where those who had been "bad" were kept on lockdown, according to my guides, sometimes for weeks or even months at a stretch. This was both boys' greatest fear when they learned they were headed for Red Wing.

"I heard it was a prison," said Kent, who had braced himself accordingly. His fears were allayed when he learned that only the security unit operated on a twenty-three-hour lockdown, not the whole facility. Nonetheless, Kent did end up in the security unit "a few times" during his first year at Red Wing. "I was a lot different," he explained. "I was hardheaded. It took me nine months to realize it wasn't working and I needed to change."

Another conundrum: Red Wing was the very model of a modern institution—a therapeutic milieu staffed by trauma-informed personnel. Its use of solitary confinement may well have been more judicious, the conditions therein more humane, than at many facilities. But both Kent and Riley had spent time on the security unit early in their stay, sometimes for a week at a stretch. Anything over fifteen hours in solitary is considered torture under international standards, even for adults, and the United Nations has declared using it with adolescents for any duration at all to be torture. Yet here at Red Wing—the loveliest facility I had yet to visit—it was part of the program, along with therapeutic interventions, upbeat slogans, and all the other trappings of a rehabilitative model.

There are, of course, many notions about what is therapeutic, multiple theories as to what helps children heal. Trust, however, is central to all of

them. At Red Wing, boys were being asked to trust adults who were permitted, under certain circumstances, to subject them to a practice that most
of the world agrees is torture.

The standard rationale for the use of isolation—that isolating dangerous individuals is sometimes necessary to maintain institutional safety—
had not reached my interlocutors. "They are showing us it can get harder
if we decide not to follow the rules," Kent explained instead.

Solitary confinement is merely the extreme end of a spectrum of correctional practices that continue to infuse even those institutions that have
been most successful in integrating treatment models. At Red Wing, for
example, I saw lines of young people walking from one place to another
in the same "chicken walk" posture (arms folded across the chest, hands
tucked into armpits) I had seen at more traditional facilities. The explanation I was given—free hands can become fists at the drop of a hat—seemed
reasonable enough inside the gates. But as I thought about it later, the contradictions loomed. You can't reach out with your hands in your armpits,
much less open up. And what did a boy forced to walk like a chicken—past
the high-minded slogans and grandly named dormitories—learn from the
posture about how he was perceived and who he might become?

On the other hand, Red Wing had been highly successful at engaging
the local community—a crucial step toward changing public perceptions
of those held there, and those who would return from Red Wing and other
juvenile facilities. Sometimes, I was told, there were so many eager to help
that each cottage had its own volunteer grandma who baked during school
hours so the boys could come back to fresh-baked cookies and milk.

"It's *privileges*," Riley made a point of clarifying, stretching out the
word as if answering a familiar challenge. "We can get this taken away
from us, so basically we're working for it. It's not just *handed* to us. Everything, you got to work for."

The biggest concern Riley and Kent seemed to have about Red Wing
was that, sooner or later, they would have to leave. No matter how much
they had changed during their stay at Red Wing, the impoverished high-
crime neighborhoods they had come from had not, and if they returned to
those same neighborhoods—as most young prisoners do—they wouldn't
have a chance, both told me.

"It's impossible," Kent insisted, to "return to your same environment and not be involved in the streets. So the only chance you got is if you move to a different environment."

Kent stopped to talk to a passing staffer for a moment, and Riley hung back as if to speak with me in private. "I'm not going to say this is Disney World because it's not," he began. "It takes a lot of work to get out of here. People have got to keep on moving. We don't stop. We move on all day. We keep pushing ourselves through all our struggles. Even though he had a brother that got shot [while he was] here." Riley lowered his voice and gestured toward Kent.

"How can you deal with that in here and you can't do nothing about it?" Riley asked rhetorically. Then he answered his own question.

When Kent learned over the phone that his sixteen-year-old brother had been shot and killed, said Riley, the first thing he did was "come to the group"—the boys on his unit who had been working together in a therapeutic group and were by then accustomed to talking with one another about things that mattered.

Riley, who had known Kent since seventh grade, went out of his way to help his friend. "Somebody to talk to, encouragement, tell him to keep on moving. I prayed for him, you know—tell him everything is going to be okay. When he needed to talk, I talked to him, tried to give him the best answers I could when he had a question."

"We don't give each other the easy way out," Riley said, his tone a poignant mixture of machismo and tenderness as he described his role in helping his friend through a terrible time. "It's sad, but he's okay now. He's safe," Riley added in a tone of reassurance.

Kent said later that his first instinct upon getting the call about his brother had been to seek vengeance. Quelling that impulse "took a lot for me," he said. "With the help of this program, what they taught me and everything, I was kind of able to control my anger and think things through before I reacted. That's one of the good things about this program. I use some of the skills and they really work. . . . I wanted revenge and everything, but I couldn't do it, because it was only going to lead to more problems."

"They teach about thinking ahead—what could happen?" Riley elaborated. "What if this? What if that?"

"I was a person who would minimize a lot," Kent added earnestly.

I mentioned that I had just seen that very word written on the board in a classroom we passed through. "These are stated beliefs," Kent nodded. "I mean, you've got minimizing, assuming the worst, blaming others, glorifying—all that."

Kent had reached Level Four when I visited, which meant he was starting the process that would bring him home. Initially, he would be released on a series of temporary furloughs. If all went well, he would go home for good, rejoining his family in a new home in the suburbs, where they had relocated shortly after Kent's brother was shot. Riley will return to a new environment also—a smaller town where his girlfriend and son are living.

"It feels good," Kent said of his imminent departure. "I am happy to see my family. But I am kind of nervous."

Kent's anxiety was not unwarranted. The court had placed both him and Riley on what Minnesota calls Extended Juvenile Jurisdiction. That meant they started out with time at Red Wing, but if they faltered post-release their juvenile status could be revoked. Both had adult sentences hanging over their heads.

"I feel like I got what I needed," Kent asserted, as if giving himself a pep talk. "It is up to me to use it."

"Going back will be stressful," mused Riley.

Would I call Red Wing a prison? I still hadn't answered their question. But I was going to walk out the gate within a matter of hours. I was more interested to know how these young men perceived it.

"If we're not free to leave?" Riley repeated, momentarily stymied, when I handed his question back to him.

"Me, personally," Kent interjected, "I call it a treatment program."

A loud, collective cheer came from a nearby classroom, where young men in hairnets were packing up rice to send to Haiti and Somalia as part of a community service project.

"That means they met their goal," Riley explained.

"They're saving a lot of lives," Kent added with evident pride. "Starvation. The people in Haiti that are suffering from the earthquake."

"Starvation," Riley repeated, staring into the distance for a moment as if trying to imagine the people of Haiti, rescued by rice that had passed through his hands.

"We feel very good," said Kent, completing, as he often did, his friend's half-spoken thought.

Kent and Riley felt safe inside Red Wing. They were doing things that gave them a sense pride, even of purpose. Did they feel free? Did it matter? *Were* they in prison, by their own accounting?

"Yes," Kent answered finally, recoiling a bit, as if he had surprised himself with his own answer.

"No," insisted Riley. "I mean, you can take elderly people to an elderly home and they can't go home. Would you call that a prison?"

"It's all about how you think of it," Riley said finally, changing his mind even as he spoke. "If it's got a gate around it, then basically, yes, it's a prison."

"I *do* feel incarcerated," Kent repeated, with a solemnity befitting a hard-won conclusion. "I do. I'm not able to make my own decisions. I'm getting told when to use the bathroom, when to shower, when I can eat. So I do feel incarcerated."

Riley remained on the fence. He felt incarcerated "in a way," he ventured, still puzzling through the question he had been the first to ask. "Incarcerated because I can't make my own decisions, but there's freedom here when you start doing what you got to do."

"Time to move on," he said finally. The all clear had sounded and we were free to continue on our way.

The O.H. Close Youth Correctional Facility in Stockton, California, was in a state of flux. As part of the settlement of a long-running lawsuit against the California Youth Authority, the state had brought in experts from the University of Cincinnati to train staff in an Integrated Behavioral Treatment Model—the latest in what one staffer half-jokingly called "two or three thousand policy changes" that had come down from the top in the years since the lawsuit was settled and the long road toward compliance began. In the most sweeping change of all, the state has shuttered all but three state juvenile facilities over the past decade and brought the population down from ten thousand to fewer than a thousand.

The physical plant at O.H. Close—a razor-wire-enclosed campus with dormitory-style units, a football field, a gymnasium, and a chapel—still had the appearance of a textbook reform school. The population when I visited was 220 young men, down from a peak of about six hundred. In the dayroom, a couple of kids were half watching something about alligators on the Discovery Channel while others played dominoes or chess. Several young men were sprawled across their chairs, dozing or staring at the wall. They all wore a uniform of khaki pants and green polos, sometimes over a white T-shirt.

Boys lived on units with names like Fir, Rivers, and El Dorado, as if the place were a suburban subdivision trying to evoke a gold rush past. Each unit of thirty-six to thirty-eight boys traveled together, marching from one destination to the next in rows of three or four across.

The staff were at work transitioning to the Integrated Behavioral Treatment Model—the approach the state had selected to transform its poorly regarded facilities into therapeutic zones.

"Change is hard," various staff members told me at O.H. Close. "Change is hard on the self."

For years, one staff member explained, "the culture was, 'We are here to provide security and the youth are here to follow our instructions.' "

Now, he explained, "We're working together. So we are a part of the team just as much as the youth are a part of the team, just as much as their families are a part of the team."

The hardest part of this change in ethos, another staffer offered, was following instructions for years, only to have a new protocol come along, complete with people "telling you how wrong you've been."

"When you put your heart and soul into something, and then you have people coming in and telling you, 'Well you're all wrong,' that's hard," she continued plaintively. "We were doing things for years that we honestly thought were helpful."

What sort of things? "Focusing on the offense. Breaking down the denial. Doing all of that—it came from an honest place. So, you know, it's not [like we are] bad, horrible people. It's more of, 'Okay, we've got to recognize that came from an honest place, now we know better, so let's work together to do even better.' "

Staff, it struck me, were facing demands that paralleled those that had long been placed on incarcerated youth: to make profound changes to the way they had always done things, and to do so both quickly and under duress.

Their anxieties about this new approach were not unfounded. A meta-analysis that compared the impact of community-based interventions and those undertaken inside juvenile facilities found that even when successful models were used, their efficacy was lower inside prison walls. Placing young people in juvenile facilities in order to offer them treatment, researchers found, "dampen[s] the positive effects of appropriate service while augmenting the negative impact of inappropriate service."

Some wards who had been in the system for years by the time the changes hit were also finding the new therapeutic regime a big adjustment. In the recent past, for example, minor infractions—"refusing to follow staff instruction; disruptive behavior"—would get a kid a write-up, which, if repeated, could lead to loss of privileges. Now, instead of taking the write-up and sucking up the consequences, a kid might have to write *himself* up, coming up with answers to difficult questions: *What were you thinking? What was the triggering event? What was going on for you?* It did not surprise me to learn that some kids would rather take their consequence and be done with it than engage in this sort of forced introspection after years of learning to shut down and keep quiet.

No dice. A kid involved in a more serious infraction—a fistfight, for example—might still be subdued with pepper spray and put in what was now called a "cool-down" room under the new way of doing things, but that was just a preliminary: now he had to *talk* about it when he got out— talk to the kid he fought with, the guard who sprayed him, and the rest of the guys on the unit, all of whom, he was told, were affected by his actions (during a fight, wards have to "get down" on their bunks, their only private space, until the conflict is over and the unit has been declared cleared). Most kids, I was told, were quick to apologize—unsurprising, given that it took a verbal commitment, or sometimes a No Violence Contract, just to get out of the "cool-down" room.

Those familiar with the history of the California Youth Authority see no small irony in the "new" rehabilitative mandates the litigation sparked. Founded in 1941 with the express purpose of rehabilitation, the California

Youth Authority was for decades seen as a model nationally and internationally. According to historians, the California system "is often cited as a turning point in American juvenile correctional history. . . . Radically breaking with traditional thinking and practice in juvenile corrections, it proposed a model of juvenile justice based on rehabilitation instead of retributive punishment and called for state-level coordination of services. The passage of the California Youth Correction Authority Act of 1941 represents the first time an elected legislative body declared that the purpose of juvenile corrections was rehabilitation rather than punishment."

That law defined the mandate of the California Youth Authority as "to protect society by substituting training and treatment for retributive punishment of young persons found guilty of public offenses." For decades, the Youth Authority relied on educators, doctors, psychiatrists, psychologists, and social workers to assess and devise treatment plans for each youth in its care. In the decades that followed, the Youth Authority became famous for its pioneering efforts to use therapeutic approaches to improve the life chances of those in its care. The "change" that current staffers were finding so hard, in other words, was merely a return to what had once been common practice.

When the national pendulum swung back toward a punitive mentality in the 1980s and 1990s, California took the lead once again, locking up growing numbers of young people under ever-harsher conditions. At its apex, the California Youth Authority held more than ten thousand youths in inhumane conditions, operating for a time at double its capacity.

Despite protests, it seemed an untouchable monolith, backed by a uniquely powerful guards' union known for handing out seven-figure contributions on both sides of the aisle. The staff called themselves "counselors," but not only did they act more like prison guards; they were dues-paying members of the California Correctional Peace Officers Association, the mighty guards' lobby that represented guards at the state's adult prisons as well and that was known for backing harsh sentencing laws and opposing reforms that would stem the flow of bodies into custody.

Then the pendulum swung once again. In 2004, the Prison Law Office won a sweeping settlement in a lawsuit (*Farrell v. Cate*) that described a system that was failing by every measure, including respecting young people's basic human rights. As the Prison Law Office put it, "Rehabilitation cannot succeed when the classroom is a cage and wards live in constant fear of physical and sexual violence from CYA staff and other wards."

The post-*Farrell* years saw the Youth Authority, under attack from multiple directions, enter what appeared to be its death throes, with fewer than a thousand youths in its care, and all but three of its facilities shuttered. Governor Jerry Brown called for the agency to be abolished entirely, with responsibility for its remaining wards handed over to the counties. Meanwhile, staff accustomed to ruling with brute force with little outside oversight are discovering that . . . well, change is hard.

The generation of staffers hired during the "tough on crime" years and trained in the "custody and control" ethos of the time are now being told that their role is that of not guards but adjunct therapists. Many are resistant, and, even if they are not, the kids have a hard time making the conceptual shift required to entrust their deepest traumas to someone who may have pepper sprayed them in the past, or might tomorrow.

If change is proving particularly hard in California, that may have to do with how very far the state has come to reach an environment that meets even minimal safety standards, much less is therapeutic. A 1999 investigation by the California Inspector General's office unearthed practices including "sealing rooms and spraying youth with mace, slamming them into walls, forcing youth into cells with human waste on the floors, or staging 'Friday night fights' between institutionalized youth." Many of these actions were taken by guards who apparently felt so little fear of reprimand that they did not even bother stepping out of range of surveillance cameras, which caught many abuses on tape.

The videotaped beatings at the N.A. Chaderjian Youth Correctional Facility in Stockton; grainy footage of guards setting dogs on unresisting boys; still images of the small steel cages used for "therapy" and "education"—these convey a horror that words cannot quite capture. This effect comes not only from the blunt intensity of the violence captured on film, or the piercing images of teenagers curled up in the fetal position to indicate surrender and to protect their vital organs from the boots and blows of the gangs of men attacking them. The real horror in these images comes from how clearly they convey, simply by their very existence, the perpetrators' confidence that they need not hide their actions. They knew they were being taped but felt certain enough, apparently, that *these* children did not matter—to the public, to outside authorities, or to prison administrators—that they saw no risk in brutalizing them in full view of the camera.

This is the culture into which outside experts were introduced, with the mandate of creating an environment that was not just humane but therapeutic. Consultants from the University of Cincinnati bent to the task, insisting that staff be trained in Effective Reinforcement; Effective Disapproval; Effective Use of Authority; Quality Interpersonal Relationships; Cognitive Restructuring; Anti-Criminal Modeling; Structured Learning/ Skill Building; and Problem Solving Techniques.

Trent, I'd been told, was the "perfect kid" to talk to about the changes that had taken place at O.H. Close and elsewhere in recent years. A husky white twenty-year-old with a blond goatee, Trent had been in various state facilities since the age of sixteen, growing from a boy to a man within the confines of the Youth Authority during a period when that institution was going through rapid changes of its own.

Trent had sampled a buffet of self-improvement offerings: anger management, gang awareness, parenting, healthy living—he has certificates in all of these and more. "This place has really helped me a lot, helped me realize I need to grow up," he said. "Staff treat us like we're their sons sometimes. They tell us they're here to help, not trying to get over on us."

These positive connections, however, were counterbalanced by the bottom line: Trent was constrained not only by bars and gates but also by the unspoken codes still in place despite official reforms. "You can't show somebody fear," he said, describing the rigorous emotional blankness Jared had dubbed the *machine down* mentality. "If you show fear or kindness, that's going to be taken as weakness . . . and then they're gonna try and use that against you."

"Basically, I am institutionalized, a little bit," Trent added. "Like, we're used to getting everything on time, not later. I'm used to getting my clothes on a certain time. I'm used to waking up on a certain time. I'm used to going outside on a certain time. . . . When I get out, [reality] is just going to smack me in the face."

More than any program, Trent said, what motivated him to shed his gang affiliations and stay on the straight and narrow was his young son, born not long after he was arrested. "I'm just trying to change my life around for my son," he insisted. "That's my world. My girlfriend and my son, that's what makes me keep going. . . . I actually got someone I can say, that's mine, you know?"

Trent's young family may have been his great love and motivation, but that did not mean he was able to see them. In fact, he had not seen his son since the boy was an infant, because the trip from Southern California is too long and too costly for his girlfriend to manage.

As another young man at O.H. Close put it, "I'm supposed to be in a 'family-focused' program, but my family is three hundred miles away. What's up with that?"

As I spoke to more of the wards at O.H. Close, it became clear to me why my hosts had described Trent as the "perfect" interview. Others, it seemed, were running into more difficulties under the new regime.

As states close down facilities, young people are often moved from one to the next. In California, a large state where—as elsewhere—most facilities were in remote rural areas, this has made keeping in touch with family nearly impossible for many. For those whose families were in Southern California, O.H. Close was a six- or seven-hour drive.

Danny and Connor were both on the sex offender unit, where, I was told, the treatment program was particularly well established. But everywhere I turned, it seemed, "institutional safety" seemed to collide with treatment goals. The logistical challenges of life on a locked unit also made therapeutic aims such as trust and positive relationships appear difficult, if not impossible, to reach.

The open dorm layout was one example. Following correctional protocol, the boys had to be "down" several times throughout the day, they explained—for count, during shift changes, during snack, and while other groups were showering. Because they had no other personal space, in all, they estimated, they spent between two and four waking hours each day prone on their bunks.

Connor, seventeen, was walking on eggshells. Arrested at thirteen, he was slated to be released at eighteen but had an adult "hold" hanging over him. "If I get into any trouble while I'm here," he translated. "I'll be put into an adult system until I'm twenty-three."

That made any conflict—no matter how peripheral—potentially devastating. "When problems go on, you get jittery, like you want to just get out of the way. You don't want to get in trouble because you know you have a chance of going home."

"Right," Danny interjected. "And then when the chances actually blow up in your face, you just feel like giving up."

Danny, like others I met, chose not to discuss the details of the charges against him. But he did describe the particular risks and stresses he faced as a nineteen-year-old convicted sex offender required to bunk with minors in a mixed-age dorm. Were one of the younger residents to make an allegation against him, no matter how brazen a lie it might be, he believed he could lose his chance to go home. This put him in an especially vulnerable position in an environment that remains very much power oriented. "All that fourteen-year-old [has to say is] 'I don't want this guy touching me' and I'll get in trouble for that. *Big* trouble."

Like others at O.H. Close, Danny was also struggling with the distance from his family. Until he was transferred several months ago, Danny had been close enough to home that his family had been able to visit every weekend. Since the transfer, he had not seen his family once. "It makes a big impact, because without family support, how are you able to move on?"

"I miss my mom," he said. "Basically, I lost everything."

Connor is fortunate in this regard: his family has committed to visiting him every other weekend, despite the distance. "They're a support system," he said. "You need one. . . . [It] gives you something to hold on to."

Distance was not the only obstacle to staying in touch with family. The coercive aspects of the therapeutic program were another barrier. If a boy is deemed not to be participating fully, Connor said, he may get a write-up for "program failure." Potential consequences include no visits, sometimes for as long as ninety days.

The irony of this was not lost on the youths. "The new program they've just introduced to us, it's basically all family oriented," Danny explained. "They want you to do phone calls and phone call meetings. Like, they'll put you on speakerphone with your family . . . and the doctor and you'll have like a family group with the doctor."

Family involvement, in other words, is mandatory, because it is considered central to successful treatment, but those deemed to be doing *poorly* in treatment can, as a consequence, be denied contact with their families. "That's why I say there's a whole lot of game with a little action," Danny concluded.

Nevertheless, Danny did feel he had benefited from the programming he had received. "It matures you and it helps you think out of what's in the box. It helps you think, 'All right, man, I did make a mistake, but *why* did I do it? What was the reason I was angry?'"

Most crucially, he developed a strong connection with a particular staff member. "I remember when I first came to the system, one staff told me, 'Believe it or not, but there's going to be one person you can open to and trust them, and when you find this person everything is going to be easier because you can express your feelings to that person.'"

This prediction had come true for Danny, who had developed a close and trusting relationship with a staff member down south. But as with his family, he lost that support when he was transferred to O.H. Close. He also lost a psychologist whom he had begun to trust. "Then a new doctor came and she wanted me to open up to her. I only knew this doctor for three months and she expected me to open up and share my life. . . . She told me, 'Do it on your own pace. I won't force you to present' [in group therapy], but at the same time, she wants me to present by force."

I asked Danny to clarify what he meant by "force." His response spoke volumes about the perils of coerced redemption.

It was made clear to him, he explained, that if he did not "open up" in group, he would receive a write-up for program failure. Danny could not afford a write-up. He wanted to go home. But getting there, under the new therapeutic model, would require revealing to yet another group of peers and professionals wounds he preferred not to talk about with strangers (including me).

"So much happened to you in the past you can't even trust people, but . . . now they want you to open up, knowing that you can't do it," Danny worried. "I understand we have to open up eventually, but it has to be on our own pace. You have to get to know the person."

The notion of giving a kid a disciplinary write-up for being unwilling, or unable, to expose his deepest traumas on a fixed time frame seems paradoxical at best. Isn't it the responsibility of a therapeutic program to *help* clients develop that degree of trust? Every time I heard about a kid who "failed the program," I wondered why the onus was always on the children. Wasn't it possible that the program had failed *the kid?*

Joseph Leavey—who served as deputy commissioner under Jerome Miller when Miller was closing Massachusetts's reform schools in the 1970s—raised similar questions at the forum on the Massachusetts experience. "It used to be that kids were 'incorrigible,'" Leavey said. "Then we got more sophisticated, and we said they were 'untreatable.' . . . But I always tell my staff, no kid is untreatable. There are quite a few kids we haven't figured out how to treat, but at least that puts the onus on us. Because we're the adults. We're getting paid for this stuff."

At O.H. Close, Connor had given the question of treatment on command some thought as well. "You can be in treatment with somebody that controls you, but you feel you can't open everything up," he said. "You feel a little bit of resentment towards them because you know that no matter what you say, they have power over you."

In group therapy sessions, according to Connor, wards were required to discuss the details of the offense for which they had been committed. Sometimes, Connor said, group leaders would compare what young people revealed in group to their court records. If a young person's account conflicted with what was in his file, he said, the paperwork trumped the testimony, and a young person might be accused of failing to "accept responsibility" or "own up to your actions"—a failure that might affect his chances before the parole board.

Most youths, he added, learn their lesson quickly. "You say what the police said happened," he said. "They want 'truth,' but they want their truth, not your truth."

Like Red Wing, O.H. Close has both a therapeutic mandate and a lockdown unit—the BTP, for Behavioral Treatment Program. According to the boys I met, you could go there for fighting, rioting, "any kind of trouble. Any kind of big conflict or write-ups." Some went for a month. Six months was the maximum. There were, they told me, twenty to thirty boys there at a time—"same as a regular unit."

What seemed to me an intrinsic contradiction—treatment and torture—was by no means limited to these two facilities. At the Giddings School, lauded in John Hubner's 2008 book *Last Chance in Texas* for what he described as a groundbreaking therapeutic program, the majority of wards—86 percent—reported being confined to their rooms for more than twenty-four hours as punishment, according to a 2012 report. Forty-five percent had been isolated as punishment ten or more times during their stay.

Beyond the question of whether a penal institution can truly be transformed into a therapeutic environment or whether the internal contradictions are simply too great, there is the matter of the quality of the treatment itself. Some institutions train their staff in therapeutic modalities; others bring in staff or contract psychologists and psychiatrists; and still others contract out services such as group therapy to outside agencies. The result, inevitably, is a mixed bag. But when therapeutic interventions are not handled with sensitivity to the unique circumstance of incarceration, or to the trauma many young prisoners bring with them—or are just not handled well—they can do more harm than good to a clientele that does not have the option of voting with its feet.

That was Gabrielle's experience. Behind bars, the greatest threat to her safety came in the guise of well-intentioned help: a group for survivors of childhood abuse. The facilitator, she recalled, "sat us in a circle with all these kids that were [physically] and sexually abused, and we told our stories. And then what? We can't help each other right now. We are all kids."

In group, Gabrielle listened to stories of abuse more horrific than her own. One young woman described being violated as a toddler.

"You all need to listen to her, not me," Gabrielle remembers thinking, sinking even deeper into self-protective silence. "Now I'm pushing myself out of the way, because that's worse than mine has ever been."

Eventually, Gabrielle did as she was told and "ran her story." Then she was instructed to list on paper the various assaults and violations she had endured and "flush it"—literally, the paper—and along with it (at least in theory) the trauma.

This strategy was, to put it mildly, ineffective. Gabrielle had breached the carefully constructed wall around her feelings only to be told to "flush them" by a well-meaning, undertrained facilitator.

Once Gabrielle had passed the first benchmark—"flushing" years of trauma—it was time for the next: phoning her abuser (in her case, her father) and demanding an explanation.

"Are you freaking serious?" Gabrielle remembers thinking. "You want me to call my dad and ask him why?"

"This is how you heal from this," the facilitator insisted. "You confront your abuser." A prisoner, Gabrielle did as she was told.

"I don't understand why you did what you did to me," she said when she reached her father by phone.

"Did what?"

"You hit me," she pressed, in search of that elusive "healing" she had been promised. "You raped me."

"Naah. I think you imagined that."

Then he hung up.

The effort to turn a locked facility into a therapeutic environment stumbles again and again on the question of coerced transformation. Changing policy is one thing, changing people quite another. Can individuals realistically be expected to change as radically, and as quickly, as the kind of culture change now taking place demands, to drop not only ingrained habits but long-held belief systems?

I am not talking, for the moment, about the youth. On or off the record, those working to institute culture change inside juvenile facilities described staff resistance as their biggest obstacle.

New York's Gladys Carrión was one of the few willing to speak on the record about this challenge. When I met with Carrión, I was touring her revamped juvenile system. My itinerary included both community-based programs and locked facilities that were transitioning to a therapeutic model.

Since Carrión took the job as commissioner of New York's Office of Children and Family Services in 2007, she has focused on closing those facilities she described as most clearly driven by "power and control and managing behavior through the use of force."

"These facilities were very much correctional in nature, in that there was a punitive environment," she elaborated. "This wasn't necessarily about looking at how you make sure that kids come out with a GED or a high school diploma or college credits. This wasn't about looking at what their clinical needs are. This wasn't about engaging families. This wasn't about creating skill sets in kids. It wasn't about trauma-informed work and understanding behavior and what the root causes were. It wasn't about any of that."

Today, Carrión said, the New York system is "the first in the country where the entire system has been trained on trauma-informed work. It's at different levels of development in each facility, but everybody has been trained." The Sanctuary Model, which New York has chosen to implement, is a well-regarded, trauma-informed therapeutic program that has shown strong outcomes elsewhere.

Nevertheless, according to the Albany *Times Union*, violence has increased fivefold over the past five years in New York's state juvenile facilities. State officials attribute some or all of this uptick to better reporting. Some of Carrión's staff, however, think she has gone too far, placing their own safety at risk by cracking down on the forcible restraints that were once commonplace. Still others implied that Carrión was being set up—that, as Jerry Miller described experiencing when he tried to reform Massachusetts's locked facilities, staff were allowing things to get out of hand, or even instigating conflict, in order to make the commissioner look bad and force her to roll back the changes.

In the pre-reform days, according to a 2009 report by the U.S. Department of Justice, facility staff "routinely" resorted to "uncontrolled, unsafe applications of force." Post-reform, investigators wrote, "staff informed us that . . . their 'hands are tied' and they are forced to just step aside when youth are defiant." Investigators found this attitude "clearly problematic," given that staff were, in fact, being trained in alternative ways of dealing with this kind of behavior.

A clinician who works with several New York state facilities offered his perspective on the roots of staff resistance. Many who work inside the system, he said, "associate the Sanctuary Model with hug-a-thug programs. They feel that Sanctuary is taking away the structure, taking away the rules, taking away authority, which is not actually what it means. Trauma-informed models of care promote consistency, fairness, shared decision making, a commitment to nonviolence, open communication."

"All [these] things fall apart," he added, when "systems are under chronic stress."

Security camera footage taken at Brookwood and Goshen Secure Centers, released in 2011 by a former employee, reveal what does indeed seem to be a system under stress. As the Albany *Times Union* describes the sometimes blurry images of mayhem, "teenage detainees gang up on a much larger staff member and pound him to the ground. In other videos, youthful prisoners attack each other with similar viciousness. Blood spills and tables are overturned. In some recordings, staff members and young residents lay unconscious from the blows."

"Now we have to wait until they take a swing at us to use a restraint, rather than nipping the behavior in the bud," a Brookwood employee told the *Times Union*. "I went to work with a constant feeling I was going to be assaulted." According to the same article, the percentage of staff out on workers' compensation claims for on-the-job injuries went from 29 percent in 2007 to 59 percent in 2010.

This high rate of absence creates stress for those still on the job, one youth aide told me. "Being mandated [to work overtime] is like breathing around here," he said, due to the precipitous rise in workers' comp claims and absences.

"You gotta suck it up," he said. "Anyway, it stacks retirement." Meaning, the more overtime you work, the more retirement you get.

In Brooklyn, I spoke with two young men who were transitioning from institutions where, they said, the Sanctuary Model had been in place. A sixteen-year-old who was on his way home after seven months at the Highland Residential Center found the program there "corny—it didn't work."

"If you're mad, you're not going to look at your safety plan and try to do any of that," he said, referring to laminated cards young people wear around their necks with personalized suggestions for calming their anger. "You not paying that no mind. It's not going to work. It's just nothing . . ."

"Get mad, look down at the safety plan that says read a book, and actually go read a book or something . . ." he mocked, his tone laced with obvious skepticism.

Despite his scorn for the safety plan, he acknowledged that his time away had changed him. "I used to get mad and fight all the time, but now I don't fight no more," he said.

His explanation for the transformation? "It's just growing up."

A seventeen-year-old who had participated in the Sanctuary program had a different take. When he arrived, he said, he had recently lost his brother and was overwhelmed by grief. "A few times in there I got real angry and just shut down," he said, but a staff member he described as his social worker helped him get through it—whether or not he was "programming" well.

"It took a little while," this young man acknowledged. "Once I sat down with him, [at first] I wasn't really talking. I'd just sit there." Unlike the boys at O.H. Close, however, he was permitted to open up at his own pace.

"Talk when you're ready," the social worker told him. Sometimes they sat in silence for as long as half an hour. What finally cemented their relationship, this young man told me, was when the social worker told him that he, too, had lost a sibling recently: his sister had died at almost the same time his client's brother had.

The advice the worker offered—"stay on the bright side"; "things could be worse"—may have been simplistic, but that didn't seem to matter. What did matter was the fact that his young client felt a genuine connection. Today, this young man is planning to go to college—out of state, if he can swing it—and enroll in the navy.

One does not even have to be buzzed in the door of the Red Hook Residential Center in New York's picturesque Duchess County along the Hudson River to sense that this is a place marked by a strong personality. The expansive, tree-dotted grounds may evoke a sanatorium of years gone by, but even before one enters the building, a different sensibility reveals itself. Whimsical plastic figures—M&M icons and other commercial memorabilia—are arranged like flower beds outside the facility. Piles of stuffed animals complete the anachronistic decor.

Red Hook is full of these personal touches: director Eddie Figueroa's troll collection arrayed along a windowsill; a tree planted in memory of

Figueroa's father; a peaceful gazebo; and a central courtyard landscaped by residents, which Figueroa showed me with evident pride. The flower beds there—planted not with figurines but with living flowers—were bright and well tended.

It didn't take ten minutes with Figueroa, who had been at Red Hook for nearly three decades, to understand what Carrión meant when she spoke of the importance of institutional leadership. Figueroa embraced the Sanctuary Model and welcomed the consistency it offered but didn't expect it to bring radical changes at Red Hook. "We were doing Sanctuary before there was a Sanctuary!" he said gleefully.

As we toured the campus, Figueroa greeted each boy who passed, calling him by name, asking after a relative, or shouting out, "Hi, papi!"

"I was them a long time ago," Figueroa said. "I lost my mom at eleven. Dad was never home. The only difference was I had sports to guide me, then the military."

I found myself thinking about a casual remark one of his staff had made earlier in the day. Sports are an important part of the curriculum at Red Hook, and kids get hurt regularly on the court and the field, he told me. Juvenile facilities such as Red Wing hold more than their share of city kids from under-resourced schools—kids who may not have had a chance to belong to a sports team before.

Figueroa greets each new arrival with the same ritual: he brings the teenagers out to the basketball court and challenges them to a game of one-on-one. If they beat him, he promises, he'll buy them a soda.

Some of the guys take pity on the retirement-aged, round-bellied, short-statured director. Others play all out. Either way, Figueroa clobbers them. That opens the door to lesson number one: he may be short, plump, and old, but he *never gives up*. Success, he is showing them, is not just about the advantages you start with; it's about how hard you try.

Lesson number two: he buys them the soda anyway. When it comes to the affection Figueroa offers, he communicates via that gesture, there are no conditions.

Figueroa supports Carrión—"I'd rather deal with a person who is principled"—and has little patience for her critics, who, he indicated, "see them [the youth] as a cash cow." The day we met, Figueroa was interviewing candidates for a youth division aide position at Red Hook. One applicant worked at another institution but wanted to transfer in order to shorten his commute. When he inquired politely as to whether he could count on "job security" at Red Hook, I thought Figueroa might pick him up by his collar and deposit him out in the parking lot.

"These are God's children," Figueroa told him sternly. "They are not here for you to make a living." The rest of the interview, I suspected, was a formality.

Figueroa had little patience for the notion that by limiting the use of force, Carrión had left staff in a vulnerable position. "*Before*, it was dangerous," he said. "Kids were getting abused. Kids *and* staff were getting hurt."

" 'Safe' for them," he scoffed, referring to Carrión's critics, means that if you ship a Brooklyn kid upstate, "you got one less juvenile delinquent in Brooklyn. But the consequence is the loss of family, friends, community."

As I was heading out, he asked me to carry a message to Carrión: "Tell her I say, 'Go, girl!' " he said, smiling broadly.

It was a school day, and the kids were in their classrooms, but the atmosphere at Red Hook had the syrupy, slowed-down feel of the summer afternoon it was. In the vast, echoing gymnasium, a staff member was shooting baskets with a single resident. In a nearby classroom, fifteen young men, all black as far as a glance could tell, were learning CPR. Inside the classroom, I saw a cluster of young men in various stages of ennui—sitting, slumping, or flat-out sleeping. One rested his cheek on the cool of his desk. Another had his T-shirt pulled up over his head. Two older white men, seemingly oblivious to their students' lack of interest, blithely continued to run through their curriculum.

At the end of the day, when my family came to pick me up, a staffer let my eleven-year-old son into the gymnasium to shoot baskets. "Don't worry," the man joked later, as he brought me to the gym to pick up my kid. "I haven't put a uniform on him."

I was reminded of the last time I'd heard this kind of joke, years ago when I was visiting Eliza in juvenile hall. A little girl was scurrying playfully around the visiting room one weekend while her teenage mother visited with the child's grandmother. "You'd better settle down," a guard with a heavy ring of keys at his belt told the little girl, "or I'll lock *you* up too." Terrified, the child dashed back to the table and hid her face in her grandmother's lap.

Despite the tremendous difference between the two institutions, it struck me that both jokes relied on the same premise: prisons are scary places, especially for children. No matter how well run or therapeutically oriented, even the best institutions I had visited—places like Red Hook—were struggling mightily to implement treatment modalities inside locked facilities. Can a young person establish a genuinely trusting and therapeutic relationship with someone who is also the keeper of the keys?

Red Hook was lovely, and Eddie Figueroa would give Red Wing's Otis Zanders a run for his money for Warden of the Year. If a kid had committed a crime serious enough to require that he be locked up for the sake of public safety, it seemed to me, he'd be hard-pressed to do better than Red Hook.

But the kids at Red Hook, as well as many at far harsher institutions, were *not* there because they posed a threat to public safety. Across the country, the more serious juvenile offenders are often not in the juvenile system at all; instead they have been transferred to adult court. In New York— one of only two states that charge all sixteen- and seventeen-year-olds as adults (the other is North Carolina)—this is especially likely.

In December 2009, New York governor David Paterson's Task Force on Transforming Juvenile Justice released *Charting a New Course: A Blueprint for Transforming Juvenile Justice in New York State*. According to that report, more than half the youth who enter state institutional placements (at a cost of more than $200,000 per child per year) have a misdemeanor as their most serious offense. "This investment," the task force concluded, "does little to protect public safety or help youth become productive, law-abiding citizens. In fact, many have concluded that it may even be making things worse."

When we met in 2012, Carrión told me that two-thirds of the kids in her system were what New York calls "step-ups"—low-level kids who started out being placed in the care of a voluntary agency and were later "modified" into state custody. Smoking marijuana, skipping school, stealing a cell phone: these were the examples Carrión offered when I asked what sorts of things could get a kid modified. At Red Hook, she told me before

I visited, "the vast majority you're going to find are going to be [there for] misdemeanors and low-level felonies." I might meet a kid who had been involved in an assault, she said, or a robbery, but "you're not going to have murderers there. You're not going to have rapists there."

In fact, 64 percent of youth at low-level facilities like Red Hook state-wide are there for misdemeanors. New York classifies these facilities as "nonsecure," a somewhat confusing term that means, per Carrión, that "it's locked and kids can't run away," but it has an open-feeling campus with no intimidating perimeter fence. The state's "limited-secure" facil-ities are different. According to the 2009 report from the governor's task force, several "look and feel exactly like secure facilities, with surrounding barbed wire." Despite this intimidating facade, however, the majority of kids in these places—56 percent—also have been convicted of nothing more serious than misdemeanor charges.

No matter how lovely the landscaping at a place like Red Hook might appear, how sincere its director and well trained its staff, there is no get-ting around the question of why kids are sent there to begin with. Does lighting a joint or skipping out on school justify the trauma inherent in incarceration; the separation from family, school, and community; the high odds of recidivism and reduced life chances?

Most kids, to be clear, can get away with missing a few days of school, getting high occasionally, or even both at once without winding up locked up. Poor youth of color, however, are granted far less leeway for "youth-ful indiscretions." In New York City, a stunning 93.5 percent of youth placed in state custody are children of color. Had the "high bar" Carrión spoke of been met for most of these kids? Carrión's conversation with the judges about who they were sending her way clearly had an impact, but the fundamental quandary has yet to be resolved. The state is still taking away young people's liberty—a grave act, as Carrión herself is the first to point out, and one that affects youth of color more than anyone—for acts that pose little or no threat to public safety, acts that better-off white kids commit on a regular basis, often with no governmental intervention at all, much less the theoretically last-ditch intervention of incarceration.

The Supreme Court itself has waffled on the question of whether placing a child in a locked building as treatment for his problems, not as punishment for his actions, constitutes imprisonment, and so demands due-process protections.

In its decision in *In re Gault*, the Supreme Court challenged the notion that benign intent could supersede the fact of the fence. Juveniles facing delinquency proceedings, the Court concluded in its 1967 ruling, had a right to counsel under the Fourteenth Amendment specifically because they faced "the awesome prospect of incarceration in a state institution."

"Commitment is a deprivation of liberty," the Court wrote in declaring that juveniles could invoke the Fifth Amendment right against self-incrimination, because "it is incarceration against one's will, whether it is called 'criminal' or 'civil.'"

Four years later, the Court changed its tune. In *McKeiver v. Pennsylvania*, the justices refused to extend further constitutional protections (most notably, trial by jury) on the grounds that confinement, when it is imposed by the juvenile court, "is aimed at rehabilitation, not at . . . imposing pains and penalties" and is therefore fundamentally different from the incarceration of adults. In this case, according to the Court, the intent of the jurist trumped the experience of the judged.

The top court's inconsistency left lower courts flummoxed when faced with similar due-process challenges on behalf of juveniles. "Sometimes punishment is treatment," the Washington Supreme Court offered in one particularly obscure ruling.

These conundrums continue to emerge to this day, as staff and administrators at juvenile facilities struggle to respond to new mandates to "treat" their captive charges. Researcher Richard Mendel, who has studied state juvenile facilities extensively, uses the term "toxic treatment environment" to describe the challenges that come with implementing even a good program in a juvenile prison. "Even if juvenile corrections facilities provide high quality education, mental health, and substance abuse treatment services," Mendel writes, "youth are unlikely to benefit when the overall environment of the facility is permeated with fear, violence, or maltreatment."

University of California, Berkeley's Barry Krisberg put it more concisely: "You can't give a motivational interview with a tear gas canister on your belt."

Having visited several therapeutic prisons, I am left ambivalent. The best of them are better—some far so—than the standard institution. If the goal is the lesser evil, then the therapeutic prison may well fit the bill. But if we hold ourselves to a higher standard—if our goal is to protect both children's rights and public safety, as well as to help traumatized children to heal—then doors that lock from the outside will always run counter to these aims.

12

ONLY CONNECT

Rehabilitation Happens in the
Context of Relationship

We are all born for love. It is the principle of existence, and its only end.
—Benjamin Disraeli

He told me that I had a soul.
How did he know?

—Valjean's soliloquy, *Les Misérables*

IT WAS A LAZY, humming, late spring afternoon, and I was standing with my daughter and her fourth-grade class atop a hill in Marin County, California, where a docent had brought us to examine bugs and leaves. The view was tremendous, encompassing the San Francisco skyline, the green hills of Berkeley, and, incongruously, the two-hundred-building complex that comprises San Quentin State Prison, looming over the San Francisco Bay like something out of a Stephen King novel.

"That's where the heroes put the bad guys," the docent said offhandedly as she pointed out the prison to the dusty, distracted children.

As the schoolchildren dutifully gazed across the water at the place they kept the "bad guys," I thought of Jared, who was nineteen years old and fresh out of San Quentin the first time I met him, having landed there at sixteen for his role in an attempted robbery. A friend brought him into the youth newspaper I edited. Hesitant at first, he quickly became one of our most prolific writers and a valued member of our editorial team.

That did not stop him from pointing a gun at my head in the office one afternoon—a "joke" that frightened me more than anything I can remember. There was no particular tension between us, and I didn't think Jared would hurt me on purpose, but he seemed visibly drunk at the time. The volatile combination of alcohol and a firearm scared me enough that it would be years before I could run into him without a wave of fear.

For a good while after that afternoon, my affection for Jared, not to mention what I'd understood until that day to be my values, was overwhelmed by a powerful desire to see him gone. It didn't matter where—I had no desire to see him suffer or "pay"—but, loath as I am to admit it today, I would have slept better had he been behind bars.

As the children rested on the hilltop, my mind wandered to a more recent afternoon, nearly two decades after that terrifying encounter. Jared leaned beneath an expansive elm, my young son, an aspiring magician, at his feet with a deck of cards. Jared watched intently, matching the earnest demeanor of his raconteur. Jared sat there patiently for at least half an hour, evincing a bottomless supply of wonder as my son ran through his entire repertoire.

We were gathered that afternoon along with friends to scatter the ashes of a man we'd all loved: a professor who had, at the urging of his wife, taken Jared into his family home. This aging iconoclast had seen past Jared's glowering visage to a bright spark of intellect and curiosity no teacher before had recognized. At his kitchen table, he had offered Jared private seminars on history, language, and religion that had fanned that spark into a lasting flame.

"This family saved my life," Jared told me days after the professor's death.

The professor's decline had been slow and agonizing, as Alzheimer's and Parkinson's ravaged first his mind and then his body. Jared had cared for him during these years, washing, feeding, and shepherding his erstwhile mentor with the patience of a monk.

Once, the professor stumbled on the stairs to his house, nearly tumbling to a devastating fall. It was Jared who caught him, the strength—both physical and psychological—he had begun to cultivate in order to survive behind bars now allowing him to cradle this elder-child with a gentle confidence.

"It's a corrupt belief," said Aaron Knipis, a clinical psychologist who was in trouble with the law himself by the time he was twelve years old, answering a reporter's questions about a twelve-year-old charged with first-degree murder, "to think you can know the heart and soul of the child and predict the course of their lifetime."

More than anyone I know, Jared has underscored Knipis's message: that a single act or even a series of acts, however menacing, is not the sum of a man and cannot tell us with any certainty who he might become, especially if that man is still a boy. My conversations with Jared have helped me to think through a central question: How *do* young people change? What rehabilitates? If not prison, what *will* keep us safe?

"At my core I'm a good dude. I know I am. I got heart. I don't mean heart as in courage, I mean *heart*," Jared told me recently, his voice dropping to a near-whisper on the final "heart." "But sometimes I may do some bad shit."

I thought of the Jared who had come out of San Quentin: the suspicion in his gaze, the gun in his hand. How had he regained his trust in humanity after what he experienced there? What had allowed *me* to regain my trust in him? How had he become the man he is today?

Like every other young person I've interviewed or known who has come back from crime and profoundly changed his life, Jared answered this question by talking about a relationship: a long-standing bond with an adult who stood by him; a connection that wouldn't evaporate overnight and wasn't contingent on his own good behavior. A bond, in other words, that was unconditional, as freely offered as it was returned, predicated on nothing besides mutual affection, evolving over time into a sense of family. *That* had changed his life, the only thing that ever does.

"I still believe in humanity because you have people like her," Jared told me, speaking of the professor's wife. She had taken him into her family without a second thought and over time had come to love him like a son, while her own sons had embraced him as a brother. "You got people like that. There's an element in her that ain't human. It's like something angelic."

"I've been places that other people haven't, experienced things that other people haven't," he continued, "and when I engage with a person, I can *see* them. I can see their core. I know who they are."

Jared was indicating, not for the first time, that he was not quick to trust, in other people and perhaps in his own future, in what life had to offer to someone with his past. But in the woman who became a second mother to him as well as a trusted friend, he found a spirit large enough to embrace him in all his complexity: a good dude who might do some bad shit, which is to say, a human being. Through their relationship of many years, Jared gained the kind of trust, in others and himself, that allows for joy even amid his constant vigilance. He can hold hands with his girlfriend, or watch his children play, and recognize in these moments his part in the web of human community. That, he taught me, is "rehabilitation"—a prerequisite, perhaps, for the cessation of crime, but something much deeper as well.

"She'll give people chances," he said, speaking again of the professor's wife, shaking his head in an abiding wonder at a quality he had so rarely encountered. "I tell my girlfriend this: if it wasn't for her, I would be dead right now. I wouldn't be alive. We wouldn't know each other. I would be fucking dead."

Instead, there he sat, in the shade of the great tree, patiently engaging with my own persistent boy even as he mourned the man who'd saved his life, whom Jared had shepherded with such tenderness through the ebbing of his own.

Like all great friendships, it struck me, theirs was a bond sustained by reciprocity, not charity. The professor and his wife had been generous toward Jared, but that was not the whole of it. They saw Jared as a young man with much to offer, not merely as someone in need. In fulfilling the unspoken promise between them, Jared had been able to glimpse his *own* promise, to see himself as more than an object of help.

Jared had been lucky in the embrace of this family, but that wasn't the whole story. A chosen son who gave as much as he was given, he had come in from the rain and grown into a man—a man he himself could describe as empathetic. Getting to this place had required a long battle, and the victory belonged to Jared himself. But without the support of this pair who had stood by his side as he found the strength to be the man they saw in him, the odds against him would have been long indeed.

In the weeks after I faced Jared's gun, I fought bitterly with the professor's wife, a dear friend of mine also, over her decision to continue their personal relationship in the immediate aftermath of that afternoon. Confused and still afraid, I felt she was placing her bond with Jared above my safety, above me. For a while—for as long, that is, as I saw myself as victim—I found her choice a bitter pill to swallow.

It was a great relief, years later, as we sat beneath that tree, to acknowledge how very wrong I had been. All of us were safer because of the chance this family had taken in welcoming Jared in and keeping him close as he stumbled his way toward stability. It struck me in that moment that I no longer feared him, a feeling far more freeing than the fleeting security I had felt when, not long after he brought the gun into the office, I learned he had been arrested for something new and was back behind bars again.

Any reason to fear Jared was long in the past and had nothing to do with the man he was today. I trusted him, I realized under that elm, in the deepest way possible. I trusted him with my child.

How? I remember asking him later. How had he gotten to where he was today, when the odds had been stacked so powerfully against him that the law itself had bet against his future by sending him to adult prison when he was not yet grown?

"I had to sit long and hard and think about it," he answered. "I analyze myself constantly. How did I go from where I was mentally, the me that was out there then, to the me now?"

"If the me that was out there then would have met the me I am now," he added, laughing, "me then would have kicked my ass."

"Would 'you now' fight back?" I asked him.

"Probably not," he said, suddenly solemn. Jared now is a man with something to lose. He has children who need him; a job he is good at; and a woman he loves, who has pledged herself to marry him. Not giving a fuck is no longer an option, as risky as letting himself care again might be.

As Jared stretched his limbs in the shade of that tree, his avuncular gaze lingering quizzically on my son, it struck me what a long road he had traveled to where he now stood, and what a narrow ledge he walked along still. Jared carries two strikes under California's unforgiving three strikes law. The slightest misstep—a moment's unchecked anger, or a stranger's misapprehension—could send him away for the rest of his life. How, I wondered, did he live with that uncertainty? How did he keep it from tipping into rage?

"It's that love factor," he answered. Then he turned to my son and drew another card.

Advances in brain science, age-old common sense—everything points to something a bit more complicated than the carrot and the stick (with the current emphasis weighted toward the stick) when it comes to changing behaviors that stem from complex and often traumatic life experiences. What does work—how change, or "rehabilitation," happens—is a question with as many answers as there are individuals. At the same time, a single thread ran through my conversations with young people who had been through the crucible of juvenile justice.

Rehabilitation happens in the context of relationship. The kids who "make it" all point to at least one consistent relationship with an adult they can trust. They have someone walking with them as they do the hard work of changing how they think, act, and respond; how they view themselves and others; with whom they spend their time; where they turn to assuage affronts and sorrows—all of which feeds into the mandate of the law: to change how they behave.

However one frames the question, the answer does not vary: children do best when they are held close. Children grow, children change, children flourish, children thrive in relationships. The "juvenile delinquent"—the one who gets caught—offers no exception to this basic rule.

The second thing young people who have managed to stay free seem to have in common is some sense of purpose: a goal of their own and a fair shot at meeting it. Whether getting into law school, saving enough for a deposit on an apartment, becoming a movie star, or getting a GED, they have something to work toward that matters to them. What justice-involved youths need, it turns out, is what anyone else does: work that gives us reason to get out of bed in the morning and someone with whom to share our setbacks as well as our successes.

These two central drives, ambition and attachment, are closely intertwined. Young people who are raised to believe that they are worthless, that they will never do or be anything of value   young people raised inside juvenile prisons—often internalize this self-defeating message. Those best equipped to resist it have someone speaking into their other ear not only a different assessment but a different set of standards——someone who aspires to more for them than not to recidivate.

I remember a conversation I once had with Eliza about the then newly named cohort "disconnected youth." There was much consternation about what should be done to help this untethered population—defined as unemployed, unmarried, not enrolled in school or enlisted in the military—get onto one or more of these presumed tracks to adulthood.

Eliza had grown up in so many "placements"—from foster homes to group homes to juvenile halls—she had lost count. As radically alone as anyone I knew, Eliza knew "disconnection" by heart.

But when I asked her what she thought should be done about the issue, she surprised me, as she often did, by challenging the premise. "Everyone says you have to get a job; you have to get an education," she said ruefully. "I'm not sure I want those things anymore. The greatest value I have right now is someone who spends time with me. I don't think many youth value success if no one cares whether they succeed."

None of this is unique to justice-involved children. What they need, in the end, is what all children need. Any difference lies not in their nature but in the extent to which that nature is denied. Teachers don't place gold stars on students' schoolwork because the shiny foil itself will motivate the children. A child will work most diligently, the teacher understands, if by doing so she can succeed in making someone proud.

Eighty to 90 percent of American teenagers, recall, will go through a period of delinquency at some point in their teens. The vast majority will grow out of it as they grow up, entering adult life unhindered by the consequences of what George W. Bush memorably described as "youthful mistakes." Seen through the lens of its near universality, juvenile delinquency begins to look less like an aberration than a developmental stage. If this is so, "What rehabilitates?" may not be the right question. More important, perhaps, is "What do children need?"

Like Freud's famous query into the hearts of women, this question has generated a mountain of research, all of which reveals what we already know: what children need is us. Children flourish in the shelter of loving adults. Not only the research but every conversation I have had with a young person leads to this same understanding.

Children need relationship in order to thrive—to navigate the maze of challenges and changes that constitutes growing up, and to ready themselves for the lifelong task of finding their place in the world. They need relationship, at the most primal level, to survive. Human infants have a longer period of dependency than any other species. Babies who are not held or touched—those in institutions, for example—may die in their cribs, even if their material needs are met.

These are human truths we deny with some difficulty. To pull it off, we rely on distancing tools such as the super-predator trope to convince ourselves that the kids who come before the juvenile court are so profoundly "other" that they do not suffer as our own would when we lock them away—so fundamentally different that isolation, against all odds and evidence, might even improve them.

Our penchant for isolation has filtered into other efforts to mold or improve children perceived as troublesome. The preschooler who won't observe "quiet time" is expelled from the circle and forced to endure a shameful and solitary time-out. Later on, in grade school, she can be suspended (pushed away) or expelled (pushed out) if she continues to act out.

"Acting out" is a broad phrase, encompassing both acts of delinquency and childhood misbehavior that falls within the law. Either way, the need for attention is the emotion that is most often being "acted out." Yet we respond with the official *withdrawal* of attention—a practice that, repeated over time, attenuates a young person's ties to the community just when she is crying out most clearly to be kept close.

Just as most of the young people I spoke with remembered the moment when they veered into delinquency, many were able to pinpoint the next fork in the road—what, or *who*, steered them back toward safety and hope. Again with remarkable consistency, young people pointed to an adult who had listened without judgment and let them know they mattered. Often that adult evolved into something like a mentor, but before an angry kid can listen to even the wisest guidance, she generally first needs to be listened to herself.

For Gabrielle to find that pivotal person, it took being treated for a drug problem she did not have. She's not clear why, finally, she was placed in a treatment program—maybe they just couldn't think of anything more to do with her. Whatever the reason, P. House—a treatment wing inside the prison where Gabrielle had landed—is where she ultimately found the sense of connection she needed to help change her trajectory.

It started with a counselor who, Gabrielle recalled, "rocked. Her and me would sit down and we would talk and talk." With the support of her counselor, Gabrielle gradually lowered her guard and began talking with some of the other P. House residents as well. "Now I'm hearing grown women tell me about what happened when they were kids, older ladies than me, and they were telling how they dealt with it and how their family dealt with it. I started to identify with some of these ladies: 'Oh, they just kind of ignored you, too? Okay, so I am not the only person . . . Then I started to learn more about myself: okay, so *that* is why I became violent."

A woman who had absorbed thirty years of abuse before finally getting "tired" enough that she killed her abuser helped Gabrielle understand why Gabrielle's mother had not left her own violent marriage sooner. Gabrielle wrote to her mother—who was now clean and on her own—and learned through their correspondence that the violence Gabrielle had thought was her solitary burden was part of an intergenerational legacy. As a child, her mother had been raped by her own father and, like her daughter, had "stuffed it" for decades. When Gabrielle had returned from Texas with the revelation that *her* father had raped her, it had shaken her mother's defenses so deeply that she had simply shut down in order not to hear it.

"I'm sorry that I didn't pay attention to you," Gabrielle's mother wrote, "but I did not know how."

Gabrielle was going through a profound transition. The spark of trust that started with one counselor who listened allowed Gabrielle not only to reach out but also to look within—to begin, to quote the poet Adrienne Rich, "diving into the wreck" of her own suppressed history, "to see the damage that was done and the treasures that prevail."

The more deeply Gabrielle delved into the sources of her anger and the bone-deep hopelessness that drove her criminality, the more clearly a new path ahead of her emerged. Somewhere along the way, she realized that she was done. *It is what it is* no longer worked for her. Prison was not where she wanted to grow old.

When her parole date came around, Gabrielle asked to be assigned to a treatment program in another city. She walked out the gates with a new sense of resolve, determined to find the life she finally believed that she might actually deserve.

"That's where I really found out who I was," she said of this next program. Once again, she was in treatment for a nonexistent drug problem, but her counselors understood that and adapted the language and framework to fit her needs.

"Everybody else, I have to worry about them relapsing by going out and using dope," the director told Gabrielle. "You, I have to worry about stealing my car."

"Relapse prevention" in Gabrielle's case translated to staving off the street. "Substance-abuse treatment" meant curbing her addiction to violence. Gangbanging was identified as her drug of choice. "Addressing grief and loss" meant mourning her brothers and her own lost childhood, but also "grieving *not* being on the streets and selling dope. . . . I had to grieve all of that, and I didn't even know you could."

Again, she found a counselor with whom she connected. "I want you to grieve," this counselor told Gabrielle as she walked her through the process of stripping herself bare enough to start to rebuild.

Each new connection opened onto the next. Gabrielle began an internship with the organization where she would rise to case manager. She met the woman who would become her wife. Day by day, the isolation that had grown so familiar gave way to a web of relationships that sustained and protected her as she started shedding skins.

If they can do it, she thought as she looked at her competent, dedicated co-workers, each with a history as complex as her own, *so can I.*

Today, at thirty-four, Gabrielle is thriving. She is married to a woman she speaks of adoringly, and she loves her job as a case manager for youth in San Francisco, where she is clearly respected by clients and colleagues alike.

A solidly built woman with broad Polynesian features and a casual style that makes her appear ageless, Gabrielle has a straightforward manner that lets her young clients know right off they will not get much by her. Before long, most find they *want* to live up to her expectations.

Dozens of young people look to Gabrielle as they navigate the rough roads she remembers so well. She's tough, the kids know that, but before she starts lecturing them about "making choices," she works to ensure that they *have* some choices besides the street. No matter how they stumble, she is there to hear them out. Because without that, she understands all too well—with no one to believe them, much less believe *in* them—how can young people feel they matter enough to "choose" a future that goes any further than a room for the night? Before a young person can choose a better, safer future, he has to be able to imagine himself in it, and before he can do *that*, he needs help believing that he is worth the trouble. That is where Gabrielle's constant unconditional presence comes in.

Now the arbiter herself of what can be expected, Gabrielle looks back on her younger self with a wry perspective but largely eschews judgment. "I think about some of the things that I did and I'm, like, 'Wow, that was messed up—and it helped me survive, too.'"

The day I met with Gabrielle in her cramped, file-filled office, the first thing she told me was not to hold back. Nothing I could ask her, she said, could be as demanding as her experience telling her story as part of a restorative justice program inside the county jail—opening her heart and history to men who were locked up for violence, often against women and girls much like herself.

She had gone as a guest speaker, her testimony intended to help the men face up to the pain they had inflicted on others. The men sat in silence as she shared with them the details of her childhood: the years of terror and sexual aggression; the day her father used her broken ribs to break through her defenses; her rape at the hands of the man she had been raised to consider her protector.

Afterwards, one of the men approached her. "He told me that he *heard* me," Gabrielle marveled, shaking her head at the memory. "That was the first time in my whole life that a male has ever told me, 'I hear what you're saying.' All of my life, it had never happened that way."

I hear what you're saying. This was the connection Gabrielle had longed for throughout her years on the street and then her long imprisonment. From there, it was a short leap to realizing that she had found her purpose: "This is what I should do—really listen to these kids."

What started as a calling has become a career, one to which her supervisors say Gabrielle is extraordinarily well suited. "I don't know," she demurred with an uncharacteristic bashfulness when I repeated this assessment. "My guys just take to me really, really well. When I say things to my guys, they know I am not going to sugarcoat it."

"They all want to be little gang members, and I am, like, 'Dude, do you know how bad it feels to have bullets in your legs when it gets cold?'"

Gabrielle has a sixth sense for the wounded child hiding behind the tough facade. She has yet to meet a kid in trouble who—if you really *listen*—is not stumbling under the weight of years of trauma.

Gabrielle answered without hesitation when I asked her a question with which others had struggled: what might have made a difference earlier in her own life?

"If somebody was there for me between fourteen and twenty-five," she answered, homing in on the years that have been identified as highest risk for crime. "Just to hear the words that I was saying to them, you know? To hear that at home it's bad, that Mom is using or I'm being hit, or I'm being abused. Even if I don't want you to do [anything] . . . I need somebody to hear me. To understand that, listen, I need to talk about this."

"A lot of my guys," she continued, "believe in the same thing I did— that what happens inside the house stays in the house. That's what we were taught."

"Nobody listens to kids," Gabrielle continued, with a fierceness that made it clear why she inspires such devotion. "Nobody hears what they're saying. . . . But I *remember* when I was a kid, and this and this happened. That's all most of them really need is just for someone to say, 'I can hear you.'"

The biggest challenge Gabrielle faces with her guys is not breaking down defenses but building up their confidence, providing a counter to the oft-repeated message that they will never be more than the sum of their crimes. "In their minds," she explained, "it's what they're *supposed* to do."

Her role as she sees it is a cross between confidante and cautionary tale. "I am here to listen to you right now, but *understand* me," she will tell her young clients. "If you keep on doing what you're doing, you are going to end up like me at twenty-nine."

She might illustrate this point by showing them a worn document stamped THREE STRIKES: 25 TO LIFE.

"I can't do this," Gabrielle remembers telling the district attorney back when she first saw that crushing piece of paper. "I can't be there forever." She was out of prison and on the road to recovery, she said, when she was accused of trying to pass a bad check (she wasn't, she added, but her word did not mean much in the face of her record). Now she was looking at life behind bars.

"I don't know why not," the DA answered, impassive. *Habitual criminal. Menace to society.* Her file, it seemed, told him all he cared to know.

"If only you knew why," Gabrielle told him.

"There is no reason why you could be this way," she remembers him responding. "There can be no 'why' for the things that you have done."

Gabrielle was a familiar face to the judge. "I am tired of seeing you in my courtroom," he told her sternly. "I saw you in juvenile all the way up to here. . . . I have seen you come in and out of here all these years. . . . What would make you stop coming back?"

"I don't know," she answered, "but I've got to find it."

To her astonishment, the judge voided the strike, giving Gabrielle one more chance to prove herself—quite likely her last.

Gabrielle held on to that act of grace like the last board in a shipwreck as she struggled once again to make her way to shore. Once she had made it there—settled into her new job and been stable long enough to trust in her new life—she sent the judge a letter. She was doing well, she told him, and also doing good; she had not squandered that single stroke of mercy.

I am doing it, she wrote. *And I am not coming back.*

Whether or not the young people I interviewed were familiar with what researchers term "resilience"—the constellation of qualities that allows some children to overcome traumas that would topple others—most were able to articulate what fostered their own strength as well as what drained it. Together, they made clear to me both why the loss of key relationships so often precedes or precipitates crime and how a connection with a caring adult (or adults) can change a life's direction.

Curtis, the "million-dollar kid" who was locked up at age ten—who had been kidnapped by his father only to be returned to a household marked by addiction, domestic violence, and unremitting chaos—remembers a childhood marked by rage and silence.

"Nobody really gave me the attention I needed," Curtis said. "Nobody sat down with me and tried to understand what I was going through or feeling, or tried to help me get through my struggles and my problems."

"Attention," he added, "was my number one goal."

At sixteen, Curtis spoke with a deliberateness that made him sound much older. As he described the defensive posture he developed growing up—the process of becoming "totally desensitized" to others' feelings and eventually his own—it was not hard to see the hurt and angry child beneath the solemn, earnest teen.

"Really, I was just a little child that was misguided, that needed some help and some direction," Curtis said of his younger self—the boy of ten who was shipped off to juvenile prison before he was old enough to use a razor.

"Fragmented" is how Curtis described his mental state during much of his incarceration. "I felt like I was cut into pieces." This sense of fragmentation worsened when, at twelve, Curtis was consigned to an isolation cell for fighting. It would be a full year before Curtis emerged and reentered the general population. He knew he could not withstand another stint in solitary but could not see a way to break free of the cycle of insult, reaction, violence, and punishment in which he was entangled.

He began paying attention to a group of wards whom he had not noticed before. Older than Curtis, they also seemed more focused. They carried books wherever they went. Several, he discovered, were college students, working toward their degrees via correspondence courses. When these boys were faced with the sort of challenges or insults that Curtis had grown used to answering with violence, they talked their way through them, and often around them.

Curtis admired these young men, but he didn't know how to approach them. Then someone told him about the Mentoring Center's Transitions program, and he went to his first meeting. Several of the young men he had noticed were there. So was Mentoring Center founder Martin Jacks.

After the class ended, Jacks approached Curtis and, to the teenager's lasting astonishment, embraced him. "Brother, you have potential," the older man told him. " 'You have the potential to be great and do great things.' I was like, 'I do? That's not what the staff on the hall is telling me. That's not what the captain and the superintendent are telling me. They're telling me I'm going to be locked up for the rest of my life!' "

"Just that hug right there—knowing that somebody cared—that sparked the good in me," Curtis believes. "Somebody was reaching out, extending themselves to me. Showing love. I was like, 'Man, I'm going to come back here.' "

Curtis marks this moment as the beginning of his long recovery from insanity, defined in a way that resonated for many young people I met: the compulsion to repeat the same actions over and over, each time expecting a different result.

"I didn't want to keep getting locked up," Curtis elaborated. "I didn't want to keep getting slammed on the ground by the staff, getting Maced, getting pepper sprayed, getting handcuffs put on me. I didn't want that life, but at the same time, I kept doing things that got those results. So I was insane in that aspect."

Turning that insight into action remained beyond Curtis for some time. He went through several cycles of the Transitions program—reading more books, according to the staff, than anyone in the program's history—but continued to fight and to suffer the consequences.

"It don't matter how much knowledge you have in your mind, but if you don't deal with your emotions . . ." Curtis's voice trailed off, then picked up again. "It's like that child in me still needed to be healed from the wounds of the past."

Eventually, Curtis began speaking about these things with a sympathetic guard. He was also seeing a psychologist twice a week and began to open himself up to the benefits of formal therapy. He describes the psychologist as "a really good man who was trying to help me. He felt for me, I believe—to a certain extent."

That caveat stems from the betrayal Curtis felt when he discovered that the sessions were not confidential. Other staff would reflect the therapist's analysis back to Curtis—"He wants to put you on meds because he feels like you can't cope"; "He says you've got a chemical imbalance."

"In the system, I'd seen people break their trust against me over and over," Curtis explained. The therapist "helped me, but I could only go so far with him. He could only take me to that place where I could see what my problems were. He couldn't help me solve them. He could diagnose me, but he didn't have no cure to heal me."

By the time I met Curtis, that healing was well under way. He described his present self as "whole, balanced, interconnected"—no longer fragmented and alone. He was growing, Curtis said, through his deepening relationship with God and its reflection in relationships with those God sent his way. When he began to list names, they were all Mentoring Center staff.

His own mentor "is like a brother, a father, a friend. He's a father because he will get on my case if I do something wrong. He's a friend because he's always there for me, no matter what. And he's a brother because there's a love there—a family bond."

Not all kids will find this kind of friend or mentor, a connection that is solid and consistent enough to sustain them through the transition to adulthood. But it is in a child's nature, when someone extends a hand in kindness, to hold on for dear life. A drowning man clings tightly, even to a stranger.

In New York, Michelle spoke of clutching at straws, until finally a few spun into gold. Twenty years old, she had grown up in a series of "placements"—a familiar trajectory from foster homes to group homes to juvenile prisons.

"I didn't meet anybody in that whole experience that genuinely cared about me," she said. "Even in the foster home that I liked, she was in it for the money. Jail, that was hard—*nobody* cared, at all."

Eventually, Michelle made it to a drug treatment facility. It was the first place she felt even the prospect of affection.

While some staff, she said, just showed up to get a paycheck, "then there are those who really love what they do. They breathe off our success. That is what makes their day. That is what keeps them alive. There are a couple people like that in here. Not many. Enough."

In Boston, Lucien underscored the importance of having an adult ally who has been in your shoes. "You've got to have people that have been in the situation and know the struggle, because they're going to vibe with you more," he said, describing something he had found post-incarceration at Roca, a community organization that focuses on building reciprocity through what they call "transformational relationships" in which "both parties experience personal change as a result of the relationship and *are expected to.* . . . Transformation is 'experienced with' someone."

"You could have a dude that has a Benz that's telling me he can feel my pain. I'm not gonna believe it," Lucien continued. "But if you got a dude that has a Toyota and three kids and he's like, 'Whatever you done I been done did it and more, I used to be a stick-up kid,' or whatever—all right, then, that's when you flip it."

When adults, such as those he encountered inside four different juvenile facilities, have *not* had this kind of personal experience, Lucien continued, "it's easier for them to lock everybody up and throw them in the system and they come out even worse. People that don't know what you've been through just look down on you, think you're fucking scum of the earth. You come out ungrateful, like life owes you, instead of you owing life."

"*Here*," he said of Roca, sounding almost astonished, "most of them actually care. They don't just do it 'cause it's their job. You end up bonding with them. They find ways to keep you pushing forward. They don't want you to [slip] back."

"What I lost was empathy," Jared said of the loveless years he spent behind bars. "It can be developed, but if somebody don't cultivate it, it's like not feeding a plant water or sunlight."

"That's that love factor," he repeated. "Being isolated takes that away. You become somebody else. You split off into a different personality. You have to, [when] all you know is 'Will I survive this day?'"

You do the crime, you do the time.

It has an appealing symmetry, but as the foundation for a justice system it doesn't have much more going for it than that. How does sitting in a locked building help build accountability, foster rehabilitation, reduce re-offending, or assist with any other goal of the juvenile court? More to the point, given the mountain of evidence that it does none of these things and often achieves just the opposite, why do we remain wedded to this particular intervention?

Will, who did six years starting at age fifteen, pushed me to consider these questions. What role does enforced idleness play in righting the wide range of wrongs for which we now invoke it? What is the relationship—*is* there a relationship?—between doing time and reducing crime?

More to the point, is that even the point? If confining juveniles in large state-run facilities fails to meet its ostensible goals—if it fails to reduce crime or enhance public safety; fails to rehabilitate those confined or improve their future prospects; fails, in fact, by every measure we've come up with, what, then, *does* it offer for the billions of dollars and millions of lives it winds up costing? Do we persist in relying on an intervention that has been demonstrated repeatedly to cause more harm than good because it offers us something psychologically, or ideologically, that we are loath to forfeit?

These are questions Will asked outright or inspired me to consider. He also helped to answer them. Our fiscal and emotional investment in juvenile incarceration, he suggested, is a manifestation of our abiding need for a population of "others." By forcibly separating "juvenile offenders" from the rest of the population—assigning them numbers, dressing them in uniforms, and imposing an arcane labyrinth of rules and restrictions that bears no relationship to life on the outside—the juvenile prison offers a concrete manifestation of our shared understanding that juvenile delinquents are different, separate, other: that "they" and "we" are in no way implicated in each other's lives.

This belief is so fundamentally reassuring that we resist relinquishing the system that sustains it, no matter how high the mountain of evidence against large-scale juvenile incarceration grows. Without the physical manifestation of otherness that the juvenile prison and its rituals provide, the broader spectrum of injustice we tolerate—the racial, economic, and educational inequities that divide our nation's children into separate castes, belying the myth of America as a land of opportunity—would be much harder to ignore or deny.

Incarceration, Will explained, functions far better as a means of defining "undesirable" people than as a means of limiting unwanted acts. It works as the "default model," he believes, only when "we identify people with the mistake that they made. It's not that you might be a good person who happened to commit a crime; you *are* your crime. You are a bad person, and we're going to remake you."

The wholesale identification of an individual with a decontextualized act may be the central pillar of an incarceration-based model of juvenile justice. If the problem is not just what you did but who you are—if you yourself are bad—your very person, it follows, must be shut away.

"But that's not a solution," Will came to understand. " 'We have to *put* him somewhere. We have to give him this amount of *time*.' Really, that suggests nothing."

Questions that might prove more relevant to the goals of rehabilitation and enhancing public safety—such as "What was he missing, and how can we provide that?"—go unasked and unanswered because they do not fit the default model of paying for one's crimes in the carceral currency of time. "You do something wrong, something bad is supposed to happen to you." The institution is that bad thing, a contemporary version of an eye for an eye, albeit out of balance: a kid steals a car stereo and loses not only his freedom but often his very future.

A system that allows us to avoid crucial questions about what children need and why so many do not have it is one that allows us to maintain the status quo, with all of its inequities, while still holding fast to the myth of equal opportunity. It is a system that—however much we may rely on the notion of "accountability" to justify harsh sentences—functions to hold none of us accountable to each other, on either side of the wall. In fact, the more I spoke with Will and others who had "done" time, the more tenuous the relationship between incapacitation and accountability came to appear.

Accountability demands both insight (a shift in the thinking that led to one's breach of the law) and action (a means of repairing the harm one has caused). Young people develop insight in the context of relationship, a commodity that incarceration radically restricts. The same goes for action: young people are hard-pressed to make better choices in an environment where they are not permitted to make choices at all.

As Jared was one of several to observe, the imperative to change while incapacitated is intrinsically contradictory. Even if one makes the internal *decision* to change, prison offers little room to practice that resolve when every movement is regimented, often down to the minute. By barring almost all self-directed action, and strictly rationing interaction with the outside world, incarceration actively *prohibits* the prisoner from acting to heal or repair any harm he has caused.

This is a lesson that crime victims who are promised "closure" through another's loss of freedom often learn the hard way. Time—the currency in which we demand payment for offenses of all varieties, from taking a pack of gum to taking a human life—turns out to have no value, except to those who lose it.

13

CONNECTION IN ACTION

Transforming Juvenile Justice

What should young people do with their lives today? Many things, obviously. But the most daring thing is to create stable communities in which the terrible disease of loneliness can be cured.

—Kurt Vonnegut

When we were in Eastern Europe we wanted a lot of things, but what we needed was hope, an orientation of the spirit.

—Václav Havel

ALONG WITH A MOUNTAIN of research exposing the wholesale failure of the juvenile prison, we have also amassed evidence about the reverse: what *does* improve the life prospects of juvenile offenders and foster public safety at the same time. This research is entirely consistent with what young people say makes the greatest difference in their lives.

Pathways to Desistance is a large, multidisciplinary study that followed 1,354 serious juvenile offenders aged fourteen to eighteen for seven years after they were convicted. A key conclusion is that even among youths who commit felony-level offenses, most simply grow out of delinquency. Sending them to prison did not make a difference on this front. What *did* make a difference was what young people said they most needed: support and connection. Those who received probation supplemented by support from the community were significantly less likely to re-offend than those who were sentenced to a juvenile facility.

The bottom line, according to the researchers: "Incarceration may not be the most appropriate or effective option, even for many of the most serious adolescent offenders." These are not the conclusions of renegade researchers or single-minded advocates. The Pathways to Desistance research was conducted under the umbrella of the U.S. Department of Justice. That makes the findings all the more striking. Nothing in the study results suggests that anything can or should be done to improve juvenile facilities. Institutional reform, in fact, is never mentioned.

At the same time, a large body of research now makes clear which interventions work better than incarceration, and which work best of all. Out of the many reform efforts around the country, a handful of models have emerged that are both evidence based (they have been studied extensively and found to work well) and intuition based (they align perfectly with what young people across the country say they need or say has worked for them). What these models have in common is that they rely on relationships—with an emphasis on supporting existing relationships, particularly with family—rather than isolation, and they offer support in the context of young people's homes and communities. These programs not only produce results far better than does incarceration; they also save vast amounts of money. Yet only a tiny proportion of young people who need and could benefit from these programs have access to them.

The models that have been studied most closely with the most positive results are Multisystemic Therapy (MST), Functional Family Therapy (FFT), and Multidimensional Treatment Foster Care (MTFC). Beyond their alphabet-soup acronyms, these programs share a single, simple premise: young people need a web of relationships to thrive—adults who will surround and support both them *and* their families in the transition from a difficult or delinquent adolescence to a stable adulthood. None of these models involves incarceration, and all have shown impressive results with young people who would otherwise often be locked up.

Dan Edwards is president of Evidence-Based Associates, which works with public agencies to implement these models. All three, he said, "focus on meeting kids in their natural ecology, where they live, in the real world," rather than shipping them out to the countryside and then bringing them back to an unchanged environment. All three also rely on a case manager who gets to know a young client as an individual and also develops a relationship with the client's family, strengthening the one support system most likely to be around long after programs and case managers have moved on.

"It is very easy to sit back and blame the families, but at the same time, they're most likely the ones that are going to have the solution," Edwards said. Staff at all three programs are trained to work intensively with even the most vulnerable families—families that the court might otherwise write off when assessing a young person's support system. They will also, when needed, search far and wide to identify and strengthen young people's natural support network even when it does not resemble traditional notions of the nuclear family.

"If you look really hard," Edwards elaborated, "a lot of the kids that [people] would have said in the past don't have a family—they've got somebody out there that cares about them." Sometimes working with a kid's family, in other words, involves tracking that family down, or helping to reconstruct it—whatever it takes to make sure each young person, including those who previously may have been on their own, has that fundamental support.

While all very similar in their guiding philosophies, each program takes a slightly different approach to the same end.

- *Multisystemic Therapy (MST)* is an intensive three- to five-month process designed for serious juvenile offenders and their families. Specially trained therapists meet their clients where they are—at home, at school, and elsewhere in the community. The thinking behind this is to help young people navigate the world in which they live, rather than removing them from it. Because MST therapists carry small caseloads, they make themselves available to families twenty-four hours a day and tackle those issues that have been shown to have a correlation with delinquency and its cessation: connecting youth with recreational activities that encourage positive friendships, supporting their efforts in school or at work, strengthening the family's ability to communicate, and helping youths and their families develop a support network that may include friends, neighbors, extended family, and others. A range of studies has found that MST reduces subsequent arrests between 25 and 70 percent.

- *Functional Family Therapy (FFT)* is similar in principle to MST. The main difference is that FFT therapists work with young people and their family members in their own offices rather than clients' homes and neighborhoods. Both programs share the aim of stabilizing a young person within, and along with, her family, and a strong focus on communication and conflict management. Key to both approaches is the priority placed on strengthening *existing* relationships over building new ones with helping professionals who, however caring, will eventually be gone.

- *Multidimensional Treatment Foster Care (MTFC)* places youths with specially trained foster families rather than in group homes or juvenile prisons. Youths stay in these homes for six to nine months and receive support similar to that offered by MST. Meanwhile, their families also receive intensive support and counseling, with the goal of reuniting the family after the treatment period. Even after families are reunited, the support does not end. Rather, youths and their families maintain contact with counselors until the home and family are deemed stable enough that they no longer need this intensive support.

As researcher Richard Mendel points out, "the most favorable real-world outcomes have occurred when MST and FFT are employed as an alternative to incarceration or other residential placements." In Florida, the Redirection Program does exactly this: provides evidence-based family treatment (primarily MST or FFT) as an alternative to incarceration or other out-of-home placement. A 2010 report from Florida's Office of Program Policy Analysis and Government Accountability found that youth in the Redirection Program did better on all fronts. Most striking was the way the benefits seemed to *increase* as time went on. Participants were 9 percent less likely to be arrested for a new crime, for example, but 35 percent less likely to end up in adult prison. The Redirection Program saved taxpayers an estimated $41.6 million over the course of four years in lowered recidivism rates and less money spent on costly residential placements.

These evidence-based interventions cost between $3,000 and $9,500 total per each youth served, and all last under a year—often well under. Juvenile incarceration, on the other hand, runs an average of $88,000 per youth, per *year*, and can last for many years. A complex cost-benefit analysis conducted by the Washington State Institute for Public Policy determined that—accounting for the difference between the cost of FFT and the cost of incarceration, and for the savings generated by reduced recidivism—each placement in FFT resulted in a total savings to taxpayers of almost $50,000. MTFC, the most expensive of the three, generated the greatest savings—an estimated $88,953 per participant.

In all three modalities, according to Dan Edwards, the therapist's job is to "figure out what's getting in the way of the family being successful and how do we address that, whether it's substance abuse or failure at school." For example, he said, there is often a disconnect between a child's school and his family, each blaming the other for perceived behavior problems. Over time, each side builds a wall against the other until communication becomes impossible. "It's the therapist's job to take that wall down somehow." (Interestingly, the Washington State Institute for Public Policy identified high school graduation as an important protective factor against recidivism, reducing it by more than 21 percent.)

Another key element of all three interventions is that they are time limited. Again, Edwards said, it is a matter of looking at what works. "We have a notion in this country that therapy takes years, but there is no evidence that sitting a kid on the couch or in a chair week after week for years really [makes a difference]." There is evidence, on the other hand, that high-intensity, carefully targeted interventions such as MST and FFT do work. A therapist may meet with a family involved in one of the evidence-based programs every day, if needed, but there is always an end point in sight. The rationale, per Edwards, is "I'm not going to stay with those kids forever, but hopefully, I'm going to be there at the point in these families' lives when they turn the corner. I'm going to help them turn the corner, and four months later, we have a graduation party, we celebrate the success, and I get out of the way."

Another defining characteristic of the evidence-based programs is that all are grounded in an understanding of the trauma that many youth who come before the court have experienced and still carry. Rather than re-traumatizing these youth, as incarceration often does, these interventions work to help them address and heal from it.

As the *Report from the Attorney General's National Task Force on Children Exposed to Violence* points out, "These youth are not beyond our ability to help if we recognize that exposure to violence causes many children to become desperate survivors rather than hardened criminals. There are evidence-based interventions that can help to repair the emotional damage done to children as a result of exposure to violence and that can put them on a course to be well-adjusted, law-abiding, and productive citizens."

Despite the widespread agreement about the effectiveness of these three evidence-based programs in particular, they remain tremendously underutilized. While a handful of states have launched major initiatives to implement these models, nationwide they remain available only to a small proportion of those who could benefit—about 5 percent of those who meet the criteria for participation, according to a 2007 study. The waste this represents is nearly incalculable, measured as it must be not only in dollars but also in lives.

Many see the failure of the juvenile prisons as evidence that those held there are themselves beyond all hope. Above and beyond their impact on the lives of those they serve, expanding efforts such as MST, FFT, and MTFC could also help to combat this defeatist perception. By demonstrating that young people, including those charged with serious offenses, *can* be reached and rehabilitated—outside of a locked environment and in their own homes and communities— these programs knock the last leg out from under the argument that juvenile incarceration is a necessary evil.

Despite the contrast between the much-documented failure of juvenile incarceration and the consistent success of the evidence-based interventions, Mendel has observed that "even in jurisdictions where such programs have been adopted, they often remain small-scale pilot projects in otherwise unreformed systems." In other words, most or even all of the travesties described in the preceding chapters—the countless children traumatized, beaten, raped, and killed inside our juvenile prisons, and the harm caused to victims of crimes that we *know* how to prevent but have chosen not to—could be avoided, if we simply acted on what we know. That we have not done so, despite all the evidence, should be occasion for shame—and for action.

All that is required is shifting the balance from favoring failure to supporting success. Interventions that have been proven effective must become the national norm, not boutique exceptions. Meanwhile, the time has come to quit studying, analyzing, investigating, and, most critically, *relying on* an intervention that has proven ineffective, destructive, and often disastrous: large-scale juvenile incarceration.

It would seem to be simplicity itself. What, then, is stopping us?

Replacing juvenile prisons with community-based programs proven to work, crucial as it may be, is also unlikely outside the context of a larger transformation. Genuine change in the way we treat young people who step outside the law must be predicated on a new way of *seeing* them—a 360-degree perspective that encompasses not only their deficits but also their strengths; not merely their offenses but also their aspirations.

One mechanism for this shift in perspective is an approach known as Positive Youth Development (PYD). A paper co-authored by New York probation chief Vincent Schiraldi, Mark Schindler, and Sean J. Goliday describes PYD as

> a combination of identifying and building on youths' strengths as well as meeting their needs . . . a PYD approach views the youth as an active participant in the change process, instead of as a client or target of change. While traditional juvenile justice work with young people has often favored control of their behavior as a central goal, for PYD, connecting the youth with community resources is the focus. For example, a traditional juvenile justice approach might involve sending a youth to job counseling and ordering community service as a punishment; PYD, in contrast, looks to engage the youth in career exploration and career-path work experience and use community service as service learning and job preparation.

That Schiraldi and his co-authors point to the importance of education and employment in the larger context of PYD is more than incidental, as both school and work themselves protect against future incarceration and point to future success. The Alliance for Excellent Education has calculated that a 5 percent increase in male high school graduation rates would reap an annual savings of approximately $18.5 billion in crime-related expenses. Other research has found that youths with jobs are less likely to break the law. Incarceration, meanwhile, both curtails a young person's education—often permanently—and limits her job prospects long after release.

Victor Rios is an assistant professor of sociology at the University of California at Santa Barbara and the author of *Punished: Policing the Lives of Black and Latino Boys*. The book examines the impact of what Rios calls the Youth Control Complex—the constellation of individuals and institutions, penal and otherwise, that converges to label young people of color living in poor neighborhoods, limiting their opportunities and criminalizing actions that are either ignored or considered "mistakes" when better-off white youths are involved.

Youth prisons are the end phase of the Youth Control Complex Rios describes, one that encompasses everything from zero-tolerance schools in which a kindergarten scuffle is more likely to lead to handcuffs than a talk with the principal; to the heavily policed streets low-income youth of color travel; to the child welfare system, which, like the public schools, has become a feeder system for juvenile lockups; to popular culture, which perpetuates the figment of hoodie-clad hordes at the gates.

As do Schiraldi and his co-authors, Rios advocates a complete shift in the way young people of color are both perceived and treated. Rios describes himself as a former gang member and juvenile detainee whose goal is to ensure that his own trajectory—going on to college and becoming a professional—does not remain an "anomaly" for youths growing up in neighborhoods like the one where he was raised.

Noting that of the forty Oakland, California, youths whose progress he studied closely, only three found mentors or the equivalent to help them toward adulthood, Rios proposes replacing the Youth Control Complex with a Youth Support Complex, "a ubiquitous system of support that nurtures and reintegrates young people placed at risk." Rios's larger vision includes a reimagined juvenile justice system but does not stop there. He calls on schools, politicians, community groups, and community members to step up to the challenge of creating an environment where all young people are held to high expectations and, at the same time, allowed to make mistakes without the devastating consequences incarceration brings.

The first step, Rios writes, "entails decriminalizing young people's style and noncriminal actions, listening to young people's analysis of the system, and asking them how to develop programs and policies that can best help them." These are questions I have spent many hours discussing with young people. Some, unsurprisingly, went straight for the bottom line. The policy they wanted to see overturned was the unwritten (although much-studied and substantiated) policy of tossing young people of color behind bars for minor transgressions that white kids commit with impunity and then just grow out of (as do virtually all kids, as long as they *don't* get locked up for them in the first place). Others spoke of more limited, yet still crucial, changes, like ensuring that youth did not lose touch with their families.

Some, like Will, offered detailed programmatic ideas. In fact, Will has already developed the blueprint for a post-prison peer support organization that would be entirely youth-run (or run, age aside, by those who had been there—a need many young people I spoke with identified). Will envisions a place where those who had gotten through the rugged early years of reentry would offer newly returned youths individualized advice and support, structured around those young people's priorities as *they* define them. Asking young people to articulate their own needs before attempting to meet them, Will believes—treating them as individuals rather than "cases" or generic "juvenile offenders" in need of improvement—might help spark the process of *de*-institutionalization that he considers crucial to recovering from prison. Requiring youths to go through a prescribed "reentry program," on the other hand, no matter how useful, risks leaving them feeling defined once again by their status ("ex-offender") rather than seen and addressed on their own terms.

This free-form but carefully thought out reentry center is only the seed of Will's larger vision. Coming together, getting to know and to trust one another, joining in conversation and common work—all this, he hopes, will lead organically to activism. The group, as he envisions it, would by that point have built the capacity to provide a public platform for youths who might otherwise be ignored, on the one hand, or else held up as "poster children"—used to carry the message of others, however worthy it might be, instead of their own.

Still others with whom I spoke, as they talked about what would have helped them most, articulated the central tenets of the most successful evidence-based practices—describing them, however, as something like pipe dreams, having never encountered these programs themselves.

I asked Jared, who had done so much to advance my thinking, what we might do better to meet children's needs. Could anyone have done something to reach him at age nine, when, as he wryly put it, "I stepped out into the world with all my vast knowledge?" What might have made a difference back then?

"My parents staying together," he responded, with a quick flash of anger he rarely allowed himself to show. "They could have fucking raised me. Instilled in me the things that I needed as a child, and built me up, and built in my mind the tools that it takes to navigate through the world."

Could anything have helped support his *parents*, I pressed, so they might have been better able to give him what he'd needed as a child?

"I don't know," he said wearily. It was a phrase I had rarely heard him use. "I don't know. All I know is they didn't work out. For whatever reason, they separated. My mom started using drugs. Heavily. My dad? He left."

"Who knows?" he said finally, still considering the question. "Maybe if this group, if the two of them, had gone to counseling . . ."

Jared, characteristically, had found his way right to the heart of the question, describing the central ingredient of MST and other interventions that have proven most successful: rather than identifying the child as the sole source of the problem, rather than responding by isolating him from home and family, they recognize that children need families, and that when those families falter children need the larger adult world to support them *and* their families.

But no one in "this group"—by which Jared meant his family—was ever offered counseling. The only hand extended was the cold hand of the law—a response that did nothing to address the root causes of the problem. Jared was not the only one who pointed out the disparity between the scant resources available to troubled youths *before* they commit an act of delinquency and the vast amount spent, later on, to incarcerate them.

A number of experts on juvenile justice—both those who had won their expertise firsthand and those who earned their credentials via more formal channels—pointed to the absence of early support for children in the context of their families, as well as its necessity. This kind of support, they told me, can help a child thrive without taking him from home, especially if we offer it early, rather than waiting until that child trips the wires of the juvenile justice system.

"The real messed-up part," concurred Will, who spent six years in a juvenile facility, "is the *before*. I was having problems at home a couple years before [getting arrested], and my mom would ask the police for help—'He's running wild'—and the police said unless he commits a crime, there's nothing we can do. So you have families crying for help before a child commits a crime, but no services to deter that. Then once they're in jail, you throw the book at them."

For nearly forty years the state of Missouri has operated a network of small, concertedly rehabilitative facilities with staff who are trained and immersed in a culture of caring. The Missouri Model, as it is often called, holds for the kids in its care the same goals a parent does for his own children, its director Tim Decker told me. Staff work closely to help young people become not merely law-abiding but happy and productive, able to pursue their own paths without restricting others.

The Missouri Model consistently shows better outcomes than traditional juvenile lockups. A state analysis of all 15,910 youth designated as juvenile offenders in Missouri in 2007 found that just over a quarter had recidivated in the strictest sense—with a "new law violation" within their first year out—a rate that is dwarfed by that of other states. Other research has found that at the three-year mark, 84 percent of Missouri system graduates are "connected": productively involved in their communities through school, work, or both.

I visited several Missouri facilities, from an alternative school for kids returning from custody (or struggling with behavior at mainstream schools) to a locked institution. I entered a bit skeptical—could values of caring and youth development truly infuse an entire state system, rather than merely individual institutions with highly committed leaders? But it did not take long for my skepticism to fade.

The facilities in Missouri do not look like prisons—in fact, their homey simplicity makes one realize how much effort it takes, in designing and maintaining a traditional juvenile prison, to drain out every element of comfort and care. More important than the lack of hardware and the comfortable atmosphere was what young people in the Missouri system told me again and again: "Here, they care about you."

I left Missouri with no doubt that the so-called dangerous few—young people who genuinely need to be removed for a time from home and society and physically contained—would benefit immensely if they were sent to Missouri-like facilities rather than large-scale, punishment-oriented juvenile prisons.

Missouri closed its old-style training schools in the 1980s, after a series of ugly scandals similar to those that have triggered less-sweeping and shorter-lived reforms in other states. In the years since, the state has developed a regional system based on a continuum of programs, from day treatments to nonsecure group homes to moderate-secure facilities (some of which are located in state parks or on college campuses) to secure-care facilities. The largest hold no more than fifty, and the secure facilities house no more than thirty-six.

Programming is not an afterthought in Missouri. It infuses every aspect of the system. "Throughout their stays in DYS [Division of Youth Services] facilities, youth are challenged to discuss their feelings, gain insights into their behaviors, and build their capacity to express their thoughts and emotions clearly, calmly and respectfully—even when they are upset or angry," Richard Mendel wrote in an article in *American Educator*.

Staff participate in each activity, rather than standing posted as symbols of supervision. Perhaps as a result of these close interactions, Decker told me, there is almost no use of solitary confinement, no handcuffs or pepper spray, and very few incidents of physical restraint. Safety lies not in restraints but in relationships.

Division of Youth Services staff work closely with families and assign each youth a case manager who works with him from entry through reentry. Across the board, staff take a trauma-informed approach, focusing not only on "What did you do?" but "Why did you do it?" as well as "What happened to you?" This, I was told, helped make the forms of physical containment used elsewhere unnecessary.

One thing that stood out particularly about the Missouri Model was the emphasis on supportive peer relationships. Caring staff are central to the work in Missouri, but I also witnessed a quality of respect and compassion in the interactions among the young people that is very rarely fostered by a traditional prison environment. Like everything else in Missouri, this is the result of conscious effort. Residents are divided into "teams" of ten or fewer, and any one of them can "call a circle" at any time if something comes up he feels needs to be addressed, or if he simply needs extra support. One of the most remarkable things I saw was a group of girls demonstrating what they do when one of their peers gets agitated enough to pose a physical risk. Staff stood back while the girls themselves formed a "trust circle" around the one playing the part of the out-of-control youth, talking to her gently, trying to help her calm herself. Only when she could not be calmed by other means did they—still collectively, and still gently—bring her to the floor until she could calm down. This was Missouri's alternative to the kind of "prone restraint" that was getting kids hurt and killed in other states.

Will had the opportunity to visit Missouri with a group of youth advocates several years ago. The experience, he said, was incredible. "A lot of times," he observed, "they just change the name, right? From 'incarceration' to 'rehabilitation.' . . . But [the reality] stays the same." Inside Missouri's youth facilities, however, Will saw something genuinely new.

"The biggest thing was the staff," he said. "Staff in California, even if they're good staff, it's obvious that they're there for a paycheck and they go home and that's it. In Missouri, they were involved. It felt like the paycheck was an afterthought. They were really there because they believed in the kids." If Will was skeptical when he arrived, that skepticism faded when he saw that young people had not been pre-selected as guides to impress the visitors. An administrator asked a nearby group for volunteers, and those who raised their hands were the ones who led the show. "They're not hiding anything," that showed Will. "They *have* nothing to hide."

The gap between the Missouri Model and the traditional prison is so vast that when young people in Missouri asked me about my book and my reporting, they simply could not believe what I told them about what I'd seen and heard in other states—not only the stories of violence and abuse, but the simple fact that teenagers like themselves would be held in places that resembled adult prisons. Their disbelief and horror was one of the strongest condemnations of the status quo I had come across.

"The institutional environment itself is a challenging place to create positive culture and opportunities for kids," Tim Decker said at one point, as we drove between one regional facility and another, "so they're really working against a lot. They're swimming upstream every day." Intended as a compliment to his staff, his words struck me as a caution as well. If the "institutional environment," no matter how well thought out, poses intrinsic challenges to meeting the goals that Decker implied were those of his system ("positive culture and opportunities for kids"), then tremendous vigilance is needed when it comes to deciding which youths require commitment to even a very good institution.

Replicating Missouri's small, therapeutic institutions could make a tremendous difference across the country, but those benefits would be maximized if strict filters were in place to ensure that only those who truly required institutional care were institutionalized. Even in Missouri, it is not clear that this is happening. The Division of Youth Services has limited control over whom it serves; initial decisions about commitment are made by the court. Just over half the youth committed to the Missouri Department of Youth Services in 2007 had been adjudicated for felonies (51 percent), while the rest had been charged with misdemeanors or what the state calls "juvenile offenses." (In fairness, some of these lower-level offenders—12 percent of the total population—were in day treatment or other nonresidential programs, and a smaller number were in one of the seven group homes across the state, each of which accommodates ten to twelve youths.)

Now and then during my visit to Missouri, the seams between the various institutions that comprise "the system" seemed to be showing. Relationships, I heard over and over, are at the heart of the Missouri Model. But sometimes this value seemed to run up against the more traditional mandates of the larger system.

At an alternative school run by the Missouri Division of Youth Services, for example, Megan said she enjoyed the small environment and "opportunities for support."

"What I dislike about being in here is I don't get to be with my friends and stuff," she added, "and I tend to think that I have to have friends."

At first, I thought Megan was talking about missing old friends from the public school she used to attend. Then it was explained to me that students at the alternative school were encouraged to develop close relationships at school but were not allowed to "associate" outside of the school. The rule came from the court, not the school, and those caught breaking it were at risk of violating their probation.

The rationale for this, I was told, was that many of the students were on probation, and "history shows us if you are hanging out with some-body that is not making good choices, and you didn't make a good choice, chances are together, you're not going to make good choices."

The administrator who explained this to me did so without much apparent conviction.

"At school, you make friends," he acknowledged. "So when you're not at a public school, and you're here, of course, they make friends, and they break the rules. We know, but if they get caught, it's an extra charge, and they get in trouble."

The gap between systems gaped most widely when I listened to Tracy McClard. Her son Jonathan had been involved in a tragic teenage melo-drama: he was still pining for an ex-girlfriend when she called and told him she was carrying his baby but that her new boyfriend was going to force her to inject cocaine in order to kill the baby. She would kill herself, she told Jonathan, before she would let that happen. Believing only he could save these two lives—the girl he loved and his unborn child—Jonathan shot and injured the new boyfriend.

The young man Jonathan shot recovered fully. Jonathan himself was not so fortunate. Although representatives from the Division of Youth Services interviewed him and found him suitable for their programs, that determination was overruled by a local judge, who sentenced Jonathan to adult prison instead. During the time he had already spent in adult jails pending sentencing, Jonathan had been attacked, beaten, and thoroughly terrified. Not long after his sentencing hearing, he hanged himself in his cell.

For his mother, who has since left her job as a teacher to become an advocate, the idea that an alternative was right there and yet denied her son has been one of the most difficult things to accept. Since her son's death, she told me, every member of her immediate family except Tracy has made a suicide attempt. The boy who was shot and the girl her son believed he was defending, she said, have also had their lives turned inside out by confusion and remorse over her son's death.

None of this decreased my respect for the Missouri Division of Youth Services. It did leave me convinced that no single system, no matter how beneficent, could undo centuries of oppressive attitudes and actions toward young people who break the law. To get to a place where no public entity traumatizes children, and all work together to improve their chances, will require changing our collective understanding of who young people are and what they might become. This will take more than the perfect model. It will take a movement.

14

THE REAL RECIDIVISM PROBLEM

*One Hundred Years of Reform and Relapse
at the Arthur G. Do{ier School for Boys*

A HUNDRED AND SOME miles inland from Florida's Emerald Coast, out of sight of the beaches and amusement parks that draw tourists to the state, children's bones lie in unidentified graves behind the Arthur G. Dozier School for Boys in Marianna, Florida. These undersized skeletons represent not only the extremity of violence behind the walls of juvenile prisons, but also its intransigence.

Dozier stands empty now, but before the state finally shut it down in 2011, the institution had been through more than a dozen investigations by organizations ranging from a local grand jury to the U.S. Senate. Again and again, the violence taking place behind its walls had been documented and decried. And still Dozier stood, for more than a century, churning out generations of walking wounded: men and boys who carried with them not only the trauma of their own experience but the memory of their dead friends as well.

The Boys of the Dark is a collaboration between journalist Robin Gaby Fisher and two Dozier survivors, Robert W. Straley and Michael O'McCarthy, who have in common unshakable memories of childhoods desecrated behind Dozier's walls. It is the kind of book one has to put down frequently, so gruesome are its depictions of adults torturing children who were powerless to resist not only because they were younger and smaller than their assailants—some were as young as five—but also because they were prisoners, mandated by the courts into the custody of their tormentors, often for offenses as minor as trespassing, smoking cigarettes, or running away from home.

In the following passage, the authors describe a night when the young O'McCarthy and his friend Woody were taken to an outbuilding known as the White House to be punished for trying to run away.

A houseman named Dixon was instructed to hold Michael down. Michael heard Hatton's [the school's director] boots pivot on the concrete floor, and the whip hit the ceiling, then the wall, before it bit into his back and his buttocks, spraying his blood on the walls. Every blow drove him deeper into the metal springs of the bloody mattress, and deeper into the grey hole of semi consciousness.

Even worse than being beaten himself, O'McCarthy recalls, was being forced to listen to his friend's cries through the door.

"No more!" Woody wailed. "Please. Oh please, God, no more!" Michael sank to his knees. He swore he heard Woody's blood splattering on the walls.

Twenty strikes. Thirty. He could hear the sounds of a scuffle breaking out. "Get him back on his stomach," Michael heard the assistant superintendent shout. Forty strikes. Woody's screams had become one long unbroken wail. Fifty strikes. Fifty-five. The more Woody screamed, the more he was beaten.

Michael covered his ears and screamed for Woody, screamed until he could no longer hear his friend, begging for mercy.

O'McCarthy never saw Woody again. Much later—after O'McCarthy, Straley, and other Dozier survivors instigated an investigation into unexplained disappearances like Woody's—thirty-one metal crosses were found behind the facility.

Over the years, Dozier has weathered more cycles of exposure, investigation, litigation, and scandal than one might think a single institution could withstand. But Dozier persisted, as did the brutality taking place behind its walls, making the institution a powerful symbol not only of the ubiquity of abuse within juvenile prisons but of the inherently toxic nature of the institution itself.

"The real recidivism problem in juvenile corrections is not the rate at which kids re-offend," the Annie E. Casey Foundation's Bart Lubow observed, "but the regularity with which state youth corrections agencies repeat the same cycle of abuse, scandal, reform and regression." This institutional recidivism, said Lubow, is evidence that "the problems with these facilities are systemic and inherent, rather than a function of individual leaders or particular eras."

Abuse of young prisoners persists in state after state, including those lauded for their reform efforts. In the long view, there is *nothing*—neither investigation, litigation, monitoring, nor oversight; not public censure, court order, or the mandates of the U.S. Constitution—powerful enough to stem the brutality that is part of daily life inside our nation's juvenile prisons, short of the courage to close the places down.

Dozier has emerged as a symbol of this cycle not only because of the extremity of the torments that children endured there, but also because of the determination of those who survived them. After the death of a boy at a Florida boot camp made the news, these now-adult survivors sought out one another, forming a coalition they called "the White House Boys," named for the outbuilding where they had been taken for beatings at Dozier. Silenced as children, these grown men, some well into retirement, found a collective voice that was strong enough to force the state of Florida to face what it had done to them and so many others—delinquent or neglected children, runaways and throwaways, anyone the state decreed in need of reform.

Reporters from the *St. Petersburg Times* interviewed a number of these men. All had discovered as children that the stately, collegiate building on the pine-dotted campus was cover for something more sinister than a "school": a torture mill through which children were churned for generations.

The men remember the same things: blood on the walls, bits of lip or tongue on the pillow, the smell of urine and whiskey, the way the bed springs sang with each blow. The way they cried out for Jesus or Mama. The grinding of the old fan that muffled their cries. The one-armed man who swung the strap.

They remember walking into the small, dark building—the White House—in bare feet and white pajamas, afraid they'd never walk out.

Roger Dean Kiser, a twelve-year-old orphan when he was sent to Dozier, went on to write a memoir about his experience there. He also wrote a letter to Florida state officials, describing what took place after a staff member accused him of cursing.

The two men picked me up and carried me into a small room, which had nothing in it except a bunk bed and a pillow. They put me down on the floor and ordered me to lie on the bed facing the wall. . . . I felt one of the men reach under the pillow and slowly pull something out. I turned over quickly and looked at the one who was standing near me. He had a large leather strap in his hand.

"Turn your damn head back toward the wall!" he yelled.

I knew what was going to happen and it was going to be very bad. I had been told what to expect by some of the boys, who were taken to the "White House." I never heard from some of them again. I also heard that this giant strap was made of two pieces of leather, with a piece of sheet metal sewn in between the halves. Again, everything was dead silent. I remember tightening my buttocks as much as I could. Then I waited and waited, and waited. I remember someone taking a breath, then a footstep. I turned over very quickly and looked toward the man with the leather strap. There was an ungodly look on his face and I knew he was going to beat me to death. . . .

Then all of a sudden, it happened. I thought my head would explode. The thing came down on me over and over. I screamed and kicked and yelled as much as I could, but it did no good. He just kept beating me over and over. . . .

God, God, God, it hurt badly. I will never forget that until the day I die.

Kiser received several responses to his letter, all of which followed a similar trajectory: sympathy, shock, and a firm effort to distance the state from his suffering by situating the abuse at Dozier in some faint and distant past.

Judge Kathleen A. Kearney, responding on behalf of then governor Jeb Bush, reassured Kiser that "corporal punishment" had been banned in Florida state institutions for more than thirty years. "I am pleased to say that children do not have to endure that kind of experience today. Now, a 24-hour abuse hotline is available to everyone and state law requires that specified state employees report any abuse or neglect that they observe."

Timothy Ring of the Client Relations Office at the Department of Children and Families professed himself "stunned that anyone could be so cruel to a child." But he was also "comforted," he assured Kiser, "to know the people . . . [at] the Department of Children and Families here in Jacksonville, really are dedicated to ensuring that all children enjoy their right to a happy and healthy childhood."

As I studied the events at Dozier, I found nothing so chilling as a video-taped deposition of an elderly Troy Tidwell, remembered by the boys as "the one-armed man" who administered many of the lashings.

Tidwell settled in with a polite smile, showing no sign of anxiety. An old man by this time, Tidwell had receding gray hair brushed straight back from his forehead and a slight quaver in his otherwise easy drawl. The attorney who took his deposition treated him with the deference reserved for the aged, even using Tidwell's preferred term for what took place in the White House: "spanking."

A weak smile flashed across Tidwell's face as the inquiry began. He leaned forward in his chair obligingly and squinted at the questioner, as if indicating a willingness to try his very best.

"When you would spank the boys," the attorney asked, "describe for us what kind of swing you would take with that leather strap you described for us."

"Well, me with one hand, I'd bring the strap back this-away and come down."

Tidwell clenched his hand around an imaginary implement, then low-ered it in slow motion from his shoulder to the table. The horror of the gesture—one that left many of those who were "spanked" with perma-nent scars—was undiminished by the liver spots on the old man's hand.

"You wouldn't ever use a full swing, maybe even nick the ceiling and come down?"

"Nah, nah, that would be somebody else that would use a different"— Tidwell repeated the swing in miniature, smiling faintly as he did so, as if trying to remain patient with a rather dim child—"than I did."

"Did others? Did Mr. Hatton?"

"Well, the tall people, you know, they would spank 'em like this, you know, and come down." That gesture again, with a longer, more powerful arc. Tidwell's heavy gold watch glinted as his arm, once more, descended.

Several of the White House Boys wrote a song about their experience at Dozier. In the video they produced to accompany it, a man stands in silhouette, bringing a leather strap down again and again in slow, deliberate strokes. These swings of the strap resemble Tidwell's own reenactment closely in their timing, pace, and particular arc. In the boys' reenactment, however, it is clear that the full force of a grown man's body is behind each stroke.

The events at Dozier have been "exposed" over and over, investigated more thoroughly than the Watergate break-in, repeatedly condemned but never contained, allowing one generation after another to suffer untold trauma.

In this regard, Dozier is anything but an anomaly. The institution may reflect the extreme end of the spectrum when it comes to the maltreatment of incarcerated youth, but it is far from unique in its apparent immunity to reform. In this, it reflects both the fundamentally dehumanizing nature of the juvenile prison and the ultimate futility of any reform effort aimed at salvaging an intrinsically corrupt institution.

Reports from state representatives assigned to investigate Dozier underscore the voices of survivors. "We found them in irons, just as common criminals," a legislative committee reported in 1903. The segregated section where black youth were held "impressed your committee as being more in the nature of a convict camp, than anything else we can think of," reported another, in 1911.

A state inspector offered the following in 1918: "Thirty five cases of pneumonia . . . boys lying under wool blankets, naked. With dirty husk mattresses on the cement floor . . . filth, body lice. . . . [Black boys' dinner] was hoe cake and bacon grease thickened with flour. The dinner of the white boys was rice and bacon grease gravy. . . . One boy said he was flogged for refusing to cook peas full of worms and that meat sent to the boys was kept until spoiled and then fed [to] them and they were all sick."

As troubling as the abuses detailed in these reports are the dates on which they and others like them were submitted: 1903 (Investigative

Committee to the Florida Senate); 1911 (Report from Investigative Committee); 1915 (Jackson County Grand Jury); and 1958 (U.S. Senate Subcommittee on Juvenile Delinquency). Reforms were ordered, according to an investigation by the *Tampa Bay Times*, in 1909, 1911, 1913, 1914, 1920, 1921, 1953, 1963, 1968, 1976, 1982, and 2007. The events at Dozier, in other words, were *never* a secret. Official findings started coming in more than a century ago and continued for decades, but still the building stood, protected by a shield not of lies but of indifference.

Again and again, official bodies looked into Dozier. Over and over, they found evidence that children were being brutalized by state employees entrusted with their care. And time after time, their reports were filed and forgotten—until the next round of investigators found the same or worse.

Boys who were paying their debt to society for stealing bicycles or cutting school learned from this that there were two sets of rules. One was for them—the powerless, with no rights worth respecting—and the other for their omnipotent captors, permitted all and accountable to none. This persistent double standard served to underscore the message that the boys were less than human. Along with post-traumatic stress from the beatings themselves, it would play a part in driving some survivors mad.

In 2008, with Dozier still open, the state of Florida acquiesced to the persistent advocacy of the White House Boys and ceremoniously shuttered the shack where boys had been tortured for decades. The day it closed the White House, the Florida Department of Juvenile Justice mounted a cautiously worded plaque on its exterior wall.

> In memory of the children who passed these doors we acknowledge their tribulations and offer our hope that they have found some measure of peace.
>
> May this building stand as a reminder of the need to remain vigilant in protecting our children as they seek a brighter future.

Tragically, the story did not end there. Nor did the abuse.

This may be the darkest turn in the White House Boys' long journey. Despite all they had experienced—unheeded cries as boys and years of silence after—the survivors kept faith in the power of their collective voice, sustaining themselves by believing that the truth would, if not set *them* free, at least protect other youths from reliving their suffering.

On this front, the state of Florida has yet to redeem their faith.

On the very day the plaque went up, it would later be revealed, 130 Dozier wards were kept inside the building, away from the press who had gathered for the ceremony.

"When the media was around, they would hide us," one of them later told the *Tampa Bay Times*. "They didn't want us saying a word to anybody, because they knew what we would say. We'd tell the truth."

The truth was that abuse remained rampant at Dozier even after the White House was formally closed—after the plaques and promises, the photo ops and the "never again"s. Throughout the decade in which the state negotiated with the White House Boys to arrange a ceremony commemorating their suffering (situating it firmly in the past in the process), even as officials reassured Kiser that children in state custody enjoyed the "right to a happy and healthy childhood," reports of abuse at Dozier continued to pour in.

Five months before the plaque went up, a boy had his ear sewn back together after a "scuffle" with staff. A month later, a guard punched a boy in the face three times and slammed him into a fence. Another reportedly "stuffed a boy in a laundry bag, and when the boy tried to chew through the strings . . . encouraged others to scratch and pinch him." Yet another broke a "broom on a refrigerator, then chased [a] boy with the sharp end. The guard grabbed the boy in a headlock and fractured his jaw." One boy, who had been kicked and stomped by other youths and then placed in isolation, asked to call the abuse hotline. His request was denied. Other boys later reported that when they asked to call the hotline to report abuse, they were warned that if they did so they could face criminal charges for false reporting. They "wipe their a— with grievances," another ward summarized.

Then there was eighteen-year-old Justin Caldwell. On February 11, 2007, he got into some kind of dispute with a guard—the details are unclear, since each side offers a different version of events. What happened next, however, was difficult to dispute. According to the *Tampa Bay Times*, "A video camera caught Justin standing still. A heavy-set guard grabs him by the throat, slams him backward on the ground, then chokes him. Guards pick up Justin and are leading him away when he falls and slams his head on a table. The guards drag him to the middle of the room where they leave him, bleeding. His legs twitch."

Both the guard involved and the superintendent eventually lost their jobs. Department of Juvenile Justice officials issued yet another call for "culture change." Only one person involved in the incident wound up facing criminal charges, however: Justin himself. He was charged with battery on a detention officer and sentenced to five years in prison, the maximum available.

The Arthur P. Dozier School for Boys was finally shuttered in 2011, amid a sweeping investigation by the U.S. Department of Justice. But even that did not stem the tide of denial—nor the cycle of institutional recidivism. Officials insisted that they were closing Dozier only as a cost-cutting measure, part of a larger state-level reorganization, not because generations of children had been tortured and killed there. And in the years since Dozier closed its doors, abuse has continued inside the private prisons on which Florida increasingly relies.

Like other states barraged by advocates, attorneys, and the press, Florida has embarked on a major reform effort in recent years, including sharp cuts in the number of youths sent to state facilities. The state has released a Roadmap to System Excellence, a commonsense-filled document issued with the lofty goal of making Florida a leader in juvenile justice.

But no ceremony, it seems—no report, reform, or road map—can put an end to the chronic violence and violation that are part and parcel of institutional justice. After countless cleansing rituals—investigations, commissions, regulations, and reforms—the abuse continues, in Florida as elsewhere.

In 2010, the privately run Thompson Academy found itself the target of a federal class action suit for its treatment of Florida youth. A group of public defenders filed a petition asking the state to stop sending youths to Thompson and to remove those already there. According to the public defenders' claim, "the children are fed so little, and the food is of such poor quality, that staff use it as 'currency.' " Images from the Thompson Academy show bare and moldering mattresses and dank, crumbling walls—a horror-show setting in which staff allegedly slammed kids into walls, broke one boy's nose and fractured another's ankle, sexually assaulted at least one girl multiple times (before and after the abuse was reported to the administration), choked the recalcitrant, and forced children who became ill to sleep on the floor.

In an official statement, the Florida Department of Juvenile Justice claimed to have sent monitors to Thompson forty-three times since 2010 and found "no deficiencies." Internal documents obtained by the *Huffington Post*, however, identify serious problems dating back at least to 2004. According to a "Personnel and Training Review for Thompson" dated March 29, 2004, for example, training files for staff contained "nothing," although wards who were interviewed said that staff "screamed, yelled, worked double shifts, [and] got mixed directives, due to lack of communication." Staff, meanwhile, confirmed that youth were not given enough to eat, adequate hot water, towels, or clothing. "It was interesting," the investigator wrote, "that youth interviewed were concerned about staff and staff interviewed were concerned about youth."

Despite what the *Huffington Post* characterizes as "voluminous evidence that inmates have suffered silence, sexual abuse and neglect inside the facilities of a private juvenile prison operator" (Youth Services International, parent company of the Thompson Academy and many other private facilities), the state of Florida continues to award contracts to that same operator—nearly $37 million worth over the course of the previous year, according to a November 2013 follow-up account in the *Huffington Post*.

In July 2011, Eric Perez died of a cerebral hemorrhage in a West Palm Beach juvenile facility after guards dropped him on his head during what officials described as "horseplay." Guards ignored his cries for hours on the grounds that he was "faking it." One was seen on videotape stepping over the boy's limp body as he lay dying on a cellblock floor. In the wake of Perez's death, the Florida Department of Juvenile Justice reaffirmed its commitment to "operating a safe and secure juvenile justice system" and promised to "clean house."

In August 2012, a guard at the Milton Girls Juvenile Residential Facility for girls was arrested after she slammed a seemingly unresisting girl face-first into a concrete wall and then sat on her for more than ten minutes, according to the *Miami Herald*. Security camera footage shows other staff members walking in and out of the room with no visible sign of alarm. One staff member joins in for a bit, sitting on the girl's legs, and another stops by to chat as casually, it appears, as if the girl pinioned beneath her colleague were a sofa or a bench. When the girl is finally allowed to stand, she appears disoriented and unsteady on her feet. The guard who has been sitting on her hands her an ice pack before escorting her out of view.

The guard's arrest did not cause her to lose so much as a single shift: she was out on bail and back at work the next day. The Florida Department of Juvenile Justice—which had given Milton a 100 percent satisfactory rating less than a year earlier, including in the category "provision of an abuse free environment"—did, however, transfer the fifteen-year-old girl to another facility. Only after the department found itself investigating charges that Milton's program director had herself thrown another girl to the ground while she was already restrained, leaving the girl with lacerations on her face and ear, did it finally move to terminate Milton's contract. Even then, revelations of past abuse continued to emerge. A mental health technician was charged next, on multiple counts of battery and sexual abuse, after six girls told investigators they had been afraid to report his frequent attacks while still in Milton's care.

Finally, in 2011, the U.S. Justice Department's Civil Rights Division released the results of its lengthy investigation into two Florida institutions: the Jackson Juvenile Offender Center and the Arthur G. Dozier School for Boys.

On the one hand, investigators wrote, "the [Department of Juvenile Justice] has a very well-developed statewide system of written procedural protections in the form of written policies and procedures."

On the other hand, no one appeared to be following them. State policy, for instance, requires that force be used only as a last resort. In practice, "staff subjected youth to force as a first resort . . . [including] impermissible uses of force such as choking."

"Harmful practices threatened the physical and mental well-being of the youth committed to these facilities," investigators wrote. "Despite its policies and procedures," the state hired abusive staff, failed to provide adequate training or supervision, and lacked an effective accountability process. "We therefore believe that the harm suffered by juveniles confined at Dozier and JJOC is not limited to those facilities. Accordingly, we are sharing these findings with the State despite the closure of these facilities."

So much, in other words, for policy and procedure, for written protections, state oversight, or federal mandates. So much for ceremonies, speeches, and plaques. So much, for that matter, for the U.S. Constitution, which forbids the practices that have taken place in Florida, as elsewhere, for more than a century. Nothing, it appears, can keep children safe behind the walls of the state institutions intended to reform them.

In August 2013, after much resistance, Florida governor Rick Scott approved a land-use agreement allowing University of South Florida anthropologists to exhume what they believe are the remains of more than one hundred children buried behind the Arthur P. Dozier School for Boys. Digging began with the exhumation of a ten-year-old boy.

As of this writing, it is unclear what the final death count will be. But Jerry Cooper—who received more than one hundred lashes during a single beating when he was a child at Dozier—offered his prediction: "There's not going to be enough crime scene tape in the state of Florida to take care of this situation," Cooper told a *Miami Herald* reporter.

The events at Dozier may be extreme, but they are by no means unique. The cycle that played out there again and again—lawsuits, investigations, scandal, and revelation; blueprints for reform followed by broken promises—is routinely repeated by institutions and agencies across the country, and has been since the dawn of the training school in America.

Louisiana is one of any number of examples of juvenile corrections systems that have, like Florida, been criticized, sued, or placed under federal oversight because of chronic abuse of the youngest prisoners, only to make temporary amends that degenerate again into unconstitutional conditions. In the late 1990s, revelations of Dozier-style horrors at the Tallulah Correctional Center for Youth began to draw attention. The *New York Times* described an institution where young people "regularly appear at the infirmary with black eyes, broken noses or jaws or perforated eardrums from beatings by the poorly paid, poorly trained guards or from fights with other boys" and where "meals are so meager that many boys lose weight [and] clothing is so scarce that boys fight over shirts and shoes."

"When I got here," said Warden David Bonnette—a twenty-five-year veteran of Louisiana's Angola State Penitentiary who was brought in to clean house—in a *New York Times* interview, "it seemed like everybody had a perforated eardrum, or a broken nose."

In an all-too-familiar cycle, revelations of brutality at Tallulah sparked lawsuits from both advocates and the Department of Justice, resulting in a merged settlement agreement. Under pressure from family members and others, the state launched a major overhaul of the state juvenile system. The Juvenile Justice Reform Act of 2003 mandated sweeping changes: a shift to a rehabilitation-based model; a commission tasked with moving the state toward a network of smaller, therapeutic facilities; the closure of Tallulah; and a commitment to investing the money saved in community-based programs.

That, anyway, was the plan. Reality followed a different and all-too-familiar trajectory. As with Dozier, Tallulah's closure was followed by reports of violence at the state's other juvenile facilities. "No Better Off: An Update on Swanson Center for Youth," a 2010 report from the Juvenile Justice Project of Louisiana, documents "significant violence" at the Swanson Center for Youth, by then home to nearly half of the youths in state secure care. Youths interviewed for the report described daily fights, some spurred on by guards, and many leading to hospitalization.

While "Louisiana's Office of Juvenile Justice . . . claims to seek the implementation of a therapeutic, rehabilitative model for youth who get in trouble," the report's authors concluded,

> According to youth at Swanson, the state has far to go in reaching that goal. The story they tell is one of mistreatment, one of violence, isolation . . . and a lack of preparation for a productive future outside of this environment. Their stories are not so different from those that advocates have heard before—first at the Tallulah facility (closed in 2003), then at the Jena facility (closed in 2004), then at Jetson Center for Youth (downsized in 2008). With every push by advocates for reform, some progress has been made. Yet too often, the challenges reappear in a different geographical location, rather than being fully addressed system wide.

So many states have gone through similar cycles of scandal, intervention, reform, and relapse that it is fair to say that institutional recidivism is the norm, not the exception. Texas, for example, has technically been operating under the constraints of a federal ruling since 1973—a mandate that did nothing to prevent the widespread sexual abuse documented in Chapter 6, nor the rapid unraveling of the reforms that were instituted in the wake of *that* scandal.

Morales v. Turman, the lawsuit that led to the 1973 ruling by the U.S. District Court for the Eastern District of Texas, identified a "widespread practice of beating, slapping, kicking, and otherwise physically abusing juvenile inmates, in the absence of any exigent circumstances, in many of the Texas Youth Council facilities."

According to author Kenneth Wooden, who attended the trial, children described a grotesque nomenclature that had evolved to categorize the various forms of suffering to which they were subjected. "The peel" involved a child kneeling shirtless with his head clamped between a guard's legs to keep him in place during a beating. "The tight" required a youngster to touch his toes while a guard beat him with a broom handle.

One epileptic boy who experienced a seizure was tossed into an isolation cell. Guards threw tear gas canisters into the cell behind him. According to court testimony, the boy left claw marks on the wall all the way to the floor. Another boy, subjected to similar treatment, emerged the following day with "skin peeling and hanging off." A girl who had been pregnant described being forced to swallow a handful of pills and then exercise vigorously until she miscarried.

After six grueling weeks of this sort of testimony came a ruling that, for the first time, established that incarcerated youth had a constitutional right to rehabilitation. *Morales v. Turman* has since been heralded for establishing the first clear standards for the nation's juvenile justice apparatus. But forty years later, incarcerated youth and their advocates are still fighting not only for an atmosphere that fosters rehabilitation but for one that merely offers some modicum of protection from chronic and vicious abuse.

In June 2012, officials hoping to curb rising violence in Texas state juvenile lockups opened the twenty-four-bed Phoenix Program inside a state facility near Waco. The idea was to isolate and contain those youths seen as the "ringleaders" and simultaneously to heal them, via a low staff-to-youth ratio and intensive therapeutic services. Early coverage praised Phoenix for offering "the kind of treatment that all 1,200 youth offenders in state facilities need."

The *Texas Observer* identified "what this program was really doing well: making it feel safer in [Texas Juvenile Justice Department] lockups. . . . There was more support here, more case managers and counselors looking out for you; and fewer distractions, a smaller chance you'd have to fight 30 or 40 people, or get jumped on your way across the room."

Youths at Phoenix went through a mandatory ten-week Aggression Replacement Training based on the premise that "aggression is a learned behavior." Posters outlining the "Anger-Control Cycle" stood as a constant reminder of where aggression might otherwise lead. "Structure and personal attention are the priorities," the *New York Times* reported admiringly. "Nearly every moment of the day is filled with counseling, school time, meals or recreation."

The problem, it later emerged, came during those intervals, however rare, when youths were *not* engaged in some sort of salubrious activity. This was when guards found time to line up the program's participants, slam them to the ground, and beat them with closed fists.

A report from the Independent Ombudsman for the Texas Juvenile Justice Department offers a window into what seems more like methodical torture than what, again, was classified as "horseplay" when initially reported to a state hotline.

> There were three staff and multiple youth visible on camera. One male staff would take youth one by one and pick them up, slam them to the floor, and lay on them, pinning them to the floor. The youth could be seen flailing his legs and arms. The staff would complete the "pinning" and then move on to another youth, repeating the act. At no time did the other staff attempt to stop the act; they only watched. During the course of 15 minutes there were 6 youth who were slammed to the floor and pinned by the staff for an extended period of time.

A grand jury declined to recommend criminal charges against the guards, but three did lose their jobs as a result of the videotape, and four were transferred to other positions. The Texas Juvenile Justice Department reiterated its "zero-tolerance" policy toward this sort of behavior as well as its intention to "continue cleaning house," and two legislative committees pledged to investigate further.

And so it goes: another group of young people left to wrestle with trauma that may never fade, another round of regret, more committees and promises of reform.

The history of Dozier, or Louisiana, or Texas—of more states, and state institutions, than it is possible to list—raises a central question: is *reforming* juvenile prisons and the larger system that operates them adequate to improving the lives and prospects of the children in their care, or even to keeping those young people safe from their keepers? Or is that system, and the various state institutions that form its foundation, itself beyond redemption? Given the long history of children being beaten, raped, and killed behind the walls of juvenile prisons, and given that these institutions remain seemingly impervious to reform, might it be time to dub the juvenile prison *itself* a "super-predator" and—in the name of public safety and the safety of our children—shut it down for good?

The myriad atrocities that take place inside juvenile prisons are not resolved simply because they happen to be revealed. The "scandals" that emerge from them have become so ubiquitous as no longer to merit the term. The cycle of revelation, reform, and recidivism has been repeated so many times over, in so many places, that we can no longer indulge in the luxury of being scandalized, of professing ourselves horrified and rushing to institute well-intentioned reforms that, with numbing regularity, erode over time, ignored or forgotten until the next "scandal" emerges, reawakening dormant outrage and setting in motion a repeat of the same cycle.

The abuse of children has become so entrenched in our nation's juvenile prisons that we are no longer justified in asserting that it betrays the values of our culture. Instead, it has come to reflect those values in their ugliest incarnation—most clearly, our belief in the myth of "other people's children" so profoundly different that somehow, when we prick them, they do not bleed or at least do not suffer the same way that "ours" would, children so devalued as to be expendable.

No scandal, revelation, ceremony, or reform can stanch the violence and violation that are, for far too many young people, part and parcel of paying their debt to society. Despite countless investigations, commissions, regulations, and reports, the abuses continue, in Florida and all across the nation.

Dozier may be closed now, but it is more than an empty building. It is an open wound.

15

AGAINST REFORM

Beyond the Juvenile Prison

If seven maids with seven mops
Swept it for half a year.
"Do you suppose," the Walrus said,
"That they could get it clear?"
"I doubt it," said the Carpenter,
And shed a bitter tear.

—Lewis Carroll, "The Walrus and the Carpenter"

AMERICANS ARE PERENNIAL REFORMERS. No sooner do we devise a new institution or program than we start picking it apart, looking for flaws and convening all manner of bodies charged with repairing it. The task force, committee, blue ribbon commission, and a near-constant flow of litigation—all are expressions of our nation's persistent optimism.

A great strength of our democracy, our reformist nature is also a critical weakness, blinding us to those occasions when a long-standing institution has a fundamental, conceptual flaw—the kind that demands not a wrench but a wrecking ball. If a reform proves inadequate, we simply try again. Another task force is assembled to supplant a now-defunct commission; new committees are assigned to exhume the wreckage of the old. Sometimes, these efforts pay off, and progress—our national religion—is attained. But there are also occasions when our reformist zeal leaves us patching the roof of a building that lacks a foundation.

The juvenile prison is a glaring example of such an edifice—flawed from the inception, failed by every measure, subject to one renovation after another, yet impervious (to date) to the genuine transformation its faulty premise and abysmal performance demand.

The past decade has seen rapid change on the juvenile justice front, especially in terms of our use of large state facilities. The number of youths in these institutions has dropped by a remarkable 40 percent. Across the country, forward-thinking officials can be found working to improve those facilities that remain, introducing therapeutic models and training staff to be trauma informed. Reform on this level has not been seen for decades, if ever.

That we are incarcerating fewer children is, without question, cause for optimism—but not yet celebration. Across the country, many thousands of young people remain behind bars in juvenile prisons—most of them convicted of minor, nonviolent offenses—despite the fact that these places are ostensibly reserved for serious offenders who pose a clear danger to those around them. Even in those states that have gone furthest in terms of reform, nearly 42 percent of confined youth are still locked up for offenses that pose no threat to public safety: breaking school rules, running away from home, missing a parole hearing, and the like. This remains so despite the fact that large-scale juvenile incarceration has been proven many times over to do absolutely nothing to reduce juvenile offending or to keep the public safer, and very often makes these problems worse. We should not break out the champagne, in other words, for doing less of a terrible thing.

Even in those states being lauded for reform, incarcerated youths continue to be abused physically, sexually, and psychologically at appalling rates. This abuse has gone on for so long, despite countless efforts to curtail it, that one must conclude it is endemic to the juvenile prison. The extreme power differentials, isolation, and coercion that characterize a locked facility are so ideal a breeding ground for abuse of all kinds that no amount of regulation, policy, or scrutiny can keep children safe behind prison walls.

Beyond that, incarceration is *intrinsically* traumatizing, all the more so during the developmental crucible that is adolescence. The years teenagers spend locked away in juvenile prisons are exactly those in which a young person's sense of himself and the world might otherwise crystal-lize, with tremendous implications for who he will become as an adult. Isolating girls and boys during a time when their malleable brains are still very much in flux flies in the face of everything we know about human development.

Nowhere in my travels did I find a way around this central conundrum—a "best practice" for keeping children away from home and community and in the care of strangers, no matter how trauma informed those strangers might be. I saw excellent programs, carefully planned and adequately funded, staffed by wise and warmhearted people. But even in the best of these, I never felt I'd stumbled upon the secret blueprint: the facility that, if replicated, could elevate our nation's juvenile justice system to meet, or even approach, its stated goals.

Children, it turns out, will never thrive in storage. We can safely stash away unwanted objects, but children are meant to be held close, not ban-ished. I came to this conclusion as, over and over, through both words and actions, young people let me know what they needed in order to change—to rehabilitate, when that was the task at hand, and, before and beyond that, simply to grow.

Over and over, in one way or another, they conveyed the same message: rehabilitation happens in the context of relationship. It is a conclusion that runs in direct contradiction to the means of correction we have chosen as the norm: isolation. Rather than building on young people's existing rela-tionships, rather than helping them forge positive new ones, we've chosen an intervention that flies in the face of all the evidence researchers can offer, everything young people tell us, and all that we know already—as parents, as people—from basic common sense.

This is where things begin to get confounding. We know what works, we know what doesn't, and we know that *persisting* with what doesn't wastes millions of dollars and destroys thousands of lives. We are clearly not getting what we say we are seeking: improved public safety and better outcomes for children. Instead, we are inflicting untold harm on the thou-sands of young people who pass through our juvenile prisons each year. Yet we persevere, through cycle after cycle of scandal, reform, relapse, and repetition.

How, knowing what we know, can we do what we do? How can we continue to deprive so many young people of what we understand as essential to their growth, if not their survival, with no evidence of any public benefit?

The facilities to which we entrust our nation's most vulnerable, most traumatized, and sometimes most dangerous children—the institutions intended to redeem, rehabilitate, and hold them accountable—do not recognize these children's fundamental humanity. How else to understand the cruelties inflicted in the name of justice, the intractable indifference that allows brutality toward captive children to perpetuate itself for decade upon decade, than to acknowledge that we see the children we consign to this failed system not only as "other people's children" but as another *breed* of children entirely, different in their very nature from those we call our own?

The mass criminalization of teenagers, taking place over decades of demographic transformation that have given us the most diverse generation this country has known, has cleared the way for the legal and literal segregation of a group of young people—the overwhelmingly poor black and brown children with whom we fill our juvenile prisons—who are indelibly marked as "other" by the experience: their names exchanged for prison ID numbers, their clothing replaced by uniforms marking them property of the state, their résumés forever tarnished by their records, every aspect of their futures constrained by the errors of their youth.

The more time I spent behind the walls of our nation's juvenile prisons, and in conversation with those who had come through them, the better I came to understand the role these institutions play both in perpetuating the exclusion of "other people's children" and in allowing us to deny that such a caste exists; in concealing behind coils of barbed wire and veils of confidentiality both the most wounded among America's children and the further injuries we inflict upon them in the name of "justice."

The frequency with which young prisoners turn to animal imagery to describe how it feels to be inside one of our youth prisons underscores the profound denial of humanity that these institutions perpetuate. Given what we know takes place behind the walls of our youth prisons—and we do *know*, despite our ability to profess ourselves shocked again and again—it is imperative that we see those contained there as somehow less than human. Because if they *are* fully human, as rich with possibility and sensitive to suffering as any other children, and we continue to countenance their chronic mistreatment inside public institutions—if that is so, then what are we?

We cannot address juvenile delinquency without considering the question of individual responsibility. Young people who are involved in delinquent acts, it goes without saying, need to make better choices. But the odds of their doing so will be vastly increased if we make some effort to ensure that they *have* better choices. Even as we ask young people to take responsibility for their actions, we must consider our own collective responsibility for the deep inequities that leave some children with many choices (and a very low risk of incarceration, despite the universal adolescent inclination to test, and to cross, the line of the law) and others with so few choices and so very much risk.

There is no single program that can achieve this goal—to bring to life the two-dimensional fantasy we hire muralists to paint on the walls of decimated neighborhoods. It's a world where parents can make a living wage and where children can play in parks that are safe and clean, attend schools as well resourced and expectation-rich as those across town, and visit the pediatrician rather than the emergency room when they get sick.

A pipe dream? Hold on. The resources are there.

Remember Curtis, the million-dollar kid? What if we spent each dollar we would otherwise spend to incarcerate Curtis *on* Curtis, without waiting for him to trigger the investment by violating the law? What if we spent the money earmarked for his incarceration *earlier*—investing it in his impoverished community, in supporting his fragmenting family, so that *they* would have the resources they needed to help Curtis grow?

At the Open Society Institute, Eric Cadora and Susan Tucker elucidated a concept they call "justice reinvestment," which centers on just such a realignment of resources. As they have written, "The goal of justice reinvestment is to redirect some portion of the $54 billion America now spends on prisons to rebuilding the human resources and physical infrastructure— the schools, healthcare facilities, parks, and public spaces—of neighborhoods devastated by high levels of incarceration. Justice reinvestment is, however, more than simply rethinking and redirecting public funds. It is also about devolving accountability and responsibility to the local level.

Justice reinvestment seeks community level solutions to community level problems."

When Oregon tested the concept with kids in Deschutes County, the results were remarkable. The state simply gave the county the roughly $50,000 per kid it would otherwise cost to incarcerate Deschutes' portion of state juvenile prisoners—with a catch. For each kid who did land in state custody, the county would now have to pay the bill itself. Beyond this, the county could spend the money with great flexibility. County leaders invested in prevention and neighborhood programs, with a strong emphasis on community service. In just a year, the number of juveniles Deschutes County sent to state institutions dropped by 72 percent.

On the notion that came to be called reinvestment, Jerome Miller was prescient. "The test for successful deinstitutionalization," he wrote, "is this. Every dollar attached to an inmate should follow that inmate into the community for at least as long as he or she would have been institutionalized."

Eliza also grasped the concept of justice reinvestment, whether or not she had heard it so named. "They could have sent me to Exeter for what they spent to lock me up," she said ruefully one afternoon in the visiting room as she waited, seemingly endlessly, for the state to come up with a suitable "placement" for her.

She was speaking hypothetically, but in fact we had tried it. While Eliza was wasting away in juvenile hall for lack of this "placement," my colleagues and I begged for permission to let her take the entrance exams that might open the doors to a boarding school. Eliza was brilliant; her scores, we believed, would have been off the charts. As for fitting in, who knows what might have happened, but she certainly did not feel she "fit" where she was. "I *want* to be preppy!" she cried out at one point (boarding school had been her idea).

All this, I was told, was irrelevant. Even if her scores put her in genius territory and she were accepted by every boarding school in the nation, the funds that were allocated to "place" her in a group home—or to keep her in juvenile hall—were not fungible. Nor, it was strongly implied, was Eliza herself. Kids like her did not go to Horace Mann.

There it was, the heart of our resistance to more than surface change: our impoverished imagination when it comes to the young people who fill our juvenile prisons.

Our treatment of the many thousands of young people who pass through our nation's juvenile prisons will not change fundamentally until our understanding of who these youth are, and who they *can* be, also changes—until and unless we hear their voices, see their faces, and accept their claim for a place at the table. Theirs is the age-old civil rights cry— the cry for equality, and with it the assertion of their humanity in the face of a system that depends on denying it.

One reason we remain so invested in practices that have long been discredited is exactly that: so many people have so much *invested* in them, financially as well as ideologically. Juvenile prisons provide jobs, and many are sited in rural regions whose economies rely on them. If the kids go home, the jobs go, too—not just the guards' but also a wide array of service positions associated with keeping captive youth alive.

In an essay published by New America Media, Will draws a troubling analogy between the kid on the corner peddling toxic palliatives and legislators who perpetuate the youth prison despite *its* proven harms. "The [guards union] is the most powerful lobby in California," Will writes. "Essentially, the Assembly is sacrificing what's right in order to please the people who are keeping money in their pockets, which to me is no different from the guy on the corner selling drugs."

In fact, the similarities are frightening. The kid on the corner ignores the long-term pain he plays a part in by fostering addiction because he needs money to survive right now. The assembly member ignores the pain his vote will cause children because he needs a job that's in jeopardy if the union doesn't get what it wants. Both want the quick dollar, so they overlook the consequences of their actions.

"The hardest thing to do in corrections is to take an existing system and try to reform it," said Dan Macallair of the Center on Juvenile and Criminal Justice. "It's much easier to start from the bottom up and build. Because once you've got an established system, you've got a constituency that is right there ready to defend it because . . . people's livelihoods are at stake. Then you have the traditions that have grown up around that institutional system—the practices, the routines that everybody has bought into. That creates a political force that keeps it in place, and that is why these systems change so little after decades and decades of evidence piling up about their ineffectiveness. It comes to a point where that [evidence] really doesn't matter, because so many people are depending on keeping it in place."

"Institutional systems are quite resilient," Macallair warned. "Even if there is a temporary fix, they tend to grow back. Their old practices and policies tend to reemerge after a very short period of time. So, sadly, I despair of the idea that you can reform these institutions to any great degree. The experience is that you can't. You have to tear down and start again."

Will made the same point, albeit more succinctly: "You can't build something effective on top of something rotten."

Many have tried, over the years, to do exactly that, and the early results have sometimes appeared promising. In the longer term, however, there may be no recidivist so persistent as the juvenile jailer. How many states, or counties, or individual institutions, have undertaken wholesale efforts to "clean house" in the wake of a lawsuit, scandal, or federal investigation? How many of those same places find themselves embroiled in similar "scandals" down the line?

Jerome Miller, now legendary for shutting down Massachusetts's reform schools in the 1970s, started out as a reformer. "I didn't go to Massachusetts to close the institutions. I went to make them decent," he has said. But the intractable resistance he faced, not only from politicians but also from his own staff, led him to abandon the notion of reform. Instead, very quickly, Miller released twelve hundred young people from state institutions and placed them under community supervision (or, less often, in other forms of residential care).

As Miller came to understand it,

The unintended by-product of the keeper-captive coupling is a bureaucracy which is by law unaccountable to those it holds and, somewhat oddly, purports to serve. That would be an unhealthy situation for even the most effective manager.

If Phillips Exeter Academy, Andover, Choate, or similar respected prep schools were filled *only* with captive students ordered there by courts and forbidden to leave under penalty of longer imprisonment, the standards of even the best of faculty and administrators would shortly go downhill. Though altruism might salvage things for a while, it makes a notoriously undependable base for long-term policy.

I thought I could get over this contradiction. We would respond sensitively to each individual youngster while recognizing our public responsibility. In the abstract, these goals aren't contradictory, but in the political arena which defines corrections, they quickly become so. Control slides toward punishment, treatment turns to threats, and decency is eaten away. Society wants its pound of flesh even as it offers sympathy. The captive client must be cooperative while suffering our ministrations. If our help fails the fault is the inmate's.

"Anything, including nothing," Miller ultimately concluded, "was better than the institutions."

As Barry Krisberg has pointed out, widespread reform has been attempted before. After Miller closed down Massachusetts's reform schools, according to Krisberg, forty other states began to follow suit. Many moved quickly, "closing facilities and moving kids to the community. Then came the moral panic of the super-predator years. The political process reversed, and they started packing places full of kids."

Without a change more profound than reform—without a genuine transformation in the way we *see* young people—there is every likelihood that this cycle will repeat itself; that the political and economic tide will turn once again, and beds that have been emptied will be filled once more. The fact that the recent decline in juvenile incarceration has brought the number confined almost exactly back to where it stood in the mid-1980s—before the super-predator scare and the years of backlash that followed—is a caution in itself. "Juvenile justice reform" has been on the table almost as long as has juvenile justice itself. It's time to get over reforming a system that isn't reforming a group of kids who need something altogether different. Providing what they need in order to grow, and what the community needs in order to be safe, demands not reform but wholesale transformation, both in how we perceive the young people we currently incarcerate and in how we respond when they step outside the law.

We need not start from scratch in enacting this transformation. Community-based interventions that eschew isolation and rely on connection have been proven many times over to protect public safety while

enhancing young lives. The challenge before us is to take these "alternatives" and make them the norm across the country, or else to give up on
another generation—a risk and a waste we cannot afford.

The first step toward deeper transformation is to take the time to listen to the young people who have passed through our juvenile prisons or
remain there today. Airlifted out of their homes and communities, hidden away behind bars and high fences, young prisoners experience what
sociologists call social death—"the condition of people not accepted as
fully human by wider society." Addressing *this* crime—the social execu-
tion of thousands of young people at exactly the moment when finding
their place in that wider society is their developmental imperative—is a
necessary first step. Only once we can see those we incarcerate as fully
human—not "delinquents," not "wards," not "other people's children"—
can we begin to understand their needs and motivations, much less answer
the challenge so many have posed: *Why should I give a fuck? No one gives
a fuck about me.*

Understanding the nihilism that can set in so early allows us to imagine responses to delinquency more profound than reform and deeper than
simply less-strict sanctions, responses that get to the heart of motive itself.
What might change in a young person's life if he were given cause to
believe he *did* have a shot at a future, that he mattered enough to deserve
attention that was not solely punitive?

America is at a crossroads when it comes to our treatment of young people who have stepped outside the law. Just as the states tripped over one
another in the super-predator era to "crack down" on kids—writing tough
new laws, building huge facilities and then packing them well past capacity, rushing to send juveniles to adult prisons—many are now moving in
the opposite direction. The drop in the number of juveniles behind bars is
as important as it is astonishing.

Visit a state like New York, which is creating innovative new programs
as quickly as it can close its much-vilified training schools; or Missouri,
which has abandoned the notion of the large-scale youth prison completely; or California, where the number of youths in state institutions is
less than a tenth of what it was a decade ago, and it's hard not to feel optimistic. Walk around a place like Red Wing in Minnesota, or Red Hook in

New York, and see wardens address kids by name, with genuine affection, hear young people earnestly repeat the hopeful mantras of Positive Youth Development, and it is tempting to believe that the problems that have plagued the youth prison since its inception are on the way to being fixed, that the kids, at last, are going to be all right.

The problem with this sort of institutional reform is that it leaves the institution itself, and its underlying premise, unchallenged. And when it comes to the juvenile prison, the grounds for such a challenge are too strong to ignore. Young people in trouble—both the many locked up for minor offenses and the few behind bars for having caused real harm—are not only propelled deeper into trouble by isolation; they are crying out, often *via* delinquent acts, for exactly the opposite: attention, relationship, connection, community. Love.

Prisons, by definition, take away two things—autonomy and connection—that are central to adolescent development. Teenagers need the opportunity to make choices, to make mistakes and learn from them—a process that banishing them to a rigid penal environment curtails rather than fosters. Children need love when they are "bad" just as they do when they are "good" (perhaps even more so; try the "my child" test on this one), and prison, no matter how thoroughly we may reform it, is fundamentally a loveless place.

Until America breaks free of the edifice complex that has made isolating youth in locked institutions far from family and community our default response to juvenile delinquency, we will neither do our children justice nor offer our citizens safety. Connection, not quarantine, must be the aim of a juvenile justice system that aims to do anything besides churn out embittered survivors—candidates, too often, for the adult prison system.

A juvenile prison is a dismal place, its atmosphere a toxic combination of rage, frustration, boredom, and fear. But something else permeates locked facilities as well: a powerful desire to communicate, to be heard. The young people I met were eager to talk—about life behind bars but also much more. They shared wrenching stories of trauma and struggle, described their aspirations and detailed their plans for pursuing them, offered keen analysis on questions of crime and punishment, and outlined detailed visions of a transformed and transformative response to youthful wrongdoing.

Above all, what young people all over the country seemed most determined to communicate was a sense of urgency. The many thousands of young people locked away today cannot afford to wait for incremental reform. They have only one chance to grow up, and those behind bars speak of feeling it slip through their fingers as one lost day fades into the next. As the decades-long debate over juvenile justice drags on, these are the young people whose lives hang in the balance. They are living in a state of emergency, and they want someone—everyone—to take notice.

A young man on lockdown writes an open letter. He has been behind bars for more than seven years at this point, the last two spent in a lockdown unit known as "The Back." Showers, clean sheets, education, worship—all are frequently denied to those in "The Back," he writes. Family visits are reserved to be taken away as punishment from young men who have little else left to lose.

But grievance was not the motive for his missive. He wanted to be known.

> I write this to represent the faceless, voiceless, the unknown strugg-l[ing] within [the] youth prison system. For we do exist. We are young, vibrant, diligent, strong minded, and remain hopeful. Not because of any outside force, but from within. Hope that sustains us, persevering and believing in what is right, just, and lawful, while humbly taking responsibility for all factors that have led us to such a predicament. . . .
>
> We call upon the Department of Corrections and this facility to provide true, meaningful, effective solutions that can offer real treatment, training, and rehabilitation—none of which we receive.
>
> And to you the public who we derive our hope from: take heed to this call, take action of which we do not have the opportunity, and stand in solidarity by supporting our cause.
>
> For the voiceless, the unknown struggle—I am WE. This is our declaration for justice.

"Ain't I a woman?" the antislavery activist Sojourner Truth asked a nation that, in taking her freedom, cast into question her very humanity.

Am I normal? Darren asked during the months he spent in solitary, his silent question echoing off the bare walls of his cell. *Does a normal kid live like this, away from his mother?*

You are not your crime, Will answers from the future, beaming in cap and gown as he graduates from college. *I am not my crime. A crime is something you did. It is not who you are.*

ACKNOWLEDGMENTS

From the beginning, assembling this manuscript has been something akin to a barn raising. The heaviest lifting was done by those whose lives are reflected in these pages, who not only lived the experiences described herein but were willing to *re*live them so that others might understand. As a reporter, I am constantly amazed by people's willingness to open their doors—to entrust their precious histories and hard-won wisdom—to someone who often arrives as a stranger. My greatest hope is to do justice to this trust.

This book is also deeply steeped in friendship and the trust reflected there. Over the past two decades, I have had the good fortune to do work that has brought into my life young people who became both dear friends and great teachers. Far too many of these young people were locked up at some point. The result has been relationships that—while they enriched my own life immeasurably—have familiarized me with the bitter taste of indifference and injustice and the particular mix of loss and helpless fury that accompanies grieving the young.

Bart Lubow at the Annie E. Casey Foundation not only supported this book; he supported its author by sharing his vast network of contacts and deep well of knowledge, offering crucial ideas and insights, and helping me get (and keep) a grip on the process as well as the subject. His wisdom, rigor, and tremendous compassion infused every aspect of this endeavor, and his life's work serves as a constant reminder that change requires patience and fortitude, but is never beyond reach.

Will Roy contributed to this work as researcher, reporter, sounding board, conscience, and friend. Will challenged, and deepened, my thinking at every turn, and his keen intellect helped me steer clear of false assumptions and received wisdom. Will is a gifted reporter, endlessly curious and profoundly empathetic, whom people trusted with their deepest truths. The stories he brought back were riveting, but it was the insights he drew out of his long conversations (technically "interviews")—the wisdom he and other survivors shared with one another—that most consistently stopped me in my tracks. It is hard to find the words to express my gratitude to Will—for his ambitious reporting, his reflective nature, his insight, his guidance, his humor, his dedication, and the relentless call to think more deeply he brought to the work (and demanded of its author). More than anything, I am grateful for his faith.

Deborah Sills Iarussi and her marvelous uncles Arthur and Peter Sills at the Sills Family Foundation understood intuitively the importance of involving those who had experienced juvenile incarceration in the development of this book. That understanding, along with their generosity, allowed me to hire Will, without whom this book might not exist. Amy Price and my allies at the San Francisco Children of Incarcerated Parents Partnership were generous in granting me a leave in order to write this book and relentless in continuing our shared effort while I was gone.

John Knight consistently went above and beyond in his role as researcher, bringing me information I asked for but also much more. His keen eye is peerless. Because Bart Lubow had the foresight to suggest that I hire a researcher and enabled me to do so—and because in John I found someone at once meticulous, knowledgeable, good-natured, and committed—I managed to finish the book without losing my mind.

Caroline Goosen contributed her time and reporting skills to this book and shared key information from her studies, as did Nabihah Azim. Grace Bauer offered insight, shared her remarkable network, and consistently inspired me with her own ferocious work at Justice for Families. I was bolstered also by her unwavering faith.

At The New Press, Jed Bickman went far beyond the call of duty, both in the early stages of assembling the manuscript and again at the end, when he worked tirelessly to speed its publication. Sarah Fan supervised the production process with exceptional precision and grace under pressure. Diane Wachtell is an editor like no other—when it comes to what stays on the page and what goes, her eye is unerring. My agent, Kathleen

Anderson, shook free the manuscript with a key piece of advice: to loosen my grip on the third person and let in my own life. My sister, Elizabeth Bernstein, lent her eye to the document at a crucial moment and helped it become a manuscript. I relied on many sources for background and statistics, but I owe particular thanks to Richard Mendel, whose report *No Place for Kids: The Case for Reducing Juvenile Incarceration* offered a meticulous and incontrovertible research-based case against the policy and practice of locking up the young.

My husband, Tim Buckwalter, did everything around the house for a period of years, while working full bore himself, so I would have time to write. He and our children, Ruby and Nicholas, spent many a dinner hour talking about juvenile justice with genuine concern and curiosity (and, if ever that flagged, great patience). Their insights are threaded throughout the book as their hearts are through my own—an everyday reminder of how grave an act it is to isolate a child.

NOTES

Introduction

5 "Caging men like animals": Quoted in Robert Perkinson, *Texas Tough: The Rise of America's Prison Empire* (New York: Metropolitan Books, 2010), p. 2.

6 "million-dollar blocks": Eric Cadora and Laura Kagan, Million Dollar Block Project, Spatial Information Design Lab, Columbia University Graduate School of Architecture, Planning and Preservation, www.spatialinformationdesignlab .org/projects.php?id=16.

6 we spend $88,000 per year to incarcerate a young person: Richard A. Mendel, *No Place for Kids: The Case for Reducing Juvenile Incarceration* (Baltimore, MD: Annie E. Casey Foundation, 2011), p. 20, www.aecf.org/OurWork/Juvenile Justice/~/media/Pubs/Topics/Juvenile%20Justice/Detention%20Reform /NoPlaceForKids/JJ_NoPlaceForKids_Full.pdf.

6 more than eight times the $10,652 we invest in her education: Expenditures were $10,652 in fiscal year 2010. Stephen Q. Cornman, Jumaane Young, and Kenneth C. Herrell, "Revenues and Expenditures for Public Elementary and Secondary Education: School Year 2009–10 (Fiscal Year 2010)," National Center for Education Statistics, 2010, nces.ed.gov/pubs2013/expenditures/findings.asp; see, e.g., Ed Mendel, "Per-Pupil Spending Rankings All Relative," *San Diego Union-Tribune*, April 13, 2008, www.utsandiego.com/uniontrib/20080413/news_1n13 pupil.html. For school spending as of 2010, see Lam Thuy Vo, "How Much Does the Government Spend to Send a Kid to Public School?" *Planet Money* blog, NPR, June 21, 2012, www.npr.org/blogs/money/2012/06/21/155515613/how -much-does-the-government-spend-to-send-a-kid-to-school.

6 youth prison: State-run juvenile facilities operate under a number of names, most of them euphemistic. I use the term "youth prison" (as well as other terms) because, based on my experience, it is the most accurate descriptor.

6 education spending dipped to less than $8,000: Cornman et al., "Revenues and Expenditures for Public Elementary and Secondary Education: School Year 2009–10 (Fiscal Year 2010)."

6 the cost of a year in a youth prison reached a high of $225,000: Susan Ferriss, "Steinberg Calls for Social Services Shift to California Counties," *Sacramento Bee*, May 30, 2010, cited in Douglas N. Evans, "Pioneers of Youth Justice Reform: Achieving System Change Using Resolution, Reinvestment, and Realignment Strategies," Research and Evaluation Center, July 2012, p. 12, johnjayresearch.org/wp-content/uploads/2012/06/rec20123.pdf.

7 66,332 American youth were confined in juvenile facilities: Annie E. Casey Foundation, "Reducing Youth Incarceration in the United States," Kids Count Data Snapshot, February 2013, p. 1, www.aecf.org/~/media/Pubs /Initiatives/KIDS%20COUNT/R/ReducingYouthIncarcerationSnapshot /DataSnapshotYouthIncarceration.pdf.

7 Most of these are boys: Office of Juvenile Justice and Delinquency Prevention, "Females Proportion of Juveniles in Residential Placement, 2010," Statistical Briefing Book, Juveniles in Corrections, www.ojjdp.gov/ojstatbb/corrections /qa08202.asp?qaDate=2010.

7 police arrest nearly 2 million juveniles each year: Charles Puzzanchera and Benjamin Adams, "Juvenile Offenders and Victims: National Report Series," U.S. Department of Justice, Office of Justice Programs Newsletter, December 2011, www.ojjdp.gov/pubs/236477.pdf.

7 one in three American schoolchildren will be arrested by the age of twenty-three: Robert Brame, Michael G. Turner, Raymond Paternoster, and Shawn D. Bushway, "Cumulative Prevalence of Arrest from Ages 8 to 23 in a National Sample," *Pediatrics*, December 19, 2011, doi:10.1542/peds.2010–3710, pediatrics.aap publications.org/content/early/2011/12/14/peds.2010–3710.abstract.

7 Sky-high recidivism rates: Mendel, *No Place for Kids*.

7 putting youth behind bars not only fails to enhance public safety: Dick Mendel, "In Juvenile Justice Care, Boys Get Worse," *Youth Today*, March 5, 2010, www .burnsinstitute.org/article.php?id=195.

7 One recent longitudinal study of 35,000 young offenders: Mary Schmich, "Locking Up Juveniles May Plant Seeds of More Crime," *Chicago Tribune*, 2013, www.modelsforchange.net/newsroom/524; and Nicholas D. Kristof, "Help Thy Neighbor and Go Straight to Prison," *New York Times*, August 11, 2013, p. SR1.

7 the single most significant factor in predicting whether a youth will offend again:

B.B. Benda and C.L. Tollet, "A Study of Recidivism of Serious and Persistent Offenders Among Adolescents," *Journal of Criminal Justice* 27, no. 2 (1999): 111–26. Cited in Barry Holman and Jason Ziedenberg, "The Dangers of Detention: The Impact of Incarcerating Youth in Detention and Other Secure Facilities," Justice Policy Institute report, November 28, 2006, www.justicepolicy.org/images/upload/06–11_REP_DangersOfDetention_JJ.pdf.

7 "A century of experience": Barry C. Feld, *Bad Kids: Race and the Transformation of the Juvenile Court* (New York: Oxford University Press, 1999).

8 Beyond this central failure: Mendel, *No Place for Kids*.

8 Physical and sexual abuse are rampant: See Chapters 5 and 6 on physical and sexual abuse, respectively, and Chapter 7 on solitary confinement.

8 Fully 80 to 90 percent of American teenagers have committed an illegal act: Adapted by Hillary Hodgdon from Elizabeth Scott and Laurence Steinberg, "Adolescent Development and the Regulation of Youth Crime," *Future of Children: Juvenile Justice* 18, no. 2 (Fall 2008), futureofchildren.org/futureofchildren/publications/highlights/18_02_Highlights_01.pdf.

8 one-third of all teens have committed a serious crime: Mendel, "In Juvenile Justice Care."

8 By the time they reach adulthood they are crime-free: Edward P. Mulvey, "Growing Up and Going Straight: Understanding Why Many Adolescent Offenders 'Age Out' of a Life of Crime," University of Pittsburgh, Office of Child Development, December 2006, www.ocd.pitt.edu/Files/PDF/89.pdf.

9 The young people who sit today inside locked facilities are, overwhelmingly, our nation's most vulnerable youth: "The Costs of Confinement: Why Good Juvenile Justice Policies Make Good Fiscal Sense," Justice Policy Institute, 2009, p. 2, www.justicepolicy.org/images/upload/09_05_REP_CostsofConfinement_JJ_PS.pdf.

9 most confined youth pose little risk to public safety: Annie E. Casey Foundation, "Reducing Youth Incarceration," p. 2.

11 Every study I've seen: See, e.g., "Building a More Effective Juvenile Justice System," Center on Early Adolescence, 2008, www.earlyadolescence.org/juvenile_justice_system; Richard A. Mendel, *The Missouri Model: Reinventing the Practice of Rehabilitating Youthful Offenders* (Baltimore, MD: Annie E. Casey Foundation, 2010), www.aecf.org/~/media/Pubs/Initiatives/Juvenile%20Detention%20Alternatives%20Initiative/MOModel/MO_Fullreport_webfinal.pdf. See also Chapter 12 and Chapter 13.

11 recidivism rates that send as many as four out of five juvenile parolees back

behind bars: Available studies of youths released from residential corrections programs find that 70 to 80 percent of youths are rearrested within two or three years. See Mendel, *No Place for Kids*, figure 3.

12 The rate of juvenile confinement has dropped a remarkable 41 percent: Annie E. Casey Foundation, "Reducing Youth Incarceration."

12 This shift has not led to a rise in youth crime: "Juvenile Arrest Rate Trends," Office of Juvenile Justice and Delinquency Prevention Statistical Briefing Book, December 17, 2012, www.ojjdp.gov/ojstatbb/crime/JAR_Display.asp ?ID=qa05200.

12 Politicians who back these changes are finding far more support: Mark W. Lipsey, James C. Howell, Marion R. Kelly, Gabrielle Chapman, and Darin Carver, "Improving the Effectiveness of Juvenile Justice Programs: A New Perspective on Evidence-Based Practice," Center for Juvenile Justice Reform, December 2010, p. 8, cjjr.georgetown.edu/pdfs/ebp/ebppaper.pdf.

12 the United States still incarcerates more of its young people: Pete Brook, "Uncompromising Photos Expose Juvenile Detention in America," *Raw File* blog, *Wired*, April 11, 2012, www.wired.com/rawfile/2012/04/photog-hopes -to-effect-policy-with-survey-of-juvenile-lock-ups/. See also American Correctional Association, *2008 Directory of Adult and Juvenile Correctional Departments, Institutions, Agencies, and Probation and Parole Authorities* (Alexandria, VA: American Correctional Association, 2008).

13 spending a total of $5 *billion*: Annie E. Casey Foundation, "Reducing Youth Incarceration," p. 2.

13 Even our closest competitor, South Africa: Scott and Steinberg, "Adolescent Development and Juvenile Justice."

13 We still fill our youth prisons primarily with young people who pose little or no threat to public safety: Annie E. Casey Foundation, "Reducing Youth Incarceration," p. 2.

13 And we persist in sending them to places where they are likely to be victimized: Annie E. Casey Foundation, "A Road Map for Juvenile Justice Reform," 2012, www.aecf.org/~/media/PublicationFiles/AEC18oessay_booklet_MECH.pdf.

13 interventions that rely on support and connection: See Chapter 13.

14 Bart Lubow: The Annie E. Casey Foundation provided funding to support this book.

1. Inside Juvenile Prison

21 Findings letter: Ralph F. Boyd, "Re: CRIPA Investigation of Oakley and Columbia Training Schools in Raymond and Columbia, Mississippi," June 19, 2003, p. 19, www.justice.gov/crt/about/spl/documents/oak_colu_miss_findinglet.pdf.

22 assigned an identification number: Many young people I met remembered this multidigit number by heart even years after their release.

22 Anything that remains will be either stored, mailed home at his expense, or destroyed: See, for example, Nebraska Department of Correctional Facilities, www.corrections.state.ne.us/ncyf.html.

23 submit to a search: *Pope v. Roulain*, Civil Action no. 05-AR-1264-S, U.S. District Court for the Northern District of Alabama Southern Division, filed June 19, 2006, www.gpo.gov/fdsys/pkg/USCOURTS-alnd-2_05-cv-01264 /pdf/USCOURTS-alnd-2_05-cv-01264-0.pdf.

23 squat and cough: While the Supreme Court has not ruled on the constitutionality of strip searches in state juvenile facilities, "some federal circuit courts require reasonable suspicion of contraband possession to justify a strip search of an adult detained for a minor offense, but require a less stringent standard to justify strip searches of juveniles." The Supreme Court has never upheld a strip search without individualized suspicion in any context other than the prison. Emily J. Nelson, "Custodial Strip Searches of Juveniles: How *Safford* Informs a New Two-Tiered Standard of Review," *Boston College Law Review* 52, no. 1 (2011): 339–74, www.bc.edu/content/dam/files/schools/law/bclawreview /pdf/52_1/06_nelson.pdf.

23 young wards still wear prison stripes: Richard Ross, "Juvenile in Justice," *Bokeh*, Juvenile Justice Information Exchange, bokeh.jjie.org/hm-age-cald well-southwest-idaho-juvenile-detention-center-id/.

28 "large-muscle exercise": After the practice of caging youth was halted, a warden reportedly told visitors that he planned to bring in dogs from the local SPCA to fill the cages previously inhabited by children. The boys would rehabilitate themselves by training the dogs, and the institution, perhaps, would rehabilitate its public image in the process. Kevin Feeney, "Experiencing Preston Youth Prison," Ella Baker Center for Human Rights, June 17, 2009, ellabakercenter .org/blog/2009/06/experiencing-preston-youth-prison.

29 A national survey: Andrea J. Sedlak and Karla S. McPherson, "Conditions of Confinement: Findings from the Survey of Youth in Residential Placement," *Juvenile Justice Bulletin*, Office of Juvenile Justice and Delinquency Prevention, May 2010, syrp.org/images/OJJDP%20Conditions%20of%20Confinement.pdf.

30 "experience violence, theft and assault": Andrea J. Sedlak, Karla S. McPherson, and Monica Basena, "Nature and Risk of Victimization: Findings from the Survey of Youth in Residential Treatment," *Juvenile Justice Bulletin*, Office of Juvenile Justice and Delinquency Prevention, June 2013, www.ojjdp.gov/pubs /240703.pdf.

30 Nearly half of those surveyed had their property stolen: See Chapters 5 and 6 for more on physical and sexual abuse, respectively, in juvenile facilities.

30 a guard was the perpetrator: Sedlak, McPherson, and Basena, "Nature and Risk of Victimization."

30 One in ten youths nationwide had suffered sexual assault: Allan J. Beck, Paige M. Harrison, and Paul Guerino, "Special Report: Sexual Victimization in Juvenile Facilities Reported by Youth, 2008–2009," Bureau of Justice Statistics, U.S. Department of Justice, January 2010, www.bjs.gov/content/pub/pdf/svjfry09.pdf.

30 Violent Crime Index offenses: Annie E. Casey Foundation, "Reducing Youth Incarceration in the United States," Kids Count Data Snapshot, February 2013, p. 2, www.aecf.org/~/media/Pubs/Initiatives/KIDS%20COUNT/R/Reduc ingYouthIncarcerationSnapshot/DataSnapshotYouthIncarceration.pdf.

31 A number of young people have died: Nancy Lewis, "Another State Bans Prone Restraints," *Youth Today*, August 26, 2008, www.youthtoday.org/view_article .cfm?article_id=2254.

31 the pervasive use of solitary confinement: See Chapter 7.

31 reported being placed in isolation: Perhaps because this practice is so out of line with international standards, the generally neutral authors of "Conditions of Confinement: Findings from the Survey of Youth in Residential Placement" present this finding with an uncharacteristic editorial comment: "Maintaining discipline and control is critical but challenging," they write. "Nevertheless, some may find SYRP findings on the prevalence of solitary confinement both surprising and problematic."

31 The more often young people are handcuffed: Sedlak, McPherson, and Basena, "Nature and Risk of Victimization," p. 6.

33 "Many of the youths informed us": Investigation of the Arthur G. Dozier School for Boys and the Jackson Juvenile Offender Center, Marianna, Florida, United States Department of Justice, Civil Rights Division, December 1, 2011, p. 25, www .justice.gov/crt/about/spl/documents/dozier_findltr_12-1-11.pdf?. For more on this facility, see Chapter 14.

35 "Friday Night Fights": James Gilligan, *Violence in California Prisons: A Proposal for Research into Patterns and Cures* (New York: Diane Publishing, 2000), p. 13.

35 Guards would place known gang rivals together: Ibid. According to subsequent investigations, wards at the facility where Mark was held were subjected to what administrators called "unofficial sanctions" for various unnamed offenses. These included being forced into cells filled with urine and feces (those who demurred were pepper sprayed) as well as a practice called "slamming," in which guards dragged their targets out of range of security cameras and slammed them repeatedly on the ground or against a cell, then kept them from receiving medical treatment for as long as twenty-four hours.

35 misses many if not most of the central developmental tasks of adolescence: "Raising Teens: Ten Tasks of Adolescent Development," MIT Work-Life Center, Massachusetts Institute of Technology, hrweb.mit.edu/worklife/raising -teens/ten-tasks.html.

2. Birth of an Abomination

38 Its managers, according to the law: Sanford J. Fox, "The Early History of the Court," *Future of Children: The Juvenile Court* 6, no. 3 (Winter 1996): 29–39, www.princeton.edu/futureofchildren/publications/docs/06_03_01.pdf.

39 "a historical milestone in the American family culture": Kenneth Wooden, *Weeping in the Playtime of Others: America's Incarcerated Children* (New York: McGraw-Hill, 1976), p. 24.

39 Social engineers of the day: Barry Krisberg, "Juvenile Corrections: An Overview," in *The Oxford Handbook of Juvenile Crime and Juvenile Justice*, ed. Barry C. Feld and Donna M. Bishop (New York: Oxford University Press, 2011), p. 749.

39 early example of racial profiling: Two centuries later, America's racial and ethnic makeup has shifted, and with it both the locus of our fears and the population of our prisons. Today, it is black and brown children from our nation's poorest neighborhoods who are painted and perceived as a threat to the social order— and who are, accordingly, locked up in greatest numbers.

39 "The lad's parents are Irish": R. Pickett, *House of Refuge* (Syracuse: Syracuse University Press, 1969), p. 6.

40 the rapid influx of confined juveniles: "Our City Charities; The New-York House of Refuge for Juvenile Delinquents," *New York Times*, January 23, 1860, www.nytimes.com/1860/01/23/news/our-city-charities-the-new-york -house-of-refuge-for-juvenile-delinquents.html.

40 agents of the House of Refuge simply roamed the streets: Barry Krisberg, "Juvenile Justice: Improving the Quality of Care," National Council on Crime and

Delinquency, 1992, p. 2, www.nccdglobal.org/sites/default/files/publication
_pdf/quality-of-care.pdf.

41 "The boys' house": "Our City Charities."

42 "While some of the children": Ibid.

43 "Injudicious friends of this": Ibid.

43 Inside the House of Refuge: Ibid.

44 As cities scrambled to keep up with a massive influx of immigrants: Barry C.
Feld, *Bad Kids: Race and the Transformation of the Juvenile Court* (New York:
Oxford University Press, 1999), p. 4.

44 "constituted the first specialized institutions": Ibid., p. 49.

44 "Children confined in the houses of refuge": A. Pisciotta, "Saving the Children:
The Promise and Practice of *Parens Patriae*, 1838–98," *Crime and Delinquency*
28 (1982): 410–25, cited in Randall G. Shelden, "From Houses of Refuge to
'Youth Corrections': Same Story, Different Day" (paper prepared for the Mid-
western Criminal Justice Association Annual Meeting, Chicago, September 29–
October 1, 2005), www.sheldensays.com/Res-twelve.htm.

44 "Punitive delinquency institutions": Feld, *Bad Kids*, p. 273.

45 Lyman School for Boys: The first to open, the Lyman School was also one of the
first to be shut down, in 1972, for "massive failure and child brutality," according to Kenneth Wooden in *Weeping in the Playtime of Others*.

45 "Those who sought to reform juvenile delinquents": Joseph F. Kett, *Rites of
Passage: Adolescence in America, 1790 to the Present* (New York: Basic Books,
1977), p. 132, cited in Feld, *Bad Kids*, p. 55.

45 "As children of immigrants and the poor": Feld, *Bad Kids*, p. 55.

45 "In an early version of 'blaming the victims'": David J. Rothman, *Conscience
and Convenience: The Asylum and Its Alternative in Progressive America* (Boston: Little, Brown, 1980), p. 24, cited in Feld, *Bad Kids*, p. 55. Similar victim
blaming continues to this day. Across the country, young people told me that
whatever indignities they were forced to endure—beatings by guards, sexual
abuse, "chemical restraints," long stints in solitary confinement—came with the
message that they had brought it upon themselves.

45 *parens patriae*: "Juvenile Justice: History and Philosophy—The Origins of the
Juvenile Court," Law Library—American Law and Legal Information, law
.jrank.org/pages/1489/Juvenile-Justice-History-Philosophy-origins-juve
nile-court.html#ixzz2PzJ1gTQr.

46 many judges did their best to advance the rehabilitative mandate: Fox, "Early
History of the Court," p. 29.

46 "courts considered what was best": Ibid.

46 "The child who must be brought into court": Wilbur R. Miller, ed., *The Social History of Crime and Punishment in America: An Encyclopedia* (Thousand Oaks, CA: Sage, 2012), p. 930.

46 "The judge on a bench": Ibid.

47 "From the very beginning": Annie E. Casey Foundation, "A Road Map for Juvenile Justice Reform," 2012, p. 4, www.aecf.org/~/media/Publication Files/AEC18oessay_booklet_MECH.pdf.

47 juvenile court was an instant sensation: Richard A. Lawrence and Craig Hemmens, "History and Development of the Juvenile Court and Justice Process," in *Juvenile Justice: A Text/Reader* (Thousand Oaks, CA: Sage, 2008), p. 59.

47 parens patriae had been invoked: Feld, *Bad Kids*, pp. 52–53.

47 *Ex parte Crouse*: Fox, "Early History of the Court," p. 32.

47 parens patriae trumped parenthood: Feld, *Bad Kids*, p. 53.

48 "may not the natural parent": *Ex parte Crouse 14*, 1839, in Jeffrey A. Jenkins, *The American Courts: A Procedural Approach* (Sudbury, MA: Jones and Bartlett, 2011), p. 175.

48 "became the precedent for 20th Century cases": Fox, "Early History of the Court," p. 32.

48 "was heavily influenced by the antagonism toward Irish parents": Krisberg, "Juvenile Corrections," p. 2.

48 Once a child was committed to a House of Refuge: Feld, *Bad Kids*, p. 54.

49 "Juvenile justice is replete": Bernardine Dohrn, "The School, the Child, and the Court," in *A Century of Juvenile Justice*, ed. Margaret K. Rosenheim, Franklin E. Zimring, David S. Tanenhaus, and Bernardine Dohrn (Chicago: University of Chicago Press, 2002), p. 295.

49 *Kent v. United States*: American Bar Association, "The History of Juvenile Justice," *Dialogue on Youth and Justice* (Chicago: American Bar Association, Division for Public Education, 2007), www.americanbar.org/content/dam/aba/migrated/publiced/features/DYJpart1.authcheck.dam.pdf.

50 a parade of investigations into the St. Charles Reformatory: Dohrn, "School, the Child, and the Court," p. 300.

50 the staff believed that a fourth of boys should not be there at all: Ibid.

50 "In the overall picture": Ibid., p. 301.

3. Other People's Children

52 "One of the underpinnings of the correction business": Deckle McLean, "Jerome Miller and the Correction Business," *Boston Globe*, November 15, 1970.

52 "What the best and wisest parent": Michael Grossberg, "Changing Conceptions of Child Welfare in the United States, 1820–1935," in *A Century of Juvenile Justice*, ed. Margaret K. Rosenheim, Franklin E. Zimring, David S. Tanenhaus, and Bernardine Dohrn (Chicago: University of Chicago Press, 1992), p. 3.

53 Survey of Youth in Residential Placement: Andrea J. Sedlak and Carol Bruce, "Youth's Characteristics and Backgrounds: Findings from the Survey of Youth in Residential Placement," *Juvenile Justice Bulletin*, Office of Juvenile Justice and Delinquency Prevention, December 2010, www.ncjrs.gov/pdffiles1/ojjdp /227730.pdf.

53 Twenty-six percent of those surveyed were locked up on assault charges: Ibid., p. 4.

53 Only 11 percent of youth in custody: Even this number may be misleading, as 55 percent of those surveyed said they were with a group when they committed their offense, and young people often do not understand that, for instance, by driving a robbery victim to an ATM they could be charged with kidnapping, or that if they are present while someone they are with uses a gun, whether or not they know the gun is there or anticipate its use, they also will be held responsible for whatever harm results.

54 the great majority of those confined as juveniles pose little to no danger to the public: Richard A. Mendel, *No Place for Kids: The Case for Reducing Juvenile Incarceration* (Baltimore, MD: Annie E. Casey Foundation, 2011), p. 13, www .aecf.org/~/media/Pubs/Topics/Juvenile%20Justice/Detention%20Reform /NoPlaceForKids/JJ_NoPlaceForKids_Full.pdf. See also Schuyler Center for Analysis and Advocacy, "Children's Policy Agenda: Policy Brief, 2010."

54 In 2008, only 12 percent of violent crime: Neelum Arya, *State Trends: Legislative Victories from 2005 to 2010 Removing Youth from the Adult Criminal Justice System* (Washington, DC: Campaign for Youth Justice), p. 14.

54 According to Lisa Thurau: Lisa Thurau, "When Asking, 'Why Me?' Means Disorderly Conduct," Viewpoints: Youth Today, September 1, 2009, strategies foryouth.org/sfysite/wp-content/uploads/2012/11/Viewpoints-YOUTH -TODAY-05-31-12.pdf.

59 Young people of color face a different reality: Miroslava Chavez-Garcia, *States of Delinquency: Race and Science in the Making of California's Juvenile Justice System* (Berkeley: University of California Press, 2012), p. 1.

59 Racism does not merely inform or infuse our juvenile justice system: Even as the number of young people behind bars has dropped in recent years, the racialization of youth incarceration has not improved. In fact, there are early indicators that reform may actually worsen the racial injustice that permeates the juvenile system, as white youth benefit most from expanded discretion and community alternatives. Recent research indicates that probation officers and other system staff—even those who are racial or ethnic minorities themselves—are subconsciously prone to attribute more negative characteristics to youths of color than to nonwhite youths, and to recommend more punitive treatment.

59 In almost every state: Spike Bradford, "Two New Reports Show Juvenile Confinement Reform in Five States," Reclaiming Futures, March 13, 2003, www.reclaimingfutures.org/blog/two-new-reports-show-juvenile-confine ment-reform-five-states.

59 Black youths are five times more likely than their white peers to be incarcerated: James Bell and Laura John Ridolfi, "Adoration of the Question: Reflections on the Failure to Reduce Racial and Ethnic Disparities in the Juvenile Justice System," W. Haywood Burns Institute, December 2008, p. 2, www.burnsinstitute .org/downloads/BI%20Adoration%20of%20the%20Question_2.pdf.

60 African American youth are 4.5 times more likely: "And Justice for Some: Differential Treatment of Youth of Color in the Justice System," National Council on Crime and Delinquency, 2007, describes in painstaking detail why, in far greater proportion than whites, youths of color enter the criminal justice system. See also Bell and Ridolfi, "Adoration of the Question"; and ACLU of Northern California and W. Haywood Burns Institute, "Balancing the Scales of Justice: An Exploration into How Lack of Education, Employment, and Housing Opportunities Contribute to Disparities in the Criminal Justice System," n.d., www.burnsinstitute.org/article.php?id=248.

60 nine times as likely to be incarcerated for crimes against persons: Mark Soler, Dana Shoenberg, and Marc Schindler, "Juvenile Justice: Lessons for a New Era," *Georgetown Journal on Poverty Law & Policy* 16, symposium issue (2009).

60 Nearly half (48 percent) of all juveniles incarcerated on drug charges are black: "Racial Inequality in Youth Sentencing," Campaign for the Fair Sentencing of Youth, fairsentencingofyouth.org/the-issue/advocacy-resource-bank/racial -inequality-in-youth-sentencing/.

60 According to research from the National Council on Crime and Delinquency: "And Justice for Some: Differential Treatment of Youth of Color in the Justice System," National Council on Crime and Delinquency, January 2007, p. 2.

61 "multi-million dollar cottage industry": Bell and Ridolfi, "Adoration of the Question," p. 15.

61 metal detectors and onsite police officers in their schools: According to research by the W. Haywood Burns Institute and the American Civil Liberties Union, young people who attend schools patrolled by police are more likely to be suspended, expelled, *and* arrested at a young age. See W. Haywood Burns Institute and American Civil Liberties Union, "Balancing the Scales."

61 "youth control complex": Victor Rios, *Punished: Policing the Lives of Black and Latino Boys* (New York: New York University Press, 2011).

63 Childhood trauma such as Curtis experienced is so widespread: Andrea J. Sedlak and Karla S. McPherson, "Survey of Youth in Residential Placement: Youth's Needs and Services," *Juvenile Justice Bulletin*, Office of Juvenile Justice and Delinquency Prevention, April 2010, www.ncjrs.gov/pdffiles1/ojjdp /grants/227660.pdf.

64 "Children exposed to violence": Robert L. Listenbee Jr., Joe Torre, Gregory Boyle, Sharon W. Cooper, Sarah Deer, Deanne Tilton Durfee, Thea James, et al., *Report of the Attorney General's National Task Force on Children Exposed to Violence*, Office of Juvenile Justice and Delinquency Prevention, December 12, 2012, pp. 171–72, www.justice.gov/defendingchildhood/cev-rpt-full.pdf.

68 "too often have become places of poor treatment and abuse": U.S. Attorney General's National Task Force on Children Exposed to Violence, University of Maryland Hearing transcript, Office of Juvenile Justice and Delinquency Prevention, pp. 45–46, www.ojjdp.gov/defendingchildhood/baltimore-hearing -transcript1-3.pdf.

4. The Rise of the Super-Predator and the Decline of the Rehabilitative Ideal

72 "more savage than salvageable": DiIulio quoted in the *Wall Street Journal*, 1997, cited in Christopher G. Robbins, *Expelling Hope: The Assault on Youth and the Militarization of Schooling* (Albany: State University of New York Press, 2008), p. 33.

72 *Body Count*: William J. Bennett, John J. DiIulio, and John P. Walters, *Body Count: Moral Poverty . . . and How to Win America's War Against Crime and Drugs* (New York: Simon & Schuster, 1996).

73 "Juvenile justice policies": A. Platt, *The Child Savers: The Invention of Delinquency* (Chicago: University of Chicago Press, 1968); and M.E. Wolfgang,

T.P. Thornberry, and R.M. Figlio, *From Boy to Man, from Delinquency to Crime* (Chicago: University of Chicago Press, 1987), cited in Barry Krisberg, *Juvenile Justice: Redeeming Our Children* (Thousand Oaks, CA: Sage, 2005).

73 super-predator "phenomenon": Fox Butterfield, *All God's Children* (New York: Alfred A. Knopf, 2002).

73 kindergartners hauled off in handcuffs: "Georgia Girl, 6, Gets Handcuffed, Arrested After Throwing Tantrum in Kindergarten Class," Smoking Gun, April 7, 2012, www.thesmokinggun.com/buster/little-girl-battery-arrest-312678; "Baltimore Police Handcuff, Arrest 4 Children Under Age 10 at Their School," CBS Baltimore, March 20, 2012, baltimore.cbslocal.com/2012/03/30/baltimore -police-handcuff-arrest-4-children-under-age-10-at-their-school/; Laura Hib-bard, "Four Maryland Children, Ages 8 and 9, Arrested and Handcuffed for Fighting at School," *Huffington Post*, April 2, 2012, www.huffingtonpost.com/2012/04/02 /four-maryland-children-arrested-and-handcuffed_n_1397622.html.

73 "demography is destiny": Robin Templeton, "Superscapegoating: Teen 'Super-Predators' Hype Set Stage for Draconian Legislation," *Extra!*, January– February 1998.

73 *San Francisco Examiner* tried to outdo Joseph Pulitzer's hyperbolic *New York World*: David Nasaw, *The Chief: The Life of William Randolph Hearst* (Boston: Houghton Mifflin, 2000).

74 "Teenage Time Bomb": David J. Krajicek, " 'Super-Predators': The Making of a Myth," *Youth Today*, April 1999, p. 1.

74 "America is being threatened": Templeton, "Superscapegoating."

74 more than half of all local news stories about youth focused on violence: Ibid.

74 "The political demonization of young black males": Barry C. Feld, *Bad Kids: Race and the Transformation of the Juvenile Court* (New York: Oxford University Press, 1999).

75 creating mechanisms to transfer many more youths to the adult system: See, e.g., National Center for Juvenile Justice, "Different from Adults: An Updated Analysis of Juvenile Transfer and Blended Sentencing Laws with Recommenda-tions for Reform," November 2008; MacArthur Foundation Research Network on Adolescent Development and Juvenile Justice, "Issue Brief 5: The Changing Borders of Juvenile Justice: Transfer of Adolescents to Adult Court." For more on the subject, see the Campaign for Youth Justice website, www.campaign foryouthjustice.org.

75 A number of states went so far as to revise their juvenile codes: Krisberg, *Juvenile Justice*, p. 3.

75 Other states made similar changes: Feld, *Bad Kids*, p. 251.

75 The result was that the number of cases heard each year in juvenile court rose
    44 percent: Krisberg, *Juvenile Justice*, p. 3.

75 "At the state level": Ibid.

76 "Since 1980": John J. Dilulio, "The Coming of the Super-Predators," *Weekly
    Standard*, November 27, 1995, p. 23, cooley.libarts.wsu.edu/schwartj/criminol
    ogy/dilulio.pdf.

76 "On the horizon": Ibid.

77 "No one in academia": Ibid.

78 violent crime arrests peaked in 1994: Isaac Wolf, "Investigation Reveals Widely
    Uneven Treatment and Oversight of Adolescents Nationwide in Adult Jails,"
    Wolf Scripps Howard News Service, November 18, 2011, www.tcpalm.com
    /news/2011/nov/18/investigation-reveals-widely-uneven-treatment-of/.

78 Between 1995 and 2004: The Annie E. Casey Foundation, "A Road Map for
    Juvenile Justice Reform," 2012, p. 11, www.aecf.org/~/media/Publication
    Files/AEC18oessay_booklet_MECH.pdf.

78 more than twice as many young people were adjudicated on charges of disor-
    derly conduct: Ibid.

79 "Super-predator thinking": E-mail correspondence with Bart Lubow, July 31,
    2013.

80 Just desert advocates: James C. Howell, "Superpredators and Other Myths
    About Juvenile Justice," in *Preventing and Reducing Juvenile Delinquency: A
    Comprehensive Framework*, 2nd ed. (Thousand Oaks, CA: Sage, 2009), p. 12,
    www.sagepub.com/upm-data/27206_1.pdf.

80 "judicial decisions": Feld, *Bad Kids*, p. 3.

5. The Fist and the Boot: Physical Abuse in Juvenile Prisons

82 But formal investigations into conditions at the CYA: Kathryn Seligman, "Peti-
    tions for Modification: Asking the Juvenile Court to Modify a Placement or
    Commitment Order After the Dispositional Hearing," First District Appellate
    Project, San Francisco, CA, January 2003, p. 30, www.fdap.org/downloads
    /news/CYA_Packet_3-04.pdf.

83 About half has experienced some kind of group punishment: Andrea J. Sed-
    lak and Karla S. McPherson, "Conditions of Confinement: Findings from the
    National Survey of Youth in Residential Placement," *Juvenile Justice Bulletin*,
    Office of Juvenile Justice and Delinquency Prevention, May 2010, www.ncjrs
    .gov/pdffiles1/ojjdp/227729.pdf.

83 Fear of abuse was equally pervasive: Ibid.

83 "Workers forced one boy": Nicholas Confessore, "4 Youth Prisons in New York Used Excessive Force," *New York Times*, August 24, 2009.

84 In Mississippi guards ripped the clothing from suicidal girls: Annie E. Casey Foundation, "Systemic or Recurring Maltreatment in Juvenile Corrections Facilities: State-by-State Summary," n.d., p. 8, www.aecf.org/OurWork/Juvenile Justice/~/media/Pubs/Topics/Juvenile%20Justice/Detention%20Reform /NoPlaceForKids/SystemicorRecurringMaltreatmentinJuvenileCorrections Facilities.pdf.

84 forced to eat their own vomit: Ralph F. Boyd Jr., "Re: CRIPA Investigation of Oakley and Columbia Training Schools in Raymond and Columbia, Mississippi: A Letter to Governor Ronnie Musgrove," June 19, 2003, i.cdn.turner .com/cnn/2008/images/04/01/oak.colu.miss.findinglet.pdf.

84 In Arkansas, young people were left naked in solitary: Annie E. Casey Foundation, "Systemic or Recurring Maltreatment," p. 1.

84 "Of these, 1,343 instances of abuse": Holbrook Mohr, "AP: 13K Claims of Abuse in Juvenile Detention Since '04," *USA Today*, March 2, 2008, cited in Richard A. Mendel, *No Place for Kids: The Case for Reducing Juvenile Incarceration* (Baltimore, MD: Annie E. Casey Foundation, 2011), p. 6, www.aecf.org/~/media /Pubs/Topics/Juvenile%20Justice/Detention%20Reform/NoPlaceForKids /JJ_NoPlaceForKids_Full.pdf.

84 Fifty-seven lawsuits: Ibid.

85 A review of all fifty states: Ibid., p. 7.

85 incarcerated youth do not forfeit their human rights: U.S. Department of Justice, Civil Rights Division, Special Litigation, "Rights of Juveniles," www .justice.gov/crt/about/spl/juveniles.php.

86 public displays of outrage and official commitments to change: Mendel, *No Place for Kids*, p. 5.

86 a range of mechanisms of assault: ABC 7, "Jail Cell Justice," Number 16370, Investigative Reporters and Editors, February 1999, www.ire.org/resource -center/stories/16370/.

86 The restraint chair: Specially designed restraint chairs, fitted out with cuffs and straps to immobilize the occupant, have been involved in several deaths behind bars and in several lawsuits. See Ann-Marie Cusac, "The Devil's Chair," *The Progressive*, April 2000, progressive.org/mag_cusacchair.

87 Witnessing violence can also have long-term effects: See, e.g., "Understanding Child Trauma," National Child Traumatic Stress Network, www.nctsn.org /resources/audiences/parents-caregivers/understanding-child-traumatic-stress;

"The Effects of Domestic Violence on Children," Domestic Violence Round-table, www.domesticviolenceroundtable.org/effect-on-children.html; Erica J. Adams, "Healing Invisible Wounds: Why Investing in Trauma-Informed Care for Children Makes Sense," Justice Policy Institute, Spring 2010, www .justicepolicy.org/images/upload/10-07_REP_HealingInvisibleWounds_JJ -PS.pdf.

88 dozens of youths went to the hospital: Fox Butterfield, "Hard Time: A Special Report: Profits at a Juvenile Prison Come with a Chilling Cost," *New York Times*, July 15, 1998.

92 "It is common practice": *Farrell v. Harper*, "Amended Complaint for Injunctive and Declaratory Relief," Superior Court for the State of California, County of Alameda, p. 5, www.clearinghouse.net/chDocs/public/JI-CA-0013-0001.pdf.

92 Outside sources corroborate Will's account: Jenifer Warren, "Youth Prison System Unsafe, Unhealthful, Reports Find," *Los Angeles Times*, February 3, 2004.

92 California law permits the use of chemical weapons: *Farrell v. Harper*.

92 272 youths were sprayed with chemical weapons: Warren, "Youth Prison System Unsafe."

93 "for extended periods of time": *Farrell v. Harper*.

95 Vincent Schiraldi: All quotations from author's interview with Vincent Schiraldi in his New York office, March 28, 2012.

95 His signal achievement there was closing down the District's Oak Hill Youth Center: John Kelly, "Three Candidates for OJJDP," *Youth Today*, January 28, 2009, www.youthtoday.org/view_blog.cfm?blog_id=82.

95 $46 million New Beginnings Youth Development Center: Cherie Saunders, "Maya Angelou Academy for DC Juveniles to Be Featured on NBC's Rock Center," *The Examiner*, July 2, 2012, www.examiner.com/article/maya -angelou-academy-for-dc-juveniles-to-be-featured-on-nbc-s-rock-center.

98 acting from their "frontal lobes": Richard Knox, "The Teen Brain: It's Just Not Grown Up Yet," NPR, March 1, 2010, www.npr.org/templates/story/story .php?storyId=124119468.

99 "The opposite of faith is not heresy": Elie Wiesel, "On Indifference," *US News & World Report*, October 27, 1986.

99 eleven thousand young people engage in suicidal behavior in juvenile facilities: Barry Holman and Jason Ziedenberg, "The Dangers of Detention: The Impact of Incarcerating Youth in Detention and Other Secure Facilities," Justice Policy Institute, 2006, p. 9, www.justicepolicy.org/images/upload /06-11_REP_DangersOfDetention_JJ.pdf.

102 "What is abnormal": "Oprah Talks to Elie Wiesel" *O, The Oprah Magazine*, November 2000, www.oprah.com/omagazine/Oprah-Interviews-Elie-Wiesel/1.

6. An Open Secret: Sexual Abuse Behind Bars

104 Review Panel on Prison Rape: Allan J. Beck, Paige M. Harrison, and Paul Guerino, "Special Report: Sexual Victimization in Juvenile Facilities Reported by Youth, 2008–2009," U.S. Department of Justice, January 2010, www.bjs.gov /content/pub/pdf/svjfry09.pdf.

104 Sexual abuse rates are higher in juvenile: Martha T. Moore, "Study: Youths Sexually Abused in Juvenile Prisons," *USA Today*, January 7, 2010, usatoday30 .usatoday.com/news/nation/2010-01-07-juvenile-prison-sexual-abuse_N.htm.

104 "In essence": David Kaiser and Lovisa Stannow, "The Crisis of Juvenile Prison Rape: A New Report," *New York Review of Books* blog, January 7, 2010, www.nybooks.com/blogs/nyrblog/2010/jan/07/the-crisis-of-juvenile -prison-rape-a-new-report/.

105 "detach physically and psychologically": Robert L. Listenbee Jr., Joe Torre, Gregory Boyle, Sharon W. Cooper, Sarah Deer, Deanne Tilton Durfee, Thea James, et al., *Report of the Attorney General's National Task Force on Children Exposed to Violence*, Office of Juvenile Justice and Delinquency Prevention, December 12, 2012, www.justice.gov/defendingchildhood/cev-rpt-full.pdf.

106 Fully 65 percent of those who had been sexually abused: Beck, Harrison, and Guerino, "Special Report."

106 81 percent had been sexually assaulted more than once: Ibid.

107 May 2012—fully ten years after PREA was signed into law: "Justice Department Releases Final Rule to Prevent, Detect and Respond to Prison Rape: Landmark Regulation Contains New Standards to Combat Sexual Abuse in Confinement Facilities," Department of Justice, press release, May 2012, www.justice.gov /opa/pr/2012/May/12-ag-635.html.

108 a small percentage of the "second chances" their keepers are granted: Allen J. Beck and Timothy A. Hughes, "Sexual Violence Reported by Correctional Authorities: 2004," U.S. Department of Justice, July 2005, bjs.gov/content /pub/pdf/svrca04.pdf.

108 "Even when prosecuted": "Deterring Staff Sexual Abuse of Federal Inmates," Office of the Inspector General, April 2005, www.justice.gov/oig/special/0504 /index.htm.

109 Under civil commitment laws: Paul Demko, "'He Was a Kid': Former Juvenile

Sex Offenders Languish in MSOP," Politics in Minnesota, October 5 2012, politicsinminnesota.com/2012/10/he-was-a-kid-former-juvenile-sex-offenders -languish-in-msop/.

109 consensual sex between two minors that is prosecuted as statutory rape: "State Civil Commitment for Sex Offenders," Criminal Defense Lawyers, www.crim inaldefenselawyer.com/resources/state-civil-commitment-sex-offenders.htm.

109 Human Rights Watch study: Nicole Pittman and Alison Parker, *Raised on the Registry: The Irreparable Harm of Placing Children on Sex Offender Registries in the US* (New York: Human Rights Watch, 2013), www.hrw.org/sites/default /files/reports/us0513_ForUpload_1.pdf.

109 "harassed and ridiculed by their peers": Ibid., p. 5.

110 "often do not believe they will be caught": "Deterring Staff Sexual Abuse of Federal Inmates," Office of the Inspector General.

110 report on girls in New York State custody: Mie Lewis, *Custody and Control: Conditions of Confinement in New York's Juvenile Prison for Girls* (New York: Human Rights Watch/American Civil Liberties Union, 2006), www.hrw.org/reports /us0906webwcover.pdf.

110 "Ebony V. stated that girls at Lansing": Ibid., p. 60.

110 Ebony's first-person account: Ibid.

111 Sheila Bedi testified: U.S. Attorney General's National Task Force on Children Exposed to Violence, University of Maryland Hearing transcript, Office of Juvenile Justice and Delinquency Prevention, November 29–30, 2011, p. 12, www.ojjdp.gov/defendingchildhood/baltimore-hearing-transcript1-3.pdf.

112 In testimony before a 2010 House Committee on Education and Labor hearing: "Survivor Testimony: National Prison Rape Elimination Commission Testimony of Pamanicka 'Chino' Hardin," Just Detention International, Boston, June 1, 2006, www.justdetention.org/en/NPREC/chinohardin.aspx.

115 "These girls in the detention center are not Little Miss Muffin": Aviva Shen, "Prison Attorneys Claim 14-Year-Old Inmate Wanted to Get Raped by Her 40-Year-Old Prison Guard," *Think Progress*, August 7, 2013, thinkprogress .org/justice/2013/08/07/2425511/louisiana-teenager-prison-rape/.

116 Commonplace incursions such as being ogled in the shower: Beck, Harrison, and Guerino, "Special Report."

116 multiple examples of staff touching girls: Lewis, *Custody and Control*, p. 68.

116 "The girl is required to take off all her clothes": Office of Children and Family Services, Policy and Procedures Manual, "PPM 3247.18: Contraband, Inspections and Searches," November 1, 1998, pp. 6–7, in Lewis, *Custody and Control*, pp. 58–59.

117 "You get strip searched": Lewis, *Custody and Control*, p. 60.

117 "the everyday rape of random body searches": David Chura, "Everyday Assaults of Young Offenders in Adult Prisons," *Juvenile Justice Information Exchange*, August 7, 2013, jjie.org/everyday-assaults-of-young-offenders-in-adult-prisons/105081/.

117 the perpetrator is a woman and the victim is a boy: Review Panel on Prison Rape, "Report on Sexual Victimization in Juvenile Correctional Facilities," U.S. Department of Justice, October 2010, p. 35, www.ojp.usdoj.gov/reviewpanel/pdfs/panel_report_101014.pdf.

117 "Violent sexual assault": Ibid., p. 2.

118 misconstrue, or misrepresent, the law: The age of consent varies from state to state, but nowhere is it below sixteen.

118 Lovisa Stannow: Just Detention International, "New Justice Report Minimizes Rampant Sexual Abuse of Detained Youth," Corrections.com, November 22, 2010, www.corrections.com/news/article/26435-new-justice-department-report-minimizes-rampant-sexual-abuse-of-detained-youth.

119 Review Panel on Prison Rape: Review Panel on Prison Rape, "Report on Sexual Victimization in Juvenile Correctional Facilities," 35.

120 *Texas Observer*'s Nate Blakeslee: Nate Blakeslee, "Hidden in Plain Sight: How Did Alleged Abuse at a Youth Facility in West Texas Evade Detection for So Long?" *Texas Observer*, February 23, 2007, www.texasobserver.org/hidden-in-plain-sight/.

121 "collected dozens of statements": Ibid.

122 *Dallas Morning News*: Michael Ainsworth, "Abuse Scandal Rocks TYC," *Dallas Morning News*, shron.wordpress.com/texas-youth-commission-scandal/.

122 "generally thought to under-represent the true extent of such abuse": Kaiser and Stannow, "Crisis of Juvenile Prison Rape."

123 Thousands of calls came in: Ralph Blumenthal, "Complaints Flood Texas Youth Hot Line," *New York Times*, March 26, 2007.

123 Texas had been neck and neck with Florida: Solomon Moore, "Troubles Mount Within Texas Youth Detention Agency," *New York Times*, October 6, 2007.

123 Employees were required to go through training: Laura Burke, "A Woman's Touch," *Texas Observer*, September 1, 2010, www.texasobserver.org/a-womans-touch/.

124 nine state facilities closed their doors entirely: Brandi Grissom, "Trial Run for Revised Juvenile Justice System," *Texas Tribune*, June 27, 2013.

124 "It's nuts that it's taken us five years": Mike Ward, "Texas Confronts Broken Juvenile Justice System, Again," *Austin American-Statesman*, July 28, 2012,

www.statesman.com/news/news/state-regional-govt-politics/texas-confronts
-broken-juvenile-justice-system-aga/nRqSD/.

125 Cherie Townsend took over: Patrick Michels, "Texas Bets on Small Fixes to
Reduce Violence in Youth Lockups," *Texas Observer*, September 6, 2012, www
.texasobserver.org/texas-bets-on-small-fixes-to-reduce-violence-in-youth
-lockups/.

125 Corsicana Residential Treatment Center: Beck, Harrison, Guerino, "Sexual
Victimization in Juvenile Facilities Reported by Youth, 2008–09."

125 Victory Field Correctional Academy: Paul Knight, "Texas' Youth Prisons
Among the Worst for Sexual Abuse, Study Finds," *Houston Press*, January 13,
2010, blogs.houstonpress.com/hairballs/2010/01/youth_molest_prison_rape
.php.

125 she was "disappointed" in the federal report: Burke, "Woman's Touch."

126 "It's a way of getting attention . . . who are very sophisticated": Ibid.

126 The "traps" set . . . "'try to manipulate them'": Review Panel on Prison Rape,
"Report on Sexual Victimization in Prisons and Jails," p. 29.

127 "some widely accepted recommended practices": Beck, Harrison, and Guerino,
"Special Report," p. 32.

127 This institution lacked all the trappings of protection: Ibid.

128 "A humane culture of care": Ibid., pp. 7–8.

7. The Hole: Solitary Confinement of Juveniles

129 "It's an awful thing": Chris Vogel, "For Their Own Good," *Houston Press*,
May 27, 2009, www.houstonpress.com/2009-05-28/news/for-their-own-good/.

129 "Little broad talking": See the First District Appellate Project, March 2004,
p. 20, www.fdap.org/downloads/news/CYA_Packet_3-04.doc: "Some wards
are forced to sleep in their underwear on concrete in cold rooms." According
to Solitary Watch, under California law, "attempted suicide for the purpose of
manipulation" is explicitly named as a "Serious Rule Violation" that, for adult
prisoners, can result in placement in the Secure Housing Unit—the equivalent
of solitary (solitarywatch.com/facts/faq/).

130 "maintained a dark, cold solitary confinement room": Douglas E. Abrams,
"Reforming Juvenile Delinquency Treatment to Enhance Rehabilitation, Personal Accountability, and Public Safety," *Oregon Law Review* 84, no. 1001 (2005),
University of Missouri–Columbia School of Law Legal Studies Research Paper
no. 2006-14, ssrn.com/abstract=904396.

131 Other facilities restrict the diet: Ian Kysel, *Growing Up Locked Down: Youth in Solitary Confinement in Jails and Prisons Across the United States* (New York: Human Rights Watch/American Civil Liberties Union, 2012), www.hrw.org /sites/default/files/reports/us1012ForUpload.pdf.

131 Of the many names for solitary confinement: Michael Jacobson, "Written Testimony," Vera Institute of Justice, June 19, 2012, www.vera.org/sites/default /files/resources/downloads/michael-jacobson-testimony-on-solitary -confinement-2012.pdf.

131 "no-touch torture": Jean Casella and Curtis Ridgeway, "Unlock the Box: The Fight Against Solitary Confinement in New York," *The Nation*, July 30– August 6, 2012, www.thenation.com/article/170276/unlock-box-fight-against -solitary-confinement-new-york#.

132 "absolute prohibition": "Torture and Other Cruel, Inhuman or Degrading Treatment or Punishment: Note by the Secretary-General," United Nations General Assembly, August 5, 2011, solitaryconfinement.org/uploads/SpecRap TortureAug2011.pdf.

132 United Nations Rules for the Protection of Juveniles Deprived of their Liberty: "United Nations Rules for the Protection of Juveniles Deprived of their Liberty," United Nations General Assembly, December 14, 1990. Section 67 of the rules states: "All disciplinary measures constituting cruel, inhuman or degrading treatment shall be strictly prohibited, including corporal punishment, placement in a dark cell, closed or solitary confinement or any other punishment that may compromise the physical or mental health of the juvenile concerned" (www.un.org/documents/ga/res/45/a45r113.htm).

132 Young prisoners in America are routinely isolated: Kysel, *Growing Up Locked Down*, p. 2.

132 A comprehensive national survey: Richard A. Mendel, *No Place For Kids: The Case for Reducing Juvenile Incarceration* (Baltimore, MD: Annie E. Casey Foundation, 2011), www.aecf.org/OurWork/JuvenileJustice/~/media/Pubs/Topics /Juvenile%20Justice/Detention%20Reform/NoPlaceForKids/JJ_NoPlace ForKids_Full.pdf.

132 "room confinement remains a standard procedure": Lindsey M. Hayes, "Characteristics of Juvenile Suicide in Confinement," Office of Juvenile Justice and Delinquency Prevention, February 2009, p. 12, www.ncjrs.gov/pdffiles1/ojjdp /214434.pdf.

133 Youth in Ohio facilities spent an average of fifty hours: Mendel, *No Place for Kids*, p. 8.

133 solitary confinement may actually be a growing problem: According to the Ella

Baker Center for Human Rights, "Ten years ago at DJJ [Division of Juvenile Justice], 16–28 percent of youth were in solitary units, and the single hour of programming or exercise they received outside of their cells was in steel cages. In 2004, the average length of stay in isolation was 42 days. By 2007, with reform efforts well underway, that number had increased to 65 days. In 2010, one prison was reporting a 59-day average, with one youth spending 246 days in isolation. And in 2011, an internal audit revealed that youth continued to be isolated for 23 or 24 hours a day, with one youth receiving only one hour out of his cell over the course of 10 days." Statement of Sumayyah Waheed and Jennifer Kim, Ella Baker Center for Human Rights, "Reassessing Solitary Confinement: The Human Rights, Fiscal, and Public Safety Consequences," Hearing Before the Senate Judiciary Subcommittee on the Constitution, Civil Rights, and Human Rights, June 19, 2012, www.judiciary.senate.gov/resources/transcripts/upload/061912RecordSubmission-Durbin.pdf.

133 "Incredibly, the practices from 10 years ago": Ibid. Another 2011 report, based on an internal audit, found that "juvenile inmates at California correctional facilities have been held in isolation nearly 24 hours straight on hundreds of occasions this year, in violation of state regulations." James Ridgeway, "Kids Put in Solitary Confinement in California's Juvie Jails," *Mother Jones*, June 16, 2011, www.motherjones.com/mojo/2011/06/kids-put-solitary-confinement-californias-juvie-jails/.

133 In New York City, nearly 15 percent of adolescents: Kysel, *Growing Up Locked Down*, p. 64.

133 "for transgressions as minor as eating a guard's food": Christie Thompson, "Solitary for Youth: The Fight in Illinois," *Juvenile Justice Information Exchange*, October 12, 2012, jjie.org/solitary-for-youth-fight-illinois/96279.

133 injured or sick youth housed in solitary: Ibid.

133 A separate look at the Harrisburg facility: Chris Bernard, "Executive Summary: Monitoring Visit to IYC-Harrisburg, March 23, 2011," John Howard Association of Illinois, p. 1, www.thejha.org/sites/default/files/IYC.Harrisburg.pdf.

133 "were restrained, hit": Douglas E. Abrams, "Reforming Juvenile Delinquency Treatment to Enhance Rehabilitation, Personal Accountability, and Public Safety," *Oregon Law Review* 84 (2005): 1032, www.njjn.org/uploads/digital-library/resource_407.pdf.

133 A survey undertaken at the Texas State facility: Benet Magnuson and Jennifer Carreon, "Youth Experiences at Giddings State School: 2012 Survey Findings," Texas Criminal Justice Coalition, March 2012, p. 8, www.texascjc.org/sites/default/files/publications/Youth%20Experiences%20at%20Giddings%20(Mar%202012).pdf.

133 In New Jersey, reports emerged in the 1990s: "Bad Girls, Bad Prison," *The Record* (Hackensack, NJ), February 20, 1994; "Jamesburg Reformatory Desperately Needs Reform," *The Record* (Hackensack, NJ), March 6, 2004; "8 a.m. Riot Is Latest Explosion for Juvie Justice System," *The Trentonian*, December 30, 2009; "Gang Members Riot at Jail for Boys," *The Trentonian*, July 29, 2008; "11 Teens Accused in Attack at Detention Center," *The Star-Ledger* (Newark, NJ), May 3, 2007; and Juvenile Law Center, "T.D. and O.S. v. Mickens et al.," www.jlc.org /legal-docket/td-and-os-v-mickens-et-al.

134 All manner of international guidelines: Kysel, *Growing Up Locked Down*, p. 73.

134 "the conditions that accompany solitary confinement": Ibid., p. 76.

134 some were locked in their cells for all but forty minutes: Ridgeway, "Kids Put in Solitary Confinement."

135 Solitary confinement is a standard response: Lindsay M. Hayes, "Juvenile Suicide in Confinement: A National Survey," National Center on Institutions and Alternatives, February 2004, p. 28, www.ncjrs.gov/pdffiles1/ojjdp/grants/206354 .pdf.

135 brief stretches of daily "recreation": "In CYA detention facilities, at any given time more than ten percent of wards are kept in solitary confinement for 23 hours a day. During the one hour per day they are permitted to leave their cells they are either shackled or caged. These lock-down units have inadequate lighting and temperature controls. . . . More than half of the wards on lock-down lack basic hygiene materials such as soap and toothpaste." Summary of the Recent Expert Reports on CYA, General Corrections Review, p. 53, in First District Appellate Project, Filing a Petition for Modification Aimed at Getting a Section 602 Juvenile Court Ward Released from the California Youth Authority (Welf. & Inst. Code Section 778 and 779), March 2004.

135 limits the isolation of juveniles to a maximum of five days: American Correctional Association, *Standards for Juvenile Detention Facilities*, 3rd ed. (Latham, MD: ACA, 1991), p. 67.

137 Writing for the majority: Atul Gawande, "Hellhole: The United States Holds Tens of Thousands of Inmates in Long-Term Solitary Confinement. Is This Torture?" *New Yorker*, March 30, 2009, www.newyorker.com/reporting/2009 /03/30/090330fa_fact_gawande.

138 A U.S. federal court has also ruled on the issue: *Morales v. Turman*, United States District Court for the Eastern District of Texas, Sherman Division, June 28, 1983, tx.findacase.com/research/wfrmDocViewer.aspx/xq/fac.19830628_0000011 .ETX.htm/qx.

141 But even the CIA shows more caution: Will Ross, "CIA's Harsh Interrogation

Techniques Described," ABC News, November 18, 2005, abcnews.go.com
/Blotter/Investigation/story?id=1322866.

142 "Placing them in solitary confinement": Sue Burrell, "Reassessing Solitary
Confinement: The Human Rights, Fiscal and Public Safety Consequences;
Hearing Before the Senate Judiciary Subcommittee on the Constitution, Civil
Rights, and Human Rights," June 19, 2012, solitarywatch.com/wp-content
/uploads/2012/06/youth-law-center2.pdf.

143 "Young people in solitary confinement": Kysel, *Growing Up Locked Down*, p. 42.

143 "For youth locked in a tiny room": Burrell, "Reassessing Solitary Confinement."

144 Researchers have found: Kysel, *Growing Up Locked Down*, p. 25.

144 "One of the paradoxes of solitary confinement": Gawande, "Hellhole."

144 "begin to see themselves": Ibid.

145 "Many of the young people": Kysel, *Growing Up Locked Down*, p. 65.

145 "It may sound weird": Ibid., p. 61.

146 "That's when I started going crazy": Ibid.

146 Facilities that rely on solitary confinement: Charles Samuels's testimony for
"Reassessing Solitary Confinement: The Human Rights, Fiscal, and Public
Safety Consequences," United States Senate Committee on the Judiciary, Subcommittee on the Constitution, Civil Rights and Human Rights, 112th Cong.,
2nd sess., June 19, 2012, www.justice.gov/ola/testimony/112-2/06-19-12-bop
-samuels.pdf.

146 These findings not only demolish "institutional safety": "Creating a Safe Cor-
rectional Environment for Youth and Staff," Texas Criminal Justice Coalition,
March 2012, www.texascjc.org/sites/default/files/publications/Creating%20
Safe%20Correctional%20Environment%20-%20Bexar%20Co%20SRRI%20
(May%202012).pdf.

147 Eddie Figueroa: For more on Red Hook, see Chapter 13.

147 "fallen angels": Author's interview with Eddie Figueroa at Red Hook, July 31,
2012.

148 "Reassessing Solitary Confinement": Senate Judiciary Subcommittee on Constitution, Civil Rights and Human Rights hearing, "Reassessing Solitary Confinement," June 19, 2012, www.hsdl.org/?view&did=713592.

8. "Hurt People Hurt People": Trauma and Incarceration

153 While only a minority of the young people: Robert L. Listenbee Jr., Joe Torre,
Gregory Boyle, Sharon W. Cooper, Sarah Deer, Deanne Tilton Durfee, Thea

James, et al., "Rethinking Our Juvenile Justice System," in *Report of the Attorney General's National Task Force on Children Exposed to Violence*, Office of Juvenile Justice and Delinquency Prevention, December 12, 2012, chap. 6, www.justice gov/defendingchildhood/cev-rpt-full.pdf.

153 Survey of Youth in Residential Placement: Andrea J. Sedlak and Karla McPherson, "Survey of Youth in Residential Placement: Youth's Needs and Services," *Juvenile Justice Bulletin*, Office of Juvenile Justice and Delinquency Prevention, December 2010, www.ncjrs.gov/pdffiles1/ojjdp/grants/227660.pdf.

153 Thirty percent had been sexually or physically abused: Andrea J. Sedlak and Karla S. McPherson, "Youth's Needs and Services: Findings from the Survey of Youth in Residential Placement," *Juvenile Justice Bulletin*, Office of Juvenile Justice and Delinquency Prevention, April 2010, www.ncjrs.gov/pdffiles1 /ojjdp/227728.pdf.

153 "Most of these girls": Text of HR 1833: Improving the Juvenile Justice System for Girls Act of 2013, www.govtrack.us/congress/bills/113/hr1833/text.

153 "first sexual encounter": Cited in ibid.

154 "The vast majority of children": Listenbee et al., *Report of the Attorney General's National Task Force on Children Exposed to Violence*, pp. 21, 171–72.

157 "Traumatized kids need to feel": Lindsey Tanner, "What Heals Traumatized Kids? Answers Are Lacking," Associated Press, February 11, 2013, bigstory.ap .org/article/what-heals-traumatized-kids-answers-are-lacking.

157 "Childhood victimization can have long lasting effects": U.S. Attorney General's National Task Force on Children Exposed to Violence, University of Maryland hearing transcript, Office of Juvenile Justice and Delinquency Prevention, hearing 1, transcript 16, www.ojjdp.gov/defendingchildhood/baltimore-hearing -transcript1-3.pdf.

158 The correlation between childhood exposure to violence: K.M. Abram, L.A. Teplin, D.R. Charles, S.L. Longworth, G.M. McClelland, and M. Dulcan, "Posttraumatic Stress Disorder and Trauma in Youth in Juvenile Detention," *Archives of General Psychiatry* 61 (2004): 403–10; J.D. Ford, J.D. Elhai, D.F. Connor, and B.C. Frueh, "Poly-Victimization and Risk of Posttraumatic, Depressive, and Substance Use Disorders and Involvement in Delinquency in a National Sample of Adolescents," *Journal of Adolescent Health* 46, no. 6 (2010): 545–52; J.D. Ford, J.F. Chapman, J. Hawke, and D. Albert, "Trauma Among Youth in the Juvenile Justice Systems: Critical Issues and New Directions," National Center for Mental Health and Juvenile Justice, 2007, www.ncmhjj.com/pdfs/publications /Trauma_and_Youth.pdf, all cited in Kristine Buffington, Carly B. Dierkhising, and Shawn C. Marsh, "Ten Things Every Juvenile Court Judge Should Know

About Trauma and Delinquency," National Council of Juvenile and Family Court Judges, 2010, p. 2, www.ncjfcj.org/sites/default/files/trauma%20bulletin _0.pdf.

158 Ninety-two percent had experienced one or more forms of abuse: Leslie Acoca, "Outside/Inside: The Violation of American Girls at Home, on the Streets, and in the Juvenile Justice System," *Crime and Delinquency* 44, no. 4 (October 1998): 565, leslieacoca.org/images/Outside-Inside_-_The_Violation_of_American _Girls_at_Home_-_On_the_Streets_-_and_in_the_Juvenile_Justice_System _by_Leslie_Acoca.pdf.

158 "The maltreatment of girls": Ibid., p. 566.

159 "Once girls have crossed the threshold": Ibid., p. 562.

160 "a source of power, prestige, security": Alex Kotlowitz, "The Price of Public Violence," *New York Times*, February 25, 2013.

161 "What happened to you?": See the National Center for Trauma-Informed Care, www.samhsa.gov/nctic/.

161 "victimization, particularly victimization that goes unaddressed": Buffington et al., "Ten Things Every Juvenile Court Judge Should Know."

166 "When you recognize from the bench": Eric Holder, "Attorney General Eric Holder Speaks at the Defending Childhood Task Force Public Meeting," Baltimore, MD, November 29, 2011, www.justice.gov/iso/opa/ag/speeches/2011 /ag-speech-111129.html.

167 Roland was "frozen": Listenbee et al., *Report of the Attorney General's National Task Force on Children Exposed to Violence.*

167 These are the risk factors for juvenile delinquency: Ibid.

167 signs and symptoms of childhood trauma: Richard A. Mendel, *No Place for Kids: The Case for Reducing Juvenile Incarceration* (Baltimore, MD: Annie E. Casey Foundation, 2011), p. 16, www.aecf.org/~/media/Pubs/Topics/Juvenile%20 Justice/Detention%20Reform/NoPlaceForKids/JJ_NoPlaceForKids_Full.pdf.

175 "It was so clear to me what incarceration did": Telephone interview with Danielle Sered.

180 mutual respect is key: See Chapter 12.

9. The Things They Carry: Juvenile Reentry

181 "Society takes upon itself the right": Oscar Wilde, *De Profundis* (1905; New York: Random House, 2000).

182 "Holding other factors constant": All cited in Richard A. Mendel, *No Place for*

Kids: The Case for Reducing Juvenile Incarceration (Baltimore, MD: Annie E. Casey Foundation, 2011), pp. 10–11, www.aecf.org/~/media/Pubs/Topics /Juvenile%20Justice/Detention%20Reform/NoPlaceForKids/JJ_NoPlace ForKids_Full.pdf.

182 roughly one hundred thousand young people under age eighteen: Because many state juvenile systems can keep young people in their care past the age of eighteen, the total number of individuals released from these facilities can be higher.

182 "are placed back into neighborhoods": National Juvenile Justice and Delinquency Prevention Coalition, "Promoting Safe Communities: Recommendations for the 113th Congress," 2013–2014, promotesafecommunities.org /images/pdfs/NJJDPC_RecstoCongress_03122013_web.pdf.

183 reduced total time spent working: Barry Holman and Jason Ziedenberg, "The Dangers of Detention: The Impact of Incarcerating Youth in Detention and Other Secure Facilities," Justice Policy Institute, 2006, www.justicepolicy.org /uploads/justicepolicy/documents/dangers_of_detention.pdf.

183 Even fifteen years down the line: Dick Mendel, "In Juvenile Justice Care, Boys Get Worse," *Youth Today*, March 5, 2010, www.burnsinstitute.org/article.php ?id=195.

184 If the applicant is black: Devah Pager, Bruce Western, and Naomi Sugie, "Sequencing Disadvantage: Barriers to Employment Facing Young Black and White Men with Criminal Records," *Annals of the American Academy of Political and Social Science* 623, no. 1 (May 2009), www.princeton.edu/~pager /annals_sequencingdisadvantage.pdf.

184 nearly half of the District's former prisoners are unemployed: June Kress, "Statement of the Council for Court Excellence before the Committee on Housing and Workforce Development Council of the District of Columbia," March 19, 2009, www.courtexcellence.org/uploads/publications/2009_Reen try_OEOA_to_DC_Council.pdf.

184 "a negative effect on the economic well-being": Holman and Ziedenberg, "Dangers of Detention."

184 "Areas with the most rapidly rising rates": Ibid.

187 "Juveniles and young adults may be incarcerated": William H. Barton, André B. Rosay, and G. Roger Jarjoura, "Applying a Developmental Lens to Juvenile Re-entry and Reintegration," *OJJDP Journal of Juvenile Justice* 1, no. 2 (Spring 2012), www.journalofjuvjustice.org/JOJJ0102/article07.htm.

190 "Reincorporation is characterized by elaborate rituals": Arnold van Gennep, *The Rites of Passage* (Chicago: University of Chicago Press, 1961), p. 166.

197 Fewer than 15 percent of kids who get locked up: R. Balfanz, K. Spiridakis,

R. Neild, and N. Legters, "Neighborhood Schools and the Juvenile Justice System: How Neither Helps the Other and How that Could Change" (paper presented at the School to Jail Pipeline Conference, Harvard University, 2003), cited in Holman and Ziederberg, *Dangers of Detention*, p. 9.

197 Completing the vicious cycle: Coalition for Juvenile Justice, "Abandoned in the Back Row: New Lessons in Education and Delinquency Prevention," 2001 annual report, www.juvjustice.org/sites/default/files/resource-files/resource _122_0.pdf; "Re-engaging High School Dropouts as Growth Strategy for PA," Operation Restart, n.d., Harrisburg, PA, www.papartnerships.org/reports /re-engaging/re-engaging_hs_dropouts.pdf.

197 Sixty-nine percent reported that they faced obstacles: "Families Unlocking Futures: Solutions to the Crisis in Juvenile Justice," Justice for Families, Data-Center, September 2012, www.njjn.org/uploads/digital-library/Fam_Unlock _Future_EXEC_SUMNOEMBARGO.pdf.

10. A New Wave of Reform

201 Over the course of a single decade: Sarah Bryer and Marc Levin, "The Comeback States: Reducing Youth Incarceration in the United States," National Juvenile Justice Network and Texas Public Policy Foundation, 2013, p. 2, www.njjn .org/uploads/digital-library/Comeback-States-Report_FINAL.pdf.

201 it has picked up speed in recent years: Annie E. Casey Foundation, "Reducing Youth Incarceration in the United States," Kids Count Data Snapshot, February 2013, p. 2, www.aecf.org/~/media/Pubs/Initiatives/KIDS%20COUNT/R /ReducingYouthIncarcerationSnapshot/DataSnapshotYouthIncarceration.pdf.

201 Fewer juvenile prisoners means fewer juvenile prisons: Richard A. Mendel, *No Place for Kids: The Case for Reducing Juvenile Incarceration* (Baltimore, MD: Annie E. Casey Foundation, 2011), www.aecf.org/OurWork/JuvenileJustice /~/media/Pubs/Topics/Juvenile%20Justice/Detention%20Reform/No PlaceForKids/JJ_NoPlaceForKids_Full.pdf.

202 about 10,000 in 1996: Barry Krisberg, Linh Vong, Christopher Hartney, and Susan Marchionna, "A New Era in California Juvenile Justice: Downsizing the State's Youth Corrections System," National Council on Crime and Delinquency, 2010, www.nccdglobal.org/sites/default/files/publication_pdf/a-new -era.pdf.

202 922 in June 2012: "Characteristics of Population: June 2012," California Department of Corrections and Rehabilitation, Division of Juvenile Justice,

www.cdcr.ca.gov/Reports_Research/docs/research/06-2012%20CHARAC
TERISTICS.pdf.

202 4,700 in fiscal year 2006: Texas Juvenile Probation Commission and Texas
Youth Authority, *Coordinated Strategic Plan Fiscal Year 2010*, www.tjjd.texas.gov
/publications/reports/RPTSTRAT201001.pdf.

202 1,500 in 2012: Texas Juvenile Justice Department, "Strategic Plan 2013–2017:
Protecting Texas by Positively Changing the Lives of Youth," June 2012, www
.tjjd.texas.gov/publications/reports/TJJD%20Strategic%20Plan%20-%20
FINAL%20-%20JULY%202012.pdf.

202 The state's juvenile incarceration rate . . . remains among the highest in the
nation: Annie E. Casey Foundation, "Reducing Youth Incarceration," p. 2.

202 A recent class action lawsuit: Susan Ferriss, "Suit Alleges Mistreatment of
California Minors with Mental Health Problems," Center for Public Integrity,
August 9, 2013, www.publicintegrity.org/2013/08/09/13152/suit-alleges
-mistreatment-california-minors-mental-health-problems.

203 "are routinely locked for days": Ibid.

203 The suit cites California law: Ibid.

203 Juvenile crime rates have been declining across the board: Mendel, *No Place for
Kids*, p. 27. See also Annie E. Casey Foundation, "Reducing Youth Incarceration," p. 2.

203 throw-the-book-at-'em regions: Mendel, *No Place for Kids*.

204 In Arkansas, an exposé: Mary Hargrove, "Welcome to Hell: Troubled
Youth in State Custody Face 'Lesson-Teaching' Beatings, Filthy Quarters,
Cramped Cells, Unwanted Sex, and Caretakers Who Don't Care," *Arkansas
Democrat-Gazette*, June 14, 1998, cited in Mendel, *No Place for Kids*.

205 in Louisiana, for example: For more on family activism in Louisiana, see Families and Friends of Louisiana's Incarcerated Children at www.fflic.org. For
more on the national family movement, see Justice for Families at www.justice
4families.org.

206 $88,000 per year: Bryer and Levin, "Comeback States," p. 2.

206 we could support about ten kids a year: Richard A. Mendel, *The Missouri Model:
Reinventing the Practice of Rehabilitating Youthful Offenders* (Baltimore, MD:
Annie E. Casey Foundation, 2010), www.aecf.org/~/media/Pubs/Initiatives
/Juvenile%20Detention%20Alternatives%20Initiative/MOModel/MO_Full
report_webfinal.pdf.

206 the Great Recession: Eileen A.J. Connelly, "Economic Crisis Timeline: '00s
Decade in Review," *Huffington Post*, December 18, 2009, www.huffingtonpost
.com/2009/12/18/economic-crisis-timeline-_n_397360.html.

206 a total state budget shortfall of $191 billion: Phil Oliff, Chris Mai, and Vincent Palacios, "States Continue to Feel Recession's Impact," Center on Budget and Policy Priorities, June 27, 2012, www.cbpp.org/cms/index.cfm?fa =view&id=711.

206 46.2 million Americans were living below the poverty line: Sabrina Tavernise, "Soaring Poverty Casts Spotlight on 'Lost Decade,'" *New York Times*, September 13, 2011.

207 This part of the brain: Claudia Dreifus, "Developmental Psychologist Says Teenagers Are Different," *New York Times*, November 30, 2009.

207 "Much adolescent involvement in criminal activity": Richard J. Bonnie, Robert L. Johnson, Betty M. Cherners, and Julie Schuck, eds., *Reforming Juvenile Justice: A Developmental Approach* (Washington, DC: National Academies Press, 2013), summary.

208 the opportunity to develop critical thinking and decision-making skills: James Swift, "National Academies Report Says Teen Neurology Should Shape Juvenile Justice Reform Efforts," *Juvenile Justice Information Exchange*, November 15, 2012, jjie.org/national-academies-report-says-teen-neurology-should -shape-juvenile-justice-reform-efforts/98667.

208 *Roper v. Simmons*: Andrew Cohen, "Should Teen Murderers Receive Life Without Parole?" *The Atlantic*, March 19, 2012, www.theatlantic.com/national /archive/2012/03/should-teen-murderers-receive-life-without-parole /254667/.

209 all relied on the understanding that there were fundamental differences: Annie E. Casey Foundation, "Reducing Youth Incarceration," p. 2.

209 Writing for the majority in *Miller*: *Miller v. Alabama*, Supreme Court of the United States, 2012, www.supremecourt.gov/opinions/11pdf/10-9646g2i8.pdf.

209 "Advocates for juvenile justice reform": National Juvenile Justice Network, "Polling on Public Attitudes About the Treatment of Young Offenders," Washington, DC, 2008, www.pendulumfoundation.com/Polling%20on%20 Public%20Attitudes.pdf.

210 Multiple polls bolster this conclusion: National Juvenile Justice Network, "Polling on Public Attitudes About the Treatment of Young Offenders," Washington, DC, www.njjn.org/uploads/digital-library/resource_633.pdf.

210 62 percent favored: Ibid.

210 several evidence-based interventions that have shown great success: See Chapter 13 for more on these evidence-based programs.

211 symposium on the legacy of another iconoclastic administrator: "Shutting Down the Massachusetts Training Schools: Reflections from the Past, Present

and Future," hosted by the Annie E. Casey Foundation and Youth Advocacy Programs, Washington, DC, December 6, 2011.

211 appointed to run the Massachusetts system: David C. Anderson, "Let His Children Go," *New York Times*, January 26, 1992.

211 "nightmarish outposts of abuse": Richard A. Hogarty, *Massachusetts Politics and Public Policy: Studies in Power and Leadership* (Amherst: University of Massachusetts Press, 2002), p. 78.

212 "Training staff in new methods": Jerome G. Miller, *Last One Over the Wall: The Massachusetts Experiment in Closing Reform Schools* (Columbus: Ohio State University Press, 1991), p. 91.

212 "It hit me with the full force of conviction": Ibid., p. 120.

212 Stubborn Child Law: John R. Sutton, "Stubborn Children: Law and the Socialization of Deviance in the Puritan Colonies," *Family Law Quarterly* 12, no. 1 (Spring 1981): 31–64.

212 Industrial School for Boys: Julie Masis, "Good, Bad of Reform School Recalled," *Boston Globe*, July 19, 2009.

212 He took the brass locks off the isolation rooms: "I'll bury Miller. He's a nut. He's insane. He belongs in an insane asylum," Democratic legislator Robert McGinn is said to have shouted, apparently advocating that not only wayward youth but also noncompliant administrators ought to be institutionalized. Ibid., 79.

213 "As a new commissioner five years ago": Gladys Carrión, presentation at "Shutting Down the Massachusetts Training Schools" symposium, December 6, 2011, author's notes.

214 a continuum of community-based and alternative programs: "ACS Joins with Juvenile Justice Leaders Citywide to Announce the Closing of Bridges Juvenile Center," New York Administration for Children's Services, press release, March 31, 2011, www.nyc.gov/html/acs/html/pr_archives/pr11_03_31.shtml.

214 New York State has closed down eighteen facilities: Elizabeth Dwoskin, "Shutting Upstate Jails Has Made a Fiery Bronx Bureaucrat a Host of Enemies," *Village Voice*, August 4, 2010, www.villagevoice.com/2010-08-04/news /gladys-carrion-upstate-jails-for-city-kids-bronx/.

215 "among the most hostile juvenile justice agencies": Mie Lewis, *Custody and Control: Conditions of Confinement in New York's Juvenile Prisons for Girls* (New York: Human Rights Watch/American Civil Liberties Union, 2006), p. 4, www.hrw .org/reports/2006/us0906/us0906webwcover.pdf.

215 "The boys had been on lockdown": Jennifer Gonnerman, "The Lost Boys of Tryon," *New York*, January 24, 2010, nymag.com/news/features/63239/.

215 the staff members involved were never indicted: Ibid.

215 the state settled with the boy's family for $3.5 million: Jamie J. Fader, "Change Is a Start, Not an End," *Times Union* (Albany), June 19, 2013, www.timesunion .com/default/article/Change-is-a-start-not-an-end-4609990.php.

215 she sat in her car and wept: Gonnerman, "Lost Boys of Tryon."

215 a video of a Tryon aide punching a boy: Ibid.

216 "a litany of abuses": Ibid.

216 That body reached the sweeping conclusion: Governor Paterson's Task Force on Transforming Juvenile Justice, *Charting a New Course: A Blueprint for Transforming Juvenile Justice in New York State* (New York: Vera Institute of Justice, 2009), p. 88, www.vera.org/sites/default/files/resources/downloads/Charting -a-new-course-A-blueprint-for-transforming-juvenile-justice-in-New-York -State.pdf.

216 Carrión faced resistance: Alysia Santo, "State's 'Insecure' Youth Centers," *Times Union* (Albany), January 6, 2013, www.timesunion.com/local/article /State-s-insecure-youth-centers-4168223.php.

216 "It's easy to say": Author interview with Gladys Carrión in her New York office, July 27, 2012.

217 "It literally broke my heart": Dwoskin, "Shutting Upstate Jails."

218 "I am not running the Economic Development Agency": Ibid.

218 "routinely used uncontrolled, unsafe applications of force": U.S. Justice Department, CRIPA Investigation of the Lansing Residential Center, Louis Gossett Jr. Residential Center, Tryon Residential Center, and Tryon Girls Center, August 14, 2009.

218 "they found that our system practices": Carrión, presentation at "Shutting Down the Massachusetts Training Schools" symposium.

219 "devastating. At least it was for me": Ibid.

219 She was carrying that flag: author interview with Gladys Carrión.

219 "At that point . . . that we institutionalize": Ibid.

221 "I came in with an opinion": Vincent Schiraldi, speaking at "Shutting Down the Massachusetts Training Schools" symposium, Washington, DC, December 6, 2011, author's notes.

11. A Better Mousetrap: The Therapeutic Prison

224 "At first I was very bitter": Marilyn Jones, *From Crack to College and Vice Versa* (Amazon Digital Services, 2013), p. 19.

224 Riley and Kent, nineteen, had been given the task of showing me around: Red

Wing was the only facility I visited where young people were permitted to show me around unattended by adult staff.

226 "to recognize that when": Edwin M. Schur, *Radical Non-intervention: Rethinking the Delinquency Problem* (Englewood Cliffs, NJ: Prentice Hall, 1973), p. 128.

227 Now he was preparing to retire: After his retirement, Zanders would go on to become the president and CEO of the St. Paul–based Ujamaa Place, which supports young African American men in turning their lives around; see ujamaa place.org.

228 "the name 'State Training School'": Otis Zanders, "MCF-Red Wing Perspectives on the State Juvenile Criminal Justice System," Council on Crime and Justice, www.crimeandjustice.org/councilinfo.cfm?pID=47.

232 Both had adult sentences hanging over their heads: Interestingly, the Extended Juvenile Jurisdiction statute includes a provision that time served in a juvenile facility be deducted from any adult sentence later imposed. The wording of this provision seems to contradict the notion that a juvenile facility is something other than a prison: "If the court revokes the probationer's extended jurisdiction juvenile status, the court shall ensure that the record accurately reflects all time spent in custody in connection with the underlying offense at juvenile facilities where the level of confinement and limitations are the functional equivalent of a jail, workhouse, or regional correctional facility. Such time shall be deducted from any adult sentence imposed pursuant to Minnesota Statutes"; see Minnesota Statutes, section 609.14, subdivision 3, in www.revisor.mn.gov/court _rules/rule.php?name=jurjdp-19.

233 brought the population down from ten thousand to fewer than a thousand: California Department of Corrections and Rehabilitation, Department of Juvenile Justice, "Population Overview as of December 31, 2012," www.cdcr.ca.gov /Reports_Research/docs/research/POPOVER2012.pdf.

235 Placing young people in juvenile facilities: D.A. Andrews, I. Zinger, R.D. Hoge, J. Bonta, P. Gendreau, and F.R. Cullen, "Does Correctional Treatment Work? A Clinically Relevant and Psychologically Informed Meta-Analysis," *Criminology* 28, no. 3 (1990): 369–404, cited in "The Costs of Confinement: Why Good Juvenile Justice Policies Make Good Fiscal Sense," Justice Policy Institute, 2009, www.justicepolicy.org/images/upload/09_05_REP_CostsofConfinement _JJ_PS.pdf, p. 12.

236 That law defined the mandate: Peggy A. Engram, "California Youth Authority," www.sagepub.com/upm-data/2791_Juvenile_Justice_samples.pdf, p. 4.

236 At its apex, the California Youth Authority: Tim Cavanaugh, "The Golden State's Iron Bars: How California Prison Guards Became the Country's

Most Powerful Union," *Reason*, July 2011, reason.com/archives/2011/06/23 /the-golden-states-iron-bars.

236 Then the pendulum swung once again: Barry Krisberg, "The Long and Winding Road: Juvenile Corrections Reform in California," University of California, Berkeley, May 2011, www.law.berkeley.edu/files/Long_and_Winding_Road _Publication-final.pdf.

243 At the Giddings School: Molly Totman, "Youth Experiences at Giddings State School," Texas Criminal Justice Association, March 2012, www.texascjc .org/sites/default/files/publications/Youth%20Experiences%20at%20 Giddings%20(Mar%202012).pdf. They also ranked family involvement as the second-most important thing to them and complained that the school's location made it difficult for them to see their family members.

245 State officials attribute some or all of this uptick: Alysia Santo, "State's 'Insecure' Youth Centers: Assaults Rise on Workers and Residents at OCFS Juvenile Detention Sites," *Times Union* (Albany), January 6, 2013, www.timesunion .com/default/article/State-s-insecure-youth-centers-4168223.php.

246 "teenage detainees gang up on a much larger staff member": Ibid.

246 "Now we have to wait": Ibid.

250 In New York: Mosi Secret, "States Prosecute Fewer Teenagers in Adult Courts," *New York Times*, March 5, 2011, p. 16. See also Governor David Paterson's Task Force on Transforming Juvenile Justice, "Charting a New Course: A Blueprint for Transforming Juvenile Justice in New York State," New York: Vera Institute of Justice, December 2009, p. 16, www.vera.org/sites /default/files/resources/downloads/Charting-a-new-course-A-blueprint-for -transforming-juvenile-justice-in-New-York-State.pdf.

250 "This investment": Ibid., p. 14.

251 64 percent of youth at low-level facilities: Ibid., p. 23.

251 the majority of kids in these places—56 percent: Ibid.

252 "the awesome prospect of incarceration": *In re Gault*, 387 U.S. 1 (1967) at 36–37, in Barry C. Feld, *Bad Kids: Race and the Transformation of the Juvenile Court* (New York: Oxford University Press, 1999), p. 123.

252 "Commitment is a deprivation of liberty": Feld, *Bad Kids*, p. 250.

252 *McKeiver v. Pennsylvania*: *McKeiver v. Pennsylvania*, 403 U.S. 528, at 551–52; Feld, *Bad Kids*, p. 246.

252 "Sometimes punishment is treatment": Feld, *Bad Kids*, p. 252.

12. Only Connect: Rehabilitation Happens in the Context of Relationship

254 "We are all born for love": Benjamin Disraeli, *Sybil, or The Two Nations*, book 5, chap. 4.

256 "It's a corrupt belief": Mark Woods, "'Baby-Faced' Boy's Case Highlights Debate About Trying Juveniles," *Florida Times-Union*, June 4, 2011, jacksonville .com/news/crime/2011-06-04/story/baby-faced-boys-case-highlights-debate -about-trying-juveniles.

260 George W. Bush: "When I was young and irresponsible, I was young and irresponsible," Bush was quoted as telling reporters who asked him about persistent rumors that he had used cocaine. The president did acknowledge that he had been pulled over for drunk driving and paid the ensuing fine. According to his former press secretary, he habitually deflected questions about both the DUI and alleged cocaine use by "segue[ing] into the broader point he wanted to emphasize: the most important message baby boomers such as himself could send to their children is that they have learned from experience and that their children should avoid repeating their mistakes"; see George W. Bush link at OntheIssues.org review of Scott McClellan, *What Happened* (New York: Public Affairs, 2008), www.ontheissues.org/What_Happened.htm.

261 Babies who are not held or touched: Daniel Goleman, "The Experience of Touch: Research Points to a Critical Role," *New York Times*, February 2, 1988.

261 it took being treated for a drug problem: This also is something I've heard many times—that in order to get anything but the most cursory therapeutic intervention under the auspices of the juvenile court, it is necessary to demonstrate the symptoms of addiction. What treatment is available for traumatized youth tends to be reserved for those who have attempted to self-medicate with illegal drugs.

262 "diving into the wreck": Adrienne Rich, "Diving into the Wreck," in *Diving into the Wreck: Poems, 1971–72* (1973; New York: W.W. Norton, 1994).

269 describing something he had found post-incarceration at Roca: Case study on Roca website, rocainc.org.

13. Connection in Action: Transforming Juvenile Justice

274 Pathways to Desistance: Edward P. Mulvey, "Highlights from Pathways to Desistance: A Longitudinal Study of Serious Adolescent Offenders," U.S.

Department of Justice, Juvenile Justice Fact Sheet, 2011, ncjrs.gov/pdffiles1
/ojjdp/230971.pdf.

277 MST reduces subsequent arrests: Richard A. Mendel, *No Place for Kids: The Case
for Reducing Juvenile Incarceration* (Baltimore, MD: Annie E. Casey Foundation,
2011), www.aecf.org/~/media/Pubs/Topics/Juvenile%20Justice/Detention
%20Reform/NoPlaceForKids/JJ_NoPlaceForKids_Full.pdf.

277 the Redirection Program: Ibid., p. 17.

278 Juvenile incarceration . . . runs an average of $88,000 per youth: Ibid.

278 an estimated $88,953 per participant: Elizabeth K. Drake, Steve Aos, and Marna
G. Miller, "Evidence-Based Public Policy Options to Reduce Crime and Criminal Justice Costs: Implications in Washington State," *Victims and Offenders* 4,
no. 2 (2009), www.wsipp.wa.gov/rptfiles/09-00-1201.pdf.

279 Despite the widespread agreement about the effectiveness: Peter W. Green-
wood, Brandon C. Welsh, Michael Rocque, "Implementing Proven Programs
for Juvenile Offenders," Association for the Advancement of Evidence-Based
Programs, December 2012, www.advancingebp.org/wp-content/uploads/2012
/01/AEBP-assessment.pdf.

279 "even in jurisdictions where such programs have been adopted": Ibid., p. 21.

281 $18.5 billion in crime-related expenses: Bill DeBaun and Martens Roc, "Sav-
ing Futures, Saving Dollars: The Impact of Education on Crime Reduction
and Earnings," Alliance for Excellent Education, September 2013, all4ed.org
/wp-content/uploads/2013/09/SavingFutures.pdf.

281 youths with jobs are less likely to break the law: Chester L. Britt, "Reconsider-
ing the Unemployment and Crime Relationship: Variation by Age Group and
Historical Period," *Journal of Quantitative Criminology* 13, no. 4 (1997): 405–28,
cited in "Costs of Confinement."

281 Victor Rios: Victor Rios, *Punished: Policing the Lives of Black and Latino Boys*
(New York: New York University Press, 2011).

281 Noting that of the forty Oakland, California, youths: Ibid., p. 162.

284 just over a quarter had recidivated in the strictest sense: "MO Juvenile Offender
Recidivism," 2009 Statewide Juvenile Court Report, Supreme Court of Missouri, Office of State Courts Administrator, September 2009.

284 84 percent of Missouri system graduates: Tim Decker, "The Missouri Division
of Youth Services and Juvenile Justice System: Brief Overview," July 23, 2009,
cited in Vincent Schiraldi, Marc Schindler, and Sean J. Goliday, "The End of
the Reform School?" New York Task Force on Transforming Juvenile Justice
Report, 2009.

285 the so-called dangerous few: At the same time, it is worth noting that Missouri

facilities hold young people on a range of charges, not only those who pose a threat to others.

285 "Throughout their stays in DYS": Richard A. Mendel, "Juvenile Confinement in Context," *American Educator*, Summer 2012, p. 7, www.aft.org/pdfs/american educator/summer2012/mendel.pdf

287 Just over half the youth committed to the Missouri Department of Youth Services: 2009 Statewide Juvenile Court Report.

287 lower-level offenders—12 percent of the total population: Richard A. Mendel, *The Missouri Model: Reinventing the Practice of Rehabilitating Youthful Offenders* (Baltimore, MD: Annie E. Casey Foundation, 2010).

14. The Real Recidivism Problem: One Hundred Years of Reform and Relapse at the Arthur G. Dozier School for Boys

290 *The Boys of the Dark*: Robin Gaby Fisher, Michael O'McCarthy, and Robert W. Straley, *The Boys of the Dark* (New York: St. Martin's Griffin, 2010).

292 Reporters from the *St. Petersburg Times*: Ben Montgomery and Waveney Ann Moore, "For Their Own Good: A St. Petersburg Times Special Report on Child Abuse at the Florida School for Boys," *St. Petersburg Times*, April 17, 2009, www.tampabay.com/features/humaninterest/for-their-own-good-a-st-peters burg-times-special-report-on-child-abuse-at/992939.

292 "The men remember the same things": Ibid.

293 letter to Florida state officials: Roger Kiser, "The Horrors of The White House," Coalition Against Institutionalized Child Abuse, www.caica.org /horrors%20of%20the%20white%20house.htm.

293 "The two men picked me up": Roger Dean Kiser, *The White House Boys: An American Tragedy* (New York: HCI, 2009).

293 Kiser received several responses to his letter: Kiser, "Horrors of the White House."

294 videotaped deposition of an elderly Troy Tidwell: "Portions of Troy Tidwell Deposition," posted by RDK (Roger Dean Kiser), www.youtube.com /watch?v=-Fr1x_Jf2nA.

295 the video they produced to accompany it: "Flowers of Marianna Video," posted by RDK (Roger Dean Kiser), www.youtube.com/watch?v=8hJDQWmzfiI.

295 Reports from state representatives: All quotations from these investigations are cited in Randy Lee Loftis, "UNT Sleuths to Help Florida Identify Remains from Boys' Reform School," *Dallas Morning News*, October 5, 2013, www.dallasnews

.com/news/metro/20131005-unt-sleuths-to-help-florida-id-remains-from-boys
-reform-school.ece.

295 "Thirty five cases of pneumonia": Ibid.

296 Reforms were ordered: Ben Montgomery and Waveney Ann Moore, "Florida Juvenile Justice: 100 Years of Hell at the Dozier School for Boys," *Tampa Bay Times*, October 9, 2009, www.tampabay.com/features/humaninterest/florida -juvenile-justice-100-years-of-hell-at-the-dozier-school-for-boys/1042880.

297 "When the media was around": Ibid.

297 The truth was that abuse remained rampant: "Investigation of the Arthur G. Dozier School for Boys and the Jackson Juvenile Offender Center, Marianna, Florida," U.S. Department of Justice, December 1, 2011, p. 6, www.justice .gov/crt/about/spl/documents/dozier_findltr_12-1-11.pdf.

297 One boy . . . asked to call the abuse hotline: Ibid.

297 Other boys later reported: Montgomery and Moore, "Florida Juvenile Justice."

298 Florida has embarked on a major reform effort: See Florida Department of Juvenile Justice, "Roadmap to System Excellence," October 2012, www.djj .state.fl.us/roadmap-to-system-excellence.

298 the privately run Thompson Academy: Susan Ferriss, "Youth Rehabilitation Facilities in Florida Under Scrutiny," Center for Public Integrity, June 2012, www .publicintegrity.org/2012/06/21/9176/youth-rehabilitation-centers-florida -under-scrutiny.

298 staff allegedly slammed kids into walls: Ibid.

299 In an official statement: Ibid.

299 Internal documents obtained by the *Huffington Post*: Chris Kirkham, "Prisoners of Profit," *Huffington Post*, October 22–23, 2013, projects.huffingtonpost.com /prisoners-of-profit/; Pam Stillwell, "Subject: FW: PROGRAM AREA," e-mail to Jerry Blanton, March 29, 2004, accessed at projects.huffingtonpost.com/prisoners -of-profit/documents/784333-stillwellprobs. Other documents about private facilities in Florida and elsewhere, including Thompson, can be accessed at projects .huffingtonpost.com/prisoners-of-profit/documents.

299 a November 2013 follow-up account: Chris Kirkham, "Troubled Youth Prison Company Wins Even More Contracts," *Huffington Post*, November 14, 2013, www.huffingtonpost.com/2013/11/14/youth-services-international-contracts _n_4269869.html.

299 Eric Perez died of a cerebral hemorrhage: Carol Marbin Miller, "As Florida Teen Lay Dying, Jail Guards Refused to Call Help, Believed He Was Faking," *Miami Herald*, October 19, 2012, www.miamiherald.com/2012/10/19/3057693 /as-florida-teen-lay-dying-jail.html.

299 In August 2012, a guard . . . was arrested: Carol Marbin Miller, "Video Shows Girl, 15, Battered in Florida Juvenile Prison," *Miami Herald*, December 12, 2012, www.miamiherald.com/2012/12/12/3139333/video-shows-15-year-old -girl-being.html.

299 Security camera footage shows other staff: The footage is posted on the *Miami Herald* website at ibid.

300 Florida Department of Juvenile Justice: Margie Menzel, "Abuse of Girls at Milton Residential Facility Exposes Flaws in Florida's Juvenile Justice," Flagler Live.com, December 18, 2012, flaglerlive.com/48291/milton-detention-abuse/.

300 Only after the department found itself investigating charges: Sarah Berres and Lynne Hough, "DJJ to Remove Girls from Facility," *Northwest Florida Daily News*, December 21, 2012, www.nwfdailynews.com/local/djj-to-remove-girls -from-facility-1.68652.

300 A mental health technician was charged next: Associated Press, "More Abuse Alleged at Panhandle Juvenile Prison," February 12, 2013, WJHG.com, www .wjhg.com/news/regional/headlines/More-Abuse-Alleged-at-Panhandle -Juvenile-Prison-190854231.html.

300 U.S. Justice Department's Civil Rights Division: "Investigation of the Arthur G. Dozier School for Boys."

301 Florida governor Rick Scott approved a land-use agreement: Lanetra Bennett, "USF Wins Federal Grant for Dozier Research," Associated Press, August 28, 2013, www.wctv.tv/home/headlines/215722331.html.

301 Digging began with the exhumation of a ten-year-old boy: Susan Donaldson James, "Florida Graves Reveal Reform School Horrors, Recall Witnesses and Families," ABC News, September 6, 2013, abcnews.go.com/US/florida -graves-reveal-reform-school-horrors-recall-witnesses/story?id=20172337.

301 it is unclear what the final death count will be: Ben Montgomery, "Cabinet Agrees to Let USF Exhume Bodies at Dozier," *Miami Herald*, August 6, 2013, www.miamiherald.com/2013/08/06/3545790/cabinet-agrees-to-let-usf -exhume.html.

301 "regularly appear at the infirmary": Fox Butterfield, "Hard Time: A Special Report: Profits at a Juvenile Prison Come with a Chilling Cost," *New York Times*, July 15, 1998.

302 "significant violence": "No Better Off: Update on Swanson Center for Youth," Juvenile Justice Project of Louisiana, November 2010, jjpl.org/site/wp-content /uploads/2011/07/no-better-off.pdf.

303 *Morales v. Turman*: Cat McCulloch, "Youth Solitary Confinement in Texas: A Two-Step in the Right Direction," ACLU, April 23, 2013, www.aclu.org/blog

/prisoners-rights-criminal-law-reform/youth-solitary-confinement texas two-step-right-direction.

303 According to author Kenneth Wooden: Kenneth Wooden, *Weeping in the Playtime of Others* (New York: McGraw-Hill, 1976), pp. 5–6.

303 After six grueling weeks of this sort of testimony: Ibid., pp. 8–9.

303 In June 2012, officials hoping to curb rising violence: Incidents of violence in state juvenile facilities more than tripled in the years since the 2007 sex scandals and ensuing reforms. *Texas Tribune* investigation, cited in Michele Deitch, Amy Madore, Kate Vickery, and Alycia Welch, *Understanding and Addressing Youth Violence in the Texas Juvenile Justice Department*, Report to the Office of the Independent Ombudsman, Lyndon B. Johnson School of Public Affairs, University of Texas at Austin, May 2013, 13, www.utexas.edu/lbj/sites/default/files/file/faculty/DeitchUnderstandingandAddressingYouthViolencein TJJDMay%202013FINAL.pdf.

304 The idea was to isolate and contain those youths: Brandi Grissom, "Giving Juveniles Intensive Treatment," *New York Times*, September 1, 2012.

304 Early coverage praised Phoenix: Ibid. See, e.g., Benet Magnuson, a juvenile justice policy analyst with the Texas Criminal Justice Coalition: "For years, advocates have called on lawmakers to shutter large institutions in remote areas and to create small treatment-focused centers close to cities. The Phoenix Program, Mr. Magnuson said, shows that plan could work."

304 "what this program was really doing well": Patrick Michels, "Texas Bets on Small Fixes to Reduce Violence in Youth Lockups," *Texas Observer*, September 6, 2012.

304 Youths at Phoenix went through a mandatory ten-week Aggression Replacement Training: "An Adolescent Anger Management Program," Episcopal Social Services, www.esswichita.org/youth/.

304 "Structure and personal attention are the priorities": Grissom, "Giving Juveniles Intensive Treatment."

304 "There were three staff and multiple youth": Independent Ombudsman for the Texas Juvenile Justice Department, *Phoenix Program Special Report*, www.documentcloud.org/documents/813666-texas-juvenile-justice-department-special-report.html. The site visits were conducted on September 18 and 20, 2013.

305 A grand jury declined to recommend criminal charges: Tommy Witherspoon, "Legislative Hearings Promised in TYC Incidents," *Waco Tribune-Herald*, November 9, 2013, www.wacotrib.com/news/courts_and_trials/legislative-hearings-promised-in-tyc-incidents/article_cc7e357e-8900-5244-bc93-266792ada832.html.

15. Against Reform: Beyond the Juvenile Prison

308 Even in those states being lauded for reform: Sarah Bryer and Marc Levin, "The Comeback States: Reducing Youth Incarceration in the United States," National Juvenile Justice Network and Texas Public Policy Foundation, 2013, p. 2, www .njjn.org/uploads/digital-library/Comeback-States-Report_FINAL.pdf.

308 large-scale juvenile incarceration has been proven many times over to do absolutely nothing to reduce juvenile offending: Mary Schmich, "Locking Up Juveniles May Plant Seeds of More Crime," *Chicago Tribune*, July 17, 2013, www .modelsforchange.net/newsroom/524.

311 "The goal of justice reinvestment": Susan B. Tucker and Eric Cadora, "Justice Reinvestment," *Ideas for an Open Society* 3, no. 3 (November 2003), www.open societyfoundations.org/sites/default/files/ideas_reinvestment.pdf.

312 In just a year, the number of juveniles: Ibid., p. 7.

312 "The test for successful deinstitutionalization": Jerome G. Miller, *Last One Over the Wall* (Columbus: Ohio State University Press, 1998), p. 154.

313 "The [guards union] is the most powerful lobby in California": Will Roy, "The Bottom Line: A Former CYA Inmate Refuses to Give Up," *Youth Outlook*, September 9, 2004, www.youthoutlook.org/news/view_article.html?article _id=150ce9ed1a4952119c53385b4c9caa97.

314 "The unintended by-product of the keeper-captive coupling": Miller, *Last One Over the Wall*, 134.

315 the recent decline in juvenile incarceration: Bryer and Levin, "Comeback States," p. 4.

PUBLISHING IN THE PUBLIC INTEREST

Thank you for reading this book published by The New Press. The New Press is a nonprofit, public interest publisher. New Press books and authors play a crucial role in sparking conversations about the key political and social issues of our day.

We hope you enjoyed this book and that you will stay in touch with The New Press. Here are a few ways to stay up to date with our books, events, and the issues we cover:

- Sign up at www.thenewpress.com/subscribe to receive updates on New Press authors and issues and to be notified about local events
- Like us on Facebook: www.facebook.com/newpressbooks
- Follow us on Twitter: www.twitter.com/thenewpress

Please consider buying New Press books for yourself; for friends and family; or to donate to schools, libraries, community centers, prison libraries, and other organizations involved with the issues our authors write about.

The New Press is a 501(c)(3) nonprofit organization. You can also support our work with a tax-deductible gift by visiting www.thenewpress .com/donate.